The Oral Gospel Tradition

The Oral Gospel Tradition

James D. G. Dunn

WILLIAM B. EERDMANS PUBLISHING COMPANY
GRAND RAPIDS, MICHIGAN / CAMBRIDGE, U.K.

Published 2013 by

Wm. B. Eerdmans Publishing Co.

2140 Oak Industrial Drive N.E., Grand Rapids, Michigan 49505 /
P.O. Box 163, Cambridge CB3 9PU U.K.

Printed in the United States of America

19 18 17 16 15 14 13   7 6 5 4 3 2 1

Library of Congress Cataloging-in-Publication Data

Dunn, James D. G., 1939-
The oral gospel tradition / James D. G. Dunn.
pages   cm
Includes bibliographical references and index.
ISBN 978-0-8028-6782-7 (pbk.: alk. paper)
1. Bible. N.T. Gospels — Criticism, interpretation, etc.
2. Oral tradition.   I. Title.

BS2555.52.D87   2013
226′.066 — dc23

2013010686

www.eerdmans.com

Contents

PART II

PART III

Acknowledgments

I am most grateful to Eerdmans for agreeing to put together these essays whose wide spread of publication could make it irksome for any who want to consult more than one or two of the essays. I am grateful too for the publishers of the original essays for permission to republish in this collected essay form. The full details of these original publications follow:

Part I

1. 'Prophetic "I"-Sayings and the Jesus-Tradition: The Importance of Testing Prophetic Utterances within Early Christianity', *New Testament Studies* 24 (1977-78) 175-98.
2. 'Altering the Default Setting: Re-envisaging the Early Transmission of the Jesus Tradition', *New Testament Studies* 49 (2003) 139-75; the version reprinted here, with texts in English, from *A New Perspective on Jesus* (Grand Rapids: Baker Academic, 2005) 79-125.
3. 'Q^1 as Oral Tradition', in M. Bockmuehl & D. A. Hagner, eds., *The Written Gospel*, G. N. Stanton Festschrift (Cambridge: Cambridge University, 2005) 45-69.
4. 'Matthew's Awareness of Markan Redaction', in *The Four Gospels: Festschrift for Frans Neirynck*, ed. F. Van Segbroeck (Leuven: Leuven University Press, 1992) 1349-59.
5. 'Matthew as *Wirkungsgeschichte*', in P. Lampe et al., eds., *Neutestament-liche Exegese im Dialog: Hermeneutik — Wirkungsgeschichte — Mat-thäusevangelium. Festschrift für Ulrich Luz* (Neukirchen-Vluyn: Neu-kirchener, 2008) 149-66.

6. 'John and the Oral Gospel Tradition', in *Jesus and the Oral Gospel Tradition*, ed. H. Wansbrough (JSNTSup 64; Sheffield: Sheffield Academic Press, 1991) 351-79.

7. 'John's Gospel and the Oral Gospel Tradition', in A. Le Donne & T. Thatcher, eds., *The Fourth Gospel in First-Century Media Culture* (LNTS 426; London: T&T Clark, 2011) 157-85.

Part II

8. 'On History, Memory and Eyewitnesses: In Response to Bengt Holmberg and Samuel Byrskog', *Journal for the Study of the New Testament* 26 (2004) 473-87.

9. 'Eyewitnesses and the Oral Jesus Tradition', *Journal for the Study of the Historical Jesus* 6 (2008) 85-105.

10. 'Social Memory and the Oral Jesus Tradition', in S. C. Barton, L. T. Stuckenbruck & B. G. Wold, eds., *Memory in the Bible and Antiquity: The Fifth Durham-Tübingen Research Symposium* (WUNT 2.212; Tübingen: Mohr Siebeck, 2007) 179-94.

11. 'Kenneth Bailey's Theory of Oral Tradition: Critiquing Theodore Weeden's Critique', *Journal for the Study of the Historical Jesus* 7 (2009) 44-62 (in response to T. J. Weeden, 'Kenneth Bailey's Theory of Oral Tradition: A Theory Contested by Its Evidence', in the same issue, 3-43).

Part III

12. Two versions of 'Remembering Jesus: How the Quest of the Historical Jesus Lost Its Way', in P. R. Eddy & J. K. Beilby, eds., *The Historical Jesus: Five Views* (Downers Grove: IVP, 2009) 199-225; also T. Holmen & S. E. Porter, eds., *Handbook for the Study of the Historical Jesus* (4 vols.; Leiden: Brill, 2011) 1.183-205.

13. 'Between Jesus and the Gospels', in *Jesus, Paul and the Gospels* (Grand Rapids: Eerdmans, 2010) 22-44.

14. 'The History of the Tradition: New Testament', *Eerdmans Commentary on the Bible* (Grand Rapids: Eerdmans, 2003) 950-71 (double-column pages).

15. 'Living Tradition', in P. McCosker ed., *What Is It That the Scripture Says? Essays in Biblical Interpretation, Translation and Reception in Honour of Henry Wansbrough OSB* (LNTS 316; London: T&T Clark, 2006) 275-89.

Abbreviations

AB	Anchor Bible
AJT	*Asia Journal of Theology*
BDAG	Danker, F. W., W. Bauer, W. F. Arndt, and F. W. Gingrich. *Greek-English Lexicon of the New Testament and Other Early Christian Literature.* 3rd ed. Chicago, 1999
BETL	Bibliotheca ephemeridum theologicarum lovaniensium
BNTC	Black New Testament Commentary
BS	Biblical Seminar
BTB	*Biblical Theology Bulletin*
BZAW	Beihefte zur Zeitschrift für die alttestamentliche Wissenschaft
BZNW	Beihefte zur Zeitschrift für die neutestamentliche Wissenschaft
CRINT	Compendia rerum iudaicarum ad Novem Testamentum
DSS	Dead Sea Scrolls
ExpTim	*Expository Times*
HBT	*Horizons in Biblical Theology*
HNT	Handbuch zum Neuen Testament
HTCNT	Herder's Theological Commentary on the New Testament
HTR	*Harvard Theological Review*
ICC	International Critical Commentary
JBL	*Journal of Biblical Literature*
JSHJ	*Journal for the Study of the Historical Jesus*
JSNT	*Journal for the Study of the New Testament*
JSNTSup	Journal for the Study of the New Testament: Supplement Series
JTS	*Journal of Theological Studies*

KAV	Kommentar zu den Apostolischen Vätern
KEK	Kritisch-exegetischer Kommentar über das Neue Testament
KuD	*Kerygma und Dogma*
LNTS	Library of New Testament Studies
NCB	New Century Bible
NEB	New English Bible
NovTSup	Supplements to Novum Testamentum
NRSV	New Revised Standard Version
NTS	*New Testament Studies*
pars.	parallels
QD	Quaestiones disputatae
RBL	*Review of Biblical Literature*
RHPR	*Revue d'histoire et de philosophie religieuses*
SBLSS	Society of Biblical Literature Semeia Studies
SNTSMS	Society for New Testament Studies Monograph Series
TDNT	*Theological Dictionary of the New Testament.* Edited by G. Kittel and G. Friedrich. Translated by G. W. Bromiley. 10 vols. Grand Rapids, 1964-76
THNT	Theologischer Handkommentar zum Neuen Testament
WBC	Word Biblical Commentary
WMANT	Wissenschaftliche Monographien zum Alten und Neuen Testament
WUNT	Wissenschaftliche Untersuchungen zum Neuen Testament
ZNW	*Zeitschrift für die neutestamentliche Wissenschaft und die Kunde der älteren Kirche*
ZTK	*Zeitschrift für Theologie und Kirche*

Introduction

My fascination with the oral tradition which lies behind the New Testament Gospels has deep roots. In my student and early scholarship days I had an instinctive sense that it must surely be important for Christians today to know about Jesus, what he taught and how he acted. To assume that the Gospel accounts were later contrivances, the wish-lists of later Christians, the ideals of good men of subsequent generations retrojected onto a much less significant historical figure, was not a perspective I could readily adapt to. Or to infer that it didn't matter whether Jesus said and did what was attributed to him (what mattered was the Christ of centuries of Christian preaching and faith) was theologically unsatisfying, a cutting and running from potentially disturbing findings.

An initial issue arose from my early research interest in the Holy Spirit, and in early Christian experience of *charismata*, 'spiritual gifts', including prophecy. The issue was posed by the then strongly presented view that many of the sayings attributed to Jesus had actually originated in prophecies within early Christian assemblies — prophecies often delivered, as in the OT, in first person ('I') terms, where the one speaking could be taken to be the risen and exalted Christ. If that was the case, it would inevitably influence how we now view the sayings attributed to Jesus and how the sayings of Jesus were regarded and handled in the beginning. I tackled that issue in the first of the essays reprinted below.

Particularly fascinating in the Gospel material were and are the different ways in which the traditions about Jesus were combined, with different versions and different emphases. I had become impressed by the diversity

1

which is in the NT: the unity of the NT was a unity in diversity, a unity constituted by its diversity, as in the image of one body made up of many diverse members.[1] But in reference to the traditions about Jesus which make up the NT Gospels, did the diversity not constitute a problem? If these were traditions about the same man, why the differences?

An early influence shaping my thought on the Gospels as oral tradition was a meeting with Kenneth Bailey in 1976 or 1977 in California. Bailey intrigued me with his accounts of how oral tradition worked in the village communities and churches in Egypt and Lebanon with which he had many years' familiarity.[2] What was so intriguing for me was that his accounts of how oral tradition functioned in the twentieth-century Middle East offered a potentially important clue to how oral tradition, particularly traditions of Jesus, might have functioned in first-century Palestine. But I was unable to investigate and exploit this potential for more than twenty years.

I was pushed to develop my ideas on the substance and variation in the Gospel tradition by a TV series, on *Jesus: The Evidence*,[3] which in effect claimed that New Testament scholarship has undermined the historical value of the Gospels. In a popular series of lectures, delivered for the Durham Council of Churches in 1984 I attempted some response.[4] The first lecture was entitled, 'The Gospels: Fact, Fiction, or What?'[5] and addressed the issues raised by the diversity of the Gospel tradition. Its conclusion to the question 'Has NT scholarship undermined the historical value of the Gospels?' was Yes and No!

> Yes! — but only for the person who comes to the Gospels with expectations they were not designed to fulfill. Whoever looks for chronological accounts, detailed conciseness in every episode recorded, pedantic precision in reproducing Jesus' teaching as given, word for word, and such like *will* be disappointed. But *not* because of anything scholars have said or done. Rather because the evangelists themselves were not concerned with such matters. The fault here, if fault there be, lies not in the scholars or in their findings, but in the false expectations with which so many have

---

1. *Unity and Diversity in the New Testament* (London: SCM, 1977, [2]1990, [3]2006).

2. I give some account of what I learned then in ch. 11 below.

3. London Weekend Television, April, 1984.

4. *The Evidence for Jesus: The Impact of Scholarship on Our Understanding of How Christianity Began* (London: SCM, 1985).

5. In the first of the Deichmann Lectures delivered at the Ben Gurion University in Beer Sheva in 2009, published as *Jesus, Paul and the Gospels* (Grand Rapids: Eerdmans, 2011), I further developed the arguments — 'Fact or Fiction? How Reliable Are the Gospels?'

come to the Gospels. The failure, if failure there be, is failure to take the Gospels as they are, on their own terms, the failure to recognize their own emphases and priorities and concerns.

No! — because all these traditions of which we have given example go back to Jesus and his ministry. All are firmly rooted in the earliest memories of his mission. In conveying the traditions of Jesus' words and deeds the evangelists were concerned to present the tradition in ways that spoke most powerfully to their readers. So while it is ever the first memories of Jesus which they retell, they do so in words often shaped by the circumstances and needs for which they were retold.

In short, far from accusing New Testament scholarship of undermining our common faith, we should be the more grateful to them. For in drawing our attention to the actual features of the Gospels themselves they have helped us the better to understand the purposes and priorities of the Gospel writers and so helped us to hear their message more clearly.[6]

In the Griffith Thomas Lectures in Oxford in February 1987,[7] I developed the case for seeing 'The Gospels as Oral Tradition'. In that lecture I argued for the probability that the first Christians were keen to retain and to pass on memories of Jesus' ministry, and developed the point that we can also see how the first Christians passed on the traditions about Jesus and thus gain a clearer perspective on what their concern to remember Jesus meant in terms of the historical value of these traditions. The conclusion was similar:

> It is clear from all this that the earliest Christians *were* concerned to remember Jesus and to pass on these memories to new converts and churches. But again and again it is equally clear that they were more concerned with the substance and meaning of what Jesus had said and done than with a meticulous level of verbal precision or with a pedantic level of historical detail. It is important to recognize the force of both points. To underestimate the former is to cut Christianity off from its historical foundation and fountainhead. But to misplace the emphasis in the latter stands in equal danger of distorting the concerns of the first Christians. The Synoptic tradition as history — yes, indeed! But the Gospels also as the living tradition of the earliest churches — that, too.

6. *The Evidence for Jesus*, 27-8.

7. Published as *The Living Word* (London: SPCK, 1987; Philadelphia: Fortress, 1987), along with two other essays; second edition (Minneapolis: Fortress, 2009) with four further essays.

We therefore can make the strong and confident affirmation that the Synoptic Gospels in particular *are* a source of historical information about Jesus; the Evangelists were concerned with the historicity of what they remembered; in burden-of-proof terms we can start from the assumption that the Synoptic tradition is a good witness to the historical Jesus unless proved otherwise. But we must be careful not to overstate our case. To claim that the Evangelists had the same level of historical concern in every phrase and sentence they used runs counter to the evidence and almost certainly misunderstands their intentions. Equally serious, such a claim *undermines* the case for the historicity of the Gospels, since it makes that case depend on a series of implausible harmonizations. Properly to recognize the Evangelists' concern for historicity in their own terms means recognizing also their other concerns and above all the character of that earliest remembering as a living word.[8]

In the years following my principal focus had to be on 'the new perspective on Paul',[9] but an invitation from Birger Gerhardsson to join an ongoing seminar on 'Jesus and the Oral Gospel Tradition', led by Henry Wansbrough, maintained my interest and curiosity in the fact and mechanics of oral transmission of the traditions about Jesus. My contribution on John's Gospel[10] was my first real effort to expand my inquiry into the tradition behind the Gospels from a focus primarily on the Synoptic Gospels to include the distinctively different Fourth Gospel. And an invitation to contribute to the Festschrift for Frans Neirynck gave me opportunity to follow up something which had caught my attention in the course of regular undergraduate seminars working directly with Synopses of the Gospels: that Matthew's failure to follow Mark's version of the Jesus tradition at various points could well best be explained by Matthew's awareness of other forms of the tradition which lacked these Markan features — a kind of redaction criticism in reverse![11] The likelihood that it was knowledge of and familiarity with other (oral) versions of the Jesus tradition which made Matthew aware that certain features of Mark's version of the tradition were Markan redaction, opened up a new vista on the oral phase of the Jesus tradition.

In 1999 I was fortunate enough to be granted two years research leave by Durham University and I determined to use it to start work on my longer

8. *The Living Word* (2009) 35.

9. *The New Perspective on Paul: Collected Essays* (Tübingen: Mohr Siebeck, 2005); revised edition (Grand Rapids: Eerdmans, 2008).

10. Reprinted below, ch. 6.

11. Reprinted below, ch. 4.

term project on *Christianity in the Making*. The first volume had to be on Jesus, naturally. The two years allowed me to mount a sustained investigation of the Gospel tradition, particularly the Synoptic tradition, at a much more detailed level than had been possible before. The character of the great bulk of the Synoptic tradition came into ever sharper focus, particularly its consistent character of 'the same yet different', coherent but flexible. The narrative accounts of what Jesus did and how he acted were again and again telling the same story, but again and again not in the same words, with different emphases and sometimes inconsistent detail. Parallel sayings of Jesus again and again conveyed the same teaching, but regularly in different groupings, and expressed in varied wording.

The best explanation I could come up with for this 'same yet different' feature is that the Synoptic tradition itself illustrates how the stories about and teaching of Jesus were communicated within and among the early Christian disciple groups. A tradition which focused on the substance and gist of what was being narrated or taught and was freely expressed in varied words, in different combinations and with different emphases, looked more and more like oral tradition — the forms in which the traditions of Jesus' mission and teaching were celebrated and taught before they were written down.

Some react against the suggestion that Jewish or Galilean society at the time of Jesus was oral. But if the findings of those who have investigated the issue are followed, then we have to accept that 10% or less of the population of Galilee was literate, and that most of Jesus' disciples would have been illiterate or at best semi-literate. For a society long accustomed to books and libraries it is hard to conceive what an oral society would be like. But a society where information would be passed from one to another by word of mouth, where teaching and story-telling would be orally communicated, is the society which we must envisage if we are talking about the earliest disciple groups in the 30s, 40s and 50s of the first century.

Others deny that there is any need to envisage a process of oral tradition behind the Gospels. Since the Gospels are in writing, and since it is entirely possible to explain every last detail of the divergent traditions by hypothesis of literary editing and redaction, there is no need to go into a pre-literary phase. The problem here is that while a good proportion of the inter-relationships between the Gospels can be explained by straightforward source and redaction criticism, that is, purely at a literary level, in an equally strong proportion of parallel traditions the divergences are so many and so inconsequential that the literary logic needed to explain them quickly becomes tortuous and increasingly unpersuasive.

Others think that oral tradition is by definition unreliable, so if the Jesus tradition is to be regarded as historically reliable its literary character must be defended at all costs. But, once again, such an attitude is simply an expression of the modern literary mind-set. Experiments in modern Western societies on how memory works can never reduplicate the reality of a first-century oral society, where memory was the first and most prized reference point. To make confidence in the reliability of the Jesus tradition depend on our being able to argue convincingly that the tradition was put in writing from the first is a counsel of despair.

Others again simply deny that one can penetrate back into the oral phase of the tradition, as though it were impossible to envisage an unwritten form or a tradition prior to its written form. That too is a counsel of despair. Since it is most likely that the earliest of the Synoptic Gospels was not written before the late 60s, and since there is no great likelihood that most of the Synoptic tradition was put in writing before, say, the late 50s, the consequence would be that we have to accept that nearly thirty years, from Jesus' crucifixion in 30, is a blank space so far as the way the Jesus tradition which came to be written down was used and how it functioned.[12]

In the essays that follow I have tried to address these and other questions. But whether the Synoptic tradition is to be explained as shaped by the oral traditioning process or not, the character of the Synoptic tradition has still to be explained — a tradition the bulk of which has this 'same yet different' character, and a tradition which overall has a coherency and consistency which is best explained as the portrayal of a historical individual whose mission and teaching it purports to describe and communicate.[13]

For myself, the key consideration is this:

- it can be assumed that Jesus made an impact on at least a number of those who heard and witnessed him;
- that impact was a disciple-forming impact, a faith-(trust in Jesus–) creating impact;
- that impact was bound to come to expression in the disciples' sharing

12. M. Goodacre, *Thomas and the Gospels: The Case for Thomas's Familiarity with the Synoptics* (Grand Rapids: Eerdmans, 2012), criticizes me for underestimating the importance of literacy among early Christian authors and tradents (130, 139-42), though his major criticism is that the contrast between an oral antiquity and a literate modernity fails to appreciate the digital revolution of the last two decades (a point well made by one well accustomed to use of Internet media). But he misses the point that most of my observations relate to the way the Jesus tradition was circulated and used before it was transcribed in written text.

13. I allude here to the quotation from C. H. Dodd quoted on several occasions in the following pages.

and communicating stories about Jesus and in discussing and passing on his teaching;

- the resulting tradition thus embodies that impact and became a means for communicating that impact to others;
- consequently from the character of the tradition we can still gain a clear impression of the one who made that impact.

If an illustration is permitted, my thesis can be summed up in the image of a gulf (the thirty years during which Jesus tradition was predominantly oral). To reach back across the gulf from the Jesus tradition as we now have it (the Synoptic tradition especially) may not get very far, since recapturing the pre-literary forms must become increasingly speculative. But we can also envisage a reaching forward from the other side of the gulf — the impact made by Jesus conveyed by and through the Jesus tradition from its earliest formulations. Oral forms of communication and transmission of that impactful tradition provide a network of supports for the resulting bridge between Jesus and the Jesus tradition in its Synoptic form. And if that explains the character of the Jesus tradition as it endures in the Synoptic tradition, then we have gained much — both a clearer idea of how the Synoptic tradition came about and how it worked for these years otherwise silent on how the Gospel tradition came to be.

Such, in summary form, was the thesis of which I became convinced when writing the first volume of my projected trilogy, *Christianity in the Making*.[14] The argument was made at about the same time for 'altering the default setting' (that of the literary mindset), and for 're-envisaging the early transmission of the Jesus tradition'.[15] Thereafter I was able to do other exploratory digs into different parts of the Jesus tradition — the Q material,[16] Matthew, following up my earlier essay on that Gospel,[17] and John, taking forward my earlier discussion on John and the oral Jesus tradition.[18] There was

---

14. *Jesus Remembered* (Grand Rapids: Eerdmans, 2003). 'Jesus in Oral Memory: The Initial Stages of the Jesus Tradition', in D. Donnelly, ed., *Jesus: A Colloquium in the Holy Land* (New York: Continuum, 2001) 84-145, was in effect a first draft of a key chapter of *Jesus Remembered* (ch. 8).

15. My presidential lecture to Studiorum Novi Testamenti Societas in Durham in 2002, 'Altering the Default Setting: Re-envisaging the Early Transmission of the Jesus Tradition', *New Testament Studies* 49 (2003) 139-75; reprinted below, ch. 2, using English texts. 'Reappreciating the Oral Jesus Tradition', *Svensk Exegetisk Årsbok* 74 (2009) 1-17, covers much of the same ground.

16. Reprinted below, ch. 3.

17. Reprinted below, ch. 5.

18. Reprinted below, ch. 7.

no need to make a particular study of Mark's tradition as such, since the early tradition of Mark was dealt with in the 'Altering the Default Setting' essay.[19] And somewhat similarly with Luke, since it is the Lukan form of the Q tradition which is generally regarded as closest to the earlier Q material.

The essays in Part II are all attempts to respond to the varied criticisms which have been made of *Jesus Remembered*. In particular, I was glad to be able to give added stress to the role of Jesus as teacher, and to that of eyewitnesses.[20] However, I was somewhat disappointed by the criticism that I did not offer a theory of memory to serve my thesis — a criticism, to be sure, to which I had left myself vulnerable by giving the volume the title I did *(Jesus Remembered)*. I am somewhat dubious about modern theories of memory applied to ancient societies where memory seems to have functioned very differently from today, and had to so function if there was to be any extensive communication or any viable historical writing. My point, however, has been that I am not working from a theory of memory, as so many today work from particular sociological theories to fill gaps in the historical evidence. From the beginning I have been working with the Jesus tradition, especially the Synoptic tradition, as it is, as it still is. My concern has been to explain how its character ('the same yet different') was formed and achieved. The best explanation, it still seems to me, is that the Jesus tradition is how the impact originally made by Jesus was passed on. This is the way Jesus was remembered. Whatever theory of memory is put forward to explain this character of the Jesus tradition, that is what has to be explained. A theory of parrot-like memorization will not do, given the variations and diversity of the tradition. A theory of freely creative memory aiming primarily to meet the needs and concerns of a later society will not do either, given the coherency and consistency of the tradition and the coherency and consistency of the impression (of Jesus) which the tradition still conveys.[21]

I was also glad to defend the integrity of Kenneth Bailey's anecdotally informed appreciation of how oral tradition still works, since it opened a window in my perspective which I have never found it necessary to close since then.[22] I should perhaps mention that I was able to respond to other critiques of *Jesus Remembered* which are less directly concerned with the oral character

19. But I am very grateful for the studies of Mark's Gospel as itself an oral presentation — particularly W. Shiner, *Proclaiming the Gospel: First-Century Performance of Mark* (Harrisburg: Trinity Press International, 2003), and now A. C. Wire, *The Case for Mark Composed in Performance* (Biblical Performance Criticism 3; Eugene, Ore.: Cascade, 2011).

20. Chs. 8 and 9 below.

21. Ch. 10 below.

22. Reprinted below, ch. 11.

of the Jesus tradition, and so have not been reprinted here.[23] Regretfully I had to omit also the 'Kontroverse' with my good friend Jens Schröter, 'Der erinnerte Jesus als Begründer des Christentums?'[24] And I should also mention the volume edited by Robert Stewart and Gary Habermas, *Memories of Jesus: A Critical Appraisal of James D. G. Dunn's Jesus Remembered*,[25] with several essays relevant to the issues in this volume, to which I was gladly able to respond,[26] but in a form also inappropriate to the present volume.

The essays in Part III are attempts to step back from the close textual work and argumentation of Parts I and II to set the thesis about the oral Gospel tradition in the wider contexts of the quest of the historical Jesus (ch. 12), the transition from Jesus to the Gospels as such (ch. 13), the broader view of the traditions which go to make the NT (ch. 14), and the whole character of the Jesus tradition in particular as *living* tradition (ch. 15), a tradition which extends from the early decades of the first century to the present, and is still *living*.

JAMES D. G. DUNN
Chichester,
June, 2012

---

23. *Expository Times* 116.1 (October 2004) included reviews by Robert Morgan, 'James Dunn's *Jesus Remembered*' (1-6), and Andrew Gregory, 'An oral and written Gospel? Reflections on remembering Jesus' (7-12), to which I was able to respond, 'On Faith and History, and Living Tradition' (13-19).

24. *Zeitschrift für das Neues Testament* 20 (2007) 46-61.

25. Nashville: B&H Academic, 2010.

26. *Memories of Jesus*, 287-323.

PART I

CHAPTER 1

Prophetic 'I'-Sayings and the Jesus-Tradition: The Importance of Testing Prophetic Utterances within Early Christianity

> The Church drew no distinction between such utterances by Christian prophets (ascribed to the ascended Christ) and the sayings of Jesus in the tradition, for the reason that even the dominical sayings in the tradition were not the pronouncements of a past authority, but sayings of the risen Lord, who is always a contemporary for the Church.[1]

This statement of Bultmann has provided the rationale for one of the most important methodological principles underlying the development and use of form criticism in historical Jesus and Synoptic Gospel research for nearly fifty years.[2] For it means not only that all Synoptic logia have their primary *Sitz im Leben* within the enthusiasm of the earliest communities, but also that there is no *a priori* reason for taking any logion in particular as a word of the earthly Jesus. Every claim to that effect has to be established by an examination of form and content. If indeed prophetic oracles were so highly regarded in the early churches, then the character of the Jesus-tradition[3] and the nature

---

1. R. Bultmann, *The History of the Synoptic Tradition* (ET Oxford, 1963), pp. 127f.

2. See particularly E. Käsemann, 'Sentences of Holy Law in the New Testament' and 'The Beginnings of Christian Theology', *New Testament Questions of Today* (ET London, 1969), chaps. III and IV; N. Perrin, *Rediscovering the Teaching of Jesus* (London, 1967), p. 15; S. Schulz, *Q Die Spruchquelle der Evangelisten* (Zurich, 1972), pp. 57-66.

3. I use the phrases 'Jesus-tradition' and '"I"-sayings' as a convenient shorthand for 'say-

---

This paper has been delivered on several occasions under the title 'Did the first Christians create sayings of Jesus? A neglected aspect of early Christian prophecy'.

of its transmission become at once clear: the tradition of Jesus' sayings was in no sense fixed but wholly fluid, subject not only to reworking but also to addition; and the communities' handling of it was by no means limited to editorial recasting and redactorial expansion of accepted logia but very much freer and independently creative. The more highly the utterances of early Christian prophets were regarded, the less distinctive was the authority accorded to sayings of the earthly Jesus, and the more liable the Jesus-tradition to massive expansion. Indeed, it would not be unjust to conclude from Bultmann's statement that prophetic oracles were regarded more highly than sayings of the earthly Jesus and only sayings which were recognizably sayings of the risen Lord were valued and preserved — the inspiration of the present being ranked more highly than the acknowledged inspiration of the past. It comes as no surprise then when we read statements like these:

> Thus it came about that *countless* 'I' sayings of the Christ who revealed himself through the mouth of prophets gained entry into the Synoptic tradition as sayings of Jesus.[4]

> According to the theory of an authentic oral tradition, the flow of tradition was from the earthly Jesus to his disciples to the apostles in the church. Actually, the flow was in the opposite direction: from the apostles in the church to the earthly Jesus.[5]

Bultmann's claim and its subsequent echoes are of course not merely assumptions, and we shall note the chief considerations in its favour in a moment (see I below). Nor has it escaped criticism; we shall elaborate the main points of this criticism below (II). But a major weakness both of the initial hypothesis and of the subsequent responses has been *the failure to inquire more carefully into what we do know of prophetic activity in the early churches.*[6] In particular, how highly regarded were prophetic utterances? Were they accepted uncritically as words of the risen Lord, or were they subjected to scrutiny and tested, some to be rejected, and only some to be accepted? If so, what were the criteria used in such testing? And what conclusions follow concern-

---

ings attributed to the earthly, pre-Easter Jesus' and 'prophetic utterances spoken in the person of the risen Jesus' respectively.

4. E. Käsemann, 'Is the Gospel Objective?', *Essays on New Testament Themes* (ET London, 1964), p. 60 (my emphasis).

5. H. M. Teeple, 'The oral tradition that never existed', *JBL* LXXXIX (1970), 67.

6. A beginning has been made in two recent monographs — U. B. Müller, *Prophetie und Predigt im Neuen Testament* (Gütersloh, 1975), and G. Dautzenberg, *Urchristliche Prophetie* (Stuttgart, 1975) — but both only touch on the particular issues raised here.

ing the relation between Jesus-tradition and prophetic oracles for the first Christians?

Here obviously is a major area of inquiry whose neglect is both surprising and unfortunate. Here is one possible way of testing the viability and validity of Bultmann's hypothesis. The pursuit of this inquiry is the primary task of this paper.

I. Considerations in Favour of Bultmann's Hypothesis

The chief points in favour of Bultmann's thesis are these.

(a) We know that there were prophets active within earliest Christianity.[7] Indeed, the primitive community was marked out precisely as a revival of the prophetic Spirit; Christianity began as an enthusiastic Jewish sect.[8] More to the point, our evidence indicates that while prophetic utterances were often attributed specifically to the Spirit (Acts xiii.2, xxi.11 — τάδε λέγει τὸ πνεῦμα τὸ ἅγιον), at least on some other occasions they were attributed alternatively or also to the risen Lord (I Thess. iv.15, Rev. ii–iii).[9] In addition, the more experience of the life-giving Spirit (including prophetic inspiration) was recognized as experience of the Risen One (Rom. viii.9-11, I Cor. xii.4ff., xv.45),[10] the less significance would the difference in attribution have (cf. Luke xxi.14f. with Mark xiii.11 pars).

(b) *Religionsgeschichtliche* parallels strengthen the probability that where prophecy had a vigorous existence most if not all of the utterances took the form of 'I'-sayings, where the 'I' was understood to be the Lord of the cult. The same picture emerges whether we look to the typical utterances of the classical prophets in the OT, or to the prophetic oracles of Hellenism typified by those of the Pythia at Delphi.[11] Bultmann and P. Vielhauer put much weight on Od. Sol. 42.6:

7. Matt. vii.15-23, x.41, xxiii.34f./Luke xi.49ff.; Acts ii.17f., xi.27, xiii.1, xv.32, xix.6, xxi.9f.; Rom. xii.6; I Cor. xii.10, 28; xiv; Eph. ii.20; I Thess. v.20.

8. See Käsemann, 'Beginnings'; J. D. G. Dunn, *Jesus and the Spirit* (London, 1975), chap. VII.

9. On I Thess. iv.15 see particularly J. G. Davies, 'The genesis of belief in an imminent parousia', *JTS*, n.s. XIV (1963), 104-7; B. Henneken, *Verkündigung und Prophetie im I. Thessalonicherbrief* (Stuttgarter Bibel-Studien 29, 1969), pp. 85-91; E. Best, *The First and Second Epistles to the Thessalonians* (London, 1972), pp. 189-93.

10. See J. D. G. Dunn, 'I Corinthians 15.45 — Last Adam, Life-giving Spirit', *Christ and Spirit in the New Testament: Studies in Honour of C. F. D. Moule* (ed. B. Lindars and S. S. Smalley, Cambridge, 1973), pp. 127-41.

11. H. W. Parke and D. E. W. Wormell, *The Delphic Oracle*, II, *The Oracular Responses* (Oxford, 1956).

And I have arisen and am among them,
And I speak through their mouth.[12]

Several of the few early Montanist prophetic utterances still extant are in an 'I'-form.[13]

And we should not ignore the jibes of Celsus in the second century:

> There are many who, although of no name, with the greatest facility and on the slightest occasion, whether within or without temples, assume the motions and gestures of inspired persons. . . . They are accustomed to say, each for himself, 'I am God; I am the Son of God'; or, 'I am the Divine Spirit.'[14]

(c) The relative lack of interest in the life and ministry of the earthly Jesus in the kerygmatic material of Acts and in Paul's letters has also to be placed on this side of the balance.[15] For, as H. M. Teeple argues, it is accompanied by a noticeable unwillingness (or inability?) to quote sayings of Jesus at appropriate points (James, Hebrews, I Peter, Rev.), and by a conviction of immediacy of inspiration and revelation (e.g. Mark xiii.11, Acts iv.31, I Cor. ii.9-13, Gal. i.11f.).[16] Taken together, these facts make the hypothesis more plausible that much of the oral tradition embodied in Q and the Synoptics derives directly from the early communities' experiences of the prophetic Spirit.

(d) Where there are echoes of sayings of Jesus in Paul (e.g. Rom. xii.14/Matt. v.44; Rom. xiii.9/Mark xii.31; Rom. xvi.19/Matt. x.16; I Cor. xiii.2/Mark xi.23; I Thess. v.2, 4/Luke xii.39) they are treated simply as part of general Christian instruction in the epistles with no real attempt being made to distinguish Jesus-tradition from Paul's own teaching.[17] Probably this simply demonstrates the degree to which the Jesus-tradition had already (unconsciously) influenced Christian paraenesis. But it could be argued that instead of Paul drawing from traditional material as the source of his paraenesis, the traditional material drew from Paul. So G. F. Hawthorne goes on to ask:

> Did some of the words of Jesus now contained in the gospel come from the parenesis, that is from the words of admonition and encouragement

12. Bultmann, *Tradition*, p. 127 n. 1; P. Vielhauer in E. Hennecke, *New Testament Apocrypha*, II (ET ed. R. M. Wilson, London, 1965), p. 606.

13. See E. Hennecke, *Apocrypha* II, pp. 686f.

14. Origen, *Contra Celsum* VII.9.

15. Though see now G. N. Stanton, *Jesus of Nazareth in New Testament Preaching* (Cambridge, 1974).

16. Teeple, pp. 63ff.

17. Cf. Perrin, *Teaching*, p. 245.

originating with the risen Lord and channeled through his prophet Paul?[18]

(e) Another relevant factor is the apparent willingness of some early Christian writers or their sources (prophetic utterances?) to quote as scripture texts which are not directly derived from any known OT text and which at best seem to be a sort of amalgam of disparate OT materials (John vii.38, I Cor. ii.9, James iv.5; cf. Luke xi.49, Eph. v.14).[19] That is to say, we have evidence of a willingness to create (under inspiration) utterances in the form of and claiming the authority of sacred tradition.[20] If thus with scripture, why not with Jesus-tradition? Conceivably then the saying attributed to Jesus in Acts xx.35 — Μακάριόν ἐστιν μᾶλλον διδόναι ἢ λαμβάνειν — is a prophetic utterance which might just as well have appeared among the Jesus-logia of the Gospels.[21]

(f) Above all, this line of argument finds a secure anchor point within the Synoptic tradition itself. I refer to Matt. xviii.20 — οὗ γάρ εἰσιν δύο ἢ τρεῖς συνηγμένοι εἰς τὸ ἐμὸν ὄνομα, ἐκεῖ εἰμι ἐν μέσῳ αὐτῶν. The saying so clearly reflects the post-Easter consciousness of the continuing presence of the risen Jesus within the community (cf. Matt. xxviii.20) that it is hardly possible to find its origin in a pre-Easter situation. Here surely, even if nowhere else, it is the risen Lord who speaks, presumably through a prophet in an early Christian assembly.[22] Other plausible examples of post-Easter prophetic utterances being incorporated among the sayings of the pre-Easter Jesus include Matt. x.5,[23] Matt. xi.28-30,[24] Luke xi.49-51[25] and Luke xxii.19b.[26] Once

18. G. F. Hawthorne, 'Christian prophecy and the sayings of Jesus: evidence of and criteria for', *SBL 1975 Seminar Papers*, II, 113.

19. Cf. also I Clem. 8.3, 17.6, 23.3f., 29.3, 46.2. But see D. A. Hagner, *The Use of the Old and New Testaments in Clement of Rome* (NovTSup XXXIV, 1973), particularly pp. 86-93.

20. See further E. E. Ellis, *Paul's Use of the Old Testament* (Grand Rapids, 1957), pp. 107-12.

21. See also Hawthorne, p. 114.

22. See e.g. E. Klostermann, *Das Matthäusevangelium* (HNT ³1938), p. 20; W. Manson, *Jesus the Messiah* (London, 1943), pp. 70f.; R. H. Fuller, *The Mission and Achievement of Jesus* (London, 1954), p. 91; W. Grundmann, *Das Evangelium nach Matthäus* (THNT, 1968), pp. 420f.

23. Cf. J. Wellhausen, *Das Evangelium Matthaei* (Berlin, 1914), p. 44; F. Hahn, *Mission in the New Testament* (ET London, 1965), pp. 54ff.

24. Perhaps an inspired utterance arising out of a prophet's meditation on the already established logion preserved in Matt. xi.25-7 and/or Ecclus. li.23-7. See further Dunn, *Jesus and the Spirit*, §5.2.

25. Cf. E. E. Ellis, 'Luke 11.49-51: An Oracle of a Christian Prophet?', *ExpTim* LXXIV (1962-3), 157f.; also, *The Gospel of Luke* (New Century Bible, 1966), pp. 170ff.

26. Hawthorne, pp. 113f.: 'Do this in remembrance of me' could have originated as a prophetic utterance (cf. I Cor. xi.23f.; Didache 10.7), or simply as a liturgical development of the ear-

we submit to the persuasiveness of this evidence the question becomes not whether prophetic utterances were included within the Jesus-tradition, but to what extent this happened: are the examples cited simply isolated instances, or merely the more perceptible tip of a very large iceberg?[27]

II. The Case against Bultmann's Hypothesis

The main weaknesses which criticism has exposed in Bultmann's thesis are as follows.[28]

1. The Lack of Substantive Parallels

There is no shortage of evidence for prophetic inspiration among the early Christians, and adequate evidence that the inspiration was attributed to the risen Jesus or the Spirit of Christ on many, if not most, occasions (though see further below). But that is not enough. Putative parallels will only demonstrate the validity of Bultmann's hypothesis if they provide evidence that sayings of the risen Jesus were incorporated within the Jesus-tradition. This evidence is lacking. *Wherever we look in the comparative material of the time the distinctive character of the prophetic utterance as the saying of a* prophet, *or as the words of the* exalted Christ *is maintained, and some sort of distinction between the words of the earthly Jesus and the prophetic inspiration of the present is implied or explicit.*

(a) In OT prophecy it is significant, as F. Neugebauer points out, that no OT book names Yahweh as its author. On the contrary, it is characteristic of prophetic literature within Judaism that it was passed down under the name of the *prophet* — so much so that unless a human recipient was named, the writing stood little chance of being accepted as inspired prophecy.[29] It may be that this feature retained its regulative force only so long as prophecy was

---

lier, briefer 'words of institution'. D. Aune has begun to catalogue the Jesus logia attributed to Christian prophets by different scholars — 'Christian prophecy and the sayings of Jesus: an index to Synoptic pericopae ostensibly influenced by early Christian prophets', *SBL 1975 Seminar Papers*, II, 131-42.

27. For further considerations in favour of Bultmann's thesis see Hawthorne, pp. 105-29.

28. See particularly F. Neugebauer, 'Geistsprüche und Jesuslogien', *ZNW* LIII (1962), 218-28; E. Cothenet, *Dictionnaire de la Bible, Supplément* VIII (1972), cols. 1285ff.; D. Hill, 'On the evidence for the creative role of Christian prophets', *NTS* XX (1973-4), 262-74.

29. Neugebauer, p. 222. Cf. *Pirke Aboth*.

thought of as confined to a few prominent individuals. In the earliest churches, where all seemed to experience the prophetic Spirit, it may have been considered unnecessary to claim authority for a saying by attributing it to any one prophet in particular. But what evidence we have tells against rather than for such a supposition: whenever Luke quotes a prophetic utterance as such he always names the prophet concerned (iii.4f., iv.17ff.); and 'the revelation of Jesus Christ' (Rev. i.1) is more precisely defined as 'to his servant John'. The implication is that the early churches were as suspicious of anonymous prophetic oracles as were their Jewish forebears, and prompts the question, Was there ever a stage when a mass of 'sayings of Jesus' were circulated without any concern as to who first gave them utterance?

(b) The most relevant evidence from Paul is I Cor. vii.10, 25, 40, where Paul seems to maintain in his own mind a clear distinction between the instruction (παραγγελία) which he is able to pass on from the Jesus-tradition (vii.10 — Mark x.11f. pars; Matt. v.32) and the opinion (γνώμη) which he offers in vii.25 — περὶ δὲ τῶν παρθένων ἐπιταγὴν κυρίου οὐκ ἔχω, γνώμην δὲ δίδωμι ὡς ἠλεημένος ὑπὸ κυρίου πιστὸς εἶναι. To be sure, he regards his 'opinion' as inspired (vii.40 — δοκῶ δὲ κἀγὼ πνεῦμα Θεοῦ ἔχειν), but this makes the distinction he holds between Jesus-tradition and inspired opinion all the more significant.[30] The distinction is one of authority: where the earthly Jesus has spoken on a subject, that word is to be regarded as an instruction or command; but an opinion, even if formed immediately by the Spirit, cannot count as a 'command of the Lord', but only be offered as advice.[31] In other words, for Paul there is a qualitative distinction between Jesus-tradition and the inspiration of the present, and the one is not a complete substitute for the other. We must therefore ask whether there was indeed a large-scale process at work whereby such sayings as II Cor. xii.9 and I Thess. iv.15 were gradually incorporated within the Jesus-tradition. The evidence from Paul points to a negative answer.

(c) Rev. ii–iii is a good example of a parallel which stops short at the crucial point. For while these chapters provide wholly adequate proof that the exalted Christ was recognized as the author of many inspired utterances within first-century Christianity, the decisive fact is that these utterances are attributed precisely to the *exalted* Christ.[32] There is no evidence here or else-

30. Teeple's suggestion that I Cor. vii.10-11, ix.14, xi.23-6 was received by Paul 'from the Lord directly, apparently by spiritual revelation' (p. 65 n. 24) has little or no support among commentators and is rightly to be rejected.

31. Cf. L. Goppelt, 'Tradition nach Paulus', *KuD* IV (1958), 224; Neugebauer, pp. 226f.; J. Roloff, *Apostolat-Verkündigung-Kirche* (Gütersloh, 1965), p. 97.

32. Hill, pp. 266f., 268ff.

where in Revelation for the transition of such sayings into the tradition ascribed to the *earthly* Jesus. And if John has incorporated earlier prophetic material into his writing, then it becomes all the more significant that as late as the end of the first century A.D. such prophetic utterances remain firmly attached to the exalted Christ and have not yet been incorporated within the Jesus-tradition. It is true of course that the second-century *Apocalypse of Peter* sets its revelatory material within the ministry of Jesus, but this provides no real parallel since the *Gattung* 'Apocalypse' is so markedly different from the *Gattung* 'Gospel'.[33]

(d) Just as significant is that parallel with the Gnostic gospels. Here too authoritative logia claim Jesus as their author. But here too it is the *exalted* Christ who speaks. Thus, for example, in *Pistis Sophia* 42 the risen Jesus says:

> Hear, Philip, thou blessed one, that I may speak with thee, for you and Thomas and Matthew are they to whom the charge is given by the first mystery, to write down all the things which I shall say and do, and all the things which ye shall see.[34]

Evidently the Gnostics felt no need to project sayings of the risen Jesus back into the Jesus-tradition; they preferred the revelations of the Risen One. This fact highlights a flaw in the logic of Bultmann's hypothesis. For if prophetic utterances were projected back into the Jesus-tradition by the earliest communities, that implies that they were of more or less equal authority for the first Christians. But if sayings of the risen Jesus were as authoritative as sayings of the earthly Jesus, then whence came the sort of (unconscious) pressure which Bultmann must presuppose to incorporate prophetic sayings into the Jesus-tradition?[35] And should we not find a goodly number of Synoptic-like sayings preserved for us in the earliest Christian literature *outside* the Synoptic Gospels? — sayings, that is, which might have been incorporated into the Synoptic tradition but which were not. The almost total absence of such evidence suggests that there were not after all so many sayings of the risen Jesus which circulated among the earliest communities as Bultmann assumes.[36]

33. Cf. Neugebauer, pp. 224ff.

34. Hennecke, I, 272.

35. Cf. F. G. Downing, *The Church and Jesus* (London, 1968), p. 121.

36. See also Hill, p. 264. The only really Synoptic-like saying of Jesus preserved outside the Synoptics in the earliest Christian literature is Acts xx.35 (see above, p. 17). But its origin as a prophetic oracle is even less likely than its place in the original Jesus-tradition. Hawthorne compares Rev. ii.10 with Matt. x.28, 22, Rev. iii.20 with John xiv.23, Rev. xvi.15 with Matt. xxiv.43f., Luke xii.39, and Rev. iii.5 with Luke xvii.8-9 (p. 112). For other possible examples in later literature see J. Jeremias, *Unknown Sayings of Jesus* (ET London, 1964).

In short, it is readily conceivable that in the earliest days of Christianity there were certain prophetic utterances of such a striking character, so manifestly words of the risen Lord, which were not unnaturally grouped with similar sayings of the earthly Jesus for one purpose or another, and whose origin in post-Easter prophecy was subsequently forgotten, so that later compilers of such sayings of Jesus took the whole group without question as authentic Jesus-tradition. But the assumption or thesis that there was a *substantial* movement of prophetic 'I'-words into the Jesus-tradition runs counter to the evidence available to us.

2. The Indecisiveness of Form-Critical Criteria

Several features of the Synoptic logia have been proffered as characteristic of the form of the prophetic oracle — particularly the ἀμήν and λέγω ὑμῖν formula,[37] and pronouncements of blessedness or woe.[38] But as formal criteria they provide no help in deciding whether a particular saying or group of sayings originated with the earthly or exalted Jesus. For if these are prophetic forms stemming from an apocalyptic background (as Schulz maintains), then we can hardly ignore the fact that Jesus was himself a prophet,[39] whose message had marked apocalyptic features.[40] That such formulae were distinctive of Jesus' utterances may very plausibly be denied; it is highly implausible to deny outright that Jesus could or did use such formulae.

The most widely acclaimed formal criterion is that suggested by E. Käsemann.[41] Sentences like I Cor. iii.17 and Gal. i.9 lead him to the conclusion that a form of prophetic speech widely recognized in the early churches was the eschatological *ius talionis*. The appearance of this form within the Synoptic tradition, most clearly Mark viii.38, enables him to conclude that these sayings originated as prophetic utterances out of the apocalyptic fervour of the period immediately after Easter. He can of course confine this form to the post-Easter period only by denying the influence of apocalyptic

---

37. V. Hasler, *Amen: redaktionsgeschichtliche Untersuchung zur Einführungsformel der Herrenworte 'Wahrlich, ich sage euch'* (Zurich, 1969); cf. K. Berger, *Die Amen-Worte Jesu* (Berlin, 1970).

38. See Schulz, pp. 57-62. See also Müller, part III.

39. See e.g. C. H. Dodd, 'Jesus as Teacher and Prophet', *Mysterium Christi* (ed. G. K. A. Bell and A. Deissmann, London, 1930), chap. III; R. Meyer, *Der Prophet aus Galiläa* (Leipzig, 1940); G. Friedrich, *TDNT* VI, 841-8; Dunn, *Jesus and the Spirit*, §14.

40. See K. Koch, *The Rediscovery of Apocalyptic* (ET London, 1972), chap. VI.

41. 'Sentences of Holy Law in the New Testament' (see p. 13, n. 2 above).

on Jesus.[42] But even more damaging is K. Berger's finding that the form is typical of exhortations in Wisdom literature; the form has much deeper roots than Käsemann supposed and cannot be confined to the charismatic prophecy of post-Easter enthusiasm.[43]

In short, formal criteria really provide no help at this point, since they do not permit any sort of clear line to be drawn between sayings of the earthly Jesus and sayings of the exalted Lord. We are in fact thrown back on judgements based on content and life-setting of individual logia.

3. The Concern to Preserve the Tradition of Jesus' Sayings

This concern is nowhere so explicit in the earliest Christian literature as is the vitality of prophetic experience. But obviously it is strongly implied by the very existence of a collection like Q. And it is implied also by the number of references to teachers, teaching and tradition within the early churches.[44] The teaching function is very clearly part of Christianity's heritage from Judaism,[45] and we must suppose that the Christian teacher shared something at least of the concern of his opposite number in Judaism to preserve and pass on that which was recognized as authoritative tradition — which for the former must have included the sayings of Jesus. The fact that prophet and teacher are so often linked — both by Paul (I Cor. xii.28, xiv.6, Eph. iv.11) and by the early tradition underlying Acts xiii.1 — strongly suggests that the creative role of prophecy was balanced to a considerable extent by the conserving role of teaching from very early days in the gatherings of the new sect. We must not of course overplay the distinction between teacher and prophet, or overestimate the conservative role of the teacher. It is evident from both Acts and Paul that teaching included charismatic interpretation and that there was no clear line between that and the prophetic *pesher*.[46] Even less justified is the thesis of B. Gerhardsson that the tradition of Jesus' message was handed

---

42. But see Koch's perceptive criticism (pp. 75-8).

43. K. Berger, 'Zu den sogenannten Sätzen heiligen Rechts', *NTS* XVII (1970-1), 10-40. See also Hill, pp. 271-4.

44. Cf. particularly Acts ii.42, xiii.1, Rom. vi.17, xii.7, xvi.17, 1 Cor. xi.2, xii.28, xiv.6, 26, II Thess. ii.15, iii.6, Jas. iii.1.

45. K. Rengstorf, *TDNT* II, 157.

46. Cf. Goppelt, pp. 213-33; Roloff, pp. 84-98; E. E. Ellis, 'The role of the Christian prophet in Acts', *Apostolic History and the Gospel* (F. F. Bruce Festschrift, ed. W. W. Gasque & R. P. Martin, Exeter, 1970), pp. 58-64; K. Wengst, 'Der Apostel und die Tradition', *ZTK* LXIX (1972), 145-62. See further Dunn, *Jesus and the Spirit*, §§33.2, 41.4, 48.2.

down by 'the apostles' in a fixed form from the first.[47] On the other hand, the role accorded to teachers in earliest Christianity should warn us against going to the other extreme by overestimating the liberty accorded to prophetic inspiration in respect to the tradition already received. In short, it would run contrary to the evidence to deny that there was a very active concern among the first Christians to preserve and pass on the sayings of the earthly Jesus.

Thus far I have merely restated and elaborated the main points which seem to emerge on both sides of the debate occasioned by Bultmann's hypothesis. To date the debate has centred principally on Bultmann's contention that there was an easy and regular transition of sayings of the risen Jesus into the Jesus-tradition, presumably via collections of sayings of Jesus indiscriminately culled from both categories. My principal inquiry is directed at an earlier stage in the postulated process — the point at which prophetic 'I'-sayings became accepted as sayings of the risen Jesus. To this inquiry we now turn.

III. The Importance of Testing Prophetic Oracles within Early Christianity

How highly regarded were prophetic utterances in the earliest churches? Prophecy certainly featured prominently in the early years of the new sect and was considered to be a key characteristic of its worship and life — that is clear enough from such passages as Acts ii.17f., I Cor. xiv, Eph. ii.20. But does that mean that whenever and wherever a prophet rose to speak, or comprehensible words were uttered under inspiration, the whole community thereupon assumed that this was the exalted Jesus or his Spirit speaking? Bultmann's hypothesis invites an affirmative answer.[48] But that would be to ignore a problem which is inextricably bound up with the prophetic phenomenon — the problem *of false* prophecy. The fact is that *wherever within the cultural and historical context of early Christianity we encounter the consciousness of inspiration by the Spirit of God, we encounter also an awareness that no inspiration or inspired utterance is self-authenticating.* Since other spiritual forces were recognized to be at work and could be the inspiration behind a prophetic word, consequently *no* prophecy could command acceptance in and of itself, and *all* prophecy had to be subjected to scrutiny and tested. The point is easily demonstrated.

---

47. B. Gerhardsson, *Memory and Manuscript* (Lund, 1961); see also *Tradition and Transmission in Early Christianity* (Lund, 1964); and earlier, H. Riesenfeld, *The Gospel Tradition and Its Beginnings* (London, 1957).

48. So Hawthorne: '. . . what he [the prophet] said was accepted by the community as the command of the Lord to be obeyed without question . . .' (p. 109).

Throughout the most vigorous period of Israelite prophecy the problem of false prophecy continually crops up and is never finally resolved. It first emerges in Judg. ix.23, I Sam. xvi.14, xviii.10f., xix.9f., II Sam. xxiv.1-17, where actions of the charismatic leader of the time are attributed to inspiration from Yahweh, even though they were manifestly evil or in the event were judged to be mistaken. These passages immediately highlight *the ambiguity of inspiration,* be it of word or deed. And thereafter the awareness of this ambiguity, of the ever-present danger of false prophecy, even in the mouth of a sincere and honourable prophet, haunts the pages of the OT. The classic expressions of this problem must include I Kings xiii, xxii, and Jeremiah. In I Kings xiii two prophets claim to exercise genuine prophetic ministry but speak conflicting oracles, and the 'false prophet' (if he is rightly so called) speaks both lies and a true word of the Lord, whereas it is the 'true prophet' who is led astray and brought to judgement. In I Kings xxii there is recounted the famous encounter between Ahab and the prophet Micaiah, with Micaiah denouncing the contrary military advice from the 400 prophets as the product of a lying spirit put in their mouth by Yahweh. Jeremiah well represents the self-questioning and misgivings which must rack the prophet whose inspired utterances are pessimistic and unpopular — particularly xv.18b and xx.7.

> Wilt thou be to me like a deceitful brook, like waters that fail? . . .
> O Lord thou hast deceived me, and I was deceived;
>   thou art stronger than I, and thou hast prevailed.
> I have become a laughing stock all the day;
>   everyone mocks me.

In these words the confident claim and counter-claim of competing prophets certain of the genuineness of their own inspiration are left far behind, and the problem of false prophecy achieves its most anguished expression, where even the consciousness of overwhelming inspiration (xx.9) gives the prophet himself no assurance that his words are true.[49]

With the revival of the prophetic Spirit at Qumran the same problem emerges, though in a different form. Clearly expressed is the awareness that inspiration and conduct may be prompted by the Spirit of perversity as well as by the Spirit of truth (1QS 3.18–4.26). Entry into the community did not mean escape from the influence of the Spirit of evil (1QS 3.18-21, 4.23, 11.9-15, 1QH 4.29-31),[50] and the threat of false prophecy and apostasy is wholly familiar to the Qumran covenanters (1QH 4.16, CD 8.1f.). Consequently it was for-

---

49. See further on this whole area J. L. Crenshaw, *Prophetic Conflict* (BZAW, 1971).
50. See Dunn, *Jesus and the Spirit,* chap. X, n. 79.

mally recognized that there was a need to examine the spirit of the member of the community not only on his entry to the covenant (וְדָרְשׁוּ אֶת רוּחוֹם) but every year (פּוֹקְדָם אֶת רוּחָם) (1QS 5.20-4; see also 6.13-23).

The early Christian churches of Syria-Palestine were certainly well aware of the danger of false prophecy: Matt. vii.15ff. — προσέχετε ἀπὸ τῶν ψευδοπροφητῶν, οἵτινες ἔρχονται πρὸς ὑμᾶς ἐν ἐνδύμασιν προβάτων, ἔσωθεν δέ εἰσιν λύκοι ἅρπαγες. In addition, Mark and Matthew have Jesus warning against the danger of false prophets (Mark xiii.22/Matt. xxiv.24, Matt. xxiv.11), and Luke attributes a saying to Jesus which warns disciples against seeking a popularity like that enjoyed by the false prophets of old (Luke vi.26). According to Luke, moreover, the first major outreach from Antioch soon encountered the false prophet Elymas in Cyprus (Acts xiii.6), just as the first major outreach from Jerusalem ran foul of Simon in Samaria (Acts viii.10 — ἡ δύναμις τοῦ Θεοῦ ἡ καλουμένη Μεγάλη).

Of the first-generation Christians no one appears to have more clearly grasped the danger of an inspiration whose source was demonic and whose utterance could not be trusted than Paul. Wherever he is confronted with prophecy as a living force he is quick to indicate that prophetic inspiration alone is no guarantee that the inspired word is of the Spirit. So much so that *every* prophetic utterance must be subjected to careful scrutiny and evaluation. Thus in listing various charismata in I Cor. xii.8-10 he is careful to link in close conjunction προφητεία and διακρίσεις πνευμάτων, the plural presumably indicating that each prophetic utterance should be accompanied by a process of διάκρισις. This suggestion is confirmed by I Cor. xiv.29 where Paul's specific instruction is that if two or three prophets speak in the assembly the others (that is, presumably, the other prophets) should evaluate what is said (διακρινέτωσαν) — that is, presumably, as to its source and/or significance.[51] So too in I Cor. ii.13, the difficult phrase πνευματικοῖς πνευματικὰ συγκρίνοντες must include the thought that inspired speech (as well as τὰ χαρισθέντα more generally) should always be subject to some sort of evaluation. In his earlier letter to a community which shared the apocalyptic enthusiasm of the earliest Palestinian groups he encourages them to welcome the prophetic Spirit, but at once adds πάντα δὲ δοκιμάζετε — 'Do not stifle inspiration, and do not despise prophetic utterances, but bring them all to the test and then keep what is good in them and avoid the bad of whatever kind' (I Thess. v.19-22 NEB). The fact that he includes the exhortation in such brief compass in the conclusion of his letter implies that the problem of false

---

51. On διάκρισις πνευμάτων as meaning 'interpretation of revelations given by the Spirit' see Dautzenberg, pp. 122-8.

prophecy was not something which had newly dawned either on Paul or on his fellow believers. At the same time the importance of testing all prophecy was apparently soon underlined for the Thessalonians by their too-ready acceptance of a prophetic utterance (διὰ πνεύματος, διὰ λόγου) to the effect that the day of the Lord had (already) come (II Thess. ii.2).[52]

At the end of the first century and into the second century the emphasis and caution are the same, only much more pronounced. Prophecy is welcome and necessary, but it must be tested; it cannot claim a hearing or demand obedience without itself being submitted to some sort of evaluation. Thus I John iv.1 — ἀγαπητοί, μὴ παντὶ πνεύματι πιστεύετε, ἀλλὰ δοκιμάζετε τά πνεύματα εἰ ἐκ τοῦ Θεοῦ ἐστιν, ὅτι πολλοὶ ψευδοπροφῆται ἐξεληλύθασιν εἰς τὸν κόσμον. Didache is even more conscious of the danger of false prophecy, and gives detailed instructions on how and when evaluation of a visiting prophet should be carried out. Not everyone who speaks ἐν πνεύματι is a prophet; therefore all who come 'in the name of the Lord' must be examined and tested (διακρίνειν, δοκιμάζειν) (Did. 11.7f., 12.1). Most detailed of all is the treatment of the eleventh Mandate, where Hermas is warned against false prophets and given careful instructions on how to test (δοκιμάζειν) whether a man has the divine Spirit or the spirit which is earthly, empty, powerless and foolish (Herm. Mand. 11.7, 11, 16).[53]

The unanimity of the evidence on this point is impressive. Wherever in pre-Christian Judaism and early Christianity men have claimed that the words they spoke were inspired by God's Spirit, there has been an accompanying recognition that their claim might be false; wherever in pre-Christian Judaism and early Christianity prophecies have been uttered 'in the name of the Lord', the need has also been stressed for some degree of discrimination and evaluation to test and discern whether they were genuine words of the Lord or not. The question then becomes, Was a similar degree of caution exercised within the earliest Palestinian communities through and from whom the bulk of the Jesus-tradition came? Was the need to test prophetic utterances, to discriminate true from false, characteristic of the early days of the new enthusiastic sect? These questions gain added point by the silence of Acts on the subject, by the fact that the Qumran parallel is of a somewhat different order from the rest of the material cited above, and by the wider *religionsgeschichtliche* fact that the more enthusiastic a new religious movement the

---

52. For individual points of exegesis see Dunn, *Jesus and the Spirit,* §41.3.

53. See also Heb. v.14 — the teacher is trained πρὸς διάκρισιν καλοῦ τε καὶ κακοῦ; I Clem. 48.5 — ἤτω τις πιστός, ἤτω δυνατὸς γνῶσιν ἐξειπεῖν, ἤτω σοφὸς ἐν διακρίσει λόγων. . . . Cf. Josephus, *Bell.* ii.258-63; vi.285-315; Rev. ii.20.

less inhibited and discriminating it tends to be in the first generation. Nevertheless it is more than likely that we shall have to answer these questions in the affirmative.

(a) When Paul speaks on this subject he does not introduce the idea of testing prophecy as something new; he rather assumes it as something already well known and underlines its importance. Nor can we assume that the need for evaluating inspired utterances was something which came into Christianity only when it spread beyond Palestine. Certainly Hellenistic religion recognized the need for ecstatic prophecy to be *interpreted;* that is, the unintelligible utterances of the god-possessed mantis had to be translated into intelligible speech. But the parallel to that in the Pauline communities was the association of glossolalia and interpretation. The need for prophecy to be accompanied by evaluation is much more likely to be part of Hellenistic Christianity's *Jewish* heritage transmitted to it through early Palestinian Christianity.[54]

(b) The rabbinic dogma that prophecy had ceased in Israel after the early post-exilic period has long roots and was already well established at the time of Jesus (see particularly Ps. lxxiv.9, Zech. xiii.2-6, I Macc. iv.46, ix.27, xiv.41).[55] It is not surprising then that the reappearance of the prophetic Spirit in John and Jesus met with scepticism and provoked several attempts to test their claims (Mark viii.11f. pars, xi.27-33 pars; cf. John i.19-23). It is entirely probable that the same response from the religious authorities greeted the outbreak of prophetic enthusiasm which marked the beginnings of the new sect after Jesus' death and resurrection (cf. Acts ii.13, v.34-9). The earliest communities could therefore hardly ignore the problem of false prophecy and must have been conscious to some degree at least of the need to exercise some caution over the prophetic oracles which were uttered in their meetings — all the more so if Zech. xiii.2f. was taken at all seriously by them (cf. Mark xiv.27 par = Zech. xiii.7).

(c) An important fact is that some of the most strongly worded warnings against false prophecy appear in contexts where apocalyptic enthusiasm is most marked (Mark xiii.6 pars — an 'I'-word; Mark xiii.21ff./Matt. xxiv.23ff.; Matt. xxiv.11; II Thess. ii.1ff.; Rev. xvi.13f., xix.20; cf. I John iv.1ff., II Pet. ii.1). Whether such warnings were the reaction to prophetic excess in the earliest days, or accompanied the initial resurgence of prophetic activity

---

54. See further Dunn, *Jesus and the Spirit,* §§41.a, 3, 7, 8.

55. For rabbinic references see P. Schäfer, *Die Vorstellung vom heiligen Geist in der rabbinischen Literatur* (Munich, 1972), pp. 89-115, 143-6. But see also pp. 116-34, 147ff. Fuller details in Dunn, *Jesus and the Spirit,* chap. IV, n. 81.

in the first Christian communities we cannot of course tell. Either way it is difficult to avoid the conclusion that the danger of false prophecy was quickly recognized by the wiser and more mature members among the first Christians, and that from early on prophetic oracles were examined with some care lest they be prompted by a lying spirit attempting to deceive the saints.

(d) The silence of Acts should not be accorded too much importance. Luke has chosen to overlook several key aspects of primitive Christianity (not least the eschatological character of early Christian enthusiasm), and almost certainly this is one of them. The fact is that he ignores the problem of false prophecy completely — as much in the latter half of his history, when we know it was a problem at Thessalonica and Corinth, as in the former. He does not even comment when his record embraces two inspired convictions on the same issue which run directly counter to each other (Acts xx.22, xxi.13).[56] Luke's silence on the matter at hand is therefore more likely the result of Luke's idiosyncrasies than of the deficiencies of primitive Christianity.

In short, it is probable that the earliest Christian communities not only rejoiced in the prophetic Spirit freely bestowed upon them, but also recognized from very early on, if not from the first, that prophecy is regularly accompanied by false prophecy, that enthusiasm all too often outruns inspiration, and that consequently *all* prophetic utterances must be tested as to their origin and significance for the congregation addressed. We may therefore already conclude, with sufficient justification, that *not every prophetic 'I'-word uttered in an early Christian assembly was taken to be a saying of the risen Jesus.* But if such discrimination was exercised by the community at large or by its acknowledged spokesmen, what criteria did they use? How was it possible to discern the source of a prophetic utterance? The answer to these questions will obviously tell us much about the sort of 'I'-word which was likely to be accepted as a saying of the Risen One, and what sort of prophetic oracles would likely have been rejected.

IV. The Criteria for Assessing Prophetic Utterances within Early Christianity

Where prophecy is a living force the community addressed cannot help but be conscious of the immediacy of divine revelation, and the atmosphere of an assembly will often be electric as it awaits a word from God. But where the

---

56. See further Dunn, *Jesus and the Spirit*, §31.3; Acts v.3f. could however be described as a 'discerning of spirits'.

danger of a false or deluded inspiration is recognized, where the problem of false prophecy has begun to be apprehended in all its seriousness, where consciousness of the demonic is as real as consciousness of the divine, a note of cautious discretion begins to mark the community's response to prophecy. In such circumstances the key question becomes, How can the individual or assembly tell when a prophecy is a 'word of the Lord' and when it is something very different — something demonic or solely human foisted upon the community wittingly or unwittingly by the over-eager or over-enthusiastic prophet? The quest for the right, or even adequate criteria, has been the inevitable concomitant of the problem of false prophecy wherever it has appeared within the religion of Israel and early Christianity.

In the most recent study of the subject J. L. Crenshaw outlines the various criteria employed within the OT.[57] He divides them into two main categories: message-centred criteria and criteria focusing upon the man. In the former category the test which is most often used is that of fulfilment and non-fulfilment. Thus, for example, the classic statement of Deut. xviii.22 — 'When the word spoken by the prophet in the name of the Lord is not fulfilled and does not come true, it is not a word spoken by the Lord. The prophet has spoken presumptuously; do not hold him in awe.' And Second Isaiah uses the criterion repeatedly — for example, xliv.7f.:

> Who is like me? Let him stand up,
> Let him declare himself and speak and show me his evidence,
> Let him announce beforehand things to come,
> Let him declare what is yet to happen.
>   Take heart, do not be afraid.
> Did I not foretell this long ago?
> I declared it, and you are my witnesses.[58]

This criterion is too bald, an oversimplification; it can only be applied to predictive prophecy and does not allow for the conditional element of prophecy — Yahweh can change his mind (II Kings xx.1ff.)! Consequently rather more refined criteria are sought. Thus the sensitive spirit of Jeremiah limits the criterion to prophecies of peace: 'If a prophet foretells prosperity, when his words come true it will be known that the Lord has sent him' (Jer. xxviii.9). In the context of Jeremiah's time the mark of the true prophet was his refusal to turn a blind eye to the disaster that lay ahead (cf. vi.14, viii.11, xiv.13ff.,

---

57. Crenshaw, pp. 49-61.

58. Translations from NEB. See also I Sam. iii.19, 1 Kings viii.56, xxii.28, Isa. xxx.8, Ezek. xxxiii.33, (II) Isa. xli.21ff., xlii.9, xliv.26, xlv.21, xlvi.10, xlviii.15f., lv.10f.

xxiii.16f.; see also I Kings xxii.5ff., Micah iii.5, Ezek. xiii.10). Elsewhere the author of Deuteronomy recognizes that the *fulfilment* of a prophet's prediction does *not* mean that everything he says should be followed: 'if he says, "Let us go after other gods", which you have not known, "and let us serve them", you shall not listen to the words of that prophet . . .' (Deut. xiii.1ff.). Here loyalty to Yahweh is the ultimate criterion.[59] The criteria focusing upon the man centre especially on the character of the prophet's conduct and his motivation. Isaiah and Jeremiah denounce the prophets of their time for drunkenness, adultery, lying and encouraging immorality in others (Isa. xxviii.7, Jer. xxiii.14). Micah denounces those who prophesy for gain or out of pique (Mic. iii.5), and both Micaiah ben Imlah and Amos demonstrate how important it is for the true prophet to retain his basic independence of all but Yahweh (I Kings xxii.5ff., Amos vii.14f.).

At Qumran the criteria for admission and for the annual examination are twofold — the individual's knowledge and understanding of the law, and his obedience to it (1QS 5.21, 24, 6.14, 18). Likewise the criterion of Matt. vii.16 focuses primarily on conduct and character — 'You will know them (false prophets) by their fruits'. For Matthew this means primarily disregard for the law: false prophecy and lawlessness (ἀνομία) go hand in hand (vii.23, xxiv.11f.; contrast Jesus, v.17-20).[60]

Paul deals with inspired utterance at greatest length in I Cor. xii–xiv. In these three chapters it can be clearly seen that he employs three different criteria of evaluation.[61] The first is the test of kerygmatic tradition: I Cor. xii.3 — 'No one speaking ἐν πνεύματι Θεοῦ says, "Jesus be cursed"; and no one can say "Jesus is Lord" except ἐν πνεύματι ἁγίῳ'. Here the test is a basic statement of the gospel — 'Jesus is Lord' — probably the basic confession of Hellenistic Christianity (cf. Rom. x.9, I Cor. viii.6, II Cor. iv.5, Phil. ii.11, Col. ii.6).[62] This gives the test of I Cor. xii.3 a particular importance. But probably in Paul's mind it is only one example of the larger criterion of kerygmatic tradition: if any inspired utterance runs counter to the gospel by which they were con-

---

59. Less satisfactory is the attempt to classify *what forms* of inspiration are acceptable — ecstatic or non-ecstatic, by dream or otherwise, by word or spirit (cf. particularly Jer. xxiii.25-8) — since the classical prophets themselves were no strangers to ecstatic and visionary experiences. See particularly J. Lindblom, *Prophecy in Ancient Israel* (Oxford, 1962), chap. III.

60. Cf. G. Barth in G. Bornkamm, G. Barth and H. J. Held, *Tradition and Interpretation in Matthew* (ET London, 1963), pp. 73ff.

61. See more fully Dunn, *Jesus and the Spirit*, §49.2.

62. See O. Cullmann, *The Earliest Christian Confessions* (ET London, 1949); V. H. Neufeld, *The Earliest Christian Confessions* (Leiden, 1963); K. Wengst, *Christologische Formeln und Lieder des Urchristentums* (Gütersloh, 1972), pp. 131-5.

verted it is to be rejected (Gal. i.8f.; cf. II Thess. ii.15, Col. ii.6). The second criterion is that of character — in particular, does it manifest love? — I Cor. xiii. Verses 4-7 are clearly polemical in intent. The Corinthian charismatics, exulting in their experiences of angelic speech (glossolalia) and the extent of their prophetic powers, had evidently become all that love was not — impatient, unkind, jealous, boastful, arrogant, rude, etc. Such a loveless character was sufficient indication that the χάρις behind their χάρισμα was not ἡ χάρις τοῦ κυρίου Ἰησοῦ Χριστοῦ (cf. Gal. v.16-24). The third test Paul applies to inspired utterance is that of οἰκοδομή — a test applied regularly throughout I Cor. xiv. In particular it is this test which demonstrates with finality for Paul that of the two most prominent types of inspired utterance in the Corinthian assembly, prophecy is superior to glossolalia; for glossolalia is a purely private, personal affair between the individual and God, whereas through prophecy God speaks to the whole congregation and builds it up by opening it more and more to God (xiv.1-5, 12, 17, 24f.). So too it is the overruling need that all things be done in the assembly πρὸς οἰκοδομήν which makes evaluation of prophetic utterance indispensable (xiv.29) and which presumably provides the means of evaluation (cf. viii.1, x.23), since for Paul prophecy is only a χάρισμα in so far as it is also a διακονία to the community (xii.4f.).

In I John the test by which the Spirit of God may be recognized is the confession that Jesus Christ has come in the flesh; whereas the spirit of antichrist refuses to make this confession (I John iv.1ff.; cf. ii.22f., iv.15, v.1). Here again we have the criterion of kerygmatic tradition. In this case the particular test is not an original form of the gospel, since 'Jesus Christ came in the flesh' is clearly a late-first-century confessional response to the threat of docetism (cf. I John v.6ff.); but in John's mind it is probably the response which ὃ ἀπ' ἀρχῆς demanded (ii.24, iii.11; cf. v.6ff., II John 9f.).[63] Other 'tests of life' which John uses throughout his letters include particularly conduct which demonstrates obedience to the commandment ἣν εἴχετε ἀπ' ἀρχῆς (ii.3-7, iii.4-10, 24, v.2f., 18; II John 5f.), and in particular, love of the brethren (ii.7-11, iii.11-18, iv.7-12, 20f., v.2, II John 5f.).

Didache urges that all wandering charismatics or visiting missionaries should be tested (12.1). It speaks primarily in terms of testing prophets (11.7-12), but teachers and apostles have to be tested too, so presumably the tests he enumerates apply in all three cases (cf. 11.5f. — an ἀπόστολος who fails the test is a ψευδοπροφήτης; 13.1f. — the same rule applies to both προφήτης and διδάσκαλος). The principal criterion is the test of conduct: ἀπὸ οὖν τῶν τρόπων γνωσθήσεται ὁ ψευδοπροφήτης καὶ ὁ προφήτης (11.8). Examples of

---

63. Cf. Rev. xix.10 — ἡ γὰρ μαρτυρία Ἰησοῦ ἐστιν τὸ πνεῦμα τῆς προφητείας.

conduct which fails the test include asking for money, even when the request or command is made ἐν πνεύματι (11.6, 12), and living off the community for more than two or three days (11.5, 12.2ff.). Here conduct is seen as evidence of motivation — the true apostle, prophet, teacher will be untrammelled with possessions and constantly driven to move on by his missionary compulsion. Here too the test also has an eye to the good of the community — those who abuse the community's hospitality can hardly bring it benefit, even when they teach the truth (cf. 11.10). Of course, if they do not even teach ἡ ἀλήθεια they are to be ignored (11.1f.). This is the other main criterion — the truth of the saying uttered charismatically. And here again the test is the teaching which has already been received previously (ταῦτα πάντα τὰ προειρημένα — 11.1) — teaching which furthers δικαιοσύνην καὶ γνῶσιν κυρίου (11.2).

Similarly in Hermas the chief criterion is the character of the prophet's conduct and life — δοκίμαζε οὖν ἀπὸ τῶν ἔργων καὶ τῆς ζωῆς τὸν ἄνθρωπον τὸν λέγοντα ἑαυτὸν πνευματοφόρον εἶναι (11.16). The false prophet is ambitious and greedy for honour; he is bold, shameless and talks too much; he lives in luxury and accepts money for his prophecies; he avoids meeting with the congregation as a whole where he would be unmasked by the righteous, and associates instead with the δίψυχοι and the κενοί, meeting with them privately (κατὰ γωνίαν) to minister to them (11.12-13).[64] Hermas also describes the character of false prophecy in a way which offers a second criterion for evaluating prophecy, although Hermas does not present it so clearly as a criterion. The false prophet prophesies on demand, by request, not at the Spirit's behest, and his prophecies are determined by the desires and wishes of those who make the request; αὐτὸς γὰρ κενὸς ὢν κενὰ καὶ ἀποκρίνεται κενοῖς (11.2f.). 'Empty' (κενός) is obviously a key word in Hermas's understanding of false prophecy (11.3, 11, 13, 15, 17). What he means by it is not altogether clear. But he also describes the false prophet's clientele as κενός and likens each to other (11.3, 4, 13). And this clientele is otherwise described as δίψυχος, κενὸς ἀπὸ τῆς ἀληθείας καὶ ἄφρων (11.1f., 4), in contrast to those who are ἰσχυροὶ ἐν τῇ πίστει τοῦ κυρίου, ἐνδεδυμένοι τὴν ἀλήθειαν. Consequently we may infer that the κενός was one who was not well-versed in the faith, the kerygmatic and confessional truth of Christianity; and further, that false prophecy was revealed as empty precisely by its failure to embody or accord with the basic message of Christian faith.[65]

---

64. See further J. Reiling, *Hermas and Christian Prophecy* (NovTSup XXXVII, 1973).

65. Reiling argues that a 'doctrinal criterion' is not applied in the Eleventh Mandate 'because neither the prophet nor the false prophet are pictured as teachers, and only indirectly in *Sim.* VIII.6.5 . . .' (pp. 67f.).

To sum up then, two important factors emerge from this part of our study. (a) First, *wherever false prophecy was recognized as a danger within the historical milieu of early Christianity, the need to test all prophecy was recognized and appropriate criteria were sought.* Indeed, the energy with which the problem of false prophecy was tackled and the variety of tests applied show just how serious the threat was that false prophecy posed to the prophetic vitality of Israelite and early Christian religion. The chief criteria which reappear again and again are, first, *the criterion of past revelation* — expressed variously in terms of loyalty to Yahweh or to the law, kerygmatic tradition, the teaching given from the beginning, the faith, the truth; the inspired utterance must not gainsay that which has already demonstrated its authenticity as divine revelation. Second, and often more prominent, is *the criterion of present conduct* — for example, immoral conduct, disobedience to the law, loveless character and act, abuse of hospitality and selling prophetic oracles as a commodity fail the test; the life of the prophet must be in accord with the message he brings. These criteria are hardly surprising, since they are the most obvious tests to be used in a religion which stems from key revelatory events in history and which is of a high moral character. A third criterion is something of an extension of the second, and features particularly in Christian circles — *the test of community benefit;* whatever harms the common life of the community and hinders its growth is not of God.

(b) Second, we should draw attention to one other striking fact — the frequency with which prophets and prophetic utterances were tested only to be *rejected* within early Christianity. Paul admonishes the Thessalonians in effect to reject the prophecy that the day of the Lord has already come (II Thess. ii.2) — just as in the Markan Apocalypse disciples are warned to reject those who say, 'I am he', 'Look, here is the Christ!', 'Look, there he is!' (Mark xiii.6, 21). In I Cor. xii.3 and I John ii.22 the test of kerygmatic tradition, the criterion of past revelation, determines that the inspired utterances, 'Jesus be cursed!' and 'Jesus is not the Christ' (?), must emphatically be rejected. The test of character, the criterion of present conduct, disqualifies the charismatics in Matt. vii.21ff., even though they prophesy in Jesus' name. For similar reasons the prophet who says, 'Give me money, or something else' must be ignored and his prophecy rejected, even though he speaks ἐν πνεύματι (Did. 11.12). And if the oracle οὐδὲν εἴδωλον ἐν κόσμῳ (I Cor. viii.4) is the inspired utterance of a Corinthian prophet, as is probable,[66] then the test of community benefit makes Paul cautious about the authority that may be ascribed to it — οἰκοδομή is more important than γνῶσις. We may com-

---

66. Dunn, *Jesus and the Spirit,* §40.4.

pare Acts xxi.4ff., where Paul apparently rejects the instruction not to go to Jerusalem even though given διὰ τοῦ πνεύματος. In short, the testing of prophetic utterances was by no means a mere formality in early Christianity. On the contrary, if the evidence available to us is at all representative, we must conclude that a great many prophetic oracles were rejected by the early Christians, either because their source was discerned to be other than the Spirit, or because their counsel was outweighed by a more important principle or revelation or element of tradition.

We may conclude therefore that if false prophecy was recognized to constitute a danger and a problem in the earliest Christian communities in Palestine, as seems probable (see III above), then it must also be judged probable that they sought to counter that threat by employing criteria similar to those which have appeared so regularly above. The regularity with which the pattern appears on both sides of the all too obscure thirty years of Christian origins (A.D. 30-60) enables us to fill in the missing elements for that period with some confidence. That is to say, the earliest Christians probably tackled the problem of false prophecy by using the test of past revelation and the test of present conduct ('By their fruits you will know them' — Matt. vii.16). And quite possibly the test of community benefit began to be formulated and used from fairly early on.

Moreover, if the evidence from elsewhere in early Christianity is anything to go by, we must also conclude that the first Christians would not have hesitated to disregard and reject any prophetic 'I'-saying which did not pass these tests. That is to say, not only were prophetic 'I'-sayings not blithely accepted at their face value as sayings of the risen Lord within earliest Christianity, but all were probably subjected to scrutiny and testing, and many were rejected. In short, 'prophetic "I"-sayings' and 'sayings of the exalted Christ' were by no means synonymous categories for the first Christians, and the transition from the former to the latter almost certainly saw the elimination of many oracles despite their manifest inspiration.

V. The Evaluation of Prophetic 'I'-Sayings in Earliest Christianity — a Test Case

How do our conclusions thus far bear upon Bultmann's hypothesis? We have concluded that the earliest groups and assemblies of Christians were probably alive to the danger of false prophecy and that the criteria most likely used in testing the spirits were the criteria of past revelation and conduct, and perhaps also of community benefit. This brings us to our final question: What prophetic utterances were likely to pass these tests and so be accepted as a word of the risen Jesus, whence they might become part of the Jesus-tradition? Assuming that something like these criteria were used as a sieve to separate true from false, can we reverse the procedure? Can we examine sayings which have been put forward by form critics as prophetic 'I'-words and determine whether or not it is likely that they would have passed these tests within the early communities? That is to say, if we assume that the sayings of Jesus which we now have in the Synoptic tradition include those prophetic utterances which passed the tests of false prophecy, can we use these tests to determine whether any particular saying within the Jesus-tradition possibly originated as a prophetic utterance which fulfilled the criteria employed? If it would have passed the tests then it could have begun life as a prophetic 'I'-saying; but *if we conclude that a logion in question would not have passed all the tests, then we must conclude that it <u>is</u> part of the authentic Jesus-tradition.*

The criterion of moral conduct and character is no help to us, since, by definition of the problem, we are dealing with utterances which have long been separated from their original speaker and from the context of his life and prophecy. The criterion of community benefit could account for the presence of a logion like Matt. x.5 within the Jesus-tradition, on the grounds that such a prophetic utterance in a Jewish Christian community in Palestine would probably have made for better relations between that community and its neighbours within Judaism and given it freer scope for its evangelism within the Jewish mission. But the most useful test for our present purposes is likely to use the criterion of past revelation. What would constitute past revelation for the first Christians? Certainly the death and resurrection of Jesus in its messianic and eschatological significance would stand at the centre (cf. Gal. i.12 — ἡ ἀποκάλυψις Ἰησοῦ Χριστοῦ). But the ministry of Jesus must also have had a revelatory significance for the earliest communities, for example in their approach to God (ἀββα — Luke xi.2, Rom. viii.15, Gal. iv.6) and in their common life together (the common meal, Lord's Supper). And the distinctive emphases of Jesus' teaching on God's kingdom and in relation to the law have also been preserved in the tradition which was transmitted through the early churches and so must have formed some sort of teaching base for the first Christians.

If then such elements provided the earliest communities with a criterion of past revelation for testing prophetic utterances, can we use this test in reverse? In fact, the test proves itself ambivalent in most cases, since most of the logia in the Jesus-tradition would probably have passed the test anyway. But there is at least one logion which offers better prospects and which provides us with something of a test case. I refer to Mark iii.28f. with its Q parallel preserved in Matt. xii.31f./Luke xii.10 — the blasphemy against the Holy Spirit logion —

Mark iii.28f.	Q — Matt. xii.32/Luke xii.10
ἀμὴν λέγω ὑμῖν ὅτι πάντα ἀφεθήσεται τοῖς υἱοῖς τῶν ἀνθρώπων τὰ ἁμαρτήματα καὶ αἱ βλασφημίαι, ὅσα ἐὰν βλασφημήσωσιν· ὃς δ' ἂν βλασφημήσῃ εἰς τὸ πνεῦμα τὸ ἅγιον, οὐκ ἔχει ἄφεσιν εἰς τὸν αἰῶνα . . .	καὶ ὃς ἐὰν εἴπῃ λόγον κατὰ τοῦ υἱοῦ τοῦ ἀνθρώπου, ἀφεθήσεται αὐτῷ· ὃς δ' ἂν εἴπῃ κατὰ τοῦ πνεύματος τοῦ ἁγίου, οὐκ ἀφεθήσεται αὐτῷ.

This is a particularly key passage in the present debate, since for many it constitutes some of the best evidence for the pneumatic and enthusiastic character of early Christianity (cf. Didache 11.7);[67] and M. E. Boring has recently offered it as a test case for identifying prophetic utterances which have found their way into the Jesus-tradition.[68] In particular, not a few scholars have argued that the Q form of the saying shows how fully convinced the early Christians were of their own inspiration — so much so that blasphemy against the Son of Man was pardonable, whereas opposition to themselves, to the Holy Spirit manifested in their mission and prophetic utterances, was quite *un*pardonable.[69] R. Scroggs puts it thus:

> If the Q logion has its place within the ecstatic communities, then it indicates the exaltation of the Spirit had so overshadowed the kerygmatic content of the gospel that one could even utter blasphemies against the Son of Man without incurring God's wrath.[70]

67. Cf. e.g. H. von Baer, *Der heilige Geist in den Lukasschriften* (Stuttgart, 1926), pp. 75f., 137f.; B. H. Branscomb, *The Gospel of Mark* (Moffatt, 1937), pp. 74f.; C. K. Barrett, *The Holy Spirit and the Gospel Tradition* (London, 1947), pp. 106f.; Teeple, p. 67.

68. M. E. Boring, 'How may we identify oracles of Christian Prophets in the Synoptic Tradition? Mark 3.28-29 as a test case', *JBL* XCI (1972), 501-21.

69. See e.g. W. Bousset, *Kyrios Christos* (1921, ET Abingdon, 1970), p. 39; A. Fridrichsen, 'Le péché centre le St. Esprit', *RHPR* III (1923), 367-72; E. Schweizer, *TDNT* VI, 397; Käsemann, 'Beginnings', p. 99; F. Hahn, *The Titles of Jesus in Christology* (ET London, 1969), p. 324 n. 88; P. Hoffmann, *Studien zur Theologie der Logienquelle* (Münster, 1972), pp. 150ff.; Schulz, pp. 247ff.

70. R. Scroggs, 'The exaltation of the Spirit by some early Christians', *JBL* LXXXIV (1965), 364.

It will at once become evident that this line of reasoning runs directly counter to the conclusions we reached above. That is to say, if the danger of false prophecy was already recognized in the first Christian assemblies, and if the criterion of past revelation was used to test prophetic utterances, then *it is wholly improbable that an utterance which ran counter to the community's kerygma would have passed that test.* In the case in point, an utterance which discounted blasphemy against the Son of Man must have jarred with the exaltation of Jesus as the Son of Man which was so basic and central a feature of the first Christians' faith, and precisely on these grounds such a prophetic oracle would most likely have been dismissed as a false prophecy. It is, of course, quite possible that such a word was *uttered* in the *hubris* of prophetic inspiration (cf. I Cor. xii.3). The decisive question, however, is whether such an oracle would have been *accepted* as a word of the risen Jesus and incorporated into collections of Jesus' sayings. And in face of the evidence reviewed above, the answer must be in the negative — unless we are to assume that Matt. x.32f./Luke xii.8f. and I Cor. xii.3 were directed against the charismatic arrogance of the early Palestinian Jewish-Christian communities! Matthew for one was very conscious of such dangers (Matt. vii.15, 22f.), and it is unlikely that he would have taken up an element of the Jesus-tradition which seemed to encourage prophetic presumption had it not been deeply rooted in the Jesus-tradition. At best, the community which heard the Q version of the blasphemy saying from the lips of a local or wandering prophet would have accepted it as a word of Jesus *only if* it was similar to or based upon a word of Jesus already in the Jesus-tradition. On these grounds it must be judged possible that the Q form ('the Son of Man') of the logion was a prophetic peshering of the earlier Markan ('sons of men') form and was accepted because the community judged it to be a justified interpretation of the original word of Jesus.[71] By the criterion of past revelation used in reverse, therefore, it seems more likely that Mark iii.28f. and/or its Q parallel (Matt. xii.31f./Luke xii.10) belonged to the Jesus-tradition from the first; and it was only because it was part of the teaching which constituted the past revelation for the first Christians that they could use it as they did.

Finally, I would like briefly to hazard the speculation that it was the practice of testing prophetic utterances which prevented inspired sayings about circumcision and clean and unclean foods from being counted among sayings of Jesus. It is hard to believe that there were no such oracles given out within the assemblies and mission of early Christianity (cf. Acts x.15, xi.9,

---

71. See further Dunn, *Jesus and the Spirit*, §8.4, where the original form of the saying is discussed.

I Cor. viii.4, x.25-26, II Cor. xi.4, Gal. i.6-8); yet none of them has found a place in the Synoptic tradition (contrast Gosp. Thos. 53). This could only be because they were either rejected as sayings of the risen Jesus, or else the Jesus-tradition was already sufficiently well established and marked out by the time such prophecies were made. It is certainly significant that Mark can make the claim that Jesus 'declared all foods clean' only by offering it as the somewhat strained *interpretation* of Jesus' sayings on defilement (Mark vii.19).

A fuller discussion at this point would require a careful examination of the nature and character of the Jesus-tradition in the Fourth Gospel; but that would extend the scope of this paper too far.[72] It must suffice to point out that the discourses in the Fourth Gospel have more the character of midrashim or meditations on original Jesus-tradition (such as the words at the Last Supper or the parable of the Lost Sheep) than of prophetic utterances. They were accepted no doubt in the event as a legitimate 're-proclamation' (John xvi.14f.) of the truth of Jesus, although, as we know, the boldness of John's re-interpretation was almost branded as gnostic by emerging orthodoxy in the second century.[73]

VI. Conclusions

The whole discussion in this paper began from the assumption that prophecy was a living and creative force in earliest Christianity. There is no disagreement between Bultmann's hypothesis and the present study on this basic issue. Where I part company with Bultmann is on the issue of what the prophetic activity of the earliest communities entailed. He assumes that the transition of a logion from prophetic oracle to accepted saying of the risen Jesus to Jesus-tradition was relatively straightforward and unhindered. My objection to Bultmann stems from the observation that *everywhere else in the historical 'trajectory' of Judaeo-Christian prophecy authentic prophecy has been accompanied by false prophecy and prophetic communities have been strongly insistent on the need to test all putative inspiration.* Consequently it seems to follow that the more we stress the liveliness of the prophetic consciousness of the first Christian assemblies (à la Bultmann), the greater the likelihood that it was accompanied by a consciousness of the danger of false inspiration hu-

---

72. This particular discussion has already begun with J. R. Michaels, 'The Johannine Words of Jesus and Christian Prophecy', *SBL 1975 Seminar Papers*, II, 233-64.

73. See J. D. G. Dunn, *Unity and Diversity in the New Testament* (London, 1977), §63.

manly contrived or demonically imposed. The more allowance we make for prophetic 'I'-words being accepted as sayings of the risen Jesus, the more room we must make in our historical-critical investigation for a degree of human scepticism and divinely given discrimination which gave a wary hearing to all prophetic oracles and refused to accept not a few of them as sayings of the risen Jesus. In short, while there is good reason to affirm the activity of prophets in earliest Christianity and the acceptance of some of their words as part and parcel of the Jesus-tradition, what we actually know of prophetic utterances and their testing suggests quite strongly that the incorporation of prophetic 'I'-words into the Jesus-tradition was by no means a large-scale affair — so that Käsemann's talk of 'countless "I"-sayings . . . gaining entry into the Synoptic tradition as sayings of Jesus'[74] must be dismissed as a considerable oversimplification and overstatement.

Moreover, if in their testing of prophetic oracles the early communities used the test of past revelation, as seems *a priori* likely and on the evidence available very probable, then a corollary of some moment for historical Jesus and Synoptic Gospel research seems to follow. As is well known, the principal criterion formulated by this research in recent decades has been the 'criterion of dissimilarity':

> the earliest form of a saying we can reach may be regarded as authentic if it can be shown to be dissimilar to characteristic emphases both of ancient Judaism and of the early Church.[75]

Perrin also proposes a second criterion, 'the criterion of coherence':

> material from the earliest strata of the tradition may be accepted as authentic if it can be shown to cohere with material established as authentic by means of the criterion of dissimilarity.[76]

It is inevitable that since the criterion *of dissimilarity* is the primary sieve, the use of these criteria will present us with a Jesus who is dissimilar to and distinct from the Jesus of the earliest Christians. But if the argument of the present paper is sound, this must be a wrong-headed approach; for it would appear that the earliest Christians also had a criterion for sifting authentic from unauthentic sayings of Jesus — and their criterion was the criterion of *similarity*. Only what was similar to the characteristic and accepted notes of Jesus'

---

74. See above, p. 14 n. 4.
75. Perrin, *Teaching*, p. 39.
76. Perrin, *Teaching*, p. 43.

ministry, death and resurrection would itself be accepted as a word of Jesus. The point is this, that if the sayings sifted out for us by the criterion of *dissimilarity* give us the authentic and characteristic voice of Jesus, that is of the earliest Jesus-tradition, then by the criterion of *similarity* few if any of the other sayings would have been accepted by the early churches as sayings of Jesus. Where modern critical research, for good and logical reasons it should be said, starts by emphasizing the *discontinuity* between Jesus and the early churches, and makes that the test of authenticity, the early churches themselves started by emphasizing the *continuity* between them and the Jesus they remembered and bore witness to, and made that the test of authenticity.

It seems to follow from this that the criterion of dissimilarity must be set aside as the *primary* critical tool, since its use will inevitably distort the evidence and make it impossible to retrieve a picture of Jesus or of his teaching which the earliest Christians would have recognized or accepted. The primary method must be a tradition criticism which endeavours to trace the earliest forms and sources of our present Synoptic traditions (thus far in company with Perrin) *by recognizing the unlikelihood of any new and strange element entering the Jesus-tradition in the post-Easter situation (pace* Perrin). Consequently, the *onus probandi* in historical Jesus and Synoptic Gospel research must shift to some extent. Perhaps indeed we should observe that the earliest stratum of Gospel material comes to us as community tradition, and make that *tradition* our starting point; and only where content and life-setting give *clear* indication of post-Easter origin should we eject it from the authentic Jesus-tradition, though always with a reserve born of respect for the critical circumspection with which that tradition was handled from the first.[77] Thus by setting out from the recognition of the importance which the early churches placed upon the testing of prophetic utterances we may be saved from portraying a Jesus to the twentieth century who is merely the construct of an artificially contrived critical tool, and who bears little resemblance either to the Jesus of history or to the Jesus of the early Church's tradition.

---

77. Cf. the way in which Bultmann in fact wrote his *Jesus and the Word* (ET New York, 1934).

CHAPTER 2

Altering the Default Setting: Re-envisaging the Early Transmission of the Jesus Tradition

Defining a Default Setting

For some time now I have been reflecting on the perils of "the default setting." For any who may be less than familiar with the pleasures and perils of computers or of word processing, let me explain. From my *Idiot's Guide to the One-Eyed Monster* I read this definition: "Default is a pre-set preference that is used by a program, the 'fallback' position." In word processing, for example, there may be a default setting for the style of type and size of font used — let us say, New York type, 12-point size; also for margins of a certain width — let us say, 2 inches.

The problems come when you want to change your default settings. You may want a broader margin (2.5 inches) and to use Palatino type in 10-point size. And so you set up all these different options; you format the document you are writing according to your own design, and override the default settings provided for you by your computer or program. All that is fine, and you produce the document according to your preferred format. The trouble is that when you

---

The presidential address at the 57th Annual Meeting of Studiorum Novi Testamenti Societas at the University of Durham, August 6-10, 2002. I wish to acknowledge my debt to Annekie Joubert for advice on current research into oral culture in southern Africa, and to Werner Kelber for several helpful comments on an earlier draft of the paper, but particularly also to Terence Mournet, who for nearly three years worked closely with me on the theme of oral tradition in the Gospels. Not only has he provided invaluable advice on bibliography and the PowerPoint oral presentation of the "live" paper, but also several of the insights and observations developed in the paper are the outcome of our joint deliberations over the past two years.

open a new document and want to start afresh, you find that, whether you wanted to or not, your format has reverted to the original default settings.

The default setting means that when you want to create something different, you need constantly to resist the default setting, you need consciously to change or alter it. But when you turn your attention elsewhere, the default setting, the preset preference, reasserts itself.[1]

The default setting is a useful image to remind us of our own preset preferences, the mind-set by which we unconsciously, instinctively process and format information. The most obvious example today is the difficulty which many (most) of my generation in Britain have in dealing with centimeters and liters. *Inches* and *feet* and *pints* are so deeply bred into us that we automatically think in these terms. They are our default settings. I *think* inches; I do not think centimeters. And when confronted with centimeters, I must consciously revise my way of looking at the item in question.

Similarly, perhaps, with languages. Many people are fluent in several languages. But the first language, the language of childhood, is likely to be the default language. In moments of stress or great emotion, our involuntary reflex is to speak in our mother tongue.

The more serious examples are the default settings that determine our attitudes and behavior toward others. Through the nineteenth and most of the twentieth centuries, the idea of *progress* was a default setting. It was the way European academics saw history and the historical role of the West. That is, we understood progress as scientific advance, as the spread of European "civilization." The consequences are still a major factor in our relationships with Africa and the Far East.

In Britain the mistakes made in investigating the tragic murder of a black London teenager in 1993 forced us to confront the reality of what the official report, the Macpherson Report, described as "institutional racism."[2] "Institutional racism" is Macpherson's term for a prejudicial mind-set toward individuals of another race, which unconsciously predetermines attitudes and actions in particular instances. "Institutional racism," in other words, is another example of a default setting — an involuntary reflex attitude, a "preset preference" in attitudes endemic within, in the case in point, the Metro-

1. On a computer, of course, the experienced operator can easily alter the default setting. My point is that it is much more difficult to alter the default setting of the "onboard mental computer." The analogy is not precise!

2. The Macpherson Report on *The Stephen Lawrence Inquiry* (London: Stationery Office, 1999) identifies "institutional racism" in "processes, attitudes and behavior which amount to discrimination through unwitting prejudice, ignorance, thoughtlessness and racist stereotyping which disadvantages minority ethnic people" (28).

politan Police force. The point is not to deny that such attitudes were being combated, not to deny that when members of the Metropolitan Police concentrated on the problem they succeeded in avoiding racist sentiments. The point rather is that when people did *not* concentrate on the problem, when they relaxed their vigilance, they fell back to their default setting; their actions expressed their involuntary preset preferences.

So too in Christian circles and in NT scholarship, it is only relatively recently that we have become aware of the default setting of centuries-old *patriarchalism*. We simply took it for granted, as an unexamined a priori, that "man" of course denotes humanity, that "brethren/brothers" of course is an appropriate way to address a Christian congregation. I recall the shock I experienced when working on Romans 16 to find commentators convinced that προστάτις *(prostatis)* in 16:2 could mean only something like "helper" (RSV), because, of course, a woman (Phoebe) could not have been a "patron," the normal meaning of the word προστάτις. Likewise, the accusative Ἰουνιᾶν must denote a man, Junias rather than Junia, because, of course, a woman could not have been "outstanding among the apostles" (16:7).[3] Was such logic not indicative of a patriarchalist mindset or default setting?

If anything, more serious has been what might be called "the institutional anti-Semitism," or more accurately anti-Judaism, which for so long disfigured Christian theology, including NT scholarship. What was it that caused our predecessors to persevere with a description of Second Temple Judaism as "*late* Judaism," *Spätjudentum*, well into the second half of the twentieth century? They must have been aware that such a description perpetuated Christian supersessionism, the belief that Judaism's only function was to prepare for Christianity. This implies that when Christianity came Judaism ceased to have a reason for existence, and that first-century Judaism was *late* Judaism, the *last* Judaism. Such a supersessionist attitude must have become so inbred over centuries, an involuntary reflex, a subconscious default setting, that our predecessors fell back to it without thinking.

A default setting, then, a computer's preset preferences, is a useful image of an established mind-set, an unconscious bias or *Tendenz*, an instinctive reflex response. The point is that to alter a default setting, to change a habitual attitude or instinctive perspective, requires a conscious and sustained or repeated effort; otherwise without realizing it we revert to the default setting, to our unexamined predispositions.

However, it is another default setting in NT scholarship that I want to speak about in this essay.

---

3. For details, see my *Romans*, WBC 38 (Dallas: Word, 1988), 888-89, 894-95.

The Literary Paradigm

We are all children of Gutenberg and Caxton. We belong to cultures shaped by the book. Our everyday currency is the learned article and monograph. Libraries are our natural habitat. We trace the beginnings of our modern discipline to the Renaissance's reassertion of the importance of studying classical texts in their original languages, to Erasmus's first Greek New Testament in 1516. Our discipline developed in the nineteenth century around the distinction between "lower criticism" (the attempt to reconstruct the original text of our NT writings) and "higher criticism" (concerned with questions of sources and genre). The dominant mode of treating the Synoptic Gospels during the last generation has been redaction criticism, the Gospels as the product of literary editing. Today a major concern for many is summed up in the word "intertextuality," where the appropriation of earlier texts, oral as well as written, is conceived in exclusively literary terms.

In a word, we naturally, habitually, and instinctively work within a *literary paradigm*. We are, therefore, in no fit state to appreciate how a *non*literary culture, an *oral* culture, functions. And if we are to enter empathetically into such a culture, it is essential that we become conscious of our literary paradigm and make deliberate efforts to step outside it and to free ourselves from its inherited predispositions. It becomes necessary to alter the default settings given by the literary-shaped software of our mental computers.

The prevalence of the literary paradigm in study of the Synoptic tradition can be readily illustrated, as also the fact that it has both shaped and restricted NT scholarship's way of envisaging the Jesus tradition and its early transmission.

I need only remind you of the eighteenth- and nineteenth-century debate about the origins of the Synoptic tradition.[4] The early solution of G. E. Lessing and J. G. Eichhorn was of an original gospel composed in Aramaic, written as early as 35, and known to the three Synoptic evangelists in different recensions.[5] Schleiermacher's "fragment hypothesis" was conceived in terms

---

4. Of the various reviews and analyses, I found the following most helpful: T. Zahn, *Introduction to the New Testament*, 3 vols. (Edinburgh: Clark, 1909), 2:400-427; J. Moffatt, *An Introduction to the Literature of the New Testament* (Edinburgh: Clark, 1911; 3rd ed., 1918), 179-217; W. G. Kümmel, *Introduction to the New Testament* (1973; ET: London: SCM, 1975), 44-80; B. Reicke, *The Roots of the Synoptic Gospels* (Philadelphia: Fortress, 1986), ch. 1; E. P. Sanders and M. Davies, *Studying the Synoptic Gospels* (London: SCM, 1989), 51-162; U. Schnelle, *The History and Theology of the New Testament Writings* (ET: London: SCM, 1998), 162-97; J. S. Kloppenborg Verbin, *Excavating Q: The History and Setting of the Sayings Gospel* (Minneapolis: Fortress, 2000), 271-408.

5. For G. E. Lessing, see his "Neue Hypothese über die Evangelisten," in *Theologie-*

of multiple written sources, on which various recollections, notes, or reports of Jesus had been written.[6] It is true that Herder and Gieseler thought more in terms of an orally formulated tradition; though Herder was evidently still thinking of a full gospel, "a history of Christ";[7] and Gieseler assumed that frequent repetition produced a fixed form of the narrative and outline of Gospel history from the Baptist onward, in which the most important events and sayings were reproduced with great uniformity, so that this Gospel survived, in spite of modifications, in its original stereotyped form.[8]

Such alternatives, however, were swamped by the dominant impression that "the Synoptic Problem" could be solved only in terms of literary sources, that the intricate variations and coincidences in the Synoptic Gospels could be realistically explained only in terms of literary dependence. As James Moffatt summed up the nineteenth-century debate:

> The gospels are books made out of books; none of them is a document which simply transcribes the oral teaching of an apostle or of apostles. Their agreements and differences cannot be explained except on the hypothesis of a more or less close literary relationship, and while oral tradition is a *vera causa*, it is only a subordinate factor in the evolution of our canonical Greek gospels.[9]

It should occasion no surprise, then, that the hypothesis that emerged in the late-nineteenth and early-twentieth centuries as the most plausible resolution of the Synoptic Problem is still known simply as the two-document hypothesis.[10] And even when some variations are offered in explanation of some of the complexities of the data, like Ur-Markus or Proto-Luke, what is

---

kritische Schriften I und II, vol. 7 of *Werke* (Munich: Hanser, 1976), 614-36; ET: *Theological Writings: Selections in Translation*, with introductory essay by H. Chadwick (London: Black, [1956]). W. G. Kümmel, *The New Testament: The History of the Investigation of Its Problems* (2nd ed., 1970; ET: Nashville: Abingdon, 1972), provides extensive excerpts from both Lessing and Eichhorn (76-79). See also Zahn, *Introduction*, 2:403-4; Schnelle, *History*, 162-63.

6. Reicke, *Roots*, 12-13, refers to F. Schleiermacher, *Über die Schriften des Lukas: Ein kritischer Versuch* (Berlin: Reimer, 1817), fifteen years before the better-known "Über die Zeugnisse des Papias von unseren beiden ersten Evangelien," *Theologische Studien und Kritiken* 5 (1832): 738-58.

7. J. G. Herder, "Vom Erlöser der Menschen," *Herder Werke: Theologische Schriften* 9/1 (Frankfurt: Deutscher Klassiker, 1994), particularly 671-87, here 679; see also Reicke, *Roots*, 9-12.

8. I echo Zahn's description (*Introduction*, 2:409).

9. Moffatt, *Introduction*, 180.

10. There is no need to rehearse the usual litany of Lachmann, Weisse, et al.; for details, see, e.g., Kummel, *New Testament*, 146-51; Kloppenborg Verbin, *Excavating Q*, 295-309.

envisaged are still written documents.[11] The literary paradigm continues to determine the way the problem and its solution are conceptualized. B. H. Streeter certainly recognized the importance of "a living oral tradition" behind the Gospels and cautioned against studying the Synoptic Problem "merely as a problem of literary criticism," but, ironically, he went on to develop "a four document hypothesis."[12]

The main development from and challenge to *source* criticism was, of course, *form* criticism, which began as a deliberate attempt to break away from the literary paradigm and to conceptualize the transmission process in oral terms. The character of the challenge was already signaled by Wellhausen's observation: "Die letzte Quelle der Evangelien ist mündliche Überlieferung, aber diese enthält nur den zerstreuten Stoff."[13] In effect, Wellhausen was combining the hypotheses of Herder and Schleiermacher — Jesus tradition as oral tradition but in small units. Bultmann took up the challenge when he defined the purpose of form criticism thus: "to study the history of the oral tradition behind the gospels."[14] His analysis of *The History of the Synoptic Tradition*, I need hardly remind you, became the single most influential exposition of Formgeschichte.[15]

Unfortunately, however, Bultmann could not escape from the literary default setting; he could not conceive of the process of transmission except in literary terms. This becomes most evident in his conceptualization of the whole tradition about Jesus as "composed of a series of layers."[16] The imagined process is one where each layer is laid or builds upon another. Bultmann made such play with it because, apart from anything else, he was confident that he could strip off later (Hellenistic) layers to expose the earlier (Palestinian) layers.[17] The image itself, however, is drawn from the literary process of editing, where each successive edition (layer) is an edited version (for Bultmann, an elaborated and expanded version) of the previous edition (layer). But is such a conceptualization really appropriate to a process of oral

11. On *Ur-Markus*, see, e.g., Kummel, *Introduction*, 61-63; and Proto-Luke, particularly V. Taylor, *Behind the Third Gospel* (Oxford: Clarendon, 1926).

12. B. H. Streeter, *The Four Gospels: A Study of Origins* (London: Macmillan, 1924), ch. 9, quotations from 229.

13. J. Wellhausen, *Einleitung in die drei ersten Evangelien* (Berlin: Georg Reimer, 1905), 43.

14. R. Bultmann (with K. Kundsin), *Form Criticism* (1934; ET: New York: Harper Torchbook, 1962), 1.

15. *Die Geschichte der synoptischen Tradition* (Göttingen: Vandenhoeck & Ruprecht, 1921; ET: Oxford: Blackwell, 1963).

16. R. Bultmann, *Jesus and the Word* (1926; ET: New York: Scribners, 1935), 12-13.

17. Bultmann, *Jesus and the Word*, 12-13.

retellings of traditional material? Bultmann never really addressed the question, despite its obvious relevance.

Similarly, Kümmel in his classic *Introduction* recognizes the importance of oral tradition, both in "fixing" the gospel material in written form and in the reworking of the earliest sources into the canonical Gospels; but his discussion focuses mainly on the two-source hypothesis, and his references to form-critical analyses do little to carry the discussion forward or to envisage how a process of oral transmission worked or how it might have influenced the shape of the tradition.[18] It may be true, as E. P. Sanders affirms, that "everyone accepts oral transmission at the early stages of the gospel tradition."[19] But in reality the role of oral tradition is either reduced to characteristically fragmentary forms[20] or unknown oral sources are postulated. In the latter case the working assumption, signaled by the word "source" itself, is usually that the source was in effect a fixed version of some Jesus tradition used by the evangelist as one would use a written document.[21]

Even more revealing are the various more-recent attempts to contest the dominance of the two-document hypothesis. W. Farmer's attempt to revive the Griesbach hypothesis (Luke dependent on Matthew, and Mark on both) only begins to make sense if the Synoptic Problem is viewed in exclusively literary terms, of one document dependent on and derived from another.[22] Sanders issued a justified critique of Bultmann's assumption of a uniform tendency in the development of the original "pure forms" of the Jesus tradition; yet his critique itself suffers from the idea of linear development evoked by the word "tendency."[23] M.-É. Boismard in turn assumes that the

---

18. Kümmel, *Introduction*, particularly 76-79; Schnelle's acknowledgment of the role of oral tradition is cursory (*History*, 174).

19. Sanders and Davies, *Studying*, 141. Sanders and Davies, and Reicke *(Roots)*, are fairly exceptional in the importance they have accorded to oral tradition in the development of the Jesus tradition.

20. ". . . those fragments of tradition that bear the imprint of orality: short, provocative, memorable, oft-repeated phrases, sentences, and stories" (R. W. Funk and R. W. Hoover, *The Five Gospels: The Search for the Authentic Words of Jesus* [New York: Macmillan/Polebridge, 1993], 4).

21. "Even now, when we have come to affirm that behind some or many of the literary works we deal with there is an oral tradition, we still manipulate such traditions as though they too were 'literary' works" (W. H. Silberman, "'Habent Sua Fata Libelli': The Role of Wandering Themes in Some Hellenistic Jewish and Rabbinic Literature," in *The Relationships among the Gospels*, ed. W. O. Walker [San Antonio: Trinity University Press, 1978], 195-218, here 215).

22. W. R. Farmer, *The Synoptic Problem* (New York: Macmillan, 1964), ch. 6.

23. E. P. Sanders, *The Tendencies of the Synoptic Tradition*, SNTSMS 9 (Cambridge: Cambridge University Press, 1969).

complexity of the Synoptic Problem can be resolved only by a complex literary solution, a multistage interaction among earlier and later versions of the three Synoptic Gospels.[24] M. D. Goulder demonstrates that once the hypothesis of literary dependence is given exclusive explanatory rights, then, with sufficient imagination and ingenuity, Matthew can be derived entirely from Mark, and Luke by a combination of the prior two.[25] And Mark Goodacre, despite acknowledging the potential importance of oral tradition, discusses individual cases in terms exclusively of literary dependence.[26]

At the present time the main focus of interest lies in Q. As the transition from the nineteenth to the twentieth century was dominated by fascination with the Gospel of Mark, so the transition from the twentieth to the twenty-first century has been dominated by fascination with the second of the two sources in the two-document hypothesis — the second source common to Matthew and Luke, the sayings source Q. That Q was a document, written in Greek, is one of the principal points of consensus. Yet overdependence on the literary paradigm again dictates, as with Mark and *Ur-Markus,* that divergences between Matthean and Lukan Q material have to be explained by postulating different versions of Q, a Q^{Mt} and a Q^{Lk}.[27] The debate, however, now focuses on the issue whether different compositional layers can be distinguished *within* Q, with Kloppenborg's hypothesis that three layers can be so discerned winning a substantial following.[28] What is of interest here is the almost explicit assumption that each layer is to be conceived as a written document, and the process of development conceived in terms of editing and redaction. It should occasion no surprise that Kloppenborg envisages his investigation of Q in terms of an archaeological dig, as *Excavating Q,* where, as with Bultmann, the process is visualized as stripping away successive layers to reach the bottom layer, or as removing the redactional elements of successive editions to recover the original edition.[29]

24. M.-É. Boismard, "The Two-Source Theory at an Impasse," *New Testament Studies* 26 (1979): 261-73; also "Théorie des niveaux multiples," in *The Interrelations of the Gospels: A Symposium Led by M.-É. Boismard, W. R. Farmer, F. Neirynck, Jerusalem 1984,* ed. D. L. Dungan, BETL 95 (Leuven: Leuven University Press, 1990), 231-43. See also the discussion in Sanders and Davies, *Studying,* 105-11.

25. M. Goulder, *Luke: A New Paradigm,* 2 vols., JSNTSup 20 (Sheffield: Sheffield Academic Press, 1989), in his attempt to dispense with Q (particularly vol. 1, ch. 2).

26. M. Goodacre, *The Case against Q* (Harrisburg, PA: Trinity, 2002), 56-59, 89-90 (despite 64-66, 188).

27. E.g., Schnelle, *History,* 187.

28. J. S. Kloppenborg, *The Formation of Q: Trajectories in Ancient Wisdom Collections* (Philadelphia: Fortress, 1987).

29. Kloppenborg does not explicitly address the issue of whether Q^1 was also a docu-

Finally, we might simply note that the discussion of possible knowledge of Jesus tradition in Paul's letters has similarly suffered from an assumption that the case depends on a quasi-literary inter-dependency. Since the case cannot be clearly made that Paul knew the form of tradition as it has been recorded in Mark or Q, the case cannot be made for such interdependency.[30] That Paul, James, and 1 Peter, not to mention the Apostolic Fathers, bear testimony to *different* versions of the *same* sayings of Jesus has been too little considered. More to the point, such allusions to what we know from the Synoptics as Jesus tradition attest a much more diverse and fluid transmission process. This situation has been allowed too little say in our conceptualization of the character of the Jesus tradition and the way it was initially passed on.[31]

In all this discussion the literary paradigm has dominated. Even when a conscious effort has been made to alter the default setting, to recall that oral tradition would not necessarily move along the grooves of literary composition, of reading and revising, the literary paradigm soon reasserts its influence and closes down the historical possibilities that may be envisaged. As soon as attention shifts from the perspective itself to the data to be discussed, the default setting clicks back into place, and the interrelationships of the data are conceived in literary terms as though no other terms were relevant.

Should this be so? Need this be so?

What Do We Mean by an Oral Culture?

We should not underestimate the difficulty for a mind-set formed within a long-established literary culture trying to shift to an oral mind-set, the difficulty for someone bred to the literary paradigm trying to enter empathetically into an oral paradigm. Walter Ong effectively illustrates the problem by

---

ment, but he does assume it (*Excavating Q*, 159, 197, 200, 208-9); see also 154-59 on the genre of Q[1].

30. Notably F. Neirynck, "Paul and the Sayings of Jesus," in *L'Apôtre Paul*, ed. A. Vanhoye, BETL 73 (Leuven: Peeters, 1986), 265-32 reprinted in *Evangelica*, vol. 2, ed. F. van Segbroeck (Leuven: Peeters, 1991), 511-68. Neirynck's many and valuable contributions on the Gospels well illustrate the dominance of the literary paradigm.

31. I of course except H. Koester, *Synoptische Überlieferung bei den apostolischen Vätern* (Berlin: Akademie-Verlag, 1957); also *Ancient Christian Gospels: Their History and Development* (London: SCM, 1980), 49-75; though Koester has not attempted to develop a model of oral transmission.

imagining how difficult it would be for those who knew only transport by automobile to visualize a horse, a horse conceptualized as an automobile without wheels.

> Imagine writing a treatise on horses (for people who have never seen a horse) which starts with the concept not of horse but of "automobile," built on the readers' direct experience of automobiles. It proceeds to discourse on horses by always referring to them as "wheelless automobiles," explaining to highly automobilized readers who have never seen a horse all the points of difference in an effort to excise all idea of "automobile" out of the concept of "wheelless automobile" so as to invest the term with a purely equine meaning. Instead of wheels, the wheelless automobiles have enlarged toenails called hooves; instead of headlights or perhaps rear-vision mirrors, eyes; instead of a coat of lacquer, something called hair; instead of gasoline for fuel, hay; and so on. . . . No matter how accurate and thorough such apophatic description, automobile-driving readers who have never seen a horse and who hear only of "wheelless automobiles" would be sure to come away with a strange concept of a horse. . . . You cannot without serious and disabling distortion describe a primary phenomenon by starting with a subsequent secondary phenomenon and paring away the differences. Indeed, starting backwards in this way — putting the car before the horse — you can never become aware of the real differences at all.[32]

The uncomfortable fact is that if we are to accomplish such a paradigm switch, we probably need to be jolted out of the one and make a conscious and sustained effort to train our thinking to the other. If we are to begin to appreciate what it must have been like to live and function in an oral society, we must shake ourselves free from the unconscious presuppositions that shape the very way we see the Synoptic Problem and envisage the early transmission or retelling of the Jesus tradition.[33]

For a start we should recall the estimate of credible authorities that literacy in Palestine at the time of Jesus would probably have been less than 10

---

32. W. J. Ong, *Orality and Literacy: The Technologizing of the Word* (London: Methuen, 1982; London and New York: Routledge, 1988), 12-13. See also M. McLuhan, *The Gutenberg Galaxy: The Making of Typographic Man* (Toronto: University of Toronto Press, 1962); and E. A. Havelock, *The Muse Learns to Write: Reflections on Orality and Literacy from Antiquity to the Present* (New Haven: Yale University Press, 1986), where Havelock sums up a scholarly lifetime of reflection on the transition from orality to literacy.

33. W. H. Kelber, *The Oral and the Written Gospel* (Philadelphia: Fortress, 1983; reprinted, Bloomington: Indiana University Press, 1996), begins with a similar protest (xv-xvi).

percent.[34] Given the importance of Torah learning in Jewish culture, that estimate can be questioned. But given equally that royal officials, priests, scribes, and Pharisees would have made up a significant portion of the 10 percent, the corollaries are probably much the same. These corollaries include the fact that knowledge of Torah for most people would have been by hearing, aural, rather than by reading. We have to assume, therefore, that the great majority of Jesus' first disciples would have been functionally illiterate.[35] That Jesus himself was literate cannot simply be assumed.[36] And even allowing for the possibility that one or two of Jesus' immediate disciples were able to read and write (Matthew) and may even have kept notes of Jesus' teaching,[37] it remains overwhelmingly probable that the earliest transmission of the Jesus tradition was by word of mouth.[38] This also means, as Herder and the early form critics appreciated, that the forms of the tradition were already becoming established in oral usage and transmission.

Second, we need to recall the character of rural Galilee, where, on almost any reckoning, the initial impulse that resulted in the Jesus tradition is to be located. We can be confident that the village and small-town culture within which Jesus predominantly operated and where the stories and teachings of Jesus were first retold was a predominantly oral culture. Through recent archaeological work in Galilee, we have a much better idea of the physical settings in which that early formulation of the Jesus tradition took place.[39]

34. Recent estimates are of less than 10 percent literacy in the Roman Empire under the principate, falling to perhaps as low as 3 percent literacy in Roman Palestine; see particularly W. V. Harris, *Ancient Literacy* (Cambridge, MA: Harvard University Press, 1989); M. Bar-Ilan, "Illiteracy in the Land of Israel in the First Centuries CE," in *Essays in the Social Scientific Study of Judaism and Jewish Society,* ed. S. Fishbane and S. Schoenfeld (Hoboken, NJ: Ktav, 1992), 46-61; C. Hezser, *Jewish Literacy in Roman Palestine* (Tübingen: Mohr Siebeck, 2001).

35. Kloppenborg Verbin properly reminds us that "'literacy' itself admits of various levels: signature-literacy; the ability to read simple contracts, invoices and receipts; full reading literacy; the ability to take dictation; and scribal literacy — the ability to compose" (*Excavating Q,* 167).

36. J. D. Crossan, *The Birth of Christianity* (San Francisco: Harper SanFrancisco, 1998), has little doubt that Jesus was illiterate (235); similarly, B. Chilton, *Rabbi Jesus: An Intimate Biography* (New York: Doubleday, 2000), 99.

37. See, particularly, A. Millard, *Reading and Writing in the Time of Jesus,* Biblical Seminar 69 (Sheffield: Sheffield Academic Press, 2000), 223-29; also E. E. Ellis, *The Making of the New Testament Documents* (Leiden: Brill, 1999), 24, 32, 352.

38. Pace W. Schmithals, "Vom Ursprung der synoptischen Tradition," *Zeitschrift für Theologie und Kirche* 94 (1997): 288-316, who continues to argue that the Synoptic tradition was literary from the first. Ellis, *Christ and the Future in New Testament History,* NovTSup 97 (Leiden: Brill, 2000), 13-14, also queries whether there was an initial oral stage of transmission.

39. See D. R. Edwards and C. T. McCollough, eds., *Archaeology and the Galilee,* South

Here a trite but necessary reminder is that in the first century there were no newspapers, no television, no radio. But have we done enough to think through what that must have meant for communities? In the villages and small towns of Galilee, when the day's work was over and the sun had set, what else was there to do but to sit around and talk, to share the news of the day, to tell stories, to recall matters of importance for the community?

Kenneth Bailey suggests that the traditional evening gathering of Middle Eastern villagers to listen to and recite the tradition of the community, the *haflat samar,* is the continuation of a practice that stretches back to the time of Jesus and beyond.[40]

Can we say more about the character of oral tradition and about oral transmission? As Sanders points out, the problem is "that we do not know how to imagine the oral period."[41] In an overwhelmingly literary culture, our experience of orality is usually restricted to casual gossip and the serendipitous reminiscences of college reunions. The burden of my essay, however, is that we must endeavor to "imagine the oral period" for the sake of historical authenticity, to re-envisage how tradition was transmitted in an orally structured society; also, that we can do so, or at least are more able to do so than has generally been realized. Here we are in the fortunate position of being able to call upon a wide range of research into oral tradition. No longer is it a matter simply of depending on the research into the Homeric and Yugoslavian sagas by Milman Parry and Albert Lord.[42] But I think also, in particular, of research into oral tradition in Africa[43] and the

---

Florida Studies in the History of Judaism 143 (Atlanta: Scholars, 1997); and particularly J. L. Reed, *Archaeology and the Galilean Jesus* (Harrisburg, PA: Trinity, 2000).

40. K. E. Bailey, "Informal Controlled Oral Tradition and the Synoptic Gospels," *Asia Journal of Theology* 5 (1991): 34-54; also "Middle Eastern Oral Tradition and the Synoptic Gospels," *ExpTim* 106 (1995): 363-67.

41. Sanders and Davies, *Studying,* 141; ironically, in the same volume Sanders has demonstrated that there is an equal problem, too little recognized, of "imagining the literary period."

42. The work of A. B. Lord, *The Singer of Tales* (Cambridge, MA: Harvard University Press, 1978), has been seminal, here especially ch. 5.

43. I refer particularly to J. Vansina, *Oral Tradition as History* (Madison: University of Wisconsin Press, 1985), a revision of his earlier *Oral Tradition: A Study in Historical Methodology* (London: Routledge & Kegan Paul, 1965); R. Finnegan, *Oral Literature in Africa* (Oxford: Clarendon, 1970); and I. Okpewho, *African Oral Literature: Backgrounds, Character and Continuity* (Bloomington: Indiana University Press, 1992). Annekie Joubert notes that a paradigm shift took place in folklore studies in the late 1970s and early 1980s, when a new emphasis on performance directed attention away from the study of the formal patterning and symbolic content of the texts to the emergence of verbal art in the social interaction between performers and audiences — quoting from R. Bauman and C. L. Briggs, "Poetics and Performance as Critical Perspectives on Language and Social Life," *Annual Review of Anthropology* 19 (1990): 59-88, here 59-60.

thirty years of personal experience of Bailey in the Middle East, recorded as anecdotes.[44]

On the basis of such research it is possible to draw up a list of characteristic features of oral tradition. The point, I will stress at once and will no doubt need to stress repeatedly, is not that an oral tradition once recorded or transcribed will necessarily look any different from a literary tradition. Transcribed oral tradition and literary tradition, not altogether surprisingly, look very much the same. My point is rather to bring home the danger of *envisaging* the process of tradition transmission in too exclusively literary terms and to suggest that it will be necessary for us deliberately to alter our print-determined default setting when we try to envisage the early transmission of the Jesus tradition.

There are five characteristic features of oral transmission of tradition that deserve attention.

First, and most obvious — or should be most obvious — an oral performance is not like reading a literary text.[45] In reading a text it is possible to look back a few pages to check what was written earlier. Having read the text, you can take it with you and read it again later. A written text can be revised, or edited, and so on. But none of that is possible with an oral tradition. An oral performance is evanescent. It is an event. It happens and then is gone. Oral tradition is not there for the auditor to check back a few pages, or to take away, or to edit and revise. It is not a thing, an artifact like a literary text. That fact alone should be sufficient to cause us to question whether models of literary editing, of intertextual dependence, or of archaeological layers are appropriate as we attempt to re-envisage the early transmission of the Jesus tradition.

Nor should we forget that even written documents like Paul's letters would not have been read by more than a very few. For the great majority of recipients, the letter would have been heard rather than read. And the public reading of the text would require careful preparation and practice if it was to be heard meaningfully. The public reading of such a letter, in other words, would itself have the character of a performance.[46] Which also means that general knowledge of and even reference back to such texts would depend much more on recollection of what had been heard when the text was read to the congregation than on an individual perusal of the text itself. In technical

---

44. See above, n. 40.

45. See, e.g., Finnegan, *Oral Literature*, 2-7.

46. The point is well made by W. Dabourne, *Purpose and Cause in Pauline Exegesis*, SNTSMS 104 (Cambridge: Cambridge University Press, 1999), ch. 8. See further P. J. Achtemeier, "*Omne verbum sonat:* The New Testament and the Oral Environment of Late Western Antiquity," *Journal of Biblical Literature* 109 (1990): 3-27.

terms, oral tradition includes the phenomenon of second orality, that is, a written text known only through oral performance of the text.

Second, oral tradition is essentially communal in character. On the literary paradigm we envisage an author writing for a reader. We speak of the intended reader, the ideal reader, the implied reader. We envisage the characteristic context of communication as the individual reader poring over the text, as the text there on a shelf to be consulted by readers functioning as individuals in separate one-to-one encounters with the text. But oral tradition continues in existence because there are communities for whom the tradition is important. The tradition is performed with greater or less regularity (depending on its importance) in the gatherings of the community, kept alive for the community by the elders, teachers, or those acknowledged as proficient performers of the tradition.[47]

The recognition of this point has enabled J. M. Foley in recent years to merge oral tradition theory fruitfully with receptionalist literary theory. For it is precisely the communal character of oral tradition, the degree to which the elders or teachers retain the tradition on behalf of the community and the performers perform it for the benefit of the community, that reminds us of the community's role in such performances. The performer's awareness that some tradition is already familiar to the community is a factor in the performance. The performance is heard within the community's "horizons of expectation." The performance's "gaps of indeterminacy" can be filled out from the audience's prior knowledge of the tradition or of like traditions. What Foley calls the "metonymic reference" of a performance enables the performer to use a whole sequence of allusions to the community's store of tradition and enables the community thus to recognize the consistency of the performance with the whole.[48]

---

47. The point was never adequately worked through by the early form critics. The model of "oral history" drawn into the discussion by S. Byrskog, *Story as History — History as Story: The Gospel Tradition in the Context of Ancient Oral History*, WUNT 123 (Tübingen: Mohr Siebeck, 2000), while valuable in other aspects, also fails at this point. Oral history envisages tradition as elicited from eyewitnesses by a historian some years or decades later, tradition that might have been latent or only casually exchanged in the meantime. But the oral tradition model put forward here, in contrast, envisages a tradition that sustained a community through its regular performance. Byrskog, in fact, has no real conception of or indeed role for oral transmission as itself a bridging factor between past and present.

48. J. M. Foley, *Immanent Art: From Structure to Meaning in Traditional Oral Epic* (Bloomington: Indiana University Press, 1991), chs. 1 and 2 (particularly 6-13 and 42-45); he is drawing on the language of H. R. Jauss and W. Iser. The argument is developed in J. M. Foley, *The Singer of Tales in Performance* (Bloomington: Indiana University Press, 1995), chs. 1-3. Foley's observation is also taken up by R. A. Horsley and J. A. Draper, *Whoever Hears You Hears Me:*

Third, as already implied, in the oral community there would be one or more who were recognized as having primary responsibility for maintaining and performing the community's tradition — the singer of tales, the bard, the elders, the teachers, the rabbis. An ancient oral society had no libraries or dictionaries or encyclopedias. It had instead to rely on individuals whose role in their community was to function as, in the words of Jan Vansina, "a walking reference library."[49] In NT terms this certainly accords with the role of the apostle in providing what can properly be called foundation tradition for the churches he founded.[50] And the prominence of teachers in the earliest communities[51] is best explained by the communities' reliance on them as repositories of community tradition.[52]

This in turn suggests that the teachers would be responsible for a body of teaching, presumably what Luke refers to as "the apostles' teaching" (Acts 2:42). There is no reason to conceive of this teaching as entirely fragmentary, a sequence of individual forms preserved randomly. In his paper on "The Gospels as Oral Traditional Literature," Albert Lord observes that "oral traditional composers think in terms of blocks and series of blocks of tradition."[53] The Synoptic tradition itself attests such groupings of parables (e.g., Mark 4:2-34) and miracle stories (4:35–5:43; 6:32-52), of Jesus' teaching on exorcism (3:23-29) or discipleship (8:34-37), of sequences of events such as a day in the life of Jesus (1:21-38), and so on.[54] Our knowledge of how oral tradition

---

Prophets, Performance, and Tradition in Q (Harrisburg, PA: Trinity, 1999), chs. 7-8. Annekie Joubert notes that "the use of allusion is normally an appeal to the audience to link the references, and the audience will have to draw on extra-performance/extra-textual information in order to interpret and to understand the web of allusive communication" (private correspondence).

49. Vansina, *Oral Tradition as History,* 37; similarly Havelock speaks of an oral "encyclopedia" of social habit and custom-law and convention (*Muse,* 57-58).

50. As in 1 Cor. 11:2, 23; 15:1-3; Phil. 4:9; Col. 2:6-7; 1 Thess. 4:1; 2 Thess. 2:15; 3:6.

51. Acts 13:1; Rom. 12:7; 1 Cor. 12:28-29; Gal. 6:6; Eph. 4:11; Heb. 5:12; James 3:1; *Didache* 13.2; 15.1-2.

52. From what we know of more formal teaching in the schools, we can be sure that oral instruction was the predominant means: "It is the 'living voice' of the teacher that has priority" (L. C. A. Alexander, "The Living Voice: Scepticism towards the Written Word in Early Christianity and in Graeco-Roman Texts," in *The Bible in Three Dimensions: Essays in Celebration of Forty Years of Biblical Studies in the University of Sheffield,* ed. D. J. A. Clines et al. [Sheffield: Sheffield Academic Press, 1990], 221-47, here 244).

53. A. B. Lord, "The Gospels as Oral Traditional Literature," in *Relationships,* ed. Walker, 33-91, here 59.

54. A fuller listing of such groupings of tradition would include the Beatitudes (Matt. 5:3, 4, 6, 11, 12//Luke 6:20b, 21b, 21a, 22, 23), the sequence of mini-parables in Mark 2:18-22 (followed by Matt. 9:14-17 and Luke 5:33-39), Jesus' responses to would-be disciples (Matt. 8:19-22//Luke 9:57-62), the cost of discipleship and danger of loss (Mark 8:34-38; again followed by Matt. 16:24-

"works" elsewhere suggests that this would have been the pattern from earliest days, as soon as the stories and sayings of Jesus began to be valued by the groups of his followers.

Fourth, oral tradition subverts the idea(l) of an "original" version. With minds attuned to the literary paradigm, we envisage an original form, a first edition, from which all subsequent editions can at least in principle be traced by form and redaction criticism. We envisage tradition-history as an archaeological tell where we can in principle dig through the layers of literary strata to uncover the original layer, the "pure form" of Bultmann's conceptualization of *Formgeschichte*. But in oral tradition each performance is not related to its predecessors or successors in that way. In oral tradition, as Lord particularly has observed, each performance is, properly speaking, an "original."[55]

The point here can easily be misunderstood or misrepresented, so let me elaborate it a little. As it applies to the Jesus tradition, the point is not that there was no originating impulse that gave birth to the tradition. In at least many cases we can be wholly confident that there were things Jesus said and did that made an impact on his disciples, a lasting impact. But properly speaking, the tradition of the event is not the event itself. And the tradition of the saying is not the saying itself. The tradition is at best the witness of the event, and as there were presumably several witnesses, so there may well have been several traditions, or versions of the tradition, from the first. We can speak of an originating event, but we should certainly hesitate before speaking of an original tradition of the event. The same is true even of a saying of Jesus. The tradition of the saying attests the impact made by the saying on one or more of the original audience. But it may well have been heard slightly differently by others of that audience, and so told and retold in different versions from the first. And if, as Kelber points out, Jesus himself used his most effective parables and aphorisms on more than one occasion, the ideal of a single

---

27 and Luke 9:23-26), the sayings about light and judgment in Mark 4:21-25 (followed by Luke 8:16-18), the "parables of crisis" (Matt. 24:42–25:13 pars.), Jesus and the Baptist (Matt. 11:2-19 par.), Jesus' teaching on his exorcisms (Matt. 12:24-45 pars.), and the sending out of the disciples on mission (Mark 6:7-13; Matt. 9:37–10:1, 7-16; Luke 9:1-6; 10:1-12).

55. "In a sense each performance is 'an' original, if not 'the' original. The truth of the matter is that our concept of 'the original,' of 'the song,' simply makes no sense in oral tradition" (Lord, *Singer*, 100-101). R. Finnegan, *Oral Poetry: Its Nature, Significance and Social Context* (Cambridge: Cambridge University Press, 1977), also glosses Lord — "There is no correct text, no idea that one version is more 'authentic' than another: each performance is a unique and original creation with its own validity" (65) — and credits Lord with bringing this point home most convincingly (79). Kelber already took up the point: "Each oral performance is an irreducibly unique creation"; if Jesus said something more than once there is no "original" (*Oral*, 29, also 59, 62).

original, authentic version once again reduces more to the figment of a literary-molded mind-set. Yes, we can and need to envisage teaching that originated with Jesus, actions that characterized his mission. But to treat the history of the Jesus tradition as though it were a matter of recovering some original version of the tradition is to conceptualize the transmission of the Jesus tradition at best misleadingly; the Jesus Seminar completely misjudged the character of the Jesus tradition at this point.[56] In oral tradition, performance variation is integral to and even definitive of the tradition.[57]

Fifth and finally, oral tradition is characteristically (I do not say distinctively) a combination of fixity and flexibility, of stability and diversity. The preceding characteristics could easily be taken to encourage the idea of oral tradition as totally flexible and variable. That would be a mistake. In oral tradition there is characteristically a tale to be told, a teaching to be treasured, in and through and precisely by means of the varied performances. Oral tradition is oral memory; its primary function is to preserve and recall what is of importance from the past. Tradition, more or less by definition, embodies the concern for continuity with the past, a past drawn upon but also enlivened that it might illuminate the present and future. In the words of E. A. Havelock, "Variability and stability, conservatism and creativity, evanescence and unpredictability all mark the pattern of oral transmission" — the "oral principle of 'variation within the same.'"[58] It is this combination, reverting to our second point, that makes it possible for the community both to acknowledge its tradition and to delight in the freshness of the individual performance.

My basic thesis, then, is that a proper recognition of the characteristics

56. Funk and Hoover, *The Five Gospels;* also R. W. Funk, *The Acts of Jesus: The Search for the Authentic Deeds of Jesus* (San Francisco: Harper/Polebridge, 1998). To recognize that variation is integral to orality likewise undercuts much of the critical criteria (particularly "contradiction with other accounts"), used by H. Reimarus, D. F. Strauss, and their successors.

57. A. Dundes, *Holy Writ as Oral Lit: The Bible as Folklore* (Lanham, MD: Rowman & Littlefield, 1999), insists "upon 'multiple existence' and 'variation' as the two most salient characteristics of folklore" (18-19). The problem of deriving a text from the recollections of a performance is well illustrated by the play *Pericles,* attributed to Shakespeare (S. Wells and G. Taylor, eds., *The Oxford Shakespeare* [Oxford: Clarendon, 1988], 1037); see further J. Bate, *The Genius of Shakespeare* (London: Picador, 1997), 75-87 (I owe the latter reference to H. D. Betz). Nor should it be forgotten that NT textual criticism has to take account of the diverse ways in which the text was performed/used, read/heard in different churches; see particularly B. D. Ehrman, *The Orthodox Corruption of Scripture: The Effect of Early Christological Controversies on the Text of the New Testament* (Oxford: Oxford University Press, 1993); D. C. Parker, *The Living Text of the Gospels* (Cambridge: Cambridge University Press, 1997); E. J. Epp, "The Multivalence of the Term 'Original Text' in New Testament Textual Criticism," *Harvard Theological Review* 92 (1999): 245-81.

58. Kelber, *Oral,* 33, 54; quoting E. A. Havelock, *Preface to Plato* (Cambridge, MA: Harvard University Press, 1963), 92, 147, 184, passim.

of oral tradition, as just outlined, requires us to alter the default setting of our typically literary mind-set. To recognize that the early transmission of the Jesus tradition took place in an oral culture and as oral tradition requires us consciously to resist the involuntary predisposition to conceive that process in literary terms and consciously to re-envisage that process in oral terms.

I have no time here to develop the theoretical model further. Suffice it to say, the model takes up the best of the insights of the early form critics, while avoiding the false paths that the literary paradigm led them down. That is to say, the recognition of the *oral* and *communal* character of the early Jesus tradition should be retrieved from the confusion caused by an unjustifiably schematic conception of the development of the tradition from pure to complex form, from simple to elaborated form.[59] Likewise, the "oral principle of 'variation within the same'" tells more heavily than has hitherto been appreciated against the assumption of Bultmann and Käsemann[60] that there was a steady inflow of fresh material from prophetic utterances into the Jesus tradition in the pre–AD 70 period.[61]

The model also recognizes the strengths of Birger Gerhardsson's response to Bultmann while, hopefully, avoiding its weaknesses.[62] That is to say, the oral tradition model recognizes that where an influential teacher was in view, there was bound to be a concern among his disciples to remember what he had taught them.[63] But it sees the more fundamental trait of oral tradition in terms of the combination of flexibility as well as fixity, so that the character of oral transmission is not adequately caught by the single term "memorization."[64]

---

59. "Das . . . Kriterium der 'reinen Gattung' stellt eine Vermischung linguistischer und sprachhistorischer Kategorien dar, die einer heute überholten Auffassung der Sprachentwicklung zuzuweisen ist" — J. Schröter, *Erinnerung an Jesu Worte*, Wissenschaftliche Monographien zum Alten und Neuen Testament 76 (Neukirchen-Vluyn: Neukirchener Verlag, 1997), 59, also 141-42. See also G. Strecker, "Schriftlichkeit oder Mündlichkeit der synoptischen Tradition?" in *The Four Gospels, 1992: Festschrift Frans Neirynck*, ed. F. van Segbroeck et al., BETL 100 (Leuven: Leuven University Press, 1992), 1:159-72, here 161-62, with other bibliography in n. 6.

60. Bultmann, *History*, 127-28: "In the primitive community at Jerusalem the spirit of Jesus continued to be active, and his ethical teaching was progressively elaborated and expressed in utterances which were then transmitted as the sayings of Jesus himself" ("The New Approach to the Synoptic Problem" [1926]; ET: *Existence and Faith* [London: Collins Fontana, 1964], 42); E. Käsemann, "Is the Gospel Objective?" *Essays on New Testament Themes* (London: SCM, 1964), 48-62.

61. See further Dunn, *Jesus Remembered* (Grand Rapids: Eerdmans, 2002), #8.2.

62. B. Gerhardsson, *Memory and Manuscript: Oral Tradition and Written Transmission in Rabbinic Judaism and Early Christianity* (Lund: Gleerup, 1961).

63. Finnegan critiques Lord in pointing out that memorization also plays a part in oral tradition (*Oral Poetry*, 79, 86).

64. E.g., "The general attitude was that words and items of knowledge must be memo-

Bailey's intermediate model of *informal controlled* tradition seems closer to the more broadly recognizable oral-tradition model than either Bultmann's informal *uncontrolled* model or Gerhardsson's *formal* controlled model.[65]

So then, in the light of these characteristics of oral tradition, how do we go about re-envisaging the early transmission of the Jesus tradition?

Re-envisaging the Early Transmission

The test of any theoretical model for the transmission of the Jesus tradition, of course, is how well it explains the data we have, how well it explains the character of the Jesus tradition as we know it. I believe the oral-tradition model passes that test with flying colors. But before illustrating the claim, I need to make three preliminary points.

First, there is no possibility of producing a knockdown argument. I cannot produce a sample from the Jesus tradition that is demonstrably oral rather than literary in character.[66] This, of course, is partly because the tradition as we now have it is in literary form. So, naturally, it is literary in charac-

---

rized: *tantum scimus, quantum memoria tenemus*" (Gerhardsson, *Memory,* 124); "Cicero's saying was applied to its fullest extent in Rabbinic Judaism: *repetitio est mater studiorum.* Knowledge is gained by repetition, passed on by repetition, kept alive by repetition. A Rabbi's life is one continual repetition" (*Memory,* 168). Sanders and Davies rightly observe that Gerhardsson tries to allow for the flexibility of verbal tradition (citing Gerhardsson, *The Gospel Tradition,* Coniectanea biblica: New Testament Series 15 [Lund: Gleerup, 1986], 39-40), but that even so the Synoptic data do not fit well with the model (*Studying,* 129-32). R. Riesner, *Jesus als Lehrer: Eine Untersuchung zum Ursprung der Evangelien-Überlieferung,* WUNT 7/2 (Tübingen: Mohr Siebeck, 1981), 65-67, 440-53, also emphasizes the role of learning by heart *(Auswendiglernen)* in Jesus' teaching. D. L. Balch, "The Canon: Adaptable and Stable, Oral and Written: Critical Questions for Kelber and Riesner," *Forum* 7.3-4 (1991): 183-205, criticizes Riesner for assuming "a print mentality" that was not true of "passing on tradition of great philosophers' teachings" (196-99).

65. I might simply add that the appeal sometimes made, by Horsley in particular (*Whoever Hears You,* 98-103; also *Hearing the Whole Story: The Politics of Plot in Mark's Gospel* [Louisville: Westminster John Knox, 2001], 157-59), to James C. Scott's use of the distinction between the "great tradition" and the "little tradition" in a community — the great tradition as expressing the dominant and dominating ruling power, the little tradition as expressing the hidden but continuing values and concerns of the oppressed community — is of little relevance for us. It is used by Scott in reference to a colonialist situation in Southeast Asia, which has little bearing on a Jewish Galilee ruled by a client Jewish king. And in the Jesus tradition, we have not so much the persistence of old tradition but the emergence of new tradition (even if much of it can be regarded as a reconfiguration of older tradition).

66. I recall that my doctor-father, C. F. D. Moule, in the mid-1960s challenged his Cambridge Seminar to produce such a knockdown example in regard to any solution of the Synoptic Problem; no example went unquestioned.

ter. But it is also true anyway that there are no distinctive characteristics of any particular sample of tradition that enable us to pronounce definitively "Oral and not literary."[67]

On the other hand, the observation cuts both ways. That is to say, we should not assume that simply because the tradition as we now have it is in literary form, therefore its current form is the outcome of a process conceived in purely literary terms. My challenge once again is for us to shake ourselves out of that literary mind-set and to attempt to revisualize the part of the process that must have been largely if not entirely oral in character. What I ask for is that we seriously attempt to re-conceptualize the parameters and constraints within which we envisage the transmission of the Jesus tradition taking place. It is not what we look at, so much as the way we look at it, that we need to reflect on.

Second, as just implied, we simply cannot escape from a *presumption of orality* for the first stage of the transmission of the Jesus tradition. In a society that was so illiterate and where the great bulk of communication must have taken place in oral mode, it would be ludicrous either to assume that the whole history of the Jesus tradition was literary in character from start to finish or to make any thesis regarding the process of its transmission dependent in effect on such an assumption. I say this in response to various recent claims either that the Jesus tradition took literary form from the first,[68] or that all differences between parallel traditions, no matter how great, can be explained in terms of literary redaction.[69] As indicated earlier, I do not for a moment

67. Note the conclusion of the symposium on *Jesus and the Oral Gospel Tradition*, ed. H. Wansbrough, JSNTSup 64 (Sheffield: Sheffield Academic Press, 1991): "We have been unable to deduce or derive any marks which distinguish clearly between an oral and a written transmission process. Each can show a similar degree of fixity and variability" (12). Strecker rightly emphasizes the continuity in transmission of the tradition from oral to written ("Schriftlichkeit," 164-65). Cf. Schröter, *Erinnerung*, 55, 60.

68. See above, n. 38.

69. B. W. Henaut, *Oral Tradition and the Gospels: The Problem of Mark 4*, JSNTSup 82 (Sheffield: JSOT, 1993), is tendentiously concerned to argue the virtual impossibility of recovering any oral tradition behind the Gospels: all differences, no matter how great, can be explained in terms of literary redaction; and oral tradition was wholly fluid and contingent on the particularities of each performance. But his conception of the oral tradition process is questionable — as though it was a matter of recovering a history of tradition through a set of sequential performances (e.g., 118). And he gives too little thought to what the stabilities of oral remembrances of Jesus might be as distinct from those in the epics and sagas studied by Parry and Lord. H. W. Hollander, "The Words of Jesus: From Oral Tradition to Written Record in Paul and Q," *Novum Testamentum* 42 (2000): 340-57, follows Henaut uncritically (351-55): he has no conception of tradition as reflecting/embodying the impact of anything Jesus said or did; and he thinks of oral tradition as essentially casual, without any conception that tradition

deny that differences within the Synoptic tradition can be explained in terms of the literary paradigm. My question is whether they should be so explained, and whether in so doing we do not lose sight of important features of the Jesus tradition, the way it was regarded and handled, and what that tells us about the earliest communities that preserved it.

Third, despite the cautionary note I am sounding, I remain convinced of the essential correctness of the two-document hypothesis. That is to say, the evidence continues to persuade me that Mark was the earliest of the Synoptic Gospels, and that there was a further document behind Matthew and Luke on which both drew (Q). The primary evidence is as it has always been: the closeness of verbal parallels between two or three of the three documents. When I look at such passages as Mark 8:34-37 and parallels (the cost of discipleship) and 13:28-32 and parallels (the parable of the fig tree),[70] the evidence forces me to the conclusion that these three versions of particular Jesus traditions are interdependent at the literary level. The evidence almost requires us to speak of sources, of sources already in Greek, of one serving as the source for the other, or of each drawing on a common literary source (the underlining indicating the extent of the agreement).

Matthew 16:24-26	Mark 8:34-37	Luke 9:23-25
[24]Then Jesus told his disciples, "If any man would come after me, let him deny himself and take up his cross and follow me. [25]For whoever would save his life will lose it, and whoever loses his life for my sake will find it. [26]For what will it profit a man, if he gains the whole world and forfeits his life? Or what shall a man give i return for his life?"	[34]And he called to him the multitude with his disciples, and said to them, "If any man would come after me, let him deny himself and take up his cross and follow me. [35]For whoever would save his life will lose it; and whoever loses his life for my sake and the gospel's will save it. [36]For what does it profit a man, to gain the whole world and forfeit his life? [37]For what can a man give in return for his life?"	[23] And he said to all, "If any man would come after me, let him deny himself and take up his cross daily and follow me. [24]For whoever would save his life will lose it; and whoever loses his life for my sake, he will save it. [25]For what does it profit a man if he gains the whole world and loses or forfeits himself?"

could have a role in forming community identity and thus be important to such communities. Similarly, Crossan seems to think of oral tradition principally in terms of individuals' casual recollection (*Birth of Christianity,* 49-93).

70. Full statistics in R. Morgenthaler, *Statistische Synopse* (Zurich and Stuttgart: Gotthelf, 1971), 239-43.

Matthew 24:32-36	Mark 13:28-32	Luke 21:29-33
		29And he told them a parable:
32"From the fig tree	28"From the fig tree	"Look at the fig tree, and all the
learn its lesson: as soon as	learn its lesson: as soon as	trees; 30as soon as
its branch becomes tender and	its branch becomes tender and	they come out in leaf, you
puts forth its leaves, you know	puts forth its leaves, you know	see for yourselves and know
that the summer is near.	that the summer is near.	that the summer is already near.
33So also, when you see all these	29So also, when you see these	31So also, when you see these
things, you know	things taking place, you know	things taking place, you know
that he	that he	that the kingdom of God
is near, at the very gates.	is near, at the very gates.	is near.
34Truly, I say to you, this	30Truly, I say to you, this	32Truly, I say to you, this
generation will not pass away	generation will not pass away	generation will not pass away
till all these things take place.	before all these things take place.	till all has taken place.
35Heaven and earth will pass away,	31Heaven and earth will pass away,	33Heaven and earth will pass away,
but my words will not pass away."	but my words will not pass away."	but my words will not pass away."
36But of that day and hour no	32But of that day or that hour no	
one knows, not even the angels	one knows, not even the angels	
of heaven, nor the Son, but	in heaven, nor the Son, but	
the Father only."	only the Father."	

The Q material has similar parallels, such as the preaching of John the Baptist in Matt. 3:7-10//Luke 3:7-9, and the parable of the returning evil spirits in Matt. 12:43-45//Luke 11:24-26.[71]

Matthew 3:7-10	Luke 3:7-9
7But when he saw many of the Pharisees and Sadducees coming for baptism, he said to them, "You brood of vipers! Who warned you to flee from the wrath to come? 8Bear fruit that befits repentance, 9and do not presume to say to yourselves, 'We have Abraham as ourfather'; for I tell you, God is able from these stones to raise up children to Abraham. 10Even now the axe is laid to the root of the trees: every tree therefore that does not bear good fruit is cut down and thrown into the fire."	7He said therefore to the multitudes that came out to be baptized by him, "You brood of vipers! Who warned you to flee from the wrath to come? 8Bear fruits that befit repentance, and do not begin to say to yourselves, 'We have Abraham as our father'; for I tell you, God is able from these stones to raise up children to Abraham. 9Even now the axe is laid to the root of the trees; every tree therefore that does not bear good fruit is cut down and thrown into the fire."

Matthew 12:43-45	Luke 11:24-26
43"When the unclean spirit has gone out of a man, he passes through waterless places seeking rest, but he finds none. 44Then he says, 'I will return to	24"When the unclean spirit has gone out of a man, he passes through waterless places seeking rest; and finding none he says. 'I will return to

71. Full statistics in Morgenthaler, *Statistische Synopse*, 258-61.

Matthew 12:43-45	Luke 11:24-26
my house from which I came.' <u>And when he comes he finds it</u> empty, <u>swept, and put in order.</u> ⁴⁵Then he goes and brings with him <u>seven other spirits more evil than himself, and they enter and dwell there; and the last state of that man becomes worse than the first.</u> So shall it be also with this evil generation."	my house from which I came.' ²⁵<u>And when he comes he finds it</u> <u>swept and put in order.</u> ²⁶Then he goes and brings <u>seven other spirits more evil than himself, and they enter and dwell there; and the last state of that man becomes worse than the first.</u>"

So, I have no problems in recognizing the probability of literary interdependence between the Synoptic Gospels. My question, once again, is whether the hypothesis of literary interdependence is sufficient to explain *all* the data of correlation between the Gospel traditions. My question is whether we should take such close parallels as the *norm* for explaining *all* parallels, whether we should simply extrapolate from such examples and conclude that all parallels are to be explained in the same way.

Consider the following cases. As you look at these passages, I ask you to consider whether literary dependence is the only or most obvious explanation for the degree of similarity between the different versions.

1. The Triple Tradition

In the triple tradition consider first the account of the epileptic boy in Mark 9:14-27 and parallels. Note the cluster of agreement at vv. 18-19, 25, evidently the core of the story, and the wide variation for the rest (again, the underlining indicating the extent of the agreement).

Matthew 17:14-18	Mark 9:14-27	Luke 9:37-42
¹⁴And when they <u>came</u> to the crowd,	¹⁴And when they <u>came</u> to the disciples, they saw <u>a great crowd</u> about them, and scribes arguing with them. ¹⁵And immediately all the crowd, when they saw him, were greatly amazed, and ran up to him and greeted him. ¹⁶And he asked them, "What are you discussing	³⁷On the next day, when they had come down from the mountain, <u>a great crowd</u> met him.
a man came up to him and kneeling	with them?" ¹⁷And one of <u>the crowd</u>	³⁸And behold, <u>a man</u> from <u>the crowd</u>

Matthew 17:14-18	Mark 9:14-27	Luke 9:37-42
before him said, 15"Lord, have mercy on <u>my son,</u> for he is an epileptic and he suffers terribly; for often he falls into the fire, and often into the water. 16<u>And I</u> brought him to <u>your disciples,</u> <u>and</u> they could <u>not</u> heal him." 17And Jesus <u>answered,</u> "<u>O faithless</u> <u>and perverse</u> <u>generation, how long am I to be</u> with <u>you?</u> How long am I <u>to put up with you?</u> Bring him here to me."	answered him, "<u>Teacher,</u> I brought <u>my son</u> to you, for he has a dumb spirit; 18and wherever it grabs <u>him,</u> it dashes him down; and he foams and grinds his teeth and becomes rigid; <u>and I</u> asked <u>your disciples</u> <u>to cast it out,</u> <u>and</u> they were <u>not</u> able." 19And he <u>answered</u> them, "<u>O faithless</u> <u>generation, how long am I to be</u> with <u>you?</u> How long am I <u>to put up with you?</u> Bring him to me." 20And they brought the boy to him; and when the spirit saw him, immediately it <u>convulsed</u> the boy, and he fell on the ground and rolled about, foaming at the mouth.	cried, "<u>Teacher,</u> I beg you to look upon <u>my son,</u> for he is my only child; 39and behold, a spirit seizes <u>him,</u> and he suddenly cries out; it convulses him till he foams, and shatters him, and will hardly leave him. 40<u>And I</u> begged <u>your disciples</u> <u>to cast it out,</u> <u>and</u> they could <u>not.</u>" 41Jesus <u>answered,</u> "<u>O faithless</u> <u>and perverse</u> <u>generation, how long am I to be</u> with <u>you</u> and <u>to put up with you?</u> Lead your son here." 42While he was coming, the demon tore him and <u>convulsed</u> him.
. . . .		
18And Jesus <u>rebuked</u> him	25And when Jesus saw that a crowd came running together, he <u>rebuked</u> the unclean spirit, saying to it, "You dumb and deaf spirit, I command you, come out of him, and never enter him again." 26And after crying out and convulsing him	But Jesus <u>rebuked</u> the unclean spirit,
and the demon <u>came out</u> of him,	terribly, it <u>came out,</u> and the boy was like a corpse; so that most of them said, "He is dead." 27But Jesus took him by the hand and	
and the boy was cured from that hour.	lifted him up, and he arose.	and healed the boy, and gave him back to his father. 43And all were astonished at the majesty of God.

Or again, note the variations in the accounts of finding the empty tomb — Mark 16:1-8 and parallels.

Matthew 28:1-8	Mark 16:1-8	Luke 24:1-11
[1]Now after <u>the sabbath</u>, toward the dawn of <u>the first day of the week</u>, <u>Mary Magdalene and</u> the other <u>Mary</u>	[1]And when <u>the sabbath</u> was past, <u>Mary Magdalene, and</u> <u>Mary the mother of James,</u> and Salome, bought <u>spices</u>, so that they might go and anoint him. [2]And very early on <u>the first day of the week</u> <u>they went to the</u> <u>tomb</u> when the sun had risen.	[1]But on <u>the first day of the week</u>, at early dawn, <u>they went to the</u> <u>tomb</u>, taking the <u>spices</u> which they had prepared.
<u>went</u> to see the sepulcher. [2]And behold, there was a great earthquake; for an angel of the Lord descended from heaven and came and <u>rolled</u> back <u>the stone</u>, and sat upon it. [3]His appearance was like lightning, and his raiment <u>white</u> as snow. [4]And for fear of him the guards trembled and became like dead men.	[3]And they were saying to one another, "Who will roll away the stone for us from the door of the tomb?" [4]And looking up, they saw that <u>the stone</u> was <u>rolled</u> away — it was very large. [5]And <u>entering</u> the tomb, they saw a young man sitting on the right side, dressed in a <u>white</u> robe; and they were amazed.	[2]And they found <u>the stone</u> <u>rolled</u> back from the tomb, [3]but when they <u>entered</u> they did not find the body. [4]While they were perplexed about this, behold, two men stood by them in dazzling apparel; [5]and as they were frightened and bowed their faces to the ground, the men <u>said to</u> them,
[5]But the angel <u>said to</u> the women, "<u>Do not be</u> afraid; for I know that <u>you seek Jesus</u> <u>who was crucified</u>. [6]<u>He is not here</u>; for <u>he has risen</u>, as he said. Come, <u>see the place where</u> he lay. [7]Then <u>go</u> quickly and <u>tell his disciples</u> that he has risen from the dead, and behold, <u>he is going before you to Galilee;</u> <u>there you will see him</u>. Lo, I have <u>told you</u>."	[6]And he <u>said to</u> them, "<u>Do not be</u> amazed; <u>you seek Jesus</u> of Nazareth, <u>who was crucified</u>. <u>He has risen</u>, <u>he is not here</u>; <u>see the place where</u> they laid him. [7]But <u>go</u>, <u>tell his disciples</u> and Peter that <u>he is going before you to Galilee;</u> <u>there you will see him</u>, as he <u>told you</u>."	"Why do <u>you seek</u> the living among the dead? [6]Remember how he told <u>you</u>, while he was still in <u>Galilee</u>, [7]that the Son of man must be delivered into the hands of sinful men, and be crucified, and on the third day rise." [8]And they remembered his words, [9]and returning
[8]So <u>they</u> departed quickly <u>from the tomb</u> with fear and great joy, and ran to tell his disciples.	[8]And <u>they</u> went out and fled <u>from the tomb</u>; for trembling and astonishment had come upon them; and they said nothing to anyone, for they were afraid.	<u>from the tomb</u> they told all this to the Eleven and to all the rest. [10]Now it was <u>Mary Magdalene</u>

Matthew 28:1-8	Mark 16:1-8	Luke 24:1-11
		and Joanna and Mary the mother of James and the other women with them who told this to the apostles; [11]but these words seemed to them an idle tale, and they did not believe them.

My question is whether such evidence is not better explained in terms of *oral* tradition — that is, as *retellings* of a familiar story, with variations dependent on the teller's foibles and the community's perceived interests. That may mean that Matthew or Luke already knew versions of the stories that differed from Mark's, and that they followed these different versions. Or, bearing in mind the characteristics of oral performance, perhaps we should envisage Matthew and Luke *retelling* the story known to them from Mark, that is, retelling it *in oral mode* — as story tellers, rather than editors — with Matthew and Luke as evidence not so much of redaction as of second orality.

2. The Q Tradition?

The Q hypothesis, which I accept, is built in the first instance on the closeness of parallel between non-Markan pericopes in Matthew and Luke. More than 13 percent of these common pericopes are more than 80 percent in verbal agreement. But the fact that the verbal agreement in over a third of the common material is less than 40 percent[72] has not been given sufficient weight. Is it to be explained solely in terms of free redaction? Consider the following examples: turning the other cheek, in Matt. 5:39b-42//Luke 6:29-30; dividing families, in Matt. 10:34-38//Luke 12:51-53 and 14:26-27; and forgiving sins seven times, in Matt. 18:15, 21-22//Luke 17:3-4 (the underlining once again indicating the extent of the verbal agreement).

---

72. See Kloppenborg Verbin's summary of Morgenthaler's data (*Excavating Q*, 63). In such cases, Kloppenborg Verbin defends a literary dependence by pointing out that Matthew and Luke show equal freedom in their use of Mark (64). But he does not consider the obvious alternative noted above, that such divergences of Matthew and Luke from Mark may indicate rather that Matthew and Luke knew and preferred to use other oral versions of the tradition, or to retell Mark's version in oral mode.

Matthew 5:39b-42	Luke 6:29-30
[39b]"But whoever hits you on your right <u>cheek</u>, turn to him <u>the other also</u>; [40]and to the one who wants to sue you and take your <u>tunic</u>, let him have your <u>cloak also</u>; [41]and whoever forces you to go one mile, go with him a second. [42]<u>Give to</u> the one <u>who asks you</u>, and do not turn away the one who wants to borrow from you."	[29]"To the one who strikes you on the <u>cheek</u>, offer <u>the other also</u>; and from the one who takes away your <u>cloak</u> do not withhold your <u>tunic also</u>. [30]<u>Give to</u> everyone <u>who asks you</u>; and from the one who takes what is yours, do not ask for them back."

Matthew 10:34-38	Luke 12:51-53; 14:26-27
[34]"Do not think that I came to bring <u>peace</u> to <u>the earth</u>; I came not to bring peace, <u>but</u> a sword. [35]For I came to set a man against his <u>father</u>, and a <u>daughter</u> against her <u>mother</u>. and a <u>daughter-in-law</u> against her <u>mother-in-law</u>; [36]and a man's foes will be members of his own household. [37]Whoever loves <u>father</u> or <u>mother</u> more than me is not worthy of me; and whoever loves son or daughter more than me is not worthy of me; [38]and he <u>who does not</u> take up <u>his</u> <u>cross and</u> follow <u>after me</u> is not worthy <u>of me</u>."	[12:51]"Do you consider that I am here to give <u>peace</u> on <u>the earth</u>? No, I tell you, <u>but</u> rather division! [52]From now on five in one household will be divided; three against two and two against three; [53]they will be divided, father against son and son against <u>father</u>, mother against daughter and <u>daughter</u> against <u>mother</u>, mother-in-law against her daughter-in-law and <u>daughter-in-law</u> against <u>mother-in-law</u>." . . . . [14:26]"Whoever comes to me and does not hate his <u>father</u> and <u>mother</u>, and wife and children, and brothers and sisters, yes, and even his own life, cannot be my disciple. [27]<u>Whoever</u> <u>does not</u> carry <u>his</u> own <u>cross and</u> come <u>after me</u> cannot be <u>my</u> disciple."

Matthew 18:15, 21-22	Luke 17:3-4
[15]"<u>If your brother sins</u> against you, go and point out the fault when you and he are alone. If he listens to you, you have regained your brother." . . . . [21]Then Peter came and said to him, "Lord, <u>if</u> my brother <u>sins against</u> me, how often should I <u>forgive him</u>? As many as <u>seven times</u>?" [22]Jesus said to him, "I tell you, not <u>seven times</u>, but seventy-seven times."	[3]"Be on your guard! <u>If your brother sins</u>, rebuke him, and if he repents, forgive him. [4]And <u>if</u> someone <u>sins against</u> you <u>seven times</u> a day, and turns back to you <u>seven times</u> and says, 'I repent,' you must <u>forgive him</u>."

My question again is simple: Is there anything in these passages that compels the conclusion that one has drawn the sayings from the other or that both

67

have drawn from a common literary source?[73] Is the assumption that only literary dependence need or should be invoked not a consequence of our literary default setting, a consequence of our reading such passages through the spectacles or with the blinkers of a mind-set formed by our print-dominated heritage? Ought we not to make the effort to *hear* these traditions as they were shaped and passed down in an oral culture? Ought we not to give more consideration to the likelihood, not to say probability that such *variation* in what is obviously the *same* essential tradition is the result of the flexibility of *oral* performance?[74]

3. Liturgical Tradition

The two most obvious examples of liturgical tradition are the Lord's Prayer and the words of the Last Supper. By liturgical tradition I mean, of course, traditions that were regularly used in worship in the early churches. That these two traditions were so used is not merely a deduction from the Gospel texts but is confirmed by *Didache* 8.2 and 1 Cor. 11:23-26. How then shall we explain the variations in the traditions of the Lord's Prayer?

Matthew 6:7-15	Luke 11:1-4
[7]"When you are praying, do not heap up empty phrases as the Gentiles do; for they think that they will be heard because of their many words. [8]Do not be like them, for your Father knows what you need before you ask him.	
	[1]He was praying in a certain place, and after he had finished, one of his disciples said to him, "Lord, teach us to pray, as John taught his disciples." [2]He said to them, "When you pray, say:
[9]Pray then in this way: Our <u>Father</u> who is in heaven, <u>hallowed be your name.</u> [10]<u>Your kingdom come.</u> Your will be done, on earth as it is in heaven. [11] <u>Give us</u> to<u>day our daily bread.</u> [12]<u>And forgive us our</u> debts, as <u>we</u> <u>also</u> have <u>forgiven</u> our <u>debt</u>ors. [13]<u>And do not bring us to the time of trial,</u> but rescue us from the evil one. [14]For if you forgive others their trespasses, your heavenly Father will also forgive you; [15]but if you do not forgive others, neither will your Father forgive your trespasses."	<u>Father,</u> <u>hallowed be your name. Your kingdom come.</u> [3]<u>Give us</u> each <u>day our daily bread.</u> [4]<u>And forgive us our</u> sins, for <u>we</u> ourselves <u>also</u> forgive everyone in<u>debt</u>ed to us. <u>And do not bring us to the time of trial.</u>"

73. My distinguished predecessor, C. K. Barrett, was asking the same question sixty years ago in his "Q: A Re-examination," *ExpTim* 54 (1942-43): 320-23.

74. As Streeter recognized (*Four Gospels*, 184-86, 229).

So too, how shall we explain the variations in the traditions of the Last Supper, as between the Matthew/Mark version on the one hand and the Luke/Paul version on the other?

Matthew 26:26-29	Mark 14:22-25
[26]While they were eating, Jesus took a loaf of bread, and after blessing it he broke it, giving it to the disciples, and said, "Take, eat; this is my body." [27]Then he took a cup, and after giving thanks he gave it to them, saying, "Drink from it, all of you; [28]for this is my blood of the covenant, which is poured out formany for the forgiveness of sins. [29]I tell you, from now on I will not drink of this fruit of the vine until that day when I drink it new with you in the kingdom of my Father."	[22]While they were eating, he took a loaf of bread, and after blessing it he broke it, gave it to them, and said, "Take; this is my body." [23]Then he took a cup, and after giving thanks he gave it to them, and all of them drank from it. [24]He said to them, "This is my blood of the covenant, which is poured out on behalf of many. [25]Truly I tell you, no more will I drink of the fruit of the vine until that day when I drink it new in the kingdom of God."

Luke 22:17-20	1 Corinthians 11:23-26
[17]Then he took a cup, and after giving thanks he said, "Take this and divide it among yourselves; [18]for I tell you that from now on I will not drink of the fruit of the vine until the kingdom of God comes."	
	[23]For I received from the Lord what I also handed on to you, that the Lord Jesus on the night when he was betrayed
[19]Then he took a loaf of bread, and when he had given thanks, he broke it and gave it to them, saying, "This is my body, which is given for you. Do this in remembrance of me." [20]Also the cup likewise after supper, saying, "This cup is the new covenant in my blood which is poured out for you."	took a loaf of bread, [24]and when he had given thanks, he brokeit and said, "This is my body which is for you. Do this in remembrance of me." [25]Likewise also the cup after supper, saying, "This cup is the new covenant in my blood. Do this, as often as you drink it, in remembrance of me." [26]For as often as you eat this bread and drink the cup, you proclaim the Lord's death until he comes.

What kind of failure in historical imagination could even suggest to us that Matthew, say, only knew the Lord's Prayer because he read it in Q?[75] Or

75. Contrast D. E. Oakman, "The Lord's Prayer in Social Perspective," in *Authenticating of the Words of Jesus,* ed. B. Chilton and C. A. Evans (Leiden: Brill, 1999), 137-86: "The differences in form are best accounted for by differing scribal traditions and interests" (151-52); with the sounder judgment of H. D. Betz, *The Sermon on the Mount,* Hermeneia (Minneapo-

that Luke only knew the words of the Last Supper because he found them in Mark? The alternative explanation positively cries out for consideration: that these were living traditions, living because they were used in regular church assemblies; that even though liturgical tradition tends to be more stable than other oral tradition, nevertheless, as is common with oral tradition, it adapted in wording to the usage of different churches — as the Lord's Prayer still adapts in different traditions today. Such liturgical traditions are special examples of oral tradition and oral transmission, but they reflect the character of oral communities far more closely than do explanations dependent solely on the literary paradigm.

4. Stylistic Features

There are several stylistic features characteristic of oral tradition: for example, parataxis,[76] rhythmic speech,[77] repetition,[78] multiple existence, and variation.[79] This is not to say, I repeat, that such features are *distinctive* of oral tradition; the written document, Mark, provides one of the best examples of parataxis. However, the question once again arises whether the tradition retold by Mark is retold *in oral mode*, rather than as a distinctively literary exercise[80]

---

lis: Fortress, 1995), 370-71: "It is characteristic of liturgical material in general that textual fixation occurs at a later stage in the transmission of these texts, while in the oral stage variability within limits is the rule. These characteristics also apply to the Lord's Prayer. The three recensions, therefore, represent variations of the prayer in the oral tradition. . . . There was never only one original written Lord's Prayer. . . . The oral tradition continued to exert an influence on the written text of the New Testament well into later times" (370). M. Goulder, "The Composition of the Lord's Prayer," *Journal of Theological Studies* 14 (1963): 32-45, argues that the prayer was written by Matthew from hints found in Mark, and that Luke was dependent on Matthew's version.

76. "One law of narrative in oral poetry, noted by specialists, takes the form of parataxis: the language is additive, as image is connected to image by 'and' rather than subordinated in some thoughtful relationship" (Havelock, *Muse*, 76).

77. Havelock, *Muse*, 70-71. Here the examples from the Jesus tradition produced by J. Jeremias, *New Testament Theology*, part 1, *The Proclamation of Jesus* (London: SCM, 1971), are very much to the point (20-27).

78. Achtemeier, "*Omne verbum sonat*," 23-24.

79. See above, n. 57.

80. See particularly J. Dewey, "Oral Methods of Structuring Narrative in Mark," *Interpretation* 43 (1989): 32-44; also "The Gospel of Mark as an Oral-Aural Event: Implications for Interpretation," in *The New Literary Criticism and the New Testament*, ed. E. S. Malbon and E. V. McKnight, JSNTSup 109 (Sheffield: Sheffield Academic Press, 1994), 145-63; Horsley, *Hearing the Whole Story*, ch. 3.

— a question once again of how we envisage the character of the tradition used by Mark, as also how we envisage Mark's use of it.

One of the best-attested characteristics of oral tradition is the pattern of threes — stories built on three episodes or illustrations. Such patterning positively invites the oral performer to vary the examples or episodes at his own whim, often quite spontaneously within the performance itself. There are some good examples of this feature within the Jesus tradition. I cite two, focusing only on the section where the pattern of threes is followed. First, Matt. 22:5-6//Luke 14:18-20, the excuses made by those invited to the great supper or royal wedding banquet; note again how little verbal agreement there is between them.[81]

Matthew 22:1-10	Luke 14:15-24
[1]Once more Jesus spoke to them in parables, saying: [2]"The kingdom of heaven may be compared to a king who gave a wedding banquet for his son. [3]He sent his slaves to call those who had been invited to the wedding banquet, but they would not come. [4]Again he sent other slaves, saying, 'Tell those who have been invited: Look, I have prepared my dinner, my oxen and my fat calves have been slaughtered, and everything is ready; come to the wedding banquet.' [5]But they made light of it and went away, one to his *farm*, another to his business, [6]while the rest seized his slaves, mistreated them, and killed them. [7]The king was angered. He sent his troops, destroyed those murderers, and burned their city. [8]Then he said to his slaves, 'The wedding is ready, but those invited were not worthy. [9]Go therefore into the streets, and invite everyone you find to the wedding banquet.'	[15]One of the dinner guests, on hearing this, said to him, "Blessed is anyone who will eat bread in the kingdom of God!" [16]Then Jesus said to him, "A certain person gave a great dinner and invited many. [17]At the time for the dinner he sent his slave to say to those who had been invited, 'Come; for it is now prepared.' [18]But they all alike began to make excuses. The first said to him, 'I have bought a *farm*, and I must go out and see it; please accept my regrets.' [19]Another said, 'I have bought five yoke of oxen, and I am going to try them out; please accept my regrets.' [20]Another said, 'I have married a wife, and therefore I cannot come.' [21]So the slave returned and reported this to his master. Then the owner of the house became angry and said to his slave, 'Go out at once into the roads and lanes of the town and bring in the poor, the crippled, the blind, and the lame.'

81. Note that in *Gospel of Thomas* 64, the performance variation runs to four different excuses.

Matthew 22:1-10	Luke 14:15-24
¹⁰Those slaves went out into the streets and gathered all whom they found, both good and bad;	
	²²And the slave said, 'Sir, what you ordered has been done, and there is still room.' ²³Then the master said to the slave, 'Go out into the roads and lanes, and compel them to come in, so that my house may be full.
so the wedding hall was filled with guests."	
	²⁴For I tell you, none of those who were invited will taste my dinner.'"

Second, the account of Peter's threefold denial, in Mark 14:66-72 and parallels.

Matthew 26:69-75	Mark 14:66-72	Luke 22:56-62
⁶⁹Now <u>Peter</u> was sitting outside <u>in the courtyard</u>. And a <u>maid</u> came up to him,	⁶⁶And as <u>Peter</u> was below <u>in the courtyard</u>, one of the <u>maid</u>s of the high priest came; ⁶⁷and <u>seeing</u> Peter warming himself, she looked at him,	⁵⁶Then a <u>maid</u>, <u>seeing</u> him as he sat in the light and gazing at him,
and said, "<u>You also were with</u> <u>Jesus</u> the Galilean."	and said, "<u>You also were with</u> the Nazarene, <u>Jesus</u>."	said, "This man <u>also was with</u> him."
⁷⁰<u>But he denied it</u> before them all, <u>saying</u>, "<u>I do not know</u> <u>what you mean</u>."	⁶⁸<u>But he denied it</u>, <u>saying</u>, "I neither <u>know</u> nor understand <u>what you mean</u>."	⁵⁷<u>But he denied it</u>, <u>saying</u>, "Woman, <u>I do not know</u> him."
⁷¹<u>And</u> when <u>he went out</u> to the porch, another <u>maid saw him</u>, <u>and</u> she <u>said to the</u> <u>bystanders</u>, "<u>This man</u> was with Jesus of Nazareth."	<u>And</u> he went out into the gateway. ⁶⁹And the <u>maid saw him</u>, <u>and</u> began again to say <u>to the</u> <u>bystanders</u>, "<u>This man is</u> <u>one of them</u>."	⁵⁸And a little later someone else <u>saw him</u> <u>and</u> <u>said</u>, "You also are <u>one of them</u>."
⁷²And <u>again he denied</u> <u>it</u> with an oath, "I do not know the man."	⁷⁰But <u>again he denied it</u>.	But Peter said, "Man, I am not."
⁷³ <u>After a little while</u> the bystanders came up and <u>said to Peter</u>, "<u>Certainly you are</u> also <u>one of</u> <u>them</u>, for your accent betrays you."	<u>And after a little while</u> again <u>the bystanders</u> <u>said to Peter</u>, "<u>Certainly you are one of</u> <u>them</u>; for you are <u>a Galilean</u>."	⁵⁹And after an interval of about an hour still another insisted, saying, "<u>Certainly</u> this man also was with him; for he is <u>a Galilean</u>."
⁷⁴Then <u>he began to invoke a curse</u> <u>on himself and to swear</u>, "<u>I do not know</u> the <u>man</u>."	⁷¹But <u>he began to invoke a curse</u> <u>on himself and to swear</u>, "<u>I do not know this man</u> of whom you speak."	⁶⁰But Peter said, "Man, <u>I do not know</u> what you are saying."
<u>And immediately</u>	⁷²<u>And immediately</u>	<u>And immediately</u>, while he was still speaking,

Matthew 26:69-75	Mark 14:66-72	Luke 22:56-62
the cock crowed.	the cock crowed a second time.	the cock crowed. [61]And the Lord turned and looked at Peter.
[75]And Peter remembered	And Peter remembered	And Peter remembered the word of the Lord,
the saying of Jesus, "Before the cock crows, you will deny me three times." And he went out and wept bitterly.	how Jesus had said to him, "Before the cock crows twice, you will deny me three times." And he broke down and wept.	how he had said to him, "Before the cock crows today, you will deny me three times." [62]And he went out and wept bitterly.

In all these cases we see what is characteristic of oral tradition — a combination of fixity and flexibility, of stability and variation. Of course, I repeat yet again, such characteristics are not exclusive to oral tradition. The difference comes in *the way we envisage the traditioning process*. In oral transmission we do not look for an explanation for the diversity in terms (only) of editorial redaction, but in terms of performance variation. The explanation lies as much or more in the character of the tradition than in the interpretative goals of the performer. And we do not look behind the variations for some original (and therefore more authentic) version or source. Rather, we recognize the character of the Jesus tradition as oral tradition, where appropriateness of performance to context is not a departure from authenticity but integral to the tradition's living character.

Had I time, I would extend the exploration to the knowledge of Jesus tradition outside the Gospels. In my judgment, discussion of possible allusions to and use of the Jesus tradition, both within the NT epistles (Paul, James, 1 Peter), within the Apostolic Fathers, and now also within the Nag Hammadi texts, has been seriously flawed by overdependence on the literary paradigm. For if we are indeed talking about largely illiterate communities, dependent on oral tradition and aural knowledge of written documents, then we have to expect *as the rule* that knowledge of the Jesus tradition will have shared the characteristics of oral tradition. That is to say, the historical imagination, liberated from the *literary* default setting and tutored in regard to *oral* culture, can readily envisage communities familiar with *their* oral tradition, able to recognize allusions to Jesus tradition in performances of an apostolic letter written to them, and to fill in "the gaps of indeterminacy" in other performances of that tradition.[82]

82. I may refer here simply to my earlier attempts to develop this theme — "Jesus Tradition in Paul," in *Studying the Historical Jesus: Evaluations of the State of Current Research,* ed. B. Chil-

The suggestion of a living oral tradition, still continuing after so much of it was written down in various Gospels, carries with it, of course, the possibility that the tradition was significantly modified in its central thrust — that the flexibility overwhelmed the stability, the diversity the continuity. Here we would have to enter the debate about the "authenticity" of the Jesus tradition in the forms that it came to take in documents like the *Gospel of Thomas* and the *Dialogue of the Savior,* not to mention the Gospel of John! That is a debate for another day — in particular, on the criteria by which a form of the tradition was recognized as true to its originating impulse, and on the role of the community in checking the performances of that tradition.[83] Here it must suffice simply to note again that any attempt to resolve the issue purely in terms of literary dependence, or of the literary concept of the "original" form of the tradition, is hardly likely to prove satisfactory in the long run. Unless we take seriously the oral character of the early transmission of the Jesus tradition, we are always going to be in the position of one who attempts to describe a horse as a wheelless automobile, with the misperception of what we are trying to describe as the unavoidable outcome.

Conclusions and Corollaries

I believe we are confronted with a stark alternative: either we continue to operate within the literary paradigm and allow it to determine the way we envisage the earliest churches, their knowledge of the Jesus tradition, and their use of it; or we deliberately alter that default setting and attempt consciously to envisage a world strange to us, a world of rampant illiteracy, a world where information was communicated orally, a world where knowledge in the vast majority of cases came from hearing rather than from reading. There is room for compromise on this alternative, but not as much as we have simply assumed. For if we allow that the Jesus tradition as it has come down to us consists to any extent of various performances, frozen in writing to be sure, but no less in the first instance *performances,* rather than edited versions of some "original," then our basic methodologies of source and form and redaction criticism become increasingly speculative in their application and uncertain in their outcome.

---

ton and C. A. Evans (Leiden: Brill, 1994), 155-78, particularly 176-78; also Dunn, *The Theology of Paul the Apostle* (Grand Rapids: Eerdmans; Edinburgh: Clark, 1998), 651-53.

83. At this point I would wish to take issue with a central thrust of Koester's magisterial contribution, *Ancient Christian Gospels.*

Consider what corollaries we are loaded with when we opt for exclusive or over-dependence on the literary paradigm. For no hypothesis is more vulnerable to reductio ad absurdum than the hypothesis of an exclusively literary explanation for the Synoptic tradition. Was there no Jesus tradition known and used and circulated before Mark (or Q) wrote it down? Of course there was. Was the tradition wholly inert until Mark gave it life by writing it down? Of course not. Did Mark have to seek out aging apostles or rummage for scraps in boxes hidden away in various elders' houses in order to gather unknown, unused tradition and set it out in writing? Of course not. Was the tradition gathered by Mark known only to Mark's church or circle of congregations? Surely not. And once Mark had gathered the tradition into his Gospel, did that mean that the tradition ceased to be oral? Of course not. Or again, when Matthew received Mark's Gospel, are we to assume that this was the first time Matthew or his church(es) had come across this tradition? Of course not.

What is the alternative? The alternative is to recognize that in an oral culture, tradition — oral tradition — is *communal memory*. A group's tradition is the means by which the group affirms and celebrates what is important about its origins and about its past. So the alternative is to envisage little groups of disciples and sympathizers, their identity as a group given by their shared response to Jesus himself or to one of his disciples/apostles — little groups who met regularly to share the memories and the traditions that bound them together, for elders or teachers to tell again stories of Jesus and to expound afresh and elaborate his teachings.

Of course, Good Friday and Easter made a difference. They brought illumination to many features of the earlier tradition. They became integral to the tradition and often more important than the earlier tradition. Easter faith became the context in which the tradition was performed. I do not question that for a moment. But the fact remains that much if not most of the pre-Easter tradition retained its pre-Easter content and perspective, and various clear indications of its Galilean provenance.[84] The very features that Q specialists read as evidence of a *post*-Easter Galilean community that knew nothing of the passion narrative are much more naturally read as evidence of Jesus' *own pre-passion Galilean* mission. That character was already impressed in and on the Jesus tradition as it was orally circulated already during the mission of Jesus.

---

84. See particularly H. Schürmann, "Die vorösterlichen Anfänge der Logientradition: Versuch eines formgeschichtlichen Zugangs zum Leben Jesu," in *Der historische Jesus und der kerygmatische Christus*, ed. H. Ristow and K. Matthiae (Berlin: Evangelische Verlag, 1961), 342-70; also idem, *Jesus: Gestalt und Geheimnis* (Paderborn: Bonifatius, 1994), 85-104, 380-97.

And of course the transition from village to city, and from Aramaic to Greek, introduced still further factors influencing the preaching, telling, and performance of the Jesus tradition. But here again, the preservation of that Galilean, pre-passion character of so much of the tradition, now in Greek, and circulating in ever-widening circles as new churches were established, indicates that it was the *same* tradition that was being thus circulated and used. The essential character of that tradition was being maintained in and through the diversity of its performances.

On this model that I ask you to envisage, we need not assume that *Mark* wrote down all the tradition known to him. We can envisage quite readily that the tradition he drew upon continued to circulate in oral communication and was known more widely than the Gospel itself. Also, we can allow that Mark's Gospel itself functioned for many as itself a kind of oral performance,[85] known only by hearing, and recalled on the basis of that hearing. We can assume that *Matthew* knew at least many of the traditions written down by Mark, and knew the tradition almost certainly in different versions, in accordance with the nature of oral tradition. Also, we can assume that in various instances Matthew probably preferred the version of the tradition that he already knew, rather than Mark's. The same with Luke.

The corollaries regarding Q are of greater consequence, particularly in the light of the latest attempt to recover the text of Q.[86] If much of the shared Matthew and Luke material attests *oral* dependency rather than *literary* dependency, then *the attempt to define the complete scope and limits of Q is doomed to failure.* It is not simply that by definition of "Q" (material common to Matthew and Luke) we cannot know its scope and limits, since wherever Matthew or Luke decided not to use "Q" we do not have "Q"![87] It is rather that the material common to Matthew and Luke itself attests the pervasiveness of *oral* Jesus tradition precisely in its *variability,* as well as whatever of that material had already become more fixed in writing (as Q).[88]

I fully appreciate that the consequences of altering the default setting so

---

85. See again n. 80, above.

86. J. M. Robinson et al., eds., *The Critical Edition of Q* (Minneapolis: Fortress; Leuven: Peeters, 2000).

87. The spate of recent work on Q has provoked several vigorous responses, particularly C. S. Rodd, "The End of the Theology of Q?" *ExpTim* 113 (2001-2): 5-12; and Goodacre, *Case against Q.* The case against Q is only as strong as it is because the case for Q has been overstated.

88. Cf. F. G. Downing, "Word-Processing in the Ancient World: The Social Production and Performance of Q," *Journal for the Study of the New Testament* 64 (1996): 29-48, reprinted in his *Doing Things with Words in the First Christian Century,* JSNTSup 200 (Sheffield: Sheffield Academic Press, 2000), 75-94, especially 92-93.

abruptly are extensive. When we abandon the hypothesis of exclusive literary dependence, *we will simply be unable to trace the tradition-history of various sayings and accounts so confidently.* The unknown factors and variations so characteristic of oral tradition put the tradition-history or, better, performance-history beyond reach. The model of linear development, layer upon layer, edition following edition, is no longer appropriate.

Let me press the point more strongly. In recognizing the oral character of the early Jesus tradition, we have to give up the idea of a *single original form* from which all other versions of the tradition are to be derived, as though the "authenticity" of a version depended on our ability to trace it back to that original. In so saying, again, I do *not* mean that it is impossible to envisage or speak of the *originating impact* of Jesus himself. Quite the contrary. What I mean is that from the first the original impact was itself *diverse* in character. What I mean is that the form of the tradition itself was from the first *multiform*. This also means that *variation in tradition does not of itself either indicate contradiction or denote editorial manipulation.* Variation is simply the hallmark of oral tradition, how the Jesus tradition functioned.

In consequence also, we see how unrealistic is the suggestion that we can define the character of a community from the character of the documents they held in their possession. And the suggestion that the character of a community can be restricted to the character of a single document (for example, the Q community) becomes little short of ludicrous. For if the Jesus tradition was relatively widespread among churches in oral form and if indeed the Jesus tradition formed a kind of network linking the churches, as apostles, prophets, and others moved among them, then there is no good reason to limit the Jesus tradition known to individual churches to a certain kind of tradition or a particular written version of some of that tradition.

Confronted by the greater uncertainty thereby implied, some may be tempted to invoke Occam's razor: Why multiply unknown factors when a simple two-document hypothesis with redaction can cover every eventuality?[89] The answer is that the simplicity envisaged is far from simple, since it has to postulate editorial ingenuity of tremendous complexity and sophistication. Much more simple in fact is the inference that the variations within the Synoptic tradition reflect more closely the kind of variations that were common in the performance traditions of the early churches. Again I stress that it

---

89. But it is a double-edged razor, since both Farmer (*Synoptic Problem*, 203) and Goodacre (*Case against Q*, 18, 77) can use it to excise one of "the two documents" (Q). It is a fallacy to assume that elegance of solution can be achieved simply by restricting the range of options that the character of the evidence invites.

need not be an either-or matter. I am not arguing for one against the other; I am arguing for both.[90]

There is much more to be said about the way the Jesus tradition was used in performance by apostles and teachers. For example, I have already noted how Lord's observation that "oral traditional composers think in terms of blocks and series of blocks of tradition" correlates well with the various groupings or clusters of pericopes evident in the Synoptic tradition.[91] We need not assume, as the early form critics did, that before the written-down stage, the tradition was used only in small, individual units.[92] And we should reexamine the old suggestion of C. H. Dodd, that already in the prewritten (oral only) Gospel stage we can detect what we might call a narrative- or kerygma-sequencing of tradition.[93] For the connectedness of the passion narrative still attests some such concern, as does the fact that Mark and Q both reflect a common intuition (practice?) of beginning their rehearsal of the Jesus tradition with John the Baptist.[94] Just as elsewhere it seems to be "taken-for-granted and familiar" that a period of Jesus' mission in Capernaum preceded his return to Nazareth (Luke 4:23), and that the mission of the Twelve was a consequence of time spent with Jesus (made explicit in Mark 3:14), and so on. Thus the sequencing of the centurion's servant after the collection of Jesus' teaching (Sermon on Mount/Plain), which provides a decisive argument for the inclusion of the centurion's servant in Q (Matt. 7:28; 8:5-13//Luke 7:1-10), may after all be better explained as a recurring feature of the various performances of the Jesus tradition in more than one community.[95]

A fuller study of the Jesus tradition as oral tradition would also need to examine more closely what balance between stability and variation, between fixity and flexibility, was actually maintained, what it means to speak of the *same* tradition being maintained through the diversity of oral performance, and how Jesus was actually remembered in and by those earliest disciple

90. Streeter had already noted the danger of imposing an oversimplified solution on more complex data (*Four Gospels*, 229).

91. Above, nn. 53-54.

92. Pace Funk and Hoover (n. 20, above), who would regard their observation as form-critical orthodoxy.

93. C. H. Dodd, "The Framework of the Gospel Narrative," *New Testament Studies* (Manchester: Manchester University Press, 1953), 1-11. See further also Reicke, *Roots*; S. Hultgren, *Narrative Elements in the Double Tradition: A Study of Their Place within the Framework of the Gospel Narrative*, Beihefte zur Zeitschrift für die neutestamentliche Wissenschaft 113 (Berlin: de Gruyter, 2002).

94. See also N. T. Wright, *The New Testament and the People of God* (London: SPCK, 1992), 442; Schröter, *Erinnerung*, 439-51.

95. This in response to Goodacre, *Case against Q*, 172 n. 6.

groups. I have attempted to press further in this direction in my study *Jesus Remembered*. In the present essay, it has been a sufficient challenge to attempt to persuade you of the need to alter our inherited literary default setting, which (in my judgment) has contorted the way we envisage the early transmission of the Jesus tradition.

Perhaps the point most to be emphasized in conclusion is that to recognize the character of the Jesus tradition as oral tradition is to recognize its character also as *living* tradition. The Jesus tradition was not at first a written text, to be read by individuals in the solitude of their studies, capable of fine literary analysis and redaction. It was not carried around like a sacred relic fixed in written form. It was living tradition, lived-in-and-through tradition. It was not so much kept as used, not so much preserved as performed, not so much read as heard. To treat it as a lifeless artifact, suitable for clinical dissection, is to lose it. Its variability, the oral principle of "variation within the same," is not a sign of degeneration or corruption. Rather, it puts us directly in touch with the tradition in its living character, as it was heard in the earliest Christian groups and churches, and can still be heard and responded to today.

In short, to alter the default setting is to refuse to treat the Jesus tradition first and only as a written text, and to insist on the importance of *hearing* it, of hearing it as it was heard in the beginning, and of hearing it also as a tradition that still lives and still demands response from its hearers as it did from the beginning.

CHAPTER 3

Q^1 as Oral Tradition

The most influential study of Q in recent years has been that of John Kloppenborg, *The Formation of Q*.[1] Kloppenborg's analysis of the 'sapiential speeches in Q'[2] leads him to the conclusion that 'a collection of sapiential speeches and admonitions was the formative element in Q', a collection 'subsequently augmented by the addition and interpolation of apophthegms and prophetic words which pronounced doom over impenitent Israel'.[3] This 'formative stratum', which can be conveniently designated Q^1, consists of six 'wisdom speeches', 'united not by the themes typical of the main redaction [Q^2], but by paraenetic, hortatory, and instructional concerns'.[4] The six 'wisdom speeches' he lists as:[5]

1. J. S. Kloppenborg, *The Formation of Q: Trajectories in Ancient Wisdom Collections* (Philadelphia: Fortress, 1987); see also his masterful *Excavating Q: The History and Setting of the Sayings Gospel* (Minneapolis: Fortress, 2000).

2. *Formation*, ch. 5.

3. *Formation*, 244.

4. *Formation*, 317; *Excavating Q* 146.

5. *Formation*, ch. 5, summarized and amended in *Excavating Q*, 146. That six collections of aphoristic sayings lie behind Q was already suggested by D. Zeller, *Die weisheitlichen Mahnsprüche bei den Synoptikern* (Würzburg: Echter, 1977) 191-2 (Q 6.20-23, 31, 36, 43-46; 10.2-8a, 9-11a, 12, 16(?); 11.2-4; 12.2-3, 8-9, 10; Matt. 6.25-33, 19-21; Q 12.35-37(?), 39-40). R. A. Piper, *Wisdom in the Q-tradition: The Aphoristic Teaching of Jesus* (SNTSMS 61; Cambridge: Cam-

---

The essay is dedicated to Graham Stanton, in token of long and much valued friendship and as a far from adequate expression of deep appreciation for all that his scholarship on the Gospels has contributed to NT studies.

1. Q 6.20b-23b, 27-35, 36-45, 46-49;
2. Q 9.57-60, (61-62); 10.2-11, 16, (23-24?);[6]
3. Q 11.2-4, 9-13;
4. Q 12:2-7, 11-12;
5. Q 12.22b-31, 33-34 (13.18-19, 20-21?);[7] and probably
6. Q 13.24; 14.26-27; 17.33; 14.34-35.

Kloppenborg is clear that 'tradition-history is not convertible with literary history', and that his concern is only with the latter; the judgment that material is redactional, secondary, is a *literary* judgment and need not imply anything about the *historical* origin or emergence of the tradition in view.[8] So he certainly does not wish his analysis necessarily to imply that redactional material from the secondary compositional phase cannot be dominical. And by the same token, it need not follow that material from Q^1 is necessarily the oldest material in the Q tradition. On the other hand, the archaeological imagery of a *lowest* 'stratum', capable of being uncovered by 'excavation', almost unavoidably promotes the implication of an *earliest* stratum, a stratum which contains the earliest artefacts of the literary 'tell' known as Q.

More to the point here, Kloppenborg works essentially with a *literary* model for the history of the Q material. Not only is Q itself, or already Q^2 a literary document,[9] but Q^1 is conceptualized in the same way. He never explicitly examines the question, but his talk of Q^2 'interpolations' into Q^1 clearly implies an established script into which insertions can be made. And in *Excavating Q* he speaks of Q^1 as 'a good example of instructional literature', and as 'the product of scribes', 'a scribal accomplishment'.[10]

It is this assumption, that the earliest grouping of Q material (Q^1) was

---

bridge University, 1989) identified five aphoristic collections: Q 11.9-13; 12.22-31; 6.37-42; 6.43-45; 12.2-9; to which he added Luke 6.27-36 and 16.9-13.

6. Kloppenborg regards 10.23-24 as part of the secondary redaction of Q, along with 10.21-22 (*Formation*, 201-3), but with some qualification (*Excavating Q*, 147 n. 63).

7. In 'Jesus and the Parables of Jesus in Q', in R. A. Piper, ed., *The Gospel Behind the Gospels: Current Studies on Q* (NovTSup 75; Leiden: Brill, 1995) 275-319, Kloppenborg suggests that Q 13.18-21 (which was not treated in his analysis of Q^1 in *Formation*, 223 n. 214) was perhaps added to Q 12.2-12, 13-14, 16-21, 22-31, 33-34, in the formative layer of Q (311).

8. *Formation*, 244-5. He has continued to make this point in subsequent writing — most recently 'Discursive Practices in the Sayings Gospel Q and the Quest of the Historical Jesus', in A. Lindemann, ed., *The Sayings Source Q and the Historical Jesus* (Leuven: Leuven University, 2001) 149-90.

9. For Kloppenborg, Q is simply Q^2 with the temptation narrative (Q 4.1-13), and a handful of other brief passages inserted (e.g. *Excavating Q*, 212-3).

10. *Excavating Q*, 197, 200, 209.

already a written text, which I wish to question. I have already raised the issue in a much more wide-ranging discussion.[11] And in *Jesus Remembered* I have expressed my doubts as to the character of the Q^1 material in a footnote,[12] with some comments on several of the passages designated as Q^1 scattered in a disjointed way through the following pages. What I would like to do in this paper is to subject the Q^1 material as a complete whole to the same sort of analysis, to see what kind of collection it is and whether there are sufficient grounds for regarding it as a single, coherent collection or scribal composition. My hypothesis is (1) that the Q^1 material consists of groups of teaching material, clusters of wisdom sayings and exhortations, used by teachers in the early Christian communities in their oral teaching role within these communities; (2) that the use made of this material by Matthew and Luke attests the flexible or variable character of the oral tradition used in such teaching — hence the difficulty which the compilers of the Q document have typically experienced in reconstructing the Q text for this material;[13] and (3) it is very unlikely that the Q^1 material formed a coherent unit or single collection used as such in the several communities which we can assume to have been familiar with the Q^1 material.

I will proceed then by examining the six clusters of Q material identified above in sequence.[14] As in *Jesus Remembered* I will lay out the key Matthew/Luke texts synoptically, along with Gospel of Thomas and other parallels where appropriate, and with the parallel (Q?) material indicated simply by underlining. Double underlining indicates material that Matthew or Luke does not share with the other but with another parallel text. To make the texts more accessible I will use English translation, but attempt to ensure as far as conveniently possible that the English translation and the underlining reflect the vagaries of the Greek.

11. 'Altering the Default Setting: Re-envisaging the Early Transmission of the Jesus Tradition', *NTS* 49 (2003) 139-75; = pp. 41-79, above.

12. *Christianity in the Making*. Vol. 1: *Jesus Remembered* (Grand Rapids: Eerdmans, 2003) 157 n. 82.

13. J. M. Robinson, P. Hoffmann, & J. S. Kloppenborg, eds., *The Critical Edition of Q* (The International Q Project; Leuven: Peeters, 2000). I will refer to this by the abbreviation *CEQ*.

14. Because of pressures of space I will have to bypass the items in Kloppenborg's list of six groups where he has put a question mark, and also those further passages which he now thinks may also belong to 'the earliest level of Q' — Q 15.4-7, 8-10; 16.(13), 16, 18; 17.1-2, 3-4, 6 ('Jesus and the Parables of Jesus in Q', 314-5; *Excavating Q*, 146 n. 62). The additional material does not make any real difference to the picture which emerges below; Luke 15.8-10 has no Matthean parallel.

1. The Sermon on the Plain — Q 6.20b-23b, 27-49

1.1. Matt. 5.3-6, 11-12/Luke 6.20-23/(GTh 54, 68, 69)

Matthew 5.3-6, 11-12	Luke 6.20-23	GTh 54, 69.2, 68
³Blessed are the poor in spirit, for theirs is the kingdom of heaven. ⁴Blessed are those who mourn, for they will be comforted. ⁵Blessed are the meek, for they will inherit the earth. ⁶Blessed are those who hunger and thirst for righteousness, for they will be filled.	²⁰Blessed are the poor, for yours is the kingdom of God.	⁵⁴Blessed are the poor, for yours is the kingdom of heaven.
	²¹Blessed are those who hunger now, for you will be filled. Blessed are you who weep now, for you will laugh.	⁶⁹·²Blessed are those who hunger, that the belly of him who desires may be satisfied.
¹¹Blessed are you when they revile you and persecute you and utter all kinds of evil against you falsely on my account. ¹²Rejoice and be glad, for your reward is great in heaven, for in the same way they persecuted the prophets who were before you.	²²Blessed are you when people hate you, and when they exclude you, revile you, and reject your name as evil on account of the Son of Man. ²³Rejoice in that day and leap for joy, for surely your reward is great in heaven; for that is what their fathers did to the prophets.	⁶⁸Blessed are you when people hate you and persecute you, and no place will be found where you have [not] been persecuted.

In every case to be examined it is obvious that the sort of variation in the texts here presented could be explained by a process of editorial manipulation of a common written source. But it is at least equally possible to infer that each of the three texts has been derived from an oral tradition, or orally preserved memory of Jesus teaching the blessedness of the poor, the hungry and the persecuted.[15] Or to put the point more accurately, given that we are talking about a predominantly oral society as the context for this tradition, each of these texts can be seen as a typical performance of a shared oral tradition. The common features of the three texts are just what one might expect to have remained firm within such a tradition, and the variations between them are better explained as the variations deemed appropriate in performances of the tradition to different communities.[16] On a literary model the

15. Cf. W. D. Davies & D. C. Allison, *The Gospel according to Saint Matthew* (ICC; Edinburgh: T&T Clark, Vol. I, 1988) 441.

16. For oral tradition as characteristically a combination of fixity and flexibility, of stability and diversity, of 'variation within the same', see my 'Altering the Default Setting', 154-5 = 57-58, above.

variations of Q 6.22-23 are hard to explain as editorial redactions: why such changes?[17] But on an oral model, such variations as part of a 'live performance' are what we should expect, without having to find a reason for them beyond the mood of the performative moment.

1.2. Matt. 5.39-47; 7.12/Luke 6.27-35/(Did. 1.3-5/P.Oxy 1224/GTh 95, 6.3)

Matthew 5.43-47	Luke 6.27-28, 32-35	Did. 1.3; P.Oxy 1224; GTh 95
[43]You have heard that it was said, 'You shall love your neighbour and hate your enemy'. [44]But I <u>say to you</u>, <u>Love your enemies</u>		
	[27]But I <u>say to you</u> that listen, <u>Love your enemies</u>, do good to <u>those who hate you</u>, [28]<u>bless those who curse you</u>, pray for those <u>who</u> abuse <u>you</u>.	[1.3d]Love <u>those who hate you</u>, and you shall have no <u>enemy</u>. [1.3b]<u>Bless those who curse you</u> and <u>pray</u> for your enemies, and fast for those who persecute you.
and <u>pray for those who</u> persecute <u>you</u>, [45]so that you may be sons of your Father in heaven; for he makes his sun rise on the evil and on the good, and sends rain on the righteous and on the unrighteous.	. . . .	P.Oxy 1224 . . . a]nd pray for your [enem]ies.
[46]For <u>if you love those who love you</u>, what reward do you have? Do not even the tax collectors do the same? [47]And if you greet only your brothers, what more are you doing than others? Do not <u>even</u> the Gentiles <u>do the same</u>?	[32]And <u>if you love those who love you</u>, what credit is that to you? For even sinners love those who love them. [33]And if you do good to those who do good to you, what credit is that to you? For <u>even</u> sinners <u>do the same</u>. [34]If you lend to those from whom you hope to receive, what credit is that to you? Even sinners lend to sinners, to receive as much again. [35]But love your enemies, do good, and lend, expecting nothing in return. Your reward will be great, and you will be children of the Most High; for he is kind to the ungrateful and the wicked.	GTh 95 If you have money do not lend at interest, but give . . . from whom you will not get it (back).

---

17. Kloppenborg concludes that Q 6.23c is Q^2 redaction (*Formation*, 190).

Matthew 5.39b-42	Luke 6.29-30	Did. 1.4b, d, 5a
[39b]But whoever hits <u>you on</u> your <u>right cheek, turn to him the other also;</u> [40]and to the one who wants to sue you and take <u>your tunic,</u> let him have <u>your cloak also;</u> [41]and whoever forces you to go one mile, go with him a second. [42]<u>Give to</u> the one <u>who asks you, and</u> do not turn away the one who wants to borrow from you.	[29]To the one who strikes <u>you on</u> the <u>cheek,</u> offer <u>the other also;</u> and from the one who takes away <u>your cloak</u> do not withhold <u>your</u> tunic also. [30]<u>Give to</u> everyone <u>who asks you;</u> and from the one who takes what is yours, <u>do not ask for it back.</u>	[4b]If someone gives <u>you</u> a blow on the <u>right cheek, turn to him the other also,</u> and you will be perfect. [4d]If someone takes <u>your cloak,</u> give him <u>your tunic also.</u> [5a]<u>Give to</u> everyone <u>who asks you, and</u> <u>do not ask for it back.</u>

Matthew 7.12	Luke 6.31	GTh 6.3
Everything, therefore, whatever <u>you wish that people should do for you,</u> so also <u>do for them</u>; for this is the law and the prophets.	And as <u>you wish that people should do for you, do for them</u> likewise.	. . . [and what you ha]te do not do . . .

If the tradition used here was typical of Q, or to be more precise, typical of the material common to Matthew and Luke which provides the basis for the whole Q hypothesis, then it is doubtful whether the Q hypothesis would ever have emerged — that is, the hypothesis of Q as a written document known to and used as such by Matthew and Luke. The level of verbal agreement in the first two sections above is just too low to support the hypothesis of a literary document underlying both.[18] But equally improbable as an explanation of the character of the agreements and non-agreements of Matthew and Luke is the usual alternative which dispenses with the Q hypothesis and argues instead that Luke derived his (Q) text by redacting Matthew (or vice-versa).[19] Such hypotheses help make sense of some details, such as Matthew's introduction (Matt. 5.43). But most of the other variations are inconsequential (e.g. Q 6.29-30),[20] and cause one to wonder why, on a literary hypothesis,

18. *The Critical Edition of Q (CEQ)*, 58, has to opt for 'so that you may become sons of your Father, for he raises his sun on bad and [[good and rains on the just and unjust]]' for Q 6.35, drawn exclusively from Matt. 5.45.

19. Most recently M. Goodacre, *The Case Against Q* (Harrisburg, PA: Trinity Press International, 2002).

20. The *CEQ* version, without the double brackets which indicate 'reconstructions that are probable but uncertain' (lxxxii) — 'probable' seems too uncritical in most cases — reads '. . . you on the cheek, offer [opting for Matthew's *strepson* rather than Luke's *pareche*] . . . the other as well; and . . . your shirt . . . the coat as well' (60).

the second author should have bothered to change the text of the first.[21] Much the more obvious explanation is that both Matthew and Luke knew a tradition about Jesus' teaching on love of enemies, and about generosity of attitude to the hostile and the poor; and that either each knew the tradition in a form already diversely elaborated in performance and/or transmission,[22] or they on their own account produced their written text in the manner and with the freedom of an oral performance (in oral mode).

1.3. Matt. 5.48; 7.1-5; 10.24/Luke 6.36-42/ (Mark 4.24-25/John 13.16/GTh 34, 26)

Matthew 5.48; 7.1-5; 10.24	Luke 6.36-42	Mark 4.24; GTh 34, 26
[5.48]Therefore, be perfect, <u>as your</u> heavenly <u>Father is</u> perfect. [7.1]<u>Do not judge</u>, so that <u>you</u> may <u>not be judged</u>. [2]For with the judgment you make, you will be judged:	[36] Be merciful, just <u>as your</u> <u>Father is</u> merciful. [37]<u>Do not judge</u>, and <u>you</u> will <u>not be judged</u>;	
	do not condemn, and you will not be condemned. Forgive, and you will be forgiven; [38]give, and it will be given to you. A good measure, pressed down, shaken together, running over,	
and <u>with the measure you give it will be measured to you.</u>	will be put into your lap; for by <u>the measure you give it will be measured</u> in return <u>to you.</u> [39]He also told them a parable:	Mk 4.24 <u>with the measure you give it will be measured to you</u>
	'Can <u>a blind man</u> guide <u>a blind man</u>? Will not <u>both fall into a pit</u>? [40]<u>A disciple is not above the teacher</u>,	GTh 34 If <u>a blind man</u> leads <u>a blind man</u>, <u>both</u> of them <u>fall into a pit</u>.
[10.24]<u>A disciple is not above the teacher</u>, nor <u>a slave</u> over his <u>master</u>. [25]It is enough for the disciple that he be <u>like his teacher</u>.	but everyone who is fully qualified will be <u>like his teacher</u>.	Jn 13.16 <u>A slave</u> is not greater than his <u>master</u>.

21. On Q 6.31 see my *Jesus Remembered*, 566-9.

22. The parallels in Did. 1.3-5 (add in P.Oxy 1224; also Rom. 12.14, 1 Cor. 4.12 and 1 Pet. 3.9) increase the probability of an oral tradition, unless it is to be argued that 1.4b is drawn from Matthew, whereas the rest is drawn from Luke! — discussion of the options in K. Niederwimmer, *Die Didache* (KAV; Göttingen: Vandenhoeck & Ruprecht, 1993) 95-100. See also H. D. Betz, *The Sermon on the Mount* (Hermeneia; Minneapolis: Fortress, 1995) 8-9: 'This wide distribution of similar but different elements points to oral tradition rather than to a dependency on written texts' (297). GTh's two parallels do not help much since they at best reflect traditions recalled with no great concern for any specific detail.

Matthew 5.48; 7.1-5; 10.24	Luke 6.36-42	Mark 4.24; GTh 34, 26
[7.3]Why do you see the speck which is in your brother's eye, but the log in your eye you do not notice? [4]Or how do you say to your brother, 'Let me take out the speck from your eye', while the log is in your own eye? [5]You hypocrite, first take the log out of your eye, and then you will see clearly to take out the speck from your brother's eye.	[41]Why do you see the speck which is in your brother's eye, but the log which is in your own eye you do not notice? [42]Or how can you say to your brother, "Brother, let me take out the speck in your eye", when you yourself do not see the log in your own eye? You hypocrite, first take the log out of your eye, and then you will see clearly to take out the speck which is in your brother's eye.'	GTh 26 The speck which is in your brother's eye, you see, but the log which is in your eye you do not see. When you take the log out of your eye, then you will see clearly to take out the speck from your brother's eye.

Unlike the first two (sets of) passages, the third gives more signs of literary dependence; the evidence suggests a transmission process more like copying than the inconsequential variations of tradition performed. The above synopsis shows it to be entirely plausible that there was a firm, written Q version (Q 6.35a, 38b-42, with a Markan doublet at Mark 4.24), which Matthew and Luke have elaborated each in his own way, Matthew adding 7.2, and Luke adding 6.37b-38a (their performance variations). The closeness of verbal parallel in GTh 26 (also 34) then invites a similar explanation. The synopsis also suggests the possibility, however, that Q 6.40 was known in an oral performance tradition, and/or in the double form of Matt. 10.24-25a,[23] a possibility strengthened by the repeated emphasis on the latter part of the Matt. 10.24b saying in John 13.16 and 15.20.[24]

1.4. Matt. 7.16; 12.35/Luke 6.43-45/(GTh 45)

Matthew 7.16; 12.35	Luke 6.43-45	GTh 45
[7.16]You will know them by their fruits. Are	[43]No good tree bears bad fruit, nor again does a bad tree bear good fruit; [44]for each tree is known from its own fruit. Figs	[1]Grapes are not

23. The *CEQ* version of Q 6.40 offers, 'A disciple is not superior to "one's" teacher. [[It is enough for the disciple that he become]] like his teacher' (78).

24. On the character of the interdependence of John on Synoptic-like tradition see my 'John and the Oral Gospel Tradition', in H. Wansbrough, ed., *Jesus and the Oral Gospel Tradition* (JSNTSup 64; Sheffield: JSOT, 1991) 351-79 = 138-63, below.

Matthew 7.16; 12.35	Luke 6.43-45	GTh 45
grapes gathered from thorns, or figs from thistles? [12.35]The good man out of his good treasure brings good things, and the evil man out of his evil treasure brings evil things.	are not gathered out of thorns, nor are grapes picked from a bramble bush. [45]The good man out of the good treasure of his heart produces good, and the evil (man) out of evil (treasure) produces evil; for it is out of the abundance of the heart that the mouth speaks.	gathered from thorns, nor are figs picked from thistles; for they give no fruit. [2]A good man produces good out of his treasure; [3]a wicked man produces evil out of his evil treasure which is in his heart, and speaks evil things; [4]for out of the abundance of the heart he brings forth evil things.

It is quite feasible to envisage a text of Q something like Luke 6.43-45, and then to propose some substantial Matthean editing (omitting Q 6.43 and 6.45b, and separating 6.44 from 6.45a), with Thomas omitting Q 6.43-44a.[25] If we had only the Matthew/Luke parallels to work with it would be easier to deduce an oral tradition which contained the recollection of two sayings of Jesus to similar effect. Moreover, the variations of grapes/thorns, figs/thistles (Matthew/Thomas) and figs/thorns, grapes/bramblebush (Luke), as also question (Matthew) or statement (Luke/Thomas), are more characteristic of oral performance than of literary copying.[26] But the Thomas evidence certainly strengthens the case for an established (written?) sequence consisting at least of Q 6.44b-45 — unless, of course, Thomas knew and used Luke!

1.5. Matt. 7.21, 24-27/Luke 6.46-49

Matthew 7.21, 24-27	Luke 6.46-49
[21]Not everyone who says to me 'Lord, Lord', will enter the kingdom of heaven, but only the one who does the will of my Father who is in heaven. . . . . [24]Everyone then who hears these my words and acts on them will be like a wise man who built his house on rock.	[46]Why do you call me 'Lord, Lord', and do not do what I tell you? [47]Everyone who comes to me and hears my words and acts on them, I will show you what he is like. [48]He is like a man building a house, who dug deeply and laid the foundation on rock;

25. Thus *CEQ*, 84-93.

26. Cf. Davies & Allison: 'Perhaps we are not dealing with Q but with variants from oral tradition' (*Matthew*, I.706). The traditional example of what is contrary to nature (a vine does not bear figs, nor an olive grapes) (Kloppenborg, *Formation*, 182 n. 52), as in Jas 3.12, is given a sharper twist (thorns, thistles, bramblebush).

Matthew 7.21, 24-27	Luke 6.46-49
[25]Torrential rain fell, the <u>floods</u> came, and the winds blew and beat on <u>that house</u>, but it did not fall, for it had been <u>found</u>ed on rock. [26]And everyone <u>who hears</u> these words of mine <u>and does not act</u> on them will be <u>like</u> a foolish man who <u>built</u> his <u>house on</u> sand. [27]Torrential rain fell, and the <u>floods</u> came, and the winds blew and beat against that house, and it <u>fell</u> — and <u>great</u> was its fall!	when a <u>flood</u> arose, the river burst against <u>that house</u> but could not shake it, because it had been well built. [49]But he <u>who hears</u> <u>and does not act</u> is <u>like</u> a man <u>building</u> a <u>house on</u> the ground without a foundation. When the <u>flood</u> burst against it, immediately it <u>fell</u>, and <u>great</u> was the ruin of that house.

In this case the indications point in the opposite direction.[27] We are back with a sequence of inconsequential variations: in particular, the 'wise'/ 'foolish' contrast and the contrast of sand with the rock are Matthew's alone; Luke fills out the story of the building of the house, and Matthew the picture of the elements battering the houses; likewise the different effects of the flood on the two houses look like free variation. These differences do not appear to be derived from an already fixed text, but rather are just the sort of variations one would expect from story tellers painting a vivid picture for a spell-bound audience.[28] Or if we want to say that one or the other (or both) felt free to thus vary from an established text, then it comes to much the same thing, for it means that however fixed in writing the tradition already was, the tradition thus written down was actually more fluid as demonstrated by Matthew's and/or Luke's use of the tradition in oral or performance mode.

To sum up this far. It is likely that the Q material known usually as 'the Sermon on the Plain' (loosely speaking Q 6.20-23, 27-49) was already well established as a familiar and shared collection of material in the teaching resources of many early churches. Whether this was because Jesus was remembered as delivering some of his teaching in some such sequence,[29] or was the work of (an) early teacher(s) or apostle(s) whose grouping of the teaching set

27. R. Morgenthaler, *Statistische Synopse* (Zürich/Stuttgart: Gotthelf, 1971) notes that Matthew's and Luke's versions show only a 24% verbal agreement.

28. Cf. Betz, *Sermon on the Mount*, 559-60. Minor variations taken as evidence that Q was known in different versions (Q[Mt] and Q[Lk]) simply illustrate how well established is the literary 'default-setting' in modern analyses of the tradition history of such texts; but the facts which lend themselves to the hypothesis of multiple Qs are, in an oral society, more simply interpreted as evidence of a variably performed oral tradition.

29. J. A. Fitzmyer, *The Gospel According to Luke I–IX* (AB 28; New York: Doubleday, 1981): 'The similarities are such that they suggest that the tradition has preserved here something from an extended sermon delivered by Jesus toward the beginning of his ministry' (627).

the pattern for other teachers,[30] it is no longer possible to tell. That some of the material was written down and known in that form is quite possible, though we must always recall that the society was predominantly oral, with only a small minority capable of *reading* any such text.[31] And the likelihood of more and more being written down (for convenient transmission) as the Jesus tradition spread ever more widely is strong. But even so, most of the 'Sermon on the Plain' was probably better known in oral form: the grouping could still be regular and firm — a standard repertoire for teachers;[32] but the variations still evident in the enduring form of most of the tradition bear the marks of a tradition variously performed in various churches, the substance stable, but the detail responding to the circumstances and the mood of the different occasions of celebration, instruction and performance.[33]

2. On Discipleship and Mission — Q 9.57-62; 10.2-11, 16

2.6. Matt. 8.19-22/Luke 9.57-62/(GTh 86)

Matthew 8.19-22	Luke 9.57-62	GTh 86
[19]A scribe then approached and <u>said</u>, 'Teacher, <u>I will follow you wherever you</u>	[57]As they were going along the road, someone <u>said</u> to him, '<u>I will follow you wherever you</u>	

30. I use 'teacher' as shorthand to denote those in the various groups/churches/communities who were recognized by these groups/churches/communities, and perhaps even charged by them to be chiefly responsible for retaining and rehearsing the traditions shared by the groups/churches/communities.

31. See e.g. my 'Altering the Default Setting', 148-9.

32. 'A repertoire of sayings of Jesus originally spoken in other contexts' (Kloppenborg, *Excavating Q*, 156). I cannot help asking whether the characteristics of the 'sermon' which Kloppenborg proceeds to describe as characteristics of Q (156-9) are better described as characteristics of Jesus' teaching preserved by the compilers of these repertoires.

33. Contrast L. E. Vaage, 'Composite Texts and Oral Mythology: The Case of the "Sermon" in Q (6:20-49)', in J. S. Kloppenborg, ed., *Conflict and Invention: Literary, Rhetorical, and Social Studies on the Sayings Gospel Q* (Valley Forge, PA: Trinity Press International, 1995) 75-97: 'The composition before us could not reflect an antecedent "oral" work with sufficient stability to be identified as the "sermon", owing to the very nature of orality. . . . The "sermon" would need to have been written down virtually at the very moment when it was first orally composed in order for the text that we now read in Q to represent the oral composition one might presume to posit' (92-3). This comment betrays the literary mind-set, where oral precedents relate to the Q text as earlier editions of the 'sermon', and fails to appreciate that the Q sermon can be seen as itself a performance of familiar groupings of teaching material.

Matthew 8.19-22	Luke 9.57-62	GTh 86
go'. ²⁰And Jesus says <u>to him,</u> <u>'Foxes have holes, and birds of</u> <u>the air have nests; but the Son</u> <u>of Man has nowhere to lay his</u> <u>head'.</u> ²¹Another of his disciples said to him, 'Lord, <u>first let</u> <u>me go and bury my father'.</u> ²²<u>But Jesus said to him,</u> 'Follow <u>me,</u> and <u>let the dead bury their</u> <u>own dead'.</u>	go'. ⁵⁸<u>And Jesus</u> said <u>to him,</u> <u>'Foxes have holes, and birds of</u> <u>the air have nests; but the Son</u> <u>of Man has nowhere to lay his</u> <u>head'.</u> ⁵⁹To another he said, '<u>Follow</u> <u>me</u>'. But he said, '[Lord], <u>first let</u> <u>me go and bury my father'.</u> ⁶⁰<u>But Jesus said to him,</u> '<u>Let the dead bury their</u> <u>own dead</u>; but as for you, go and proclaim the kingdom of God'. ⁶¹Another said, 'I will follow you, Lord; but let me first take leave of those at my home'. ⁶²Jesus said to him, 'No one who puts a hand to the plough and looks back is fit for the kingdom of God'.	¹[Foxes have] their [holes] <u>and birds</u> <u>have</u> [their] <u>nests</u>, ²<u>but the son</u> <u>of man has nowhere to lay his</u> <u>head</u> and rest.

It was to be expected that various sayings of Jesus about discipleship, or the call to discipleship, or the cost of discipleship would be located together in a pigeonhole of the memory of the typical teacher in early disciple groups. It was, after all, in response to such challenges that the members of these groups had become disciples. The fact that they are remembered as a cluster of 'discipleship sayings' distinct from the nearest equivalent cluster in Mark 8.34-38 pars., and that the latter are heavily marked by the lead saying on 'taking the cross' (8.34 pars.),[34] suggests that the former cluster (here being considered) reflects more the pre-Easter understanding of discipleship.[35] That is to say, the cluster may already have been in place before the events of Jesus' own passion. At all events, the three-fold tradition clearly indicates one or two sayings of Jesus which had bitten deeply into the shared memory of one or more disciple groups. At the same time, the different frameworks within which the sayings were presented indicate both the lack of concern to recall any precise context in which the sayings were initially delivered and the freedom of the different

34. The Matthew/Luke parallels to Mark 8.34–9.1 are best explained as drawn almost entirely from Mark; the sequence is one of the best examples of literary interdependence between the three Synoptics. The Q material includes the parallels to Mark 8.34-38 of Matt. 10.38/Luke 14.27, Matt. 10.39/Luke 17.33 and Matt. 10.33/Luke 12.9, so that there does not seem to have been such a widespread desire to retain them as a cluster, at least in performance. On Matt. 10.38-39 par. See below ##6.16-17.

35. The *CEQ* reconstruction omits Luke/Q 9.61-62.

tradents to provide their own framework, as presumably was appropriate in the differing variety of circumstances in which the sayings were recalled.

2.7. Matt. 9.37-38; 10.7-16/Luke 10.2-11/(GTh 73, 39.3, 14.2)

Matthew 9.37-38; 10.7-16	Luke 10.2-11	GTh 73, 39, 14
³⁷Then he said to his disciples, 'The harvest is plentiful, but the labourers are few; ³⁸therefore ask the Lord of the harvest to send out labourers into his harvest'	²He said to them, 'The harvest is plentiful, but the labourers are few; therefore ask the Lord of the harvest to send out labourers into his harvest.	⁷³The harvest is plentiful, but the labourers are few; ask the Lord to send out labourers into his harvest.
¹⁰·¹⁶'See, I am sending you out like sheep in the midst of wolves; so be wise as serpents and innocent as doves. ⁹Take no gold, or silver, or copper in your belts, ¹⁰ᵃno bag for your journey, or two tunics, or sandals, or a staff. ¹¹Whatever town or village you enter, find out who in it is worthy, and stay there until you leave. ¹²As on entering into the house, greet it. ¹³And if the house is worthy, let your peace come upon it; but if it is not worthy, let your peace return to you.	³Go on your way. See, I am sending you out like lambs in the midst of wolves. ⁴Carry no purse, no bag, no sandals; and greet no one on the road. ⁵Into whatever house you enter, first say, "Peace to this house!" ⁶And if anyone is there who shares in peace, your peace will rest upon him; but if not, it will come back to you. ⁷Remain in the same house, eating and drinking whatever they provide, for the labourer deserves his pay. Do not move about from house to house. ⁸Whenever you enter a town and its people welcome you, eat what is set before you; ⁹cure the sick who are here,	39.3 But you, be wise as serpents and innocent as doves. ¹⁴·²And if you enter into any land and wander in the countryside, and if they take you in, (then) eat what is set before you.
¹⁰ᵇfor the labourer deserves his food. ⁸Cure the sick, raise the dead, cleanse the lepers, cast out demons. You received without payment; give without payment. ⁷As you go, proclaim the good news, "The kingdom of heaven has come near". ¹⁴If anyone will not welcome you or listen to your words, as you leave that house or town shake off the dust from your feet'.	and say to them, "The kingdom of God has come near to you". ¹⁰But whenever you enter a town and they do not welcome you, go out into its streets and say, ¹¹"Even the dust of your town that clings to our feet, we wipe off in protest against you. Yet know this: the kingdom of God has come near"'.	Cure the sick among them.

The tradition history of the mission commissioning of the twelve is particularly complex, since we have to include the further variants of Mark 6.7-13/

Matt. 10.1, 7-11, 14/Luke 9.1-6. Without attempting to unravel that complexity[36] it is fairly clear that Matthew and Luke knew a tradition independent of Mark 6.7-13 but overlapping with it. The evidence presented above (#2.7) is sufficient to indicate material that was used and re-used in a variety of permutations. This is as might be expected in churches and communities of disciples/believers active in promulgating their faith, including the sending out of missionaries/apostles with a specific charge to evangelise. That is to say, the content and order of the material almost certainly reflect the diverse ways in which the tradition of Jesus' commissioning of the twelve was adapted and varied to suit the different circumstances of diverse contexts. At the same time, there are certain recurring elements, which could be included at different points as deemed appropriate. And the tightness of the strictures (no bag, no sandals) and the message of the kingdom's imminence (not attested in preaching after Easter) suggest elements given an enduring shape already in the pre-Easter context of Jesus' own mission.[37] At all events, the data are best explained as drawn variously from an oral memory of Jesus' own commissioning, as an oral resource from which differing (versions of) commission(s) could be constructed, rather than as a single established written text which the different Evangelists shredded and reconstructed at will.[38]

2.8. Matt. 10.40/Luke 10.16/(John 13.20; Mark 9.37 pars.)

Matthew 10.40	Luke 10.16	John 13.20
He who receives you receives me, and he who receives me receives him who sent me.	He who hears you hears me, and he who rejects you rejects me; but he who rejects me rejects him who sent me.	Truly, truly, I tell you, he who receives one whom I send receives me; and he who receives me receives him who sent me

36. See, e.g., the brief discussions in J. A. Fitzmyer, *The Gospel According to Luke X–XXIV* (AB 28A; New York: Doubleday, 1985) 842-3; W. D. Davies & D. C. Allison, *The Gospel according to Saint Matthew* (ICC; Edinburgh: T&T Clark, Vol. II, 1991) 163-4.

37. On Luke 10.4 and 7 see *Jesus Remembered* 505 and 601 respectively.

38. The *CEQ* reconstruction is therefore remarkably bold — not only Q 10.2-3 (including 3a) and 9, but also 10.4 and most of 10.5-8, 10-11a (160-79). Contrast J. Schröter, *Erinnerung an Jesu Worte: Studien zur Rezeption der Logienüberlieferung in Markus, Q und Thomas* (WMANT 76; Neukirchen-Vluyn: Neukirchener, 1997): 'Eine Betrachtung der verschiedenen Versionen, in denen diese Logien begegnen, erbrachte, dass der Überlieferungsprozess in diesen Fällen nicht nach dem Modell literarischer Abhängigkeit, sondern des Weiterfliessens des mündlichen Traditionsstromes vorstellen ist' (211; also 236-7).

Matthew 18.5	Luke 9.48	Mark 9.37
Whoever receives one such child in my name receives me.	Whoever receives this child in my name receives me; and whoever receives me receives him who sent me.	Whoever receives one of such children in my name receives me; and whoever receives me receives not me but him who sent me.

Here is a typical example of a saying where the substance *(die Sache)* is consistent and constant while the wording *(die Sprache)* varies in content and detail. This initial impression from the Q material is strengthened by the fact that Mark 9.37 has a different saying to the same effect, apparently followed/ copied by Matthew and Luke, giving both Matthew and Luke an effective doublet of the saying. Rather than insisting that the Q material has to be explained in terms of literary dependence, in the same way that the 'child' version of the saying can be explained by literary dependence on Mark, it makes better sense of all the data to recognize something Jesus said, probably more than once, which was recalled in its substance and reused in varying forms in the course of performing and transmitting the Jesus tradition.[39]

The second block of putative Q[1] material (##2.6-8) therefore shares the characteristics of the first (##1.1-5), the last two units in particular (##2.7-8) indicating the likelihood of tradition widely and frequently cited and reworked. To conceptualize that reuse and reworking as a sequence of layers of tradition, equivalent to sequential literary editions, each subsequent edition redacting the written text of its predecessor, is hardly realistic in communities where literacy was at a premium. Much the more obvious explanation is that the tradition was known and used orally in various forms and combinations, and that the literary forms which have actually come down to us are actually frozen performances, normatively typical in their combination of stability and flexibility, rather than one or more fixed forms.

---

39. C. H. Dodd, *Historical Tradition in the Fourth Gospel* (Cambridge: Cambridge University, 1963) 343-7: 'Any attempt, I submit, to account for these phenomena [variations] by a theory of literary dependence must be fruitless. The hypothesis that the evangelists drew upon different branches of a common oral tradition, and that the language they employ, within a form or pattern which remains largely constant, was in large measure determined by variations in that tradition, appears to me the hypothesis which best explains the facts' (347); see further my *Jesus Remembered*, 558.

3. On Prayer — Q 11.2-4, 9-13

3.9. Matt. 6.9-13/Luke 11.2-4; (Did. 8.2)

Matthew 6.9-13 = Did. 8.2	Luke 11.2-4
⁹Pray then in this way: Our <u>Father</u> who is in heaven, <u>hallowed be your name</u>. ¹⁰<u>Your kingdom come</u>. Your will be done, on earth as it is in heaven. ¹¹<u>Give us to</u><u>day our daily bread</u>. ¹²<u>And forgive us our</u> debts, as <u>we</u> also have <u>forgiv</u>en our debtors. ¹³<u>And do not bring us to the time of trial</u>, but rescue us from the evil one.	²He said to them, "When you pray, say: <u>Father</u>, <u>hallowed be your name</u>. <u>Your kingdom come</u>. ³<u>Give us</u> each <u>day our daily bread</u>. ⁴<u>And forgive us our</u> sins, for <u>we</u> ourselves also <u>forgive</u> everyone in<u>debt</u>ed to us. <u>And do not bring us to the time of trial</u>."

These are the earliest forms of the Lord's Prayer known to us. There is nothing to suggest that the individual petitions of the prayer were known as having been used by Jesus separately, or that the prayer was the composition of some unknown disciple.[40] It is remembered only as a prayer taught by Jesus. On the 'default setting' of a literary mindset the tendency is to think in terms, as usual, of literary dependency — of Matthew and Luke both having access to an established written text (Q), or, a minority would argue, of Luke copying from Matthew and thus producing his own version. But in either case one has to work hard to find reasons why either (or both) made the changes to the text which we find here. The case for transmission by copying is much clearer in Didache's evident use of Matthew. But in the case of the Matthew/Luke parallel much the more obvious solution is that these were the forms of the prayer which were being prayed in the churches of Matthew and Luke respectively. In other words, the two forms exemplify a living liturgical tradition.[41] As still today, where among English-speaking churches there are three or four slightly different versions of the Lord's Prayer in use, so already in the earliest years of Christianity we can justifiably infer that regular congregational use of the prayer produced the variations which we see in Q 11.4 and the elaborations evident in Matthew's text.[42]

---

40. The two alternatives suggested respectively by R. W. Funk & R. W. Hoover, eds., *The Five Gospels: The Search for the Authentic Words of Jesus* (New York: Macmillan, 1993) 148-50, and J. D. Crossan, *The Historical Jesus: The Life of a Mediterranean Jewish Peasant* (San Francisco: Harper, 1991) 294. Crossan's assumption that a prayer taught by Jesus would have been more uniform in content (294) takes no account of the character of oral tradition, as well enough attested in the variations of the Synoptic tradition.

41. See further my *Jesus Remembered*, 227-8, with bibliography.

42. The trend continues with the subsequent but still very early addition of the final doxology (see again my *Jesus Remembered*, 228 and n. 232).

This is not to deny that the Lord's Prayer may have been written down at an early stage. It is simply to observe that derivation of the prayer by Matthew and/or Luke from a written source is not the most obvious explanation for the character of the Matthean/Lukan versions.[43] The congregations served by Matthew and Luke almost certainly knew the prayer because they prayed it regularly, not because they read it, or because someone read it to them from a written document, Q or whatever.

3.10. Matt. 7.7-11/Luke 11.9-13/(GTh 2, 92.1, 94)

Matthew 7.7-11	Luke 11.9-13	GTh 2, 92, 94
[7]Ask, and it will be given you; seek, and you will find; knock, and the door will be opened for you. [8]For everyone who asks receives, and everyone who seeks finds, and for everyone who knocks, the door will be opened. [9]Or what person among you who, if his son asks for bread, will give him a stone? [10]Or if he asks for a fish, will give him a snake? [11]If you then, who are evil, know how to give good gifts to your children, how much more will your Father who is in heaven give good things to those who ask him.	[9]So I say to you, Ask, and it will be given you; seek, and you will find; knock, and the door will be opened for you. [10]For everyone who asks receives, and everyone who seeks finds, and for everyone who knocks, the door will be opened. [11]What father among you who, if your son asks for a fish, will give a snake instead of a fish? [12]Or if the child asks for an egg, will give a scorpion? [13]If you then, who are evil, know how to give good gifts to your children, how much more will the heavenly Father give the Holy Spirit to those who ask him!	[92]Seek and you will find. But those things about which you asked me during those days, I did not tell you on that day. Now I am willing to tell them, and you do not inquire about them. [94]He who seeks will find . . . , it will be opened. [2]He who seeks must not stop seeking until he finds; and when he finds, he will be bewildered; and if he is bewildered, he will marvel, and will be king over the All. (similar in P.Oxy. 654.1 = Gosp.Heb. in Clement, Strom. 2.9.45).

In this case one can readily envisage a written text copied quite faithfully for most of Q 11.9-11, 13, but with slight editorial redaction (addition or omission) in 11.11-12, and the interesting modification ('good things'/'Holy Spirit') in 11.13.[44] On the other hand, the variation in the illustration of a son

43. Cf. Betz: 'It is characteristic of liturgical material in general that textual fixation occurs at a later stage in the transmission of these texts, while in the oral stage variability within limits is the rule. These characteristics also apply to the Lord's Prayer. The three recensions, therefore, represent variations of the prayer in the oral tradition. . . . (T)here was never only *one original written* Lord's Prayer' (*Sermon on the Mount*, 370).

44. Of course, the sayings of Q 11.9-10 and 13 could be sufficiently memorable to have retained a very stable form in oral performance and transmission. But Thomas indicates that only

asking of his father (bread/stone, fish/snake, egg/scorpion) is just the sort of elaboration which can be expected in oral performance, as the teacher/preacher presses home the point by multiplying examples. So, even assuming dependence on a written Q, here at least we could speak quite justifiably of both Matthew and Luke reusing the Q tradition in oral mode. The material can then count in part at least as a good illustration of the way tradition, including tradition already in writing, would be used in an oral society.

Given the amount of teaching Jesus presumably gave on prayer,[45] the slimness of the Q^1 collection (#3) is somewhat surprising. The evidence suggests, however, that no single collection of that teaching became dominant, or rather that his teaching on prayer (and example of prayer) was too pervasive in his mission for the resulting Jesus tradition to be restricted to specific collections and that his teaching (and example) served rather as a stimulus to further reflection (and practice).

4. Encouragement to Fearless Confession — Q 12.2-7, 11-12

4.11. *Matt. 10.26-31/Luke 12.2-7/(GTh 5.2, 6.4, 33.1)*

Matthew 10.26-31	Luke 12.2-7	GTh 5.2, 6.5, 33.1
		[5.2]Know what is before your face, and what is hidden from you will be revealed to you; for there
[26]So have no fear of them; for <u>nothing is covered</u> <u>that will not be uncovered, and nothing secret that will not become known.</u> [27]What I say to you <u>in the dark,</u> <u>say</u> <u>in the light;</u> <u>and what you</u> hear <u>into the ear,</u> <u>proclaim</u> <u>upon the housetops.</u>	[2]<u>Nothing is covered</u> up <u>that will not be uncovered, and nothing secret that will not become known.</u> [3]Therefore whatever <u>in the dark</u> you have <u>said in the light</u> will be heard, <u>and what you</u> have said to <u>the ear</u> behind closed doors will be <u>proclaimed</u> <u>upon the housetops.</u>	is <u>nothing</u> hidden <u>that will</u> <u>not</u> become manifest. [6.5]For there is <u>nothing</u> hidden <u>that will</u> <u>not become</u> manifest, and there is nothing covered that shall remain without being revealed. [33.1]What you shall hear <u>into the</u> <u>ear</u> <u>proclaim</u> into the other ear <u>upon the housetops.</u>
[28]<u>Do not</u> <u>fear those who kill the body</u> but cannot kill the soul;	[4]I tell you, my friends, <u>do not</u> <u>fear those who kill the body,</u> and after that can do nothing more.	

---

the 'seek and you will find' saying retained such stability over the years, though John 16.23-24 looks like an elaboration of the 'ask and it will be given you' saying (cf. Dodd, *Historical Tradition* 351-2). For the debate as to whether Q 11.9-10 and 11-13 were two originally independent traditions see Kloppenborg, *Formation*, 204 n. 140.

45. E.g. Mark 9.29; 11.24-25 par.; 14.32-42 pars.; Matt. 5.44/Luke 6.28; Matt. 6.5-7; Luke 5.33; 18.1-8, 10-14; 22.32.

Matthew 10.26-31	Luke 12.2-7	GTh 5.2, 6.5, 33.1
rather <u>fear him who</u> can destroy both soul and body in <u>hell</u>. [29]<u>Are not</u> two <u>sparrows sold for</u> a <u>penny</u>? <u>Yet not one of them</u> will fall to the ground apart from your Father. [30]And <u>even the</u> <u>hairs of your head</u> are <u>all</u> <u>counted</u>. [31]So <u>do not be afraid;</u> <u>you are of more value than many</u> <u>sparrows</u>.	[5]But I will warn you whom to fear: <u>fear him who</u>, after he has killed, has authority to cast into <u>hell</u>. Yes, I tell you, fear him. [6]<u>Are not</u> five <u>sparrows sold for</u> two <u>pennies</u>? <u>Yet not one of them</u> is forgotten before God. [7]But <u>even the</u> <u>hairs of your head</u> have <u>all been</u> <u>counted</u>. <u>Do not be afraid;</u> <u>you are of more value than many</u> <u>sparrows</u>.	

The grouping here consists of three distinct units — Q 12.2-3, 4-5 and 6-7. The first (12.2) has parallels in Mark 4.22 and a doublet in Luke 8.17 (presumably following Mark), as well as the two Thomas versions (GTh 5.2 and 6.5). To this has been added to form the Q cluster the second and third units (Q 12.4-5 and 6-7) which do not appear to be recalled anywhere else.[46] An interesting variation, however, is that the first unit (Q 12.2-3) has also been appended to a different saying about revelation, by both Mark and Luke (Mark 4.21/Luke 8.16). At this point the interest quickens further, since the same saying is also preserved elsewhere in Q material (Matt. 5.15/Luke 11.33), as well as in GTh 33.2.

Matthew 5.15	Mark 4.21	Luke 8.16	Luke 11.33	GTh 33.2
Nor do they ignite <u>a lamp</u> and <u>put</u> it <u>under a bushel</u>, <u>but</u> <u>on</u> <u>a lampstand</u>, and it gives <u>light</u> to all in the house.	Is <u>a</u> <u>lamp</u> brought in to be <u>put</u> <u>under a bushel</u>, or under a <u>bed</u>? Is it not to be put <u>on</u> <u>a lampstand</u>?	<u>No one lights a</u> <u>lamp</u> and hides it <u>under a</u> jar, or puts it under a <u>bed</u>, <u>but</u> puts it <u>on</u> <u>a lampstand</u>, that those who enter may see the <u>light</u>.	<u>No one lights a</u> <u>lamp</u> and <u>puts it</u> in a hidden place or <u>under a bushel</u>, <u>but</u> <u>on</u> <u>a lampstand</u>, that those who enter may see the radiance.	<u>No one lights a</u> <u>lamp</u> and <u>puts it</u> <u>under a bushel</u>, or in a hidden place, <u>but</u> puts it <u>on</u> <u>a lampstand</u> that all who enter and leave may see its <u>light</u>.

So we have a fascinating sequence of permutations, where the same or similar material (Q 12.2/Mark 4.22/Luke 8.17) has been linked one way (#4.11 above), in another way with a different revelation saying (Mark 4.21/Luke 8.16), known in two versions (also Matt. 5.15/Luke 11.33), with Thomas providing a

---

46. Some more detail is provided in *Jesus Remembered*, 496-7, 552 n. 47.

further variation by linking the other variations together in GTh 33 (33.1/Q 12.3; 33.2/Mark 4.21/Q 11.33).

All this indicates a motif in the remembered teaching of Jesus which provided stimulating teaching material for many of the early Christian communities, with the result that it has come down to us in multiplied and varied forms. The variations are hardly to be explained on a hypothesis of Matthew and Luke knowing such tradition in only two written documents (Q and Mark), as though tradition to be transmitted had to be written, and as written formed the only two streams of tradition of the material available. By far the more obvious explanation is that the tradition of the sayings was much used and reused, reflected on and discussed in the various disciple and early Christian groupings.[47] This is not finished tradition, already shaped into final canonical form. It is living tradition. In these passages the twenty-first-century reader is able to overhear the varied forms of the tradition as they were rehearsed and mulled over in the earliest Christian assemblies.

4.12. Matt. 10.19-20/Luke 12.11-12/(Mark 13.11; John 14.26)

Matthew 10.19-20	Luke 12.11-12	Mark 13.11	John 14.26
[19]When they hand you over, do not worry how or what you will speak; for it will be given to you in that hour what you will speak; [20]for it is not you who are speaking, but the Spirit of your Father speaking in you.	[11]When they bring you before the synagogues, the rulers, and the authorities, do not worry how or what you will defend yourselves or what you are to say; [12]for the Holy Spirit will teach you in the same hour what you ought to say.	And when they take you, handing you over, do not worry what you will speak, but whatever is given to you in that hour speak; for it is not you who are speaking, but the Holy Spirit.	But the Advocate, the Holy Spirit, whom the Father will send in my name, he will teach you everything, and remind you of all that I have said to you.

Jesus here is remembered as encouraging his disciples with the promise of inspiration in the hour of persecution (cf. Luke 21.12-15). A curiosity is the decision of most Q specialists to include the passage in Q.[48] For on normal

---

47. Cf. Schröter, *Erinnerung,* 369.

48. J. S. Kloppenborg, *Q Parallels* (Sonoma, CA: Polebridge, 1988) 126; *CEQ* reconstructs the text on the basis of Luke's version — 'When they bring you before synagogues, do not be anxious about how or what you are to say; for [[the Holy Spirit will teach]] you in that . . . hour what you are to say'.

reckoning of literary dependence and redactional modification, Matthew is more obviously explained as drawn directly from Mark. Consequently the basic agreement between Matthew and Luke (independent of Mark) on which the whole Q hypothesis is predicated ceases to exist; the indications that Matthew knew a second (Q) version of the saying are wholly lacking. Nonetheless, the variations, including John, could be adequately explained on an oral hypothesis: Luke demonstrating the kind of variation and elaboration which one might find in a particular performance of a familiar saying (whether known in written or only in oral forms); whereas in John the saying has been given a different direction to become the core or basis of a major strand of the extended discourses in John 14–16.

This fourth group of sayings (##4.11-12) hardly seems to form any kind of coherent unit. Quite why #4.12 should be separated from #5.13 which follows, or indeed why Q 12.6-7 has been held apart from Q 12.22-31 is not at all clear. Is it simply that some hortatory repertoires had linked sayings with slightly different purposes and the links were retained through the various transitions of the Q (and larger) tradition? In any case, the material in these sections evidently allowed a fair variety of ordering, probably typical of the permutations and combinations of many different teaching occasions rather than evidence of a careful composition.

5. The Right Priorities — Q 12.22-31, 33-34

5.13. Matt. 6.25-33/Luke 12.22-31/(P.Oxy. 655/GTh 36)

Matthew 6.25-33	Luke 12.22-31	P.Oxy 655/GTh 36
[25]Therefore I tell you, do not worry about your life, what you will eat or what you will drink, or about your body, what you will wear. Is not life more than food, and the body more than clothing? [26]Look at the birds of the air; they neither sow nor reap nor gather into barns, and yet your heavenly Father feeds them. Are you not of more value than they? [27]And can any of you by worrying add a single hour to your span of life?	[22]Therefore I tell you, do not worry about your life, what you will eat, or about your body, what you will wear. [23]For life is more than food, and the body more than clothing. [24]Consider the ravens: they neither sow nor reap, they have neither storehouse nor barn, and yet God feeds them. Of how much more value are you than the birds! [25]And can any of you by worrying add a single hour to your span of life? [26]If then you	Jesus said: Do not worry from morning to evening and from evening to morning what you will eat or about your robe what you will wear.
[28]And why do you worry about clothing? Consider the lilies of the field, how they	are not able to do so small a thing as that, why do you worry about the rest? [27]Consider the lilies, how (they	You are much better than the lilies which do not card nor spin.

Matthew 6.25-33	Luke 12.22-31	P.Oxy 655/GTh 36
grow; they neither toil nor spin, [29]yet I tell you, that even Solomon in all his glory was not clothed like one of these. [30]But if God so clothes the grass of the field, which is alive today and tomorrow is thrown into the oven, will he not much more clothe you, you of little faith? [31]Therefore do not worry, saying, 'What will we eat?' or 'What will we drink?' or 'What will we wear?' [32]For it is the nations that strive for all these things; and indeed your heavenly Father knows that you need all these things. [33]But seek first the kingdom of God and his righteousness, and all these things will be given to you as well.	grow): they neither spin nor weave; yet I tell you, even Solomon in all his glory was not clothed like one of these. [28]But if God so clothes the grass in the field, which is alive today and tomorrow is thrown into the oven, how much more will he clothe you, you of little faith! [29]And do not keep striving for what you are to eat and what you are to drink, and do not keep worrying. [30]For it is the nations of the world that strive for all these things, and your Father knows that you need them. [31]Instead, seek his kingdom, and these things will be given to you as well.	And having one clothing . . . you . . . Who might add to your span of life? He will give you your clothing.

This is one of the better examples of the strength of the case for a written Q, a judgment which I have no wish to dispute.[49] Even so, the variations between Matthew and Luke are of no great weight,[50] apart from the final verse of each, and smack more of performance variation than of careful editing. It is possible that the tradition recalls a sustained sequence of teaching given by Jesus on one or more occasions and held in that shape in the tradition that was gathered by Q.[51] Alternatively, more disparate tradition was put into its present shape by Q or earlier, presumably to provide some teaching resource for church teachers.[52] This tradition continued to be known in oral form and in different sequence (P.Oxy. 655/GTh 36 paralleling Q 12.22, 27, 25).[53]

49. Other examples in *Jesus Remembered*, 147 n. 29.

50. Matt 6.31 sounds like the product of a more vigorous performance than Luke 12.29.

51. In an oral community the transition from original teaching to well-formed and stable tradition would not require it to be written down, either to retain the impact of the original teaching or to ensure that the stability was retained in transmission.

52. For the more common debate see Kloppenborg, *Formation*, 216-8.

53. Cf. Betz, *Sermon on the Mount*, 466-8. For the debate as to whether P.Oxy. 655 or Q 12.22-31 is the earlier see bibliography in my *Jesus Remembered*, 552 n. 45.

5.14 Matt. 6.19-21/Luke 12.33-34/(GTh 76.3)

Matthew 6.19-21	Luke 12.33-34	GTh 76.3
[19]Do not store up for yourselves treasures on earth, where moth and rust consume and where thieves break in and steal; [20]but store up for yourselves treasures in heaven, where neither moth nor rust consumes and where thieves do not break in and steal. [21]For where your treasure is, there will be also your heart.	[33]Sell your possessions, and give alms. Make purses for yourselves that do not wear out, an unfailing treasure in the heavens, where no thief comes near and no moth destroys. [34]For where your treasure is, there also your heart will be.	You also must seek for his treasure which does not perish, which abides where no moth comes near to eat and (where) no worm destroys.

Here is a case, somewhat like #1.5 above, where some teaching has been preserved by Matthew and Luke attached to a proverbial saying of Jesus (Matt. 6.21/Luke 12.34).[54] As is typically the case with such proverbs or epigrams, it has a stable form. The teaching which precedes the proverb has a common theme elaborated, and once again with the sort of variant illustrative detail which could be expected in a live performance (Matthew's 'rust', Luke's 'purses'). It is entirely possible that Jesus' teaching, perhaps on more than one occasion (why not?), provided the theme and the climactic proverb (cf. Mark 10.21 pars. — 'treasure in heaven').[55] The theme is retained (without the proverb) in GTh 76.3, and Jas. 5.2-3 reads like a further variant on the same theme.[56] Such variation has the character of an oral tradition played out with variations in the course of many performances more than of literary editing where the climactic punch-line has been dropped as a deliberate editorial decision.[57]

In this case (#5) one can readily see that two such themes of personal counselling might be grouped into a composite unit.

---

54. The fact that there are partial parallels in contemporary Jewish exhortation (see Kloppenborg, *Formation*, 221-2 nn.206-208) may only mean that Jesus was remembered as putting his own stamp on such a familiar theme.

55. See further *Jesus Remembered*, 521 n. 158.

56. The discussion by P. J. Hartin, *James and the Q Sayings of Jesus* (JSNTSup 47; Sheffield: JSOT, 1991), here 179-81, assumes an 'original wording' of Q, that is a tradition known only in a single fixed (written) form.

57. Contrast the typical discussion of sources by Fitzmyer, *Luke*, 981, where the 'sources' assume a literary fixedness.

6. The Challenge of Discipleship — Q 13.24; 14.26-27; 17.33; 14.34-35

6.15. Matt. 7.13/Luke 13.24

Matthew 7.13-14	Luke 13.24
[13]Enter through the narrow gate; for the gate is wide and the road is easy that leads to destruction, and there are many who enter through it. [14]For the gate is narrow and the road is hard that leads to life, and there are few who find it.	[24]Strive to enter through the narrow door; for many, I tell you, will try to enter and will not be able.

Once again we encounter a saying in which it is hard to envisage the thought processes behind a literary derivation. Why would Luke omit the bulk of a longer written text (= Matt. 7.13-14)? Or why should Matthew elaborate so extensively a shorter written text (= Q 13.24)?[58] The more obvious explanation is that a saying of Jesus about the challenge and difficulty of entering upon the way of discipleship, using the memorable imagery of a narrow entrance, has been variously formulated and used in different versions in the various congregations which cherished Jesus' teaching and reflected often on the traditions of that teaching. Matthew('s community) was familiar with one version, Luke('s) with the other. An identifiable Q version (= Luke 13.24) is quite possible, but an unnecessary hypothesis. And if Matthew did know a Q 13.24, he handled it with the liberty of a seasoned raconteur, free to elaborate as the dynamic of rapport with a live audience prompted.

6.16. Matt. 10.37-38/Luke 14.26-27/(GTh 55, 101)

Matthew 10.37-38	Luke 14.26-27	GTh 55	GTh 101
[37]He who loves father or mother more than me is not worthy of me; and he who loves son or daughter more than me is not worthy of me. [38]And he who	[26]If anyone comes to me and does not hate his father and mother, wife and children, brothers and sisters, yes, and even life itself, he cannot be my disciple. [27]Whoever	Jesus said: Whoever will not hate his father and his mother will not be able to be my disciple; and whoever will not hate his brothers and his	Jesus said: Whoever will not hate his fa[ther] and his mother as (I do), will not be able to be my d[iscip]le. And whoever will [not] love his [father and] his

58. Davies & Allison attribute 7.13-14 to M, Q^{Mt}, or Q + heavy redaction (*Matthew*, I.694).

Matthew 10.37-38	Luke 14.26-27	GTh 55	GTh 101
does <u>not</u> take <u>his</u> <u>cross and</u> follow <u>after</u> <u>me</u> is not worthy of me.	does <u>not</u> <u>carry</u> <u>his</u> own <u>cross and</u> come <u>after</u> <u>me</u> cannot be my disciple.	sisters and will not <u>carry his</u> cross as I have, will <u>not</u> be <u>worthy of me</u>.	mother as I do, will not be able to be my d[isciple], for [my mother] . . .

That Jesus was remembered as posing the challenge of discipleship in extreme terms (the disciple must 'hate his father and mother') is almost universally accepted.[59] Matthew's editorial hand is most evident in the softening of the saying's offensiveness ('love' less, rather than 'hate'), and in insertion of the motif 'is not worthy of me' in vv. 37 and 38.[60] On the hypothesis that the only forms of tradition available and known to Thomas were written, we would have to conclude that Thomas knew both Luke, or Luke's version of Q (not only the word 'hate', but also talk of 'carrying' his cross), and Matthew as well (Matthew's distinctive 'not worthy of me', possibly also the confused talk of 'loving father and mother' in GTh 101.2). But it is more plausible that two sayings of Jesus, about the disciple hating his parents and about the disciple having to carry his cross, circulated orally in the early churches in various permutations, of which the four versions above are probably a fair sample.

6.17. Matt. 10.39/Luke 17.33/(John 12.25)

Matthew 10.39	Luke 17.33	John 12.25
He who finds <u>his life</u> <u>will lose it</u>, and he who <u>loses</u> his life for my sake will find <u>it</u>.	Whoever seeks to make <u>his life</u> secure <u>will lose it</u>, and whoever <u>loses</u> (it) will preserve <u>it</u>.	He who loves <u>his life</u> <u>loses it</u>, and he who hates his life in this world will keep <u>it</u> for life eternal.

The theme of discipleship and its cost evidently featured regularly in Jesus' teaching as it was recalled in disciple communities. We have already noted the collection of sayings in #2.6 above and Mark 8.34-38 pars. Now we add Q 17.33 as well as Q 14.26-27 (#6.16). Notable is the evidence of diverse selection and grouping from a larger resource of such sayings: in Matthew the last two/three sayings are put together (Matt. 10.37-39), whereas in Luke they are quite separate (Luke 14.26-27; 17.33); and the #6.17 saying has quite a close

---

59. Bibliography in *Jesus Remembered*, 592 n. 217.

60. *Axios* ('worthy') is a thematic term for Matthew in this chapter; note also Matt. 10.10-13.

parallel in Mark 8.35 pars. ('Whoever wishes to save his life will lose it, but whoever loses his life for my sake . . . will save it'). In addition, John 12.25 indicates a wider knowledge of a saying of Jesus posing the same essential challenge (he who cherishes his life will lose it), once again indicating a Synoptic-like saying of Jesus used as a springboard for John's own reflections.[61] To explain all this in terms of literary derivation from one or two texts (Mark and Q) requires ingenuity of explanation for the variations in setting and inconsequential detail. Much the simpler is to infer a flexible repertoire of teaching on discipleship[62] known to most teachers in the early churches and taught in various combinations and forms as occasion permitted, to which variety and flexibility the present state of the tradition bears ready witness.[63]

6.18 Matt. 5.13/Luke 14.34-35/(Mark 9.49-50)

Matthew 5.13	Luke 14.34-35	Mark 9.49-50
[13]You are the salt of the earth; <u>but if the salt has become tasteless, by what will it be</u> restored? It is no longer good for anything, but is <u>thrown out</u> to be trampled under foot.	[34]So <u>salt is good</u>; <u>but if</u> even <u>the salt has become tasteless, by what can it be seasoned?</u> [35]It is fit neither for the earth nor for the manure heap; they <u>throw</u> it <u>out</u>.	[49]For everyone will be salted with fire. [50]<u>Salt is good</u>; <u>but if the salt</u> has become without content, <u>by what will</u> you <u>season</u> it? Have salt in yourselves, and be at peace with one another.

The saying has the same character as we have already noted in ##1.2, 1.5, 2.8, 5.14 and 6.15. A tightly worded proverb has retained its essential point across the enduring strands of tradition, though the corollary has not been deemed so important as to be retained in fixed form. This suggests a proverb referred back to Jesus, but its corollary formulated and elaborated as individual teachers deemed appropriate.

As a group (#6) one can see some sort of link in terms of the challenges and responsibilities of discipleship. But to suppose that these four units formed a single group in Q^1 seems rather far-fetched, given the diverse loca-

---

61. See above n. 24.

62. The range of the repertoire could be easily extended; see e.g. the material discussed in *Jesus Remembered*, 425-6, 503-5.

63. So Dodd, *Historical Tradition*, 338-43: 'The least difficult hypothesis to account for the likenesses and differences . . . is that this very fundamental saying had a place in many separate branches of oral tradition . . .' (343).

tions of the material in Matthew and Luke. The middle two items (##6.16-17) would much more naturally have been linked with other groups, as in Mark 8.34-38 pars. That they formed part of a much wider repertoire of many early Christian apostles and teachers I have already suggested, and that is probably how the four units should be seen, not as a single cluster but as one permutation of elements from the larger resources of the widely known oral Jesus tradition.

To conclude. Kloppenborg suggests that the material reviewed above forms a coherent group and, in all likelihood, 'a discrete redactional stratum' = Q^1, 'the formative stratum' of Q. He offers two principal reasons for this conclusion. (1) 'These clusters share a common rhetoric — the rhetoric of persuasion, rather than that of prophetic pronouncement or declamation', in contrast to the rhetoric of defence or attack that characterizes the rhetorical strategy of the main redaction (Q^2). (2) The subcollections display 'a common structure, beginning with programmatic sayings (6.20b-23; 9.57-60; 11.2-4; 12.2-3; 13.24), continuing with second person imperatives, and concluding with a saying that underscores the importance of the instructions (6.47-49; 10.16, 23-24; 12.33-34; 14.34-35).'[64]

As regards the first argument (1), 'the rhetoric of persuasion' is a very broad and indiscriminating category. It applies to a wide range of the teaching material in the Jesus tradition; indeed, it can embrace most of the material grouped by Matthew in his several collections (Matt. 5–7, 10, 13, 18). What becomes clear from Kloppenborg's reasoning is that the decisive consideration for him is not the presence of rhetoric common to the Q^1 material, but the *absence* of the warnings of coming judgment, which he judges, not unfairly, to be evidence of Q^2 redaction (particularly Q 6.23c; 10.12, 13-15; 12.8-10).[65] But even on the hypothesis of Q as a written document, that hardly constitutes evidence of more than that the compiler of Q used the theme of coming judgment as a means of linking disparate teaching material which the compiler may have been ordering into a whole for the first time. It is equally possible, on the Q hypothesis, that the compiler selected material and versions, or gave his own 'performance' of well-known material and themes in the oral Jesus tradition, drawing the material from a wider pool available in a variety of measures in the various churches known to him. It does not follow that the Q

---

64. *Excavating Q,* 144-5. It is not clear how the further material suggested by Kloppenborg for inclusion in Q^1 (above nn. 7, 14) fits in with this analysis.

65. *Formation,* 242-3; similarly, Q 13.25-27, 28-30, 34-35 and 14.16-24 are omitted from the #6 material because of its 'polemical thrust' (*Formation,* 235-7).

material shorn of its polemical and threatening material[66] formed an already coherently organised single block of material, let alone that it was known in a single written form.[67]

The argument of a common structure (2) is rather tendentious. To describe ##1.1, 2.6, 3.9, 4.11, 6.15 as 'programmatic sayings' is a substantial overstatement (#5 apparently lacks such a saying). Almost any of the sayings in any of the sections could have been placed first and been designated 'programmatic'.[68] Likewise Kloppenborg's observation that the clusters conclude 'with a saying that underscores the importance of the instructions' (but ##3 and 4 apparently lack such a saying) is more in the eye of the beholder than in the text: the explanation works well with #1,[69] but in ##5 and 6, different sayings could have served that function.[70] The reality is that the groups for the most part are simply that, groups of sayings on a similar theme; and the two in #4 don't seem to form a particularly coherent unit anyway.

In short, then, the case for designating the material reviewed above as a discrete compositional unit or stratum is weak. Just as unconvincing is the hypothesis that this material was the formative stratum of Q, that compositional techniques can so readily be distinguished from redactional techniques.[71] Much the more likely hypothesis is that this material, both in the variation of individual content and detail and in the diversity of groupings of the individual units, reflects the pattern of oral tradition. That is, the material as we still have it reflects the flexibility of oral performance, of teachers draw-

---

66. Did teachers never utter threats and warnings to outsiders mixed with their exhortations to their communities? Kloppenborg's neat distinction between a tone which is 'hortatory and instructional' and one which is 'polemical and threatening', or between proverbs and wisdom sayings 'to reinforce ethical imperatives' and those 'to undergird the pronouncements of judgment' (*Formation*, 238-9) evokes more the clinical dissection of an anatomy class than the rhetoric of a fervent teacher.

67. C. M. Tuckett, *Q and the History of Early Christianity* (Edinburgh: T&T Clark, 1996): 'It is not clear why the Q^1 layer should be considered as a unity at all. . . . it is a big step to jump from earlier (possibly disparate) material to a unified collection of sapiential speeches in a Q^1' (71; see further 71-4). The disagreements with Zeller and Piper (n. 5 above) also give cause for pause. Zeller gives a negative answer to the question, 'Eine weisheitliche Grundschrift in der Logienquelle?', in F. van Segbroeck et al., eds., *The Four Gospels*, F. Neirynck FS (Leuven: Leuven University, 1992) 389-401. See also those cited in my *Jesus Remembered*, 156 n. 80.

68. Piper notes that each of his collections, which cut across Kloppenborg's, 'begins with a rather general aphoristic saying' 'usually followed by a general maxim in statement form which provides ostensible support for whatever is being encouraged' (*Wisdom*, 61).

69. Kloppenborg, *Formation*, 185-7.

70. Note again Piper in regard to *his* collections: 'The final unit of the aphoristic collections always provides the key for interpreting the meaning' (*Wisdom*, 63).

71. See further *Jesus Remembered*, 155-7, with bibliography.

ing upon resources of Jesus tradition, much at least of it shared with other churches and teachers, and re-teaching it with variant details and emphases which reflect their own idiosyncracies, the vagaries of live performance and the needs of particular congregations. In a word, the so-called Q^1 material is best understood as oral tradition.

CHAPTER 4

Matthew's Awareness of Markan Redaction

Some years ago, while preparing undergraduate lectures on Mark's Gospel, I noted a number of instances where the Markan text was not reproduced in Matthew, and which included a high proportion of texts frequently attributed to Markan redaction.[1] Of course, some will immediately add: Markan redaction *of Matthew*. But I remain convinced on other grounds that Markan priority is much the most plausible way of explaining the agreements and disagreements between the Synoptics,[2] and gladly acknowledge the benefit I have derived from Professor Neirynck's studies on this theme.

The alternative hypothesis therefore seemed to be worth exploring, that the passages in question might serve as evidence that Matthew was aware of such elements having been added by Mark. This in turn would constitute evidence that Matthew had access to variant oral versions of much of Mark's material (other than Q), versions which lacked the details of Markan redaction and thereby alerted Matthew to the presence of that redaction. For some time I assumed that the hypothesis must have been put forward at some earlier stage in the lengthy debates about the Synoptic problem. But having been advised that this was not the case, by those who have made a greater specialist study in this area of New Testament research than I have been able to do,[3] it occurred to

---

1. See e.g. the data compiled by E. J. Pryke, *Redactional Style in the Marcan Gospel* (SNTSMS 33) (Cambridge: Cambridge University Press, 1978), pp. 10-24, 139-48.

2. For example, I find it hard to explain the differences between Mark 6,3 and Matt 13,55, or between Mark 10,17-18 and Matt 19,16-17, or between Mark 5 and the Matthean parallels, on any other plausible ground than Markan priority.

3. The discussion, e.g., in B. H. Streeter, *The Four Gospels. A Study of Origins* (London:

me that a brief investigation of the possibilities on this point might serve as a modest but fitting offering to honour one who has done more than any other in the last thirty years to clarify the detailed relations between the Gospels.

I

Let me first clear the ground. I am taking it for granted that the churches of the middle and late decades of the first century were provided with substantial, but no doubt varying amounts of (oral) traditions of Jesus' teaching and ministry. I cannot conceive that churches founded in the name of Jesus would be uninterested in the events of Jesus' mission and in his teaching, as well as in the kerygma of cross and resurrection. I assume that such tradition is alluded to in passages like 1 Cor 15,3; 1 Thess 4,1; 2 Thess 2,15; 3,6; and Col 2,6; that responsibility for retelling these traditions lay with the teachers who were clearly a prominent feature of these churches (Acts 13,1; 1 Cor 12,28; Gal 6,6); and that Paul alludes to these traditions quite frequently, particularly in the paraenetical sections of his letters.[4] I also assume that the Gospels and their sources did not spring from a vacuum but indicate the sort of traditions which must have been familiar in one form or another to such churches. I assume furthermore that when Mark did put these traditions in writing, these traditions did not immediately cease to be known in oral form in other churches (the point is perfectly obvious, but seems to need to be said).

It follows, therefore, that when the churches with which we associate Matthew received copies of Mark's Gospel, many at least of the traditions contained therein must already have been known to them, and known in variant forms. Consequently, we should not be surprised to find that Matthew produces significantly variant versions of various Markan traditions. No doubt, as we shall note in a moment, many of these variants stem directly from Matthew's editing of Mark's text. But we should *not* assume that Matthew's knowledge of the traditions contained in Mark was dependent solely on his having access to a copy of Mark; *nor* that the relation between the variant traditions in Mark and Matthew is purely literary in character. On the contrary, it is my contention that the most plausible way to make sense of Matthew's omission

---

Macmillan, 1924), pp. 162-72, obscures the issues because it is so oriented to the question of written sources.

4. See e.g. my 'Paul's Knowledge of the Jesus Tradition. The Evidence of Romans', in K. Kertelge, T. Holtz, C.-P. März (eds.), *Christus Bezeugen. Festschrift für Wolfgang Trilling* (Leipzig: St. Benno Verlag, 1989), pp. 193-207; M. Thompson, *Clothed with Christ. The Example and Teaching of Jesus in Romans 12,1–15,13* (JSNTSup 59; Sheffield: JSOT Press, 1990).

of a number of Markan details and passages is that the oral traditions known to him from his own churches lacked these details and passages, and that Matthew was able therefore to choose a different version of the tradition in a significant number of occasions. We may add, if desired: a different version to guide him in his own redaction of Mark. The point remains the same.

The passages I have in mind are not the variations in such obviously editorial sections as introductions to pericopes,[5] conclusions to pericopes,[6] or summary or link-passages.[7] And I would be quite happy to accept that the majority of omissions of Markan text by Matthew are to be attributed to Matthew's editing of Mark, either because that is the only version known to Matthew, or the version which he has chosen to follow. For example, it is fairly obvious that at various places Matthew has preferred alternative material or variant versions of the same material,[8] that in others he has made some major abbreviations and omissions,[9] and minor abbreviations or omissions,[10] often for stylistic reasons or simply to save space, and that in others again he has made modifications to material which gave potential for misunderstanding[11] or could be taken as unnecessarily demeaning of Jesus or his disciples.[12] At other points we can deduce that he has made significant and distinctively Matthean additions to Mark's text, apart from the larger tracts of material usually designated (special) M(atthean).[13]

5. Mark 1,1; 1,40a; 2,1-2; 2,13; 2,18a; 3,22; 4,13; 4,21; 4,30; 4,35-36a; 5,21; 9,14-16; 9,33; 10,1; 10,17; 11,11; 11,15; 11,20; 11,27; 12,1; 12,28; 12,35; 12,37b; 14,1; 16,1.

6. As in Mark 1,45; 2,12c; 9,29; 12,12; 12,27b; 12,34.

7. Mark 1,21-22; 1,33-34a; 1,39; 3,8-11; 6,30-31; 6,56; 7,31-37; 11,18-19.

8. Mark 4,26-29; 9,48-50 (preferring to use Q material elsewhere rather than Mark's contrived sequence); 11,21-25; 13,33-35a; 16,2-8.

9. Mark 2,1-12; 4,36b-41; 5,1-20. 21-43; 6,17-29; 7,1-5; 8,19-21; 8,38; 9,17-28; 9,33-41; 9,45; 10,30. 35; 10,46-52; 11,4-6; 11,16; 12,28-34 (unnecessarly repetitive?); 12,41-44; 13,35b-37 (unnecessarily repetitive?); 14,12-17; 15,44-45a. Cf. J. C. Hawkins, *Horae Synopticae. Contributions to the Study of the Synoptic Problem*, 2nd edition (Oxford: Clarendon Press, 1909), p. 159. The division between the material in this and the following note is rough and ready.

10. Mark 1,13b; 1,20 *(meta tōn misthōtōn);* 2,15b-16; 2,19b (unnecessarily repetitive?); 3,6 (Herodians); 3,23; 3,31b-32a; 4,19b. 23. 24c; 6,15 (possibly because same material appears later — 8,28 = Matt 16,14); 6,32-44 (6,34 retained elsewhere); 8,15 (Herodians); 10,12 (to exclude talk of wife divorcing husband); 10,19-22; 10,36-39; 11,12-14; 12,1-12; 14,3-9 (weakening rebuke of disciples); 14,35 (preferring repetition later); 14,56-61b. 65; 14,66-69. Cf. Hawkins, pp. 129-42.

11. Most obviously Mark 2,7b; 6.3. 5a and 10,17b-18.

12. Mark 1,41a. 43; 3,5; 6,48d; 8,12. 32a. 33a; 9,1d; 9,6; 10,24. 32; 14,40c. Cf. Hawkins, pp. 117-26.

13. E.g. Matt 12,5-7 and 11-12 (to make the exchange more intelligible within the categories of Jewish discussion); 14,28-31; 16,16c-19; 19,3c and 9c (to make the exchange more intelligible within the categories of Jewish discussion); 26,28c *(eis aphesin hamartiōn).*

The passages which I have in mind are particularly the following. I cite them in the order of the Markan text, only quoting the Matthean parallel where there is overlapping material. In each case underlining indicates the material which is to be found only in Mark. Luke occasionally retains this Markan material, but in most cases its absence also from Luke strengthens the probability that its distinctively Markan character was widely recognized, as indicated by the editing of Luke as well as of Matthew. I focus the issue on Matthean redaction of Mark, however, simply because so much of the Markan material falls in sections which Luke has omitted as a whole (as the following table also indicates), thereby obscuring the issue of specific Markan redaction of older material known to be Markan redaction as such.[14]

	Mark	Matthew
1,1	_archē tou euangeliou Iēsou Christou_	(not used by Luke either)
1,14b-15	_kērussōn_ to euangelion tou theou _kai legōn . . . metanoeite kai pisteuete en tō euangeliō_	apo tote ērxato ho Iēsous kērussein kai legein: metanoeite (Luke also omits)
1,34b	_kai ouk ēphien lalein ta daimonia, hoti ēdeisan auton_	(Luke retains the sense)
2,27	_kai elegen autois: to_ sabbaton _dia ton anthrōpon egeneto, kai ouch ho anthrōpos dia to sabbaton_	(Luke also omits)
3,11-12	_kai ta pneumata ta akatharta . . . ekrazon legontes hoti su ei ho huios tou theou._ kai polla epetima autois hina mē auton phaneron poiēsōsin	(Luke has variant elsewhere) kai epetimēsen autois hina mē phaneron auton poiēsōsin
3,17b	kai Iōannēn ton adelphon tou Iakōbou, _kai epethēken autois onoma Boanērges, ho estin huioi brontēs_	kai Iōannēs ho adelphos autou (Luke also omits)
3,20-21	_kai erchetai eis oikon; kai sunerchetai palin ho ochlos, hōste mē dunasthai autous mēde arton phagein. kai akousantes hoi par' autou exēlthon kratēsai auton; elegon gar hoti exestē_	(Luke also omits)

14. Whether we should speak of 'Markan redaction' in every case, or at least in some cases speak alternatively of pre-Markan redaction of still older material, does not need to be either clarified or resolved for the purposes of this enquiry.

3,29b-30	*alla enochos estin aiōniou* *hamartēmatos. hoti elegon:* *pneuma akatharton echei*	(Luke also omits)
4,10-12	*. . . ērōtōn auton hoi peri* *auton sun tois dōdeka tas* *parabolas. kai elegen autois:* *humin to mustērion dedotai* *tēs basileias tou theou; ekeinois* *de tois exō en parabolais ta* *panta ginetai hina blepontes* *. . . mēpote epistrepsōsin kai* *aphethē autois*	*. . . hoi mathētai eipan autō:* *dia ti en parabolais laleis* *autois? ho de apokritheis eipen:* *hoti humin dedotai gnōnai ta* *mustēria tēs basileias tōn* *ouranōn, ekeinois de ou* *dedotai . . . hoti blepontes . . .* (Luke also omits last clause)
4,34	*chōris de parabolēs ouk elalei* *autois, kat' idian de tois* *idiois mathētais epeluen panta*	*chōris parabolēs ouden elalei* *autois* (Luke omits entirely)
5,43	*kai diesteilato autois polla hina* *mēdeis gnoi touto*	(retained by Luke)
6,52	*ou gar sunēkan epi tois artois,* *all' ēn autōn hē kardia pepōrōmenē*	(Luke also omits)
7,2-4		(Luke also omits)
7,15	*ouden estin exōthen tou anthrōpou* *eisporeuomenon eis auton ho dunatai* *koinōsai auton; alla ta ek tou* *anthrōpou ekporeuomena . . .*	(Luke omits whole) *ou* *to eiserchomenon eis to stoma* *koinoi ton anthrōpon, alla to* *ekporeuomenon ek tou* *stomatos . . .*
7,17	*kai hote eisēlthen eis oikon apo* *tou ochlou, epērōtōn auton* *hoi mathētai autou*	*tote proselthontes* *hoi mathētai legousin autō*
7,18-19	*ou noeite hoti pan to exōthen* *eisporeuomenon eis ton anthrōpon* *ou dunatai auton koinōsai, hoti ouk* *eisporeuetai autou eis tēn kardian* *all' eis tēn koilian, kai eis ton* *aphedrōna ekporeuetai, katharizōn* *panta ta brōmata . . .*	*ou noeite hoti pan to* *eisporeuomenon eis to stoma* (Luke omits whole section) *eis tēn koilian chōrei kai eis* *aphedrōna ekballetai . . .*
7,24b	*kai eiselthōn eis oikian oudena* *ēthelen gnōnai, kai ouk ēdunēthē* *lathein*	(Luke omits whole section)
7,36	*. . . kai diesteilato autois hina* *mēdeni legōsin . . .*	(Luke also omits)
8,17b-18	*oupō noeite oude suniete . . .* *pepōrōmenēn echete tēn kardian* *humōn . . . ophthalmous echontes ou* *blepete, kai ōta echontes ouk akouete . . .*	(Luke also omits)

8,35c	*heneken emou <u>kai tou euangeliou</u>*	*heneken emou* (Luke also omits)
9,10	<u>*kai ton logon ekratēsan pros heautous suzētountes ti estin to ek nekrōn anastēnai*</u>	contrast Matt. 17.13 (Luke also omits)
9,28	*kai eiselthontos autou <u>eis oikon</u> hoi mathētai autou kat' idian epērōtōn auton*	*tote proselthontes hoi mathētai tō Iēsou kat' idian eipon*
9,30b	<u>*kai ouk ēthelen hina tis gnoi*</u>	(Luke also omits)
9,32	<u>*hoi de ēgnooun to rēma, kai ephobounto auton eperōtēsai*</u>	(retained by Luke)
10,10	<u>*kai eis tēn oikian palin hoi mathētai peri toutou epērōtōn auton*</u>	(Luke omits whole section)
10,29c	as 8,35c	(Luke also omits)
11,17	*ho oikos mou oikos proseuchēs klēthēsetai <u>pasin tois ethnesin</u>*	*ho oikos mou oikos proseuchēs klēthēsetai* (Luke also omits these words)
14,51-52	<u>*kai neaniskos tis sunēkolouthei autō peribeblēmenos sindona epi gumnou, kai kratousin auton; ho de katalipōn tēn sindona gumnos ephugen*</u>	(Luke also omits)
14,58	*egō <u>katalusō</u> ton naon touton <u>ton cheiropoiēton</u> kai dia triōn hēmerōn <u>allon acheiropoiēton</u> oikodomēsō*	*dunamai katalusai ton naon tou theou kai dia triōn hēmerōn oikodomēsai* (Luke omits the whole section)
15,21	*Simōna Kurēnaion <u>erchomenon ap' agrou, ton patera Alexandrou kai Rouphou</u>*	*Kurēnaion, onomati Simōna* (Luke omits last 5 words)
15,42b	<u>*epei ēn paraskeuē, ho estin prosabbaton*</u>	cf. Mark 7.2-4 (Luke also omits)
16,8	*eichen gar autas tromos kai ekstasis; <u>kai oudeni ouden eipan; ephobounto gar</u>*	*meta phobou kai charas megalēs* *edramon apangeilai tois mathētais autou* (Luke similar to Matthew)

Given this interesting range of special Markan material is it plausible to argue that it (the underlined material) consists of Markan redaction of older material, recognized as such by Matthew, and omitted by Matthew in part at least for that reason?

II

What then are we to make of the above set of Markan passages?

In some cases the indications of Markan redaction are strong and immediately compelling. Mark 1,1; 1,14b-15; 8,35c; 10,29c and 13,10 provide strong support for the view that *to euangelion* is a Markan formulation, and probably that it was Mark who introduced it into the Synoptic tradition.[15] Matthew has a variation of 1,14b-15 in Matt 4,23, and of 13,10 in Matt 24,14. In Matt 9,35 he reformulates what was probably the Q form using the verb (as in Luke), probably under the influence of Mark. And his only other use of the term is dependent directly on Mark (26,13). Luke, in contrast, makes no use of the noun whatsoever.

Another widely accepted example would be the secrecy motif in Mark. There is a strong probability that 1,34b (a summary passage); 3,11-12; 4,34; 5,43; 7,24b; 7,36; 8,26(?); 9,10; 9,28. 30b; 10,10 and 16,8 reflect Markan emphases at this point. Again this is not to say that Matthew and Luke were unaware of the motif or that they were hostile to it. Their reproduction of Mark 1,44; 8,30 and 9,9, and the appearance of the *oikia* motif in Matt 13,36 and 17,25, show that they were happy to make use of the secrecy motif on their own account. Nor would I wish to argue that Mark has created the whole theme; on the contrary I remain strongly of the view that the motif was given him in the tradition.[16] Nevertheless, the indications are strong that Mark chose to elaborate and emphasize that theme to a considerable extent, and the consistency of Matthean omission of these elaborations suggests at least the strong possibility that Matthew was aware that they were Mark's elaborations.

The same is true of a third Markan theme — his emphasis on the dullness of the disciples in 6,52; 8,17b-18;[17] 9,32 and again 16,8.[18] The fact that Matthew and Luke have not reproduced it in the same degree indicates either a hesitation to disparage the disciples quite so strongly, or a recognition that the theme has been strengthened by Mark for his own purposes, or, I would suggest, both. Since they retain the theme elsewhere on their own account (e.g. Matt 13,36; 16,22; 17,16; 26,8. 35), we can fairly deduce that Matthew and

---

15. W. Marxsen, *Mark the Evangelist* (Nashville: Abingdon, 1969), chap. 3; see also R. A. Guelich, 'The Gospel Genre', in P. Stuhlmacher (ed.), *Das Evangelium und das Evangelien* (WUNT 28; Tübingen, J. C. B. Mohr, 1983), pp. 183-219.

16. See my 'The Messianic Secret in Mark', *Tyndale Bulletin* 21 (1970) 92-117; reprinted in shortened form in C. Tuckett (ed.), *The Messianic Secret* (London: S.P.C.K., 1983), pp. 116-31.

17. The language of 'hardening' *(pōroō* and *pōrōsis)* occurs in the Synoptics only in Mark 3.5, 6.52 and 8.17.

18. See further n. 12 above.

Luke are not antipathetical to the theme itself. Their criterion for judging whether to retain it or not at particular points was probably in part at least determined by their awareness that at several points in Mark its presence was to be attributed to Markan redaction.

In each case Matthew demonstrates consistent but not total disregard for what are clearly strong Markan themes. These omissions cannot be attributed to Matthew's dislike for the themes, since he reproduces them elsewhere. That the omissions are motivated by merely stylistic or theological concerns or by Matthew's desire to abbreviate will provide part of the answer.[19] But the frequency of omission and the careful excisions often involved suggest another hypothesis: that Matthew was aware that these elements were the result of Markan redaction of tradition which was otherwise common in greater or less degree to the different communities with which Mark and Matthew were associated.

Other examples are less clear because the sample is less numerous. Nevertheless, we may deduce that the personal references in 14,51-52 and 15,21 were Mark's addition to common tradition because the information was personal to him, or, in the latter case, to his readers as well.[20] The omission of these references by Matthew and Luke likewise suggests their awareness of their personal character. Likewise the explanations of Jewish traditions added by Mark in 7,2-4 and 15,42b were probably recognized to be just that — additions by Mark — and therefore omitted as also (in Matthew's case at any rate) being unnecessary. In contrast, Matthew's omission of the *cheiropoiēton/ acheiropoiēton* antithesis from the trial accusation (Mark 14,58) probably indicates his awareness that this was a hellenized version of the accusation, whose hellenisation dates back to the Hellenists' (or Stephen's) appeal to the tradition that Jesus had spoken against the Temple (Acts 6,14; 7,48; cf. John 2,19).[21]

So too we can probably cite Matthew's treatment of the 'Markan sandwich' in Mark 3,20-35: he destroys the sandwich by omitting 3,20-21 (and also weakens the coherence of the sequence of exorcism sayings by omitting 3,30) and by inserting more material before the passage on Jesus' family (3,31-35). This cannot be because he disliked the 'sandwich' format (as his retention of Mark 5,21-43, albeit in much abbreviated form, shows). But he also destroys the sandwich achieved by Mark through the insertion of the 'cleansing of the

---

19. See again nn. 9-10 above.

20. Should 3.17b be included here?

21. See further my *The Partings of the Ways between Christianity and Judaism* (London: SCM, 1991), particularly pp. 68-9.

Temple' between the two halves of the cursing of the fig tree episode (11,12-14// 11,15-19//11,20-26). Once again the likelihood is that Matthew knew another form of the tradition which enabled him to recognize that these sandwiches were Markan contrivances.

In at least two cases where Matthew makes a theologically motivated modification of Mark's text we may deduce that he could do so because he was aware of a variant version of the tradition. I have in mind the significant softening of the Markan form of Mark 4,10-12 and 7,15 and 19. What is notable in these cases is both the extent to which Matthew departs from the Markan text, and the possibility in each case of recognizing an Aramaic form of the tradition which could have given rise to the Matthean version independently of Mark.[22] In contrast, the theologically motivated modifications of Mark 10,2 and 9 and Mark 10,17-18 stick very closely to Mark's text, suggesting both that Matthew knew no significantly variant version of these traditions and that in making his modifications he wished to remain as close as possible to the wording of the Markan form of the tradition. In other words, in these cases the possibility is given us of deducing from the character of Matthew's redaction of Mark that in some (here the former) cases he already knew a variant form of the tradition, while in others (here the latter) he knew only Mark's version.

More puzzling is the omission of *pasin tois ethnesin* in Mark 11,17, even though all three evangelists cite the Isa 56,7 text, and despite the fact that both the Hebrew and Greek form of the text include these words. A plausible logic can be offered in each case. In the light of Matt 10,5-6 and 15,24 we could deduce that Matthew omitted these words because he saw the worldwide commission (Matt 28,19-20) as belonging strictly to the post-Easter period (cf. 24,14). Likewise in the light of what happens in Acts, we may deduce that Luke omitted the phrase conceivably because he saw the Christian mission as a going out *from* Jerusalem, rather than in terms of the nations coming *into* Jerusalem's Temple.[23] But was there a tradition of Jesus quoting Isa 56,7 only in the abbreviated form? The choice between the argument that Mark added these words (because of his own Gentile-mission perspective — cf. Mark 7), and the alternative argument that Matthew and Luke, both for their own reasons, modified a common tradition containing these words (as attested by

22. See e.g. discussion in R. A. Guelich, *Mark 1-8* (Word Biblical Commentary 34A; Dallas: Word, 1989), pp. 210-2; and my 'Jesus and Ritual Purity: A Study of the Tradition-History of Mark 7,15', in *A cause de l'évangile, Mélanges offerts à Dom Jacues Dupont* (Lectio Divina 123; Saint-Andreé: Editions du Cerf, 1985), reprinted in my *Jesus, Paul and the Law. Studies in Mark and Galatians* (London: S.P.C.K., 1990), pp. 37-60.

23. See further my *Partings*, chap. 4.

Mark), is difficult to resolve. Equally unclear is what the citation of this particular text (Isa 56,7) without these words specifically quoted would be taken to imply anyway, given that the whole context in Isaiah (56,3-8) has in view the incoming of all categories hitherto disqualified by origin, disability or dispersion. The case is inconclusive for the present purposes.

Most difficult of all is Mark 2,27. If anything, the verse looks like the natural conclusion to the episode, serving in the form of a pronouncement story as the climax to Jesus' teaching at this point; and, if there is an addition, 2,28 looks more likely to be it, added to bend the point of the episode in a christological direction.[24] Alternatively, it could be argued, with the modest support of W and the Sinaitic Syriac, that the earlier form of the tradition omitted verse 27b — leaving the more balanced Semitic form,

lego de humin, hoti to sabbaton dia ton anthrōpon ektisthē,
hōste kurios estin ho huios tou anthrōpou kai tou sabbatou,

with 'son of man' having the force of 'man' in the original Aramaic (as in Ps 8,4). But why Matthew and Luke should both omit the whole of verse 27 remains a puzzle. Perhaps it is just that they both wished to focus the climactic saying solely on Jesus. Perhaps, in addition, both reflect the degree to which the sabbath had ceased to be observed even in the Christian Jewish congregations of Matthew; in which case, paradoxically, Mark presumably retained the verse because it was what Jesus was remembered as having said, despite any degree of irrelevance already seen in the saying among the Gentile churches for whom Mark wrote. Given the semitically balanced form of the saying (whether verses 27-28, or verses 27a, 28) one naturally hesitates to conclude that verse 27 was added by Mark. So perhaps the simplest solution is that Matthew and Luke independently omitted verse 27 for their own reasons, and that this instance does *not* add to the case for seeing behind Matthew's redaction awareness of a variant, briefer version.

Even so, however, the examples already reviewed do build up cumulatively to quite a strong case in favour of the hypothesis that Matthean omission of Markan passages or clauses is in a significant number of instances best explained by assuming that Matthew knew of different versions of the tradition which lacked these Markan details and which indicated to Matthew that these details had been added to the tradition by Mark and could therefore be set aside without interfering with or damaging the tradition itself.

---

24. See e.g. the review of the discussion on these verses in Guelich, *Mark 1-8*, pp. 123-7.

III

This, then, is the hypothesis I wish to put forward. It has three corollaries which are worth drawing attention to, in conclusion.

First, if the variant tradition known to Matthew was close enough for Matthew to be able thus to recognize Markan redaction, it also tells us that the shared tradition spread throughout the churches of the (north) eastern quadrant of the Mediterranean at this time remained strikingly similar in form and detail. Such a conclusion should not surprise us, since although the Synoptics evince tremendous diversity within the Jesus-tradition, the diversity of form and content in fact remains quite limited or restricted in extent; in most cases the substance of the shared memory of what Jesus said or did is clear. The importance of the present deduction, however, is that Matthew's sensitivity to Markan redaction strengthens the impression that the variant form of the tradition known by Matthew was well within the bounds of the diversity also attested to us by the Synoptics; when Mark's Gospel arrived in the Matthean churches they were able to recognize from their own traditions both its degree of closeness to their own versions and the Markan editing.

Secondly, if so, this further indicates that the process of writing down what had hitherto been principally oral tradition, both by Mark and by Matthew, did not constitute a significant transformation in the content and character of the tradition. The indication is rather of a continuity between the oral forms of the tradition and their written Gospel forms, sufficient for an evangelist's redaction to be evident to those aware of the traditions preserved and recycled within their own churches.

Thirdly, that so few of the references listed above come from the passion narrative may be further indication that the passion narrative was relatively more fixed at a very early stage. Although the traditions contained within the passion narrative were almost certainly an important part of any early church's stock of Jesus tradition, it is striking that there is so little evidence that Matthew knew significant variant versions of its content.

CHAPTER 5

Matthew as *Wirkungsgeschichte*

The *Wirkungsgeschichte* of a historic text has become a prominent emphasis in the study of NT writings since Hans-Georg Gadamer gave currency to the term.[1] And the study of 'the history of the effect' of a text like the Gospel of Matthew has been highly productive of fresh insights into the text and the history of its interpretation — as Ulrich Luz has demonstrated so fully and to such good effect.[2] My concern in this small birthday offering to one for whom my admiration knows hardly any bounds, is to press the point that the Gospel of Matthew is itself *Wirkungsgeschichte*. That is, to be more precise, Matthew itself has to be seen as part of the history of the effect of an earlier impulse, that is, of the Jesus tradition, or indeed, ultimately part of the effect that Jesus himself had on his first disciples. It is not necessary to this thesis that the author of Matthew himself had been one of these first disciples, although the name attached to the Gospel strongly suggests that the disciple called Matthew had at least a major part in the formation and transmission of the tradition of which his Gospel consists and which achieves its enduring form in the written Gospel of Matthew.[3] But, of course, it would fit my thesis

1. H.-G. Gadamer, *Truth and Method* (ET New York: Crossroad, [2]1989) 300-307.
2. I refer of course to U. Luz, *Das Evangelium nach Matthäus* (KEK 1; 4 vols; Zürich: Benziger, 1985/2002, 1990, 1997, 2002).
3. To argue that an eyewitness would not have used the book of a non-eyewitness as his chief source (Luz, *Matthäus* 1.105; followed by U. Schnelle, *The History and Theology of the New Testament Writings* [ET London: SCM, 1998] 219), however, indicates both an assumption of overwhelming *literary* dependency and a lack of appreciation of the traditioning process in an

well if the author 'Matthew' had indeed been the toll-collector Matthew who became an early disciple of Jesus (Matt. 9.9).

I

My basic point is that the Gospel of Matthew should not be seen simply as the beginning of a process of *Wirkungsgeschichte,* even when the question has been 'What evidence is there of the influence of Matthew's Gospel as such on subsequent writers and artists?' For the traditions and texts on which Matthew drew were part of a process already in effect, and the composition of Matthew's Gospel neither began a new form of the process nor ended the earlier form of the process. Rather, Matthew's Gospel was one way in which the earlier impact of Jesus and of the Jesus tradition continued to have its/their effect on succeeding generations.

Those who are familiar with my recent work on the Jesus tradition will be aware that I am here continuing to develop an earlier attempt to bring to the fore what I have termed (for want of a better term) the 'impact' of Jesus — the impact of Jesus as evidenced in the content and character of the Jesus tradition, particularly in its diverse Synoptic form.[4] So, it is the pre-Matthean phase of the material used by Matthew on which I wish to focus, particularly the degree of fluidity of its forms and content. That includes not only the oral character of that material, but also the transition from oral to literary which I believe Matthew's Gospel represents. The point being that Matthew's Gospel is a testimony to the character and effect of that material, to its fluidity and adaptability, much more than is often recognized by redaction critics. The content and shape of the material preserved for us in Matthew's Gospel owe a good deal more to the effect of the earlier Jesus tradition and indeed to the originating impact of Jesus himself than is often allowed. Matthew is not simply the voice of his community or only a creative editor,[5] but, much more important for Matthew himself, a faithful re-teller and re-cycler of traditions which were constitutive of a wide range of gatherings of the earliest Christians.[6]

---

oral culture both of which I regard as anachronistic; I briefly develop my alternative view in the first section below.

   4. See my *Jesus Remembered* (Grand Rapids: Eerdmans, 2003); also *A New Perspective on Jesus* (Grand Rapids: Baker Academic/London: SPCK, 2005).

   5. For Luz's views of Matthew as a coherent composition and of the Matthean community see his *Matthäus,* 1.27-39, 82-99; more briefly, *The Theology of the Gospel of Matthew* (Cambridge: Cambridge University, 1995) ch. 1.

   6. That Matthew expresses his self-understanding of his own role in 13.52 is widely recognized (Luz, *Matthäus,* 1.83, 2.364 n. 21).

To avoid any misunderstanding I should make it clear that it is also important for me that Matthew's editorial hand in the composition of Matthew's Gospel be fully recognized. I need hardly argue the point since it is familiar to all students of Matthew. But to underline my own acceptance of the point I may simply illustrate it by citing some of the most obvious evidence of Matthew's composition and redaction:

- the Gospel structured to present the teaching of Jesus in five blocks,[7] presumably in some mimicry of the five books of Moses;[8]
- the editorial introduction given, for example, to the Sermon on the Mount (5.1-2);
- the presence of distinctive terms, like *anomia, dikaiosunē, oligopistos// oligopistia* and *sunteleia tou aiōnos* in the Matthean form of the tradition, clearly indicating distinctively Matthean emphases;[9]
- the various indications of a later perspective, as in the 'community rule' in ch. 18,[10] and the allusion to the destruction of Jerusalem in 22.7.

The problem from my perspective on the most recent phase of Gospel scholarship is that as more and more attention has been focused on Matthean redaction, or on the theology and narrative of Matthew, or on the sociology of the Matthean community reflected in his Gospel, less attention has been given to Matthew as transmitter of earlier tradition, as performer of a lively and diverse oral tradition. My concern is not to downplay the creativity of author or influence of community setting, but to shine more light on the phase before Matthew composed his Gospel, and thus to gain a clearer impression of the decades during which the tradition was both shaping and being shaped.

I confess that I also continue to react against the over-dependence of too much Gospel criticism on what I call the 'literary paradigm'. By this I refer to the assumption either that Matthew is to be understood solely in terms of Matthew copying and editing tradition already in written form, particularly,

7. Matt. 5–7, 10, 13, 18, 24–25; their conclusions marked by the same formula (7.28; 11.1; 13.53; 19.1; 26.1).

8. A popular suggestion usually traced back to B. W. Bacon, *Studies in Matthew* (London: Constable, 1930); see W. G. Kümmel, *Introduction to the New Testament* (ET Nashville: Abingdon/London: SCM, 1975) 106.

9. *anomia* — 7.23; 13.41; 23.28; 24.12; *dikaiosunē* — 3.15; 5.6, 10, 20; 6.1, 33; 21.32; *oligopistos// oligopistia* — 6.30; 8.26; 14.31; 16.8; 17.20; *sunteleia tou aiōnos* — 13.39, 40, 49; 24.3; 28.20; see further Luz, *Matthäus* 1.57-75.

10. Cf. Luz, *Matthäus*, 3.8.

of course, Mark and Q.[11] Or the assumption that Matthew's use of earlier material, whether written or oral, is to be understood in quasi-literary terms, as though oral tradition took firm shape and outline which could be and was edited in the way that written texts are edited. Or the assumption that if the variations of Matthew's tradition from other forms of the same tradition can be understood in terms of Matthean redaction, then that should stand as a sufficient explanation for the variations and no other explanations need be considered.[12] As I have already observed elsewhere,[13] it is ludicrous to approach the material in Matthew which is parallel to material in Mark (or Q) as though Matthew's reading of Mark (and Q) was the first time Matthew had encountered all or most of that material.[14] Almost certainly, even on *a priori* grounds, it is more than likely that Matthew knew different versions of that material and in several cases at least chose to follow the version he knew rather than the one he encountered in Mark (or Q).

The basis of my approach is as before:[15]

- that the communities in which the Jesus tradition was preserved and circulated during the first fifty to sixty years of Christianity were predominantly oral communities, that only a small minority of the first Christians would have been literate (but more than likely including Matthew the toll-collector), and that knowledge of written documents (predominantly the Torah) would have been from hearing rather than reading;
- that the bulk of the Jesus tradition formed an important part of the foundation stratum laid down when a new church was established, that

11. E.g., in his *Theology of the Gospel of Matthew,* Luz frames his discussion of 'Matthew's Predecessors' in terms of 'various "recensions" or critical revisions of Q', deutero-Mark, and a further written source for the Sermon on the Mount, with only 'most of the remaining Matthean special sayings' drawn from oral tradition' (6-8); more fully *Matthäus,* 1.47-52. Not dissimilarly, W. D. Davies & D. C. Allison, *Matthew* (ICC; 3 vols.; Edinburgh: T & T Clark, 1988, 1991, 1997), who, though more interested in the question of tradition-history behind Matthew's material, nevertheless frame their discussion of Matthew's sources almost exclusively in terms of written sources (1.97-127). D. A. Hagner, *Matthew* (WBC 33; 2 vols.; Dallas: Word, 1993, 1995), however, takes more account of oral tradition (1.xlvi-l).

12. This was the burden of my protest in 'Altering the Default Setting: Re-envisaging the Early Transmission of the Jesus Tradition', *NTS* 49 (2003) 139-75; reprinted with Gospel texts in English in *New Perspective,* 79-125 (= 41-79, above).

13. 'Altering the Default Setting', 170-1; *New Perspective,* 120-1.

14. I do not dispute that Matthew knew Mark in written form and that he did indeed draw on and edit much of the Markan material; see *Jesus Remembered,* 144 n. 15.

15. For elaboration I refer again to *Jesus Remembered* and *New Perspective.*

it was regularly drawn on by the founding apostle(s) and continuing teachers in the regular gatherings of the young congregations for worship and instruction;

• and that the character of the use (or performance) of that tradition was typical of what we know of performance of oral tradition in other communities past and present, that is, the same substance of the narrative, but varied in detail, the same teachings but differently formulated and grouped.

What has always impressed me about the Synoptic tradition is precisely this 'same but different' character of most of the material. It was precisely the attempt to explain this character of the Synoptic tradition which led me to explore the possibility that it might reflect a tradition already shaped at the oral stage of its transmission. The fact that the same character is evident when the tradition had long since been put into Greek says to me that the translation of Aramaic into Greek and the transition from a setting in Galilean village to one in Hellenistic city cannot have made all that much difference to the shape and character of the tradition. So too, the fact that the tradition gives such a powerfully coherent and consistent picture of the Jesus who inspired it,[16] persuades me that most of the units of the tradition had already been given their enduring form during the oral stage of the tradition. And not least, the fact that so much of the tradition retains its Galilean character and in individual items is unaffected by the theology of cross and resurrection says to me that this tradition took shape during Jesus' Galilee mission and prior to Good Friday and Easter Sunday.[17]

Can a study of Matthew give more substance to these claims and provide some clarification of the role of Matthew and of Matthew's Gospel within what was already a well-developed and ongoing process? I think so. The thesis can be argued simply by drawing out examples already offered.

16. C. H. Dodd made the point well in his *The Founder of Christianity* (London: Collins, 1971): 'The first three gospels offer a body of sayings on the whole so consistent, so coherent, and withal so distinctive in manner, style and content, that no reasonable critic should doubt, whatever reservations he may have about individual sayings, that we find here reflected the thought of a single, unique teacher' (21-22).

17. The alternative explanation, current in Q scholarship, that this material only reflects continuing Galilean communities of Jesus' disciples who knew nothing of or were opposed to the passion-centred gospel (as of Mark), I find much less plausible.

II

One of my earliest forays into this arena was to suggest that Matthew in using Markan tradition showed himself to be aware of Mark's own input to the tradition in the form in which Mark transcribed it.[18] The essay has been reprinted above using transliterated Greek texts,[19] but for convenience I repeat many of the examples using the English (NRSV) translation. They should demonstrate my thesis that Matthew was aware of Mark's earlier editing of the oral Jesus tradition. More to the point, if I am right, this evidence shows that Matthew was aware of a good many instances at which Mark had given the tradition he was using a characteristic tweak.

	Mark	Matthew
1.14b-15	proclaiming <u>the good news of God</u> and saying, '. . . repent, <u>and believe in the good news</u>'.	From that time Jesus began to proclaim, 'Repent . . .' (Luke also omits the underlined words)
1.34b	<u>and he would not permit the demons to speak because they knew him.</u>	(Luke retains the sense)
2.27	<u>Then he said to them, 'The sabbath was made for humankind, and not humankind for the sabbath'.</u>	(Luke also omits)
3.11-12	<u>Whenever the unclean spirits saw him, they fell down before him and shouted, 'You are the Son of God!'</u> But he sternly ordered them not to make him known.	(Luke has something similar) and he ordered them not to make him known.
3.20-21	<u>Then he went home; and the crowd came together again, so that they could not even eat. When his family heard it, they went out to restrain him, for people were saying, 'He has gone out of his mind'.</u>	(Luke also omits)
3.29b-30	. . . <u>but is guilty of an eternal sin — for they had said, 'He has an unclean spirit'.</u>	(Luke also omits)
4.34	He did not speak to them except in parables, <u>but he explained everything in private to his disciples.</u>	without a parable he told them nothing (Luke omits entirely)
6.52	<u>. . . for they did not understand about the loaves, but their hearts were hardened.</u>	(Luke also omits)
7.2-4		(Luke also omits)

---

18. 'Matthew's Awareness of Markan Redaction', in *The Four Gospels: Festschrift F. Neirynck* (BETL 100; Leuven University, 1992) 2.1349-59 = 109-19, above.

19. Ch. 4 above pp. 109-19. As there, the underlining in the following texts indicates the material distinctive to Mark.

7.18-19	'Do you not see that whatever goes into a person from outside <u>cannot defile,</u> <u>since it enters not the heart but</u> the stomach, and goes out into the sewer?' <u>(Thus he declared all foods clean.)</u>	Do you not see that whatever goes into the mouth (Luke omits whole section) enters the stomach, and goes out into the sewer?
7.24b	<u>He entered a house and did not want</u> <u>anyone to know he was there. Yet he</u> <u>could not escape notice.</u>	(Luke omits whole section)
8.17b-18	Do you still not perceive or understand? <u>Are your hearts hardened? Do you have</u> <u>eyes, and fail to see? Do you have ears,</u> <u>and fail to hear?</u>	Do you still not perceive? (Luke also omits)
8.35c	for my sake, <u>and for the sake of the gospel.</u>	for my sake (Luke also omits)
9.10	<u>So they kept the matter to themselves,</u> <u>questioning what this rising from the dead</u> <u>could mean.</u>	contrast Matt. 17.13 (Luke also omits)
9.30b	<u>He did not want anyone to know it.</u>	(Luke also omits)
9.32	<u>But they did not understand what he was</u> <u>saying and were afraid to ask him.</u>	(retained by Luke)
10.10	<u>Then in the house the disciples asked him</u> <u>again about this matter.</u>	(Luke omits whole section)
13.10	<u>And the good news must first be</u> <u>proclaimed to all nations.</u>	(Luke also omits)
14.58	I <u>will</u> destroy this temple <u>that is made</u> <u>with hands,</u> and in three days I will build another, <u>not made with hands.</u>	I am able to destroy the temple of God and to build it in three days. (Luke omits the whole section)
16.8	for terror and amazement had seized them; <u>and they said nothing to anyone, for</u> <u>they were afraid.</u>	with fear and great joy, and ran to tell his disciples. (Luke similar to Matthew)

Now, such an awareness could have emerged from Matthew's own careful analysis of Mark, such as is common in twentieth- and twenty-first-century scholarship. But the implied portrayal of Matthew in the guise of a modern scholar is highly anachronistic and hardly persuasive. Such awareness can best be explained by the hypothesis that Matthew knew the tradition retold by Mark but *in a different form,* a form prior to or other than the version in Mark's Gospel. The data alone, in other words, serve as evidence that the traditions coming to Matthew in Mark's Gospel were not unknown to him. Matthew knew them in a different form, a form which enabled him to recognize the distinctive editing of Mark. The appropriate deduction, then, when Matthew omits, or perhaps better, ignores a distinctive Markan feature, is that Matthew preferred the version he knew without Mark's modifications. It is not necessary to further infer that Matthew wanted to convey an earlier or purer version of the tradition 'uncontaminated' by Mark's redaction. For my understanding of oral tradition is that there was no such pure or solely authentic form of the tradition, but that it existed from the first in variant forms as different apostles and teachers rehearsed the Jesus tradition in different settings and for different purposes.[20]

The data also reinforces the objection to the early form-critical assumption that development in the tradition-history of the forms was always or predominantly from 'purity' and simplicity in the direction of greater complexity.[21] The idea of a linear development from individual aphorisms through increasing accretion to the developed structure of the written Gospels, or even of two, three or four lines of development linked to particular individuals[22] or centres,[23] was always more convenient to would-be analysts of the Synoptic tradition than realistic — as though the Synoptic tradition could be likened to one or more snowballs rolled down a snowy slope and gathering more and more material as they neared the bottom. In contrast, Matthew's discarding of Mark's interpretative additions speaks more of a repertoire of material which could be used selectively, abbreviated or elaborated, aggregated or taken in different sequences — more like a musical score which includes several cadenzas, where the soloist is free to improvise in elaborating a theme within a structured movement, and may (but need not) follow the pattern of cadenzas in previous performances.

The point, then, is that Matthew's use of Markan tradition in a non-Markan form, or stripped of (some of) its Markan embellishments, gives us an important insight into the character of the oral Jesus tradition, into the traditioning process in which the tradition was celebrated and used in the gatherings of believers in Messiah Jesus and circulated among the Christian gatherings, and into Matthew's own role within that process.

---

20. See below at n. 33, where I return to this point.

21. E. P. Sanders, *The Tendencies of the Synoptic Tradition* (SNTSMS 9; Cambridge: Cambridge University, 1969) effectively squashed the earlier view, particularly of Bultmann; see further *Jesus Remembered*, 194.

22. Most recently R. Bauckham, *Jesus and the Eyewitnesses: The Gospels as Eyewitness Testimony* (Grand Rapids: Eerdmans, 2006); but the diversity of the tradition, its multi-form interweavings and variations, indicate a more complex tradition-history than simply the recollections of three or four individuals.

23. B. H. Streeter, *The Four Gospels: A Study of Origins* (London: Macmillan, 1924) famously linked Mark with Rome, Q and Matthew with Antioch, M with Jerusalem, L with Caesarea, and Luke perhaps with Corinth (diagram on 150).

III

The dominant solution to the 'Synoptic problem' (Markan priority and Matthew's and Luke's dependence on a Q source) has been built on a solid foundation of the close verbal similarity of various passages between two or three of the Synoptics (double- or triple-tradition). Again, I have no wish to challenge the basic logic which gives rise to this solution.[24] Where I lodge my protest is at two points:

- first, that the passages which point to this conclusion, although a significant proportion of the Synoptic tradition, are still a minority of the whole material, even of the parallel material;
- and second, that the other parallel passages are then drawn in and fitted to that conclusion, usually by assuming a considerable editorial freedom on the part of the later Evangelist in editing his earlier material.

That seems to me to be an unwise procedure. Better to consider the whole range of parallels, including, not least, the passages where the parallel is not close, and then ask how it is that such a range of parallel material (some verbally close, some verbally quite different) could come about. Again without denying the likelihood of editorial improvements in at least several instances, there are other cases where the parallels are so diverse that the most obvious conclusion is rather that Matthew knew and preferred a different form of the tradition.

I consider, first, a few Mark/Matthew parallels:[25]

Mark 4.35-41	Matthew 8.23-27
[35]On that day, when evening had come, he said to them, "Let us go across to the other side". [36]And leaving the crowd behind, they took him with them in the boat, just as he was. Other boats were with him. [37]A great stormwind arose, and the waves beat into the boat, so that the boat was already being filled. [38]But he was in the stern, asleep on the cushion; and <u>they woke him up</u> and said to him, "Teacher, do you not care that <u>we are perishing</u>?"	[23]And when he got into the boat, his disciples followed him. [24]A great storm arose on the sea, so great that the boat was being swamped by the waves; but he was asleep. [25]And they went and <u>woke him up</u>, saying, "Lord, save us! <u>We are perishing!</u>"

24. I list the most persuasive Q passages in *Jesus Remembered*, 147 n. 29; and see n. 14 above.

25. I will use English text for convenience; the underlining indicates somewhat crudely use of the same words; space limits the examples to four.

Mark 4.35-41	Matthew 8.23-27
³⁹<u>He got up and rebuked the</u> <u>wind</u>, and said to the <u>sea</u>, "Be quiet! Silence!" Then the wind ceased, <u>and there was a</u> dead <u>calm</u>. ⁴⁰He said to them, "Why are you <u>afraid</u>? Have you still no <u>faith</u>?" ⁴¹And they were filled with great awe and said to one another, "Who then <u>is this, that even the wind and</u> the sea <u>obey him?</u>"	²⁶And he said to them, "Why are you <u>afraid</u>, you of little <u>faith</u>?" Then <u>he got up and rebuked the</u> <u>wind</u>s and the <u>sea</u>; <u>and there was a</u> dead <u>calm</u>. ²⁷The men were amazed, saying, "What sort of man <u>is this, that even the winds and</u> the sea <u>obey him?</u>"

Mark 7.24-30	Matthew 15.21-28
²⁴From there he set out and went away to the region of Tyre. He entered a house and did not want anyone to know he was there. Yet he could not escape notice, ²⁵but a woman whose little daughter had an unclean spirit immediately heard about him, and she came and bowed down at his feet. ²⁶Now the woman was a Gentile, of Syrophoenician origin. She begged him to cast the demon out of her daughter. ²⁷He said to her, "Let the children be fed first, for <u>it is not</u> <u>fair to take the children's food and throw it to the</u> <u>dogs</u>". ²⁸But she answered him, "<u>Certainly, lord,</u> and <u>the dogs</u> under the table <u>eat from the crumbs</u> of the children". ²⁹So he said to her, "For saying that, you may go, the demon has left your daughter". ³⁰So she went to her home, and found the child lying on the bed, and the demon gone.	²¹Jesus left that place and went off to the district of Tyre and Sidon. ²²Just then a Canaanite woman from that region came out and started shouting, "Have mercy on me, lord, son of David; my daughter is tormented by a demon". ²³But he did not answer her at all. And his disciples came and urged him, saying, "Send her away, for she keeps shouting after us". ²⁴He answered, "I was sent only to the lost sheep of the house of Israel". ²⁵But she came and knelt before him, saying, "Lord, help me". ²⁶He answered, "<u>It is not</u> <u>fair to take the children's food and throw it to the</u> <u>dogs</u>". ²⁷She said, "<u>Certainly, lord,</u> for <u>also the dogs</u> <u>eat from the crumbs</u> that fall from their masters' table". ²⁸Then Jesus answered her, "Woman, great is your faith! Let it be done for you as you wish". And her daughter was healed from that hour.

Mark 9.14-27	Matthew 17.14-18
¹⁴And when they <u>came</u> to the disciples, they saw a great <u>crowd</u> about them, and scribes arguing with them. ¹⁵And immediately all the crowd, when they saw him, were greatly amazed, and ran up to him and greeted him. ¹⁶And he asked them, "What are you discussing with them?" ¹⁷And one of <u>the crowd</u> answered him, "Teacher, I brought <u>my son</u> to you, for he has a dumb spirit; ¹⁸and wherever it grabs <u>him</u>, it dashes him down; and he foams and grinds his teeth and becomes rigid; and I asked <u>your disciples</u> to cast it out, <u>and</u> they were <u>not</u> able."	¹⁴And when they <u>came</u> to the <u>crowd</u>, a <u>man</u> came up to him and kneeling before him said, ¹⁵"Lord, have mercy on <u>my son</u>, for he is an epileptic and he suffers terribly; for often he falls into the fire, and often into the water. ¹⁶And I brought him to <u>your disciples</u>, <u>and</u> they could <u>not</u> heal him."

Mark 9.14-27	Matthew 17.14-18
[19]And he <u>answered</u> them, "<u>O faithless generation, how long am I to be</u> with <u>you</u>? How long am I <u>to put up with you</u>? Bring him to me." [20]And they brought the boy to him; and when the spirit saw him, immediately it convulsed the boy, and he fell on the ground and rolled about, foaming at the mouth. . . . . [25]And when Jesus saw that a crowd came running together, he <u>rebuked</u> the unclean spirit, saying to it, "You dumb and deaf spirit, I command you, come out of him, and never enter him again." [26]And after crying out and convulsing him terribly, it <u>came out</u>, and the boy was like a corpse; so that most of them said, "He is dead." [27]But Jesus took him by the hand and lifted him up, and he arose.	[17]And Jesus <u>answered</u>, "<u>O faithless</u> and perverse <u>generation, how long am I to be</u> with <u>you</u>? How long am I <u>to put up with you</u>? Bring him here to me." [18]And Jesus <u>rebuked</u> him, and the demon <u>came out</u> of him, and the boy was cured from that hour.

Mark 9.33-37	Matthew 18.1-5
[33]Then they came to Capernaum; and when he was in the house he asked them, "What were you arguing about on the way?" [34]But they were silent, for on the way they had argued with one another about <u>who</u> was <u>greater</u>. [35]He sat down, called the twelve, and said to them, "Whoever wants to be first must be last of all and servant of all". [36]Then he took <u>a little child and put it</u> among them; and taking it in his arms, he said to them, [37]"<u>Whoever welcomes one</u> of <u>such little children</u> <u>in my name welcomes me</u>, and whoever welcomes me welcomes not me but the one who sent me".	[1]At that time the disciples came to Jesus and asked, "<u>Who</u> is <u>greater</u> in the kingdom of heaven?" [2]He called <u>a little child, and put it</u> among them, [3]and said, "Truly I tell you, unless you turn and become like little children, you will never enter the kingdom of heaven. [4]Whoever humbles himself like this little child is greater in the kingdom of heaven. [5]And <u>whoever welcomes one</u> <u>such little child in my name welcomes me</u>".

Many of the variations from Mark can, of course, be explained by Matthew's editing of the text as he received it from reading Mark. And I have no doubt that at least some of the variations can be explained by Matthean redaction of the (already) written tradition.[26] But such treatment of the tradition by Matthew should not be regarded as something wholly innovative. Rather, it probably exemplifies the way the tradition was already being handled by other tradents; indeed, Matthew's redaction, like Mark's before him, is

26. In *Jesus Remembered* I cite Matt. 13.58/Mark 6.5 and Matt. 19.16-17/Mark 10.17-18; see further 145 n. 20.

probably best seen as of a piece with the performance variations which were characteristic of the varied use of the tradition in different settings and contexts, and from the first.[27] In other words, whether Matthew was giving his own 'spin' to the tradition, or only recording faithfully a different version, either way his handling or use of the tradition bears witness to the freedom which performers and transmitters of the tradition felt free to exercise in the way they dealt with the tradition. Either way, then, whether the variations between the Markan and Matthean versions are to be explained by Matthew's knowledge of a variant tradition, or by Matthew's freedom in recasting the tradition which he received via Mark, the inference to be drawn is the same: that the material reflects the same but different character of the traditioning process in a predominantly oral society.

IV

A similar picture comes from the so-called Q material in Matthew. Here once more I do not dispute that the closeness of verbal parallel in a fair number of cases is best explained by Matthew's literary dependence on written material.[28] But here once more I have to question whether literary dependence is the best solution to parallel material which is not close. For convenience I draw the following examples solely from one section of Matthew (the Sermon on the Mount) and in the Matthean order but put Luke in the first column, since the Lukan form of the text is usually regarded as more closely reflecting a putative 'original' text on which both Matthew and Luke drew.[29]

Luke 6.29-30	Matthew 5.39b-42
[29]To the one who strikes you on the <u>cheek</u>, offer <u>the other also;</u> and from the one who takes away <u>your</u> <u>cloak</u> do not withhold <u>your</u> <u>tunic also.</u> [30]<u>Give to</u> <u>everyone</u> <u>who asks you; and</u> from the one who takes what is yours, do not ask for it back.	[39b]But whoever hits <u>you</u> <u>on</u> your <u>right</u> <u>cheek</u>, turn to him <u>the other also;</u> [40]and to the one who wants to sue you and take <u>your</u> <u>tunic</u>, let him have <u>your</u> <u>cloak also;</u> [41]and whoever forces you to go one mile, go with him a second. [42]<u>Give to</u> the one <u>who asks you, and</u> do not turn away the one who wants to borrow from you.

27. The oral character of Mark's Gospel has been noted in recent Gospels study, particularly by Joanna Dewey; details and further in *Jesus Remembered*, 202 n. 158.

28. See above n. 24.

29. See of course J. M. Robinson, P. Hoffmann & J. S. Kloppenborg, *The Critical Edition of Q: Synopsis* (Leuven: Peeters, 2000).

Luke 6.27-28, 32-35	Matthew 5.43-47
²⁷But I <u>say to you</u> that listen, <u>Love your enemies</u>, do good to those who hate you, ²⁸bless those who curse you, <u>pray for those who</u> abuse <u>you</u>. . . . . ³²And <u>if you love those who love you</u>, what credit is that to you? For even sinners love those who love them. ³³And if you do good to those who do good to you, what credit is that to you? For <u>even</u> sinners <u>do the same</u>. ³⁴If you lend to those from whom you hope to receive, what credit is that to you? Even sinners lend to sinners, to receive as much again. ³⁵But love your enemies, do good, and lend, expecting nothing in return. Your reward will be great, and you will be children of the Most High; for he is kind to the ungrateful and the wicked.	⁴³You have heard that it was said, "You shall love your neighbour and hate your enemy". ⁴⁴But I <u>say to you,</u> <u>Love your enemies</u> and <u>pray for those who</u> persecute <u>you</u>, ⁴⁵so that you may be sons of your Father in heaven; for he makes his sun rise on the evil and on the good, and sends rain on the righteous and on the unrighteous. ⁴⁶For <u>if you love those who love you</u>, what reward do you have? Do not even the tax collectors do the same? ⁴⁷And if you greet only your brothers, what more are you doing than others? Do not <u>even</u> the Gentiles <u>do the same</u>?

Luke 11.1-4	Matthew 6.7-15

¹He was praying in a certain place, and after he had finished, one of his disciples said to him, "Lord, teach us to pray, as John taught his disciples". ²He said to them, "When you pray, say: <u>Father,</u>
    <u>hallowed be your name.</u>
<u>Your kingdom come.</u>
    ³<u>Give us</u> each <u>day our daily bread.</u> ⁴<u>And forgive us our</u> sins, for <u>we</u> ourselves also <u>forgive</u> everyone in<u>debt</u>ed to us. <u>And do not bring us to the time of trial</u>."
	⁷When you are praying, do not heap up empty phrases as the Gentiles do; for they think that they will be heard because of their many words. ⁸Do not be like them, for your Father knows what you need before you ask him.
	    ⁹Pray then in this way: Our <u>Father</u> who are in heaven, <u>hallowed be your name.</u> ¹⁰<u>Your kingdom come.</u> Your will be done, on earth as it is in heaven. ¹¹<u>Give us</u> to<u>day our daily bread.</u> ¹²<u>And forgive us our</u> debts, as <u>we</u> also have <u>forgiven</u> our <u>debt</u>ors. ¹³<u>And do not bring us to the time of trial</u>, but rescue us from the evil one. ¹⁴For if you forgive others their trespasses, your heavenly Father will also forgive you; ¹⁵but if you do not forgive others, neither will your Father forgive your trespasses.

Luke 12.33-34	Matthew 6.19-21
³³Sell your possessions, and give alms. Make purses for yourselves that do not wear out, an unfailing <u>treasure in</u> the <u>heavens, where</u> no <u>thief</u> comes near and no <u>moth</u>	¹⁹Do not store up for yourselves treasures on earth, where moth and rust consume and where thieves break in and steal; ²⁰but store up for yourselves <u>treasures in heaven, where</u> neither <u>moth</u> nor rust consumes and <u>where thieves</u> do not break in

Luke 13.24	Matthew 7.13-14
destroys. [34]<u>For where your treasure is, there</u> also your heart <u>will be</u> .[24]Strive to <u>enter through the narrow</u> door; for <u>many</u>, I tell you, will try to <u>enter</u> and will not be able.	and steal. [21]<u>For where your treasure is, there</u> <u>will be</u> also your heart. [13]<u>Enter through the narrow</u> gate; for the gate is wide and the road is easy that leads to destruction, and there are <u>many</u> who <u>enter</u> through it. [14]For the gate is narrow and the road is hard that leads to life, and there are few who find it.

Luke 6.46-49	Matthew 7.21, 24-27
[46]Why do you call me "<u>Lord, Lord</u>", and do not <u>do</u> what I tell you? [47]<u>Everyone</u> who comes to me and <u>hears</u> <u>my</u> <u>words</u> <u>and acts on them</u>, I will show you what he is <u>like</u>. [48]He is like a man <u>building</u> a <u>house</u>, who dug deeply and laid the <u>foundation</u> <u>on rock</u>; when a <u>flood</u> arose, the river burst against <u>that house</u> but could not shake it, because it had been well built. [49]But he <u>who hears</u> <u>and does</u> <u>not act</u> is <u>like</u> a man <u>building</u> a <u>house on</u> the ground without a foundation. When the <u>flood</u> burst against it, immediately it <u>fell</u>, and <u>great</u> was the ruin of that house.	[21]Not everyone who says to me "<u>Lord, Lord</u>", will enter the kingdom of heaven, but only the one who <u>does</u> the will of my Father who is in heaven. . . . . [24]<u>Everyone</u> then who <u>hears</u> these <u>my</u> <u>words</u> <u>and acts on them</u> will be <u>like</u> a wise man who <u>built</u> his <u>house</u> <u>on rock</u>. [25]Torrential rain fell, the <u>floods</u> came, and the winds blew and beat on <u>that house</u>, but it did not fall, for it had been <u>founded</u> on rock. [26]And everyone <u>who hears</u> these words of mine <u>and does</u> <u>not act</u> on them will be <u>like</u> a foolish man who <u>built</u> his <u>house on</u> sand. [27]Torrential rain fell, and the <u>floods</u> came, and the winds blew and beat against that house, and it <u>fell</u> — and <u>great</u> was its fall!

Here again an explanation of these variations in terms of Matthean dependence on a written source is less rather than more probable. After all, as the whole history of the Synoptic problem reminds us, the impetus to a hypothesis of literary dependence is precisely the closeness of verbal parallel. Without that degree of parallel, the evidential pressure for literary dependence disappears. And if a modern perspective still finds itself unable to envisage other than literary sources, such evidence as just reviewed pushes us to the ironic conclusion that Matthew did not bother much with the detail of his source and felt entirely free to reformulate the teaching in his own terms — a very 'oral' perspective!

In contrast, all these passages, in my opinion, illustrate well the features which are characteristic of oral tradition — the same substance, but differently expressed, and often with individual points elaborated as the tradent thought appropriate in the circumstances.[30] Of course it is possible to infer that Mat-

---

30. Of course, I do not deny that such features/variations can be and are found in literary forms (the Gospels are all written!). What I question is the *de facto* assumption that the varia-

thew (and/or Luke differently) edited a written text. But as redaction, the differences are regularly so inconsequential that one wonders why a faithful tradent would introduce them in the first place. It is much the more realistic inference to see in such passages the ways in which the Jesus tradition was told and retold, with detail freely varied according to the whim (or inspiration) of the moment as well as (in other instances) to make a theological or pastoral point. And in either case the faithfulness of the tradent is of a quite different order from that of one who attempts to pass on the record of the tradition as accurately as possible. Faithfulness (and we may presuppose a concern to be faithful to the tradition) was faithfulness to the substance; the detail was quite obviously secondary and adaptable to a more effective rendering of the tradition in different tellings of the narrative and different groupings of the teaching. How can one conclude otherwise, given the enduring forms of the Synoptic tradition?

The point is that all this refers to Matthew as well, and to Matthew in particular. Matthew's rendering of the Jesus tradition certainly tells us much about Matthew's own concerns, theological and pastoral, and, no doubt too, something of the community within which and for which Matthew rehearsed the tradition. But it also exemplifies the character of the tradition prior to Matthew's writing it down and the diverse forms and versions by means of which the tradition was utilized, celebrated and transmitted in the communities before Matthew.

V

The final set of examples are the doublets familiar to students of the Synoptic problem. Sir John Hawkins long ago provided a detailed list of these, a total of twenty-two in Matthew.[31] It will be sufficient to list them (see p. 135): all but five are sayings tradition.

At the time when Hawkins made this contribution the question was one of sources, that is, of written sources, as the way of explaining the same but different character of the Synoptic tradition. The obvious answer given by such material to *that* question was that Matthew had been able to draw on two different sources (Mark and Q, as it was becoming known). But when we rephrase the question in terms of the *oral* culture within which the Jesus tra-

---

tions in the Synoptic tradition should be or even have to be explained in terms of literary interdependence.

31. J. C. Hawkins, *Horae Synopticae: Contributions to the Study of the Synoptic Problem* (Oxford: Clarendon, [2]1909) 80-99.

	Matthew A	Matthew B	Parallels
1.	5.29-30	18.8-9	Mk 9.43, 45, 47
2.	5.32	19.9	Lk 16.18; Mk 10.11-12
3.	7.16-18	12.33-35	Lk 6.43-45
4.	10.15	11.24	Lk 10.12
5.	10.22a	24.9b	Mk 13.13a/Lk 21.17
6.	10.22b	24.13	Mk 13.13
7.	10.38	16.24	Lk 14.27; Mk 8.34/Lk 9.23
8.	10.39	16.25	Mk 8.35/Lk 9.24; Lk 17.33
9.	12.39	16.4	Lk 11.29; Mk 8.12
10.	13.12	25.29	Mk 4.25/Lk 8.18; Lk 19.26
11.	17.20	21.21	Lk 17.6; Mk 11.23
12.	19.30	20.16	Mk 10.31; Lk 13.30
13.	20.26-27	23.11	Mk 10.43-44; 9.35
14.	24.42	25.13	Mk 13.35
15.	4.23	9.35	Mk 1.39/Lk 4.44; Mk 6.6b
16.	9.27-31	20.29-34	Mk 10.46-52/Lk 18.35-43
17.	9.32-34	12.22-24	Lk 11.14-15
18.	12.38-39	16.1-2	Lk 11.16; Mk 8.11-12
19.	3.2	4.17	Mk 1.4/Lk 3.3; Mk 1.14-15
20.	3.10	7.19	Lk 3.9
21.	9.13	12.7	
22.	16.19	18.18	

dition was initially shaped and which still provided the social context of Matthew's Gospel, the material invites different answers.

It suggests, first, that much if not most of the Jesus tradition circulated and was known and used in different versions — not just one or two, but in many, perhaps as many as there were churches using it! Such an inference does not open the door to the conclusion that the Jesus tradition took form and content of unlimited diversity; the doublet tradition is itself testimony to tradition being the *same* in subject and emphasis even when *different* in wording and detail.

It suggests, secondly, that much of the duplication of such material was the result of it having duplicate or similar forms and content from a very early period — and probably because there never was a single version of the material.

Perhaps indeed we should see in such material evidence that Jesus gave the same teaching on more than one occasion, so that such differences are the result of the different versions which Jesus *himself* used.[32] After all, what teacher gives his instruction only once? As much today, but still more in the ancient world, teaching involved repetition, driving the same point home in different words, by different examples. In other words, the presupposition that there was a single original version of most of the Jesus tradition, especially the sayings tradition, is *a priori* dubious and undermined by the doublet tradition in particular. And when 'single original version' becomes also single *authentic* version, then a wrong turn has definitely been taken. For it assumes that variations of the 'original' version are less authentic, are corruptions of the one true version. It assumes that the Matthean variations have to be explained as evidence of theological Tendenz and as moving ever further away from the 'original'. But students of oral tradition have long observed that in oral tradition there is no 'original', but only variations on a theme.[33] And this is also the testimony of the doublet tradition: either that Jesus repeated much of his teaching in different versions (so that there never was a single original); or that Jesus' single teaching impacted different hearers in different ways and was remembered in different detail; or that the Jesus tradition was always celebrated and transmitted in the various forms which they still retain within the written Synoptic tradition.

The point once again is that Matthew reflects this vitality and fluidity of the Jesus tradition, and not least in the fact that he was quite content to use the same or similar tradition more than once, reflecting, no doubt, his master in this too. In short, since I hardly need to belabour the point, Matthew opens for us a window into the way the Jesus tradition must have been passed down and used in the years between himself and Jesus, and beyond. And not simply in terms of his knowledge of written sources, as though there were only two streams of Jesus tradition known throughout the Eastern end of the Mediterranean. But rather as evidencing a panorama of Jesus tradition, in wide-ranging oral form and diversity, spread across a wide range of Christian congregations, but retaining the character in form and substance of the impact made by the first tradents and by Jesus himself. It is Matthew as testimony to the living character of the Jesus tradition in these first decades of emerging Christianity that I want to celebrate in this essay.

32. The most obvious examples are the parables of the wedding banquet/great supper (Matt. 22.1-14; Luke 14.15-24) and of the talents/pounds (Matt. 25.14-30; Luke 19.11-27).

33. The point has been brought home most effectively by A. B. Lord, *The Singer of Tales* (Cambridge, MA: Harvard University, 1978); see 'Altering the Default Setting', 153 n. 55 = *New Perspective*, 97 n. 55.

Matthew as Wirkungsgeschichte

*   *   *

I have entitled this essay 'Matthew as *Wirkungsgeschichte*', although it could fairly be said in response that a more appropriate title would be 'Matthew as part of *Wirkungsgeschichte*', that is of the history of the effects of Jesus and of the earliest Jesus tradition. But I stick with the briefer title, in order to make the point that Matthew's Gospel is neither the start nor the end of the process of *Wirkungsgeschichte*, nor is it simply like a stream of tradition frozen in the single 'instant' of composition. The value of the Jesus tradition in Synoptic version is precisely that we can actually see something of the process itself. In the light of the Synoptic parallels we can see Matthew 'in performance', selecting, abbreviating, grouping, polishing, elaborating, giving his own distinctive nuance to the material he had to hand, from oral community tradition and particular written precedents. To reduce that process to one of literary cutting and pasting, copying and redacting, is to restrict our vision and appreciation of the process and to lose sight of the vitality of the Jesus tradition which Matthew's *Wirkungsgeschichte* so vividly represents.

CHAPTER 6

John and the Oral Gospel Tradition

1. Introduction: The Final Form of the Johannine Tradition

In a previous paper on John's Gospel, for a symposium which was also concerned to shed light on the tradition behind the Gospels, I found it necessary to spend all the time in the preliminary task of clarifying the historical context and character of the Fourth Gospel.[1] The reason is obvious: the "primary" context of the material within the Gospel is the Gospel itself. Only when we have understood it within that context will we be able to undertake any systematic study of its earlier forms. If the Evangelist has used his material to address contemporary needs and concerns, and if that usage has shaped and moulded the material in any degree, we need to be aware of these needs and concerns and how they may have shaped the material, in order to make allowance for the Evangelist's redaction and editorial work. Since any attempt to penetrate "below the surface" is a hazardous business, with firm criteria usually lacking, we need to have as many checks and controls as possible in place before we begin, and one of the main checks and controls is a clear perspective on why and how the Evangelist used the material available to him.

I hope I was successful, or as successful as our state of knowledge of the period allows. Certainly I will need to assume the findings of that earlier paper if we are to make any progress on this one! My conclusions, so far as they bear upon our present concern, can be summed up thus.

---

1. "Let John Be John. A Gospel for Its Time", *Das Evangelium und die Evangelien*, ed. P. Stuhlmacher (WUNT 28; Tübingen: Mohr-Siebeck, 1983) pp. 309-39.

(1) John's Gospel was written in the late first century, in a context where the Evangelist was in dialogue with other strands of the Judaism of the period, including apocalyptic and mystical strands, and most polemically with the emerging rabbinic authorities ("the Jews" of 9.22 and elsewhere).

(2) His main concern was to portray Jesus as the embodiment of divine Wisdom, as the one who reveals God in a full and final way, and who therefore has supplemented and shown to be inadequate any other claims to knowledge of God and of heavenly things.

(3) In so doing he has given the christology of his Gospel its characteristic and distinctive emphases, which both develop the christology of the earlier NT writers and reflect the concerns of these dialogues with the other strands of late-first-century Judaism — including, not least, the thoroughgoing portrayal of the Son sent from the Father, conscious of his pre-existence, the talk of the descending-ascending Son of Man, and the profundity of the 'I am' sayings. All this has been put in a framework of signs correlated with often elaborate dialogues and discourses which are both characteristically and distinctively Johannine, and markedly different from the characteristic teaching style of the Synoptics, and which therefore have to be attributed almost entirely to the Evangelist rather than to his tradition, or at least to its earlier forms. This is fairly standard critical evaluation of the Fourth Gospel and I trust I do not need to elaborate it further here.[2] But it can be complemented now by the effective analysis of the literary design of the Gospel by Alan Culpepper, who has succeeded better than most in making us aware of the unity and coherence, in terms of thematic development, spectrum of character and subtle comment, stamped upon the material by the author.[3]

At the same time I pointed out how many roots of this developed tradition are still visible in the Fourth Gospel. For example, geographical details like "Aenon near Salim" (3.23), the pool of Bethzatha (5.2), and "a town called Ephraim" (11.54), serve no discernable theological purpose and can be reckoned as part of the historical reminiscence from which such passages as these

2. This of course is not to deny that the Synoptics are also theological presentations of Jesus, but simply to point up the self-evident fact that John's theological reworking of earlier material is more thoroughgoing and more far-reaching than in the Synoptics. For a popular treatment of John's christology which makes my point more fully see my *The Evidence for Jesus* (London: SCM, 1985) ch. 2.

3. A. Culpepper, *Anatomy of the Fourth Gospel. A Study in Literary Design* (Philadelphia: Fortress, 1983).

developed. The parallel traditions regarding John the Baptist, the calling of the first disciples, the cleansing of the Temple, the healing miracles, the feeding of the five thousand, and the passion narrative overlap to a sufficient degree with their Synoptic counterparts that it would be churlish to deny their historical rootage in the same or very similar earliest memories of Jesus' ministry. And we can see how even the most fully developed christological themes have maintained their earlier shape: the Father and Son is much developed in John, but the much briefer motif in the Synoptics is sufficient to explain where it came from; the pattern of "Son of Man" sayings appearing only on Jesus' lips is maintained by John, even though the characteristic ascending-descending motif is new to him; and even the striking and distinctive "I am" formula can be paralleled by or even traced back to its numinous use in Mark 6.50.

In the light of this the task at the end of that previous paper was to investigate further the actual tradition-history process which led from these earlier traditional elements to the much elaborated treatment of the Fourth Evangelist. Given that we have a reasonably clear appreciation of at least some of the main factors which helped determine the final shape of the tradition, and given too that we can recognize at least some of the points within that tradition from whose beginnings it grew to its present shape, what can we say about the process in between?[4] In terms of the issues confronting this symposium can we say anything about the oral tradition of Jesus' ministry and about the traditioning process, whether oral or literary, which resulted in the Gospel of John?

2. The Beginnings of the Johannine Tradition

Most of the details in the penultimate paragraph of §1 were drawn from C. H. Dodd's masterly study, *Historical Tradition in the Fourth Gospel*.[5] This remains the basic starting point for any discussion of the earliest forms of the Johannine tradition, or of the historical roots from which it grew. It remains unsurpassed in its detail and in the balanced maturity of its judgment. What has followed has in effect, on this subject anyway, merely dotted a few 'i's and crossed a few 't's. Particularly to be mentioned here are the sequence of studies by

4. It will be noted that my concern therefore is not with the issue of the historicity of the Johannine tradition, but with the issue of its earlier forms and the processes by which it reached its present Johannine "shape".

5. Cambridge: Cambridge University Press, 1963.

B. Lindars,[6] and the various attempts to illuminate the stages of the tradition's development and their backgrounds.[7] It will be sufficient for our purposes, therefore, to summarize Dodd's main findings, with a view to providing a starting point for our own analysis.

If we work with a distinction between narratives and sayings, the most important of the positive results of Dodd's analysis for the historical value of the Johannine tradition can be summarized simply and in the sequence of the Gospel itself (page references in brackets).

Narratives:[8]

1.19-21	John the Baptist — dialogue with Jerusalem delegation (256-9, 262-5) (Bailey 9-11)
23, 26-27	John the Baptist — his preaching (251-6)
28	John the Baptist — geographical details (249)
32-34	John the Baptist — descent of dove, heavenly voice (253-6, 259-61)
35-44	The first disciples — complement Synoptics (302-10)
2.1-11	Miracle of wine — parable nucleus(?) (223-8)
12	Transitional passage — Capernaum (235-6)
13-16	Cleansing of Temple — Synoptic parallel (156-62)

---

6. B. Lindars, *Behind the Fourth Gospel* (London: SPCK, 1971); also *John* (NCB; London: Oliphants, 1972) especially pp. 46-54; also "Traditions behind the Fourth Gospel", *L'Évangile de Jean: Sources, rédaction, théologie,* par M. de Jonge (BETL XLIV; Leuven University, 1975) pp. 107-24; also "John and the Synoptic Gospels: A Test Case", *NTS* 27 (1980-81) pp. 287-94; also "Discourse and Tradition: The Use of the Sayings of Jesus in the Discourses of the Fourth Gospel", *JSNT* 13 (1981) pp. 82-101. Note also J. A. T. Robinson, *The Priority of John* (London: SCM, 1985), particularly pp. 300-322.

7. R. E. Brown, *John* (AB 29-30; New York: Doubleday/London: Chapman, 1966, 1971) particularly pp. xxxiv-xxxix; also *The Community of the Beloved Disciple* (London: Chapman, 1979); J. L. Martyn, *History and Theology in the Fourth Gospel* (Nashville: Abingdon, 1968, ²1979); also "Glimpses into the History of the Johannine Community", *The Gospel of John in Christian History* (New York: Paulist, 1978) ch. 3; D. M. Smith, "Johannine Christianity" (1976), *Johannine Christianity. Essays on Its Setting, Sources and Theology* (Columbia: University of South Carolina, 1984) pp. 1-36; K. Wengst, *Bedrängte Gemeinde und verherrlichter Christus. Der historische Ort des Johannesevangeliums als Schlüssel zu seiner Interpretation* (Neukirchen: Neukirchener, 1981); U. C. von Wahlde, *The Johannine Commandments. 1 John and the Struggle for the Johannine Tradition* (New York: Paulist, 1990).

8. I append some references to J. A. Bailey, *The Traditions Common to the Gospels of Luke and John* (NovTSup VII; Leiden: Brill, 1963) who concludes that the many parallels between John and Luke, mostly in the passion narrative, are usually to be explained by John's dependence on Luke.

3.22-23	Transitional passage — geographical details (236, 249)
4.1-3	Transitional passage — geographical details (236-8)
43-45	Transitional passage — geographical details (238-41)
46-49, 51	Healing at Cana — Q parallel (188-95)
5.1-9	Healing at Bethzatha — geographical detail/Synoptic parallel (174-80)
6.1-13	Feeding of 5,000 — Synoptic parallel (199-217)
16-21	Walking on water — Synoptic parallel (196-9)
22-25	Transitional passage — geographical details, Synoptic parallel
29	Request for sign — Synoptic parallel (218-9)
69	Peter's confession (219-20)
7.1-2	Transitional passage — geographical detail (241)
23-24	Healing on Sabbath (332-3)
8.	
9.1-7	Healing at Siloam — Synoptic parallel in form (181-8)
10.	
11.1-44	Raising of Lazarus — some points of parallel (228-32)
54	Transitional passage — geographical details
12.1-8	Anointing at Bethany — Synoptic parallel (162-73) (Bailey 1-8)
12-15	Triumphal entry — OT quotations (152-6) (Bailey 22-7)
13-20	Passion narrative — use of testimonia (31-49)
13.17-20	Passion narrative — broad structure (21-30) (Bailey 29-102)
18.1	Geographical detail
3-5, 10-12	Arrest of Jesus (65-81)
13, 15-16, 18, 20	Trial before Sanhedrin (88-96)
17, 25-27	Peter's denial (83-8)
28a, 33, 37	Trial before Pilate (96-120)
39-40	Jesus or Barabbas (100-101)
19.1-3	The mocking of Jesus (101-3)
16-19, 24b, 25	The crucifixion of Jesus (121-36)
29, 30b	The death of Jesus
38, 40-42	The burial of Jesus (137-9)
20.1-2	The women at the tomb (140-2)
19-20	Appearance of Jesus to the twelve (142-4)

Sayings:[9]

1.15, 29, 30, 36(?)	(269-75)
26-27, 33/Mk 1.8 pars.	(253-6) (Bailey 9-11)
40-42/Mt 16.17-18	(306-9)
51/Mk 14.62	(JATR)
2.10/Lk 5.39	(BL)
18/Mt 12.38-39	(330)
19/Mk 14.58 par.	(89-91)
3.2/Mk 12.14	(328-9)
3, 5/Mt 18.3	(358-9)
8/Mk 4.27	(364-5) (DEA 148)
29/Mk 2.19	(280-7) (DEA 149)
35/Mt 11.27	(JATR)
4.31-34	(325-7)
35-38/Mt 9.37-38 par.	(404-5) (DEA 150)
44/Mk 6.4 par.	(239)
5.19-20a/Mt 11.27	(386n) (DEA 151)
23/Mt 10.40 par.	(BL 116-7)
30/Lk 22.42	(363-4)
6.20/Mk 6.50 par.	(197)
26/Mk 8.11f. pars.	(BL)
30/Mt 12.38-39 par.	(330)
33/Mt 6.11	(333-4)
38/Lk 22.42	(363-4)
51	(58-9)
67-70	(219-21)
7.4/Mk 4.22 par.	(322-5)
8.31-35/Mt 3.8-9 par.	(330-2) (DEA 152)
9.2-5	(185-8)
38-41	(327-8)
10.1-5/Mt 18.12-13	(382-5)
15/Mt 11.27	(359-61)

9. For the sake of completeness I have added in other suggestions culled from RR = R. Riesner, "Jesus as Preacher and Teacher", in H. Wansbrough, ed., *Jesus and the Gospel Tradition* (JSNTSup 64; Sheffield: JSOT, 1991) pp. 185-210; DEA = D. E. Aune, "Oral Tradition and the Aphorisms of Jesus", also in Wansbrough, ed., *Jesus and the Gospel Tradition,* pp. 211-65; BL = B. Lindars, "Traditions"; and JATR = J. A. T. Robinson, *Priority.*

11.9-10	(DEA 153)
12.7-8/Mk 14.6-8 par.	(164-6)
24	(DEA 154)
25/Mk 8.35 pars.	(338-43)
26/Mt 16.24	(352-3)
27(-28)/Lk 22.42(f.)	(69)
47/Lk 9.56 v.l.	(355)
13.13-16/Mt 10.24-25 pars.	(335-8)
17/Lk 11.28, Mt 24.46 par.	(353-4)
20/Mt 10.40 pars.	(343-7)
21/Mk 14.18 par.	(55)
38/Mk 14.30 par.	(55)
14.13-14	(349-52)
15.18/Mk 13.13, Lk 6.22	(408)
20/Lk 21.12 par.	(409)
21/Mk 13.13 pars.	(409)
16.2/Mt 24.9	(409)
21	(DEA 155)
23-24/Mt 7.7 par., 21.22	(349-52)
33/Mt 24.9	(409)
17.2/Mt 28.18	(361-3)
11, 15	(333-4)
25/Mt 11.27	(JATR)
18.20/(Mk 4.21-25)	(RR)
19.	
20.23/Mt 18.18	(347-9)
29/Mt 13.16 par.	(354-5)

Dodd also notes that the discourses contain a number of parables not dissimilar to the more characteristic Synoptic form (3.29; 5.19-20a; 8.35; 10.1-5; 11.9-10; 12.24; 16.21)[10] and three sequences of sayings again closer to the Synoptic pattern (4.31-38; 12.20-26; 13.1-20).[11] In addition, we could note the clustering of earlier sayings material, particularly in 12.25-28, 13.13-17, 20-21 and 15.18-21. And I have already observed in my previous study that several pas-

10. Dodd, *Historical Tradition*, pp. 366-87; see also Lindars, "Traditions", p. 33. Robinson, *Priority*, pp. 319-20, notes 13 or 14 Johannine parables.

11. Dodd, *Historical Tradition*, pp. 388-405.

sages could be ascribed to "the beloved disciple" as the source and validator of these traditions, and therefore to that extent at least probably a historical individual (19.35; 20.2-9; cf. 21.24).[12]

Given the overall striking and sustained contrast between the portrayals of Jesus in the Synoptics on the one hand and in John on the other, these are impressive findings. Even if the argument cannot be sustained (for direct dependence on early historical tradition) in a proportion of the examples cited,[13] nevertheless the overlap with and echo of Synoptic tradition at point after point must indicate a dependence on early tradition and a lack of reworking so that the parallel is still clearly visible. More to the point is Dodd's finding again and again that the overlap or parallel cannot be satisfactorily explained by Johannine dependence on one or another of the Gospels,[14] and is better explained by John's knowledge of Synoptic-like tradition but not of the Synoptic version of it.[15]

We are now in a position to go further into the question of John and the oral Gospel tradition. In the light of our (albeit provisional) grasp now of both the end and the beginnings of the Johannine tradition, of both the final form and its roots in earlier tradition, we can go on to ask what this tells us about the oral forms of the Gospel tradition and about the process of development from such beginnings to the end which John devised. Two points call for particular attention: (1) the degree to which the earliest forms of the historical tradition within John and their Synoptic parallels had already diverged; (2) the degree of freedom-within-limits which the Johannine development displays in relation to these earlier traditions. We will continue to use the simple distinction for purposes of analysis between narratives and sayings.

---

12. Dunn, "John", p. 315.

13. Examples which could be cited include the distinctive Baptist testimony to Christ (1.15, 29, 30, 36), the wine miracle (2.1-11), the opening of ch. 7, and the raising of Lazarus (11).

14. The view however is still maintained quite strongly that John knew at least Mark; see e.g. those cited and discussed by Smith in *Johannine Christianity*, chs. 6 and 7.

15. The significance of the Johannine elements in Papyrus Egerton 2 is unclear: they reflect both Johannine narratives and sayings and suggest a knowledge of the Johannine (and Synoptic) traditions, though not necessarily of the written text; see the evaluation by J. Jeremias in E. Hennecke, W. Schneemelcher, and R. McL. Wilson, *New Testament Apocrypha*, Vol. 1 (London: Lutterworth, 1963) pp. 94-7.

3. The Oral(?) Diversity of the Earliest Traditions of Jesus — the Narratives

What we have in mind here is a diversity in tradition which cannot be attributed solely to the Evangelists' reworking and which must go back to much earlier stages in the traditioning process. So far as narratives are concerned, the most interesting examples are (a) the healing at Cana (4.46-54), (b) the feeding of the five thousand and the walking on the water (6.1-21), and (c) the anointing at Bethany and the triumphal entry (12.1-8, 12-19).

a) The Healing at Cana (4.46-54)

Since the time of Irenaeus,[16] the suggestion has been held as highly plausible that this is a variant version of the story of the centurion's servant/boy in Matt 8.5-13/Luke 7.1-10. Although at first sight the two (the Synoptics' and John's) seem quite distinct, on closer examination the strength of the case becomes increasingly persuasive. Note the following points of contact.

(1) a person of rank (Mt/Lk — centurion; John — *basilikos*),

(2) having heard of Jesus (Luke 7.3a/John 4.47a),

(3) "asked Jesus to come and heal" (Luke 7.3b/John 4.47b)

(4) his boy or close personal servant (all three call him *pais,* but Luke also describes him as *doulos,* and John as *huios* and *paidion*),

(5) who was ill, close to death (Luke 7.2b — *ēmellen teleutan;* John 4.47c — *ēmellen apothnēskein*)

(6) in Capernaum.

(7) Matt and John indicates some hesitancy on Jesus' part (Matt 8.7;[17] John 4.48).

(8) All three emphasize the word of healing (Matt 8.8, 13/Luke 7.7; John 4.50),

(9) and that the healing took place at a distance.

(10) Matt and John note that the healing happened "at that hour" (*ekeinē tē hōra* — Matt 8.13/John 4.53).

(11) Not least of importance is the fact that in all three, but particularly Matthew and John, the principal thematic focus is on the faith of the centurion/official.

16. Irenaeus, *Adv. haer.* 2.22.3 (PG 7.783).

17. Jesus' reply in Matthew should probably be punctuated as a question — "Am I to come and heal him?"

These amount to a very impressive list, which, taken together, are probably too many to be explained as coincidence, either of similar events, or similarly told stories. The stronger probability is that the whole constitute variants of a single original. And since the coincidences are more of substance than of vocabulary, we may deduce that the single original was in oral rather than written form (or indeed a common event witnessed and retold by one or more present on the occasion and able to ratify the effect of Jesus' word subsequently).[18]

In addition we can fairly easily detach the distinctive Johannine emphases introduced in the Johannine reworking/retelling of the story.

(1) 4.47 — the connecting link with the previous material in John. Instead of Luke's "having heard concerning Jesus", John reads, "having heard that Jesus had come from Judea into Galilee". Otherwise the introduction is closely parallel in detail to the Lukan version.

(2) The contrast between inadequate faith (4.48) and a faith rooted in word and confirmed by sign (4.50, 54; cf. e.g. 2.23ff).

(3) The emphasis on the life-giving word of Jesus: most of the otherwise surprisingly extensive conclusion seems designed chiefly to provide occasion for the threefold repetition of the point, "Your son lives" (4.50, 51, 53). Similar redaction analysis can, of course, be applied to the other two versions of the story. Out of the common core of the story (Matt 8.7-10, 13/Luke 7.6-10), Luke has chosen to pick out and emphasize the theme of humility, the centurion's unworthiness/worthiness (Luke 7.4, 6-7) — hence the more elaborate introduction (7.1-5) and the addition of v. 7a. Out of the same core, Matthew has highlighted the theme of faith (Matt 8.10, 13), with vv. 11-12 sandwiched between the two references, so that the centurion can be seen as a paradigm for Gentile faith.

What is interesting for us here is that the common core diverges as much as it does.[19] Two points are particularly notable.

(1) The chief figure of the story (apart from Jesus) is identified differently. In the Synoptics he is a centurion; whether or not this means that he was a Gentile, both Synoptic versions assume this to have been the case and make it the basis of the different elaborations of and lessons they draw from

18. See also the discussion in R. Schnackenburg, *John*, Vol. 1 (HTCNT; London: Burns & Oates, 1968) pp. 471-5; Brown, *John*, pp. 192-3.

19. Cf. E. Haenchen, *Johannesevangelium* (Tübingen: Mohr-Siebeck, 1980): "Das Verhältnis dieser Perikope zur Erzählung Mt 8.5-13/Lk 7.1-10 lehrt, wie stark sich eine Geschichte nicht nur durch die Redaktionsarbeit eines Evangelisten, sondern auch in der mündlichen Überlieferung wandeln kann" (pp. 260-61) — summarising his treatment in "Johanneische Probleme", *Gott und Mensch* (1965) pp. 82-90.

the story.[20] In John he is a member of Herod's court, and probably a Jew, although John makes no effort to exploit the fact. Here we may deduce that in one stream of story telling the implication that the suppliant was a Gentile was deemed important; but in another the exact nature of the person's rank was not thought a matter of importance to be preserved in future retellings. Had we only the Synoptic version we could make a fairly confident historical judgment that the original suppliant thus remembered was a Gentile centurion, surprising (or dubious) though that might be in terms of the historical probability of a Roman centurion being stationed at this time in Capernaum. But when John's version is added to the evidence, we have to conclude: either that the earliest version(s) recalled only a person of rank (in Herod's service?), whom each version (Synoptics' and John's) particularized as was deemed appropriate; or that an/(the) earlier more specific reminiscence of the suppliant's status became more vague in a retelling where the suppliant's status was not integral to the storyteller's[21] thrust. The uncertainty on this point means that we today can have no certainty as to the original suppliant's status.

(2) In Matthew and Luke the common tradition focuses on the dialogue between Jesus and the centurion, and emphasizes the centurion's faith, though containing another emphasis which Luke was able to exploit and develop. In John we do not have that crucial snatch of dialogue, but we do have an equivalent snatch of dialogue which also focuses on the faith of the suppliant, and which also provides occasion for him to express his faith, but which otherwise serves as an occasion for a characteristic Johannine theme. Moreover, Matthew has exploited his version of the suppliant's faith by emphasizing that it preceded and drew forth Jesus' word of healing. In contrast, the faith of the royal retainer in John has to be cajoled and evidently does not become fully effective till he has seen the result of Jesus' life-giving word (4.53). Here again, had we the Synoptics alone, we could be confident that the almost word for word agreement between Matthew and Luke regarding the dialogue between Jesus and the centurion puts us in touch with a first-hand memory of such an exchange in Jesus' ministry. With John's evidence added in, however, the memory appears to have become vaguer (an exchange which served to highlight the suppliant's faith), or at least to have become even more adapt-

20. Since Herod's army was modelled on the Roman pattern, the "centurion" of the Synoptic account could have been a Jew.

21. It should be noted that I do not use "storyteller" as a technical folk-lore term, but simply as a way of referring to those who took it upon themselves or were appointed within the earliest Christian congregations to recall and retell such episodes from the ministry of Jesus within the gatherings, formal or otherwise, of the first congregations.

able than in Matthew and Luke, so as to serve the more characteristic Johannine emphasis the more effectively. That is to say, John attests to the flexibility or vagueness of a traditioning process which we might otherwise have regarded as more stable and fixed at least in such core elements.

Such diversity may well indicate an oral traditioning process, since marks of possible literary interdependence are so slight.[22] There was a story about Jesus healing the boy of a person of rank, in Capernaum, at a distance, which brought out the suppliant's faith. We need not doubt that it was a story which recalled an event of Jesus' ministry in faithful detail, at least to the extent just outlined. But in the retelling of the story, different versions developed and diverged. Matthew and Luke knew one version, where the dialogue between Jesus and the suppliant allowed them to develop further divergent versions. John's tradition picked up another version, which allowed a different identification of the suppliant and a different emphasis on the suppliant's faith. Whether that implies a story recalled after many years, or one worn smoother by much retelling, we cannot say.[23] The point is the degree of divergence already evident behind the earliest forms we can identify.

b) The Feeding of the Five Thousand and the Walking on the Water (6.1-21)

There is no question that these are the same traditions in each of the Gospels — all four for the former, with Luke alone omitting the latter. Given that the same event/tradition is here retold in each case, the striking thing once again is the divergence of the traditions.

In the case of the feeding miracle, there are verbal echoes and parallels in almost every line in the version shared by the Synoptics. As for John, with one exception, the verbal parallels are remarkable by their fewness, amounting to little more than the barest outline of detail without which there would be no story in the first place — "crowd followed" (v. 2), seeing a "great crowd" (v. 5), "buy loaves", "eat" (v. 5), "grass", "sat" (v. 10), and "took the loaves" . . .

---

22. This is not to imply, of course, that use of a literary source cannot be very free.

23. The discussion here is not affected by the issue as to whether the version of the story used by John came to him in a "Signs Source" (see particularly R. Fortna, *The Gospel of Signs: A Reconstruction of the Narrative Source Underlying the Fourth Gospel* [SNTSMS 11; Cambridge University, 1970], here pp. 38-48), since we are concerned with the common tradition which lay behind the material which John used. If, however, John is reacting to the form and emphasis of the story in his source (as at 4.48), then we would have to speak of a further version of the story, though one once again focusing on the suppliant's faith.

gave (v. 11).[24] The interesting exception is that in every case where a number is given, there is precise agreement between all four Gospels — 200 denarii (v. 7), 5 loaves and 2 fish (v. 9), 5,000 men (v. 10), 12 baskets of fragments (v. 13). Such agreement confirms that all four versions go back to a single original (whether story or event).[25] But it would appear that, as between the versions of the Synoptics and John at least, there was no strong desire felt to preserve a standard version of the story. The fixed points seem to have been the numbers; the other details of agreement are mostly contingent on them and would almost inevitably be involved in the unfolding of a story round these details. But this is precisely what we would expect in oral tradition — fixed points of detail which the Christian retelling the story would elaborate in his own words, so that while language and other detail might diverge, and diverge quite markedly (e.g. 6.2b-4; 6.8-9a), the substance of the story remained constant.[26]

With the walking on the water we see something the same. In John's version, the briefest of the three versions, the points of contact at first again seem to be only those without which the story could not have been told — "his disciples" "embarking into a boat" to go "across" the lake (6.16-17), a "wind" (6.18). But then come a couple of close verbal parallels: they see him "walking on the lake" . . . "but he says to them, 'It is I' *(egō eimi)*. Do not fear *(mē phobeisthe)*'" (6.19-20). Finally John ends the story abruptly, with only the phrase "into the boat", but differently used, in common (6.21). Here again we can see what may well be the effect of oral story telling: a constant common core, on which the whole story depends, and from which it can be derived, or by means of which it could be retained; and an elaboration differently to make different points. In Mark's case a quasi-ghost story (Mark 6.48-50) and

24. Cf. the fuller discussion in Brown, *John*, pp. 236-44; Lindars, *John*, pp. 237-8.

25. The case for recognizing behind the feeding miracle a historical event is strengthened by the uncontrived way in which John 6.15 and Mark's surprising use of "compelled" (Mark 6.45) fit together, each giving separate halves of the climax to the occasion which together make a strikingly coherent whole: the crowd enthused by what had happened (whatever it was!), seeking to force a role of military leadership on Jesus; the disciples caught up in the enthusiasm, with Jesus having forcibly to despatch them on to the lake late in the evening, before he could (only then) dismiss the too excited crowd, and retreat into the hills to pray (in the face of some temptation?).

26. The fact that there is a further Synoptic version of the feeding miracle (the feeding of the 4,000 — Mark 8.1-10/Matt 15.32-39), and with a similar but different scatter of overlapping details, but also different numbers, indicates still further diversity in the retelling of this episode, where the fixed point was simply the fact of a feeding miracle itself. There may, of course, be a theological significance in the number of baskets in each of the two feeding miracles: in the first, 12 baskets representing the 12 tribes of Israel, in the second, 7 baskets representing the nations.

an occasion to emphasize the disciples' hardness of heart (6.52). In Matthew's an opportunity to insert an episode about Peter, as the example of little-faith discipleship (Matt 14.28-31), and to round off the story on a note of worship and confession (14.33). In this case John seems to have made little effort to build on to the earlier material: the mention of darkness (John 6.17) to echo his strong light/darkness motif; and probably the *egō eimi* saying because it fitted into and may indeed be the traditional root or inspiration for his whole "I am" christological emphasis. At the same time, he makes no attempt to build a discourse or dialogue out of this miracle, as was his usual practice. The discourse which follows, of course, leapfrogs the walking on the water episode back to the feeding miracle. What we can say, however, is that John's decision to retain the walking on the water episode in conjunction with the feeding miracle must assuredly indicate that these episodes were linked from the beginning.[27] So firmly linked, in fact, that even John, with all his freedom in using miracle traditions to express his "signs" theology, and even though he has no dialogue or discourse to draw out from this episode, found it desirable or necessary to keep the two together. Here, we may say, was another fairly constant element in the tradition, oral and written — the conjunction of these two miracle stories — somewhat similar to the integration in the Synoptics of the raising of Jairus' daughter and the healing of the woman with internal bleeding (Mark 5.21-43 par.).

c) The Anointing at Bethany and the Entry into Jerusalem (12.1-8, 12-19)

The anointing at Bethany is one of the strongest pieces of evidence for those who think John knew and used Mark.[28]

(1) Both set the episode in a house in Bethany (Mark 14.3/John 12.1).

(2) Both use the phrase *murou nardou pistikēs polutimou* — "costly ointment of pure nard" (Mark 14.3/John 12.3).

(3) In both the complaint is made in more or less the same words: "this ointment (could) have been sold for 300 denarii and given to the poor" (Mark 14.5/John 12.5).

(4) Jesus' response is again very close, though the sequence of clauses dif-

---

27. So most commentators.

28. So particularly C. K. Barrett, *The Gospel According to St. John* (London: SPCK, [2]1978), here p. 409; F. Neirynck, *Jean et les Synoptiques: Examen critique de l'exégèse de M.-E. Boismard* (Leuven: Leuven University, 1979).

fers: "Jesus said. 'Let her be . . . for my burial . . . for the poor you have always with you, but me you do not always have'" (Mark 14.6, 7, 8/John 12.7-8).

At one notable point, however, the Johannine version diverges completely from Mark and closely parallels the different story of Luke 7.36-50, at the point where a woman anoints Jesus' feet (in Mark it is Jesus' head which is anointed) and wipes his feet with her hair (Luke 7.38/John 12.3). Further divergences between John and Mark are to be seen in the identification of the householder (Simon the leper — Mark/Matt; Pharisee — Luke; Lazarus — John), in the identification of the woman (unnamed — Matt/Mark; a sinner — Luke; Mary, sister of Lazarus — John), and in the identification of the complainant (the disciples — Matt; "some" — Mark; Simon the Pharisee — Luke; Judas Iscariot, with the added note about him being the group's treasurer and a thief — John).

The proper deduction to be drawn, I would suggest, is not that John knew and used Mark; for John's divergence from Mark at all these places then becomes a puzzle.[29] But rather that we see a further likely example of an oral transmission of tradition, together with the strengths and weaknesses of that process. Its strengths once again are the degree to which it could retain as fixed elements a substantial amount of detail on which the effectiveness of the story hung, and round which a particular retelling could be artistically contrived. In this case the fixed elements as between two versions of the story were substantial, but still only the skeleton of the story — place of happening, the richness of the ointment, the complaint reinforcing the uncalculating generosity of the act, and the climactic saying suggesting a pronouncement story formulated early on.[30] What was not so fixed in the telling was whether it was Jesus' head or feet which were anointed, and who it was who did the anointing (in the near East of the time it was remarkable enough that Jesus should have accepted such an act of devotion from a woman, whoever she was). The conflation at this point of a detail, from what was probably a different event (Luke),[31] with the outline common to Mark and John, is the sort of thing which can be readily envisaged as happening in oral retelling; a confu-

29. So e.g. Lindars, *John*, pp. 412-14, who also notes that "in all the cases of verbal agreement we must seriously reckon with the possibility of assimilation after the Gospels were written, in the process of transcription".

30. In Mark's version the rather compressed ending attested by John has been filled out to an unusually lengthy concluding exhortation by Jesus — Mark 14.6-9.

31. So e.g. those cited by G. R. Beasley-Murray, *John* (Word Biblical Commentary 36; Waco, TX: Word, 1987) p. 206.

sion at literary level is much harder to explain. The other divergent details are likewise best explained as evidence of oral retelling: where the fixed core had not specified particular characters in the story, the implication is that there was some liberty to make plausible identifications as best fitted the occasion or the themes of a more connected teaching/story telling. The tradition bearer/reteller within the community had evidently not been charged to retain such stories as though they were already sacred text, to be passed on by word for word memorization, but rather (s)he served both the demands of the tradition (a living tradition), and the needs of the community (for a word which spoke to the situation), by embroidering these fixed elements of the tradition as occasion invited or dictated.[32]

Similar points can be drawn out with regard to the triumphal entry, and we need not labour the case.[33] The only detail which John shares with the other Gospels is the cry which greeted Jesus, using Ps 118.26 — "Hosanna! Blessed is he who comes in the name of the Lord".[34] In addition, both Matthew and John explicitly cite Zech 9.9 (adapted). But otherwise the details diverge quite markedly.[35] In the Synoptics, the disciples are in primary focus in setting up the entry. In John, by way of contrast, it is the crowds who take the initiative in the shout of praise; Jesus then finds a young donkey himself; and the disciples only appear in a reflective role towards the end, where the distinctive notes of Johannine themes are clear (disciples' misunderstanding clarified by Jesus' "glorification", the crowd "bearing witness", "sign", Lazarus, "the world"). Here again we have evidence of a memory of an event in Jesus' mission which was maintained in the tradition by the combination of common theme (entry into Jerusalem on a donkey at a festival) and single fixed element (the shout of praise using the words from Ps 118.26). But whereas the Synoptics indicate a sequence of literary contacts, and the second half of John's account (12.16-19) indicates an attempt to nest the story within the literary motifs of the Gospel, the other differences between John and the Synoptics are probably better explained in terms of an oral story-telling which allowed just the sort of diverse elaboration as we find between the Synoptics and John.

32. Cf. again Haenchen, *Johannesevangelium*, pp. 434-5.

33. Fuller discussion may be found in Brown, *John*, pp. 459-61.

34. "Hosanna" is not part of Ps 118.26. But since it is the only place where it occurs in the NT, and is common to the accounts of John as well as Matthew and Mark, the implication is that its place was fixed in the tradition precisely in its conjunction with Ps 118.26; it is, of course, repeated in the Mark and Matthew version (Matt 21.9/Mark 11.10).

35. "They differ in every point where it is possible to differ in relating the same incident" (Dodd, *Historical Tradition*, p. 155).

The picture, then, is fairly clear. In John's Gospel we can cite four or five narratives which are probably best explained in terms of an oral traditioning process: (1) episodes which are evidently the same episodes, but so different in detail that a literary interdependence cannot be demonstrated (though, of course, it also cannot be entirely ruled out); (2) the marks of such a traditioning process being a substantial similarity in content and theme, with the story in each case built round certain fixed points — faith in Jesus' word for healing at a distance, the numbers involved, the central encounter, snatches of dialogue, the cry of greeting. In the latter case we could probably say that these are the universal marks of the retold story — substantial continuity of theme and fixed points on which the story and its effects depend, allowing a variety of detail and application as may be deemed appropriate.[36] At all events, the Johannine tradition in the cases examined certainly seems to fit that pattern.

4. The (Oral?) Diversity of the Earliest Traditions of Jesus — the Sayings

So far as the sayings tradition is concerned, the character of the traditioning process is less easy to establish than with the narrative tradition, since in most cases it is an isolated saying which forms the principal evidence.[37] Moreover, the more that parallel sayings diverge, the less easy is it to be confident that they stem from the same original, without the supporting detail which a fuller narrative provides. Nonetheless a number of sayings listed in the table in §2 invite closer examination. I have made no attempt to include all those listed in §2 which could have been considered; the choice is illustrative rather than exhaustive.[38]

(a) 1.27 — "he who comes after me"; "I am not worthy to loose the thongs of his sandal". The first phrase is verbally identical in Matthew and

36. Cf. A. B. Lord, "The Gospels as Oral Traditional Literature", in W. O. Walker, *The Relationships Among the Gospels. An Interdisciplinary Dialogue* (San Antonio: Trinity University, 1978) pp. 37-8.

37. The groups of sayings noted by Dodd (see above pp. 143-4) do not change the basic problem of comparing the Johannine and Synoptic versions, except that they confirm that some of the individual sayings were conveyed in clusters, formed in terms of similarity of theme or as an aid to memory.

38. For example, discussion of 5.19-20a's relation with Matt 11.27 par. would have to be more extensive than is possible in this paper; see further my *Jesus and the Spirit* (London: SCM/Philadelphia: Westminster, 1975) pp. 27-34.

John. The second clause has just the variations, as between a united Synoptic witness and John, which we would expect in two different translations or Greek versions of a common Aramaic original: different synonyms for "worthy", different constructions for the subordinate clause, singular/plural — sandal(s).

(b) 1.26, 33 — "I baptize in water . . . the one who baptizes in the Holy Spirit". The variations as between the Synoptics and John in the first clause could be editorial or could indicate oral diversity (substance constant, wording diverse). The two parts are separated, as in Matthew and Luke. In the second clause John or his tradition has the abbreviated form, as in Mark ("and fire" is missing), adapted to the flow of the Baptist's speech at this point.

(c) 2.18 and 6.30. The tradition recalls a request to Jesus for a sign — doubled in Matthew as well (Matt 12.38; 16.1). Most interesting here is the variety of settings in which the request is recalled. Mark locates his single reference immediately following the feeding of the four thousand (Mark 8.11; as also Matt 16.1), which parallels John 6.30 and suggests a memory of such a demand being put to Jesus in the wake of the incident on which the traditions of the feeding miracle(s) are based. Matthew locates his first reference, like the somewhat parallel Luke 11.29, shortly after the collection of exorcism sayings (Matt 12.25-32/Luke 11.15-26), suggesting another fairly firm setting preserved in the early churches' use of the Jesus tradition. John 2.18's setting within the cleansing of the Temple has no parallel, except to the extent that all three Synoptics report that Jesus was asked for proof of his authority shortly after the Temple incident (Mark 11.27-28 pars.), suggesting that such a juxtaposition was fairly well established within the passion narrative. Otherwise we would have to speak of freedom of editorial usage, betokening the teacher's sense of freedom to incorporate such memories of Jesus' ministry at appropriate points in his teaching, appropriate not least in terms of his own teaching concerns and objectives.

(d) 2.19 is particularly interesting, as when compared with Mark 14.58.

John — *lusate ton naon touton,*
     kai en trisin hēmerais egerō auton
Mark — *egō katalusō ton naon touton . . .*
     kai dia triōn hēmerōn allon . . . oikodomēsō

The wording is so close that it must be judged highly likely that the two forms stem from a common original. What is striking is that whereas Mark attributes the saying to false testimony against Jesus, John has it on Jesus' own lips. We need not pursue the fascinating questions as to how far one or other or both have diverged or been adapted from the original. All that is necessary to be noted here is that Jesus must have been remembered or reported as having said something of the sort, and that whereas Mark has been concerned to deny that Jesus said his version, John has been prepared to affirm and interpret appropriately what he heard as attributed to Jesus. The complications in this and the diverse reasoning of Mark and John surely reflect the pressures operating upon tradition, oral and written, in the public forum and the problems confronting the Christian teachers in the weight they gave to such tradition and the way they used it.

(e) 3.3, 5 is certainly plausible as a variant of Matt 18.3. particularly as it is the only passage in John which echoes the normal kingdom language of the Synoptics.

John —	*amēn amēn legō soi,*	
	ean mē tis	*gennēthē anōthen,*
	ou dunatai	*eiselthein eis tēn basileian . . .*
Matt —	*amēn*	*legō humin,*
	ean mē . . .	*genēsthe hōs ta paidia,*
	ou mē	*eiselthēte eis tēn basileian . . .*

Such a radicalizing of the saying (from "become a child", to "be born again"), which simply serves to reinforce and not at all to alter the point of the saying, may be regarded as a legitimate (responsible and effective) teaching device.

(f) 3.29 looks like an adaptation of the mini-parable of Jesus, in which he likened himself to a bridegroom, or the mood of his ministry to that of a wedding feast, and drew corollaries from this for his disciples (Mark 2.19 pars.). The adaptation makes the same identification (bridegroom), applies it to those with the bridegroom, and makes an equivalent deduction (they should celebrate/rejoice). It should be noted, however, that in John the words appear on the lips of the Baptist.[39] Here again we may see the flexibility of the traditioning process — the use and application of a particular image stemming from and associated with Jesus, but freely adapted to different contexts while making the same point.

(g) 4.35ff. The use of harvest as an encouragement to mission in 4.35ff. is probably drawn from "the same reservoir of tradition" (Dodd) as Matt 9.37-38 par. All the more interesting, therefore, is the fact that Matthew uses it to introduce a mission charge which deliberately excludes a Samaritan mission (Matt 10.5), whereas in John the same imagery is sandwiched between the two

---

39. Lindars, *John*, pp. 168, 283, cites 1.34, 2.10, and 7.4 as parallels.

halves of the description of the woman's testimony to her fellow Samaritans and introduces the report of its success (John 4.39). This somewhat remarkable contrast shows how the same tradition, or the same remembered imagery as coined by Jesus, could be turned to different account in different teaching and ecclesiastical contexts.

(h) 4.44, "Jesus himself testified that a prophet has no honour in his own country", clearly echoes the saying reported in direct speech in the Synoptics (Mark 6.4 pars.). They however all retain it within the rejection at Nazareth episode. John, though retaining it within a Galilean setting, evidently felt no stronger compulsion from the tradition to locate it or attach it more firmly, and used it only in a traditional sequence.

(i) Apart from 6.30 already mentioned, the middle chapters of John are not strong in close parallels. But 12.25, "He who loves his life loses it, and he who hates his life in this world will keep it for eternal life", looks to be a close variant of Mark 8.35 pars., with further variations in Matt 10.39/Luke 17.33 — indicating, probably, a theme of Jesus' teaching remembered and transmitted in slightly varying forms, and adaptable to being used in different catechetical combinations.

(j) 13.20, "Truly, truly, I say to you, he who receives any one whom I send receives me; and he who receives me receives him who sent me", is certainly a variation of a saying which likewise appears in various forms — Mark 9.37 pars., and Matt 10.40, not to mention Luke 10.16 and John 5.23. Whereas Matthew and Luke use it very naturally in a mission context (Matt 10.40 and Luke 10.16), John 13.20 is closer to the setting of Mark 9.37 pars. — a rebuke to the disciples regarding ambition and a false evaluation of greatness. Only John sets it in the context of the last supper, but it was a theme which lent itself to the context of the meal table and menial service (as Mark's resumption of the theme in Mark 10.42-45 indicates). Consequently it is not hard to envisage a teaching theme within the table fellowship of the earliest communities in which such words of Jesus were recalled in a whole sequence of variations according to how the teacher used and reformulated the tradition.

(k and l) 13.21, 38. The verbal closeness of 13.21 with its Synoptic counterpart — *amēn (amēn) legō humin hoti heis ex humōn paradōsei me* (Matt 26.21 = Mark 14.18 = John 13.21) — indicates clearly a motif or remembered utterance of Jesus so deeply rooted in the tradition and so fixed by repeated recollection that the words had become invariable. This is all the more striking when so much of the passion narrative attests a remembering more concerned with substance than detail. The same is almost as true for the memory of Jesus' prediction of Peter's denial in 13.38 (Matt 26.34 = Mark 14.30/Luke 22.34/John 13.38). It is probably significant that it is just these two predictions which are so fixed when most of the other details vary, and may very well suggest that the notes of betrayal and denial were fixed points within the early retelling of the passion, a retelling which followed a similar broad outline and sequence of events, but which otherwise left it to the individual re-teller to put the account into his or her own words. At this point, of course, we should recall the similarly fixed points in the narratives reviewed in §3, particularly John 6.20/Mark 6.50 par. and John 12.7-8/Mark 14.6-8 par.

(m) 20.23. Finally we should note that 20.23 (authority to declare sins forgiven) quite closely parallels in substance Matt 18.18 (power to bind and loose). In both cases a post-resurrection setting is implied (Matthew's context presupposing an established church structure). But whereas Matthew treats it as an in-house ruling to regulate relationships within the community, John gives it a missionary thrust (John 20.21-23).

To sum up, in all these cases we can speak of utterances of Jesus (and others) recollected as such, but used and reused in a wide variety of ways — in a form attributed to Jesus or denied to him (d), in terms unique within John (e), remembered as a word of the Baptist (f), in different and contradictory contexts (g), as an example of repeated themes or emphases in Jesus' teaching (j), as fixed points in larger stories (k, l), and so on. Such diversity reflects teaching situations in the earliest churches where memories of what Jesus said were preserved often with fixed verbal details, but often also as a substance which could be adapted to different contexts — at any rate not as completely set in form and details, far less tightly controlled by a group of formally recognized teachers/apostles, and passed on by word for word memorization.

5. The Johannine Development of Earlier Tradition

Having looked at the beginnings and earliest forms of the tradition which the Fourth Evangelist used, it remains for us to remind ourselves of how extensive his reworking and elaboration of the tradition could be.

(a) *John the Baptist.* We have no reason to doubt that John has drawn on good tradition as the basis of his portrayal of the Baptist (§4 a, b, f). What needs to be noted now is the point made by W. Wink:[40] that John has done a thoroughgoing editorial job in reworking the traditions regarding the Baptist. First, by eliminating all the other emphases in the Baptist tradition — partic-

---

40. W. Wink, *John the Baptist in the Gospel Tradition* (SNTSMS 7; Cambridge: Cambridge University, 1968) pp. 87-106.

ularly his message of repentance (Mark) in the face of coming wrath (Q) —
and focusing everything on his role as witness to Jesus as the Christ. Second,
by greatly expanding and elaborating the Baptist's role as witness (1.6-7, 15, 19-
36; 3.25ff.; 5.31-36; 10.41). In so doing he integrates the portrayal of the Baptist
with his high christology, probably in part as a polemic against a group of
Baptist disciples (hence particularly 1.8-9, 20; 3.28-31), and has the Baptist
speaking in characteristically Johannine language (1.15, 30, 34; 3.27, 31). This
too is an example of how extensively a theme might be elaborated in course of
transmission and use. It is not an arbitrary process, it should be noted: the
Baptist's role as a witness to Jesus was part of the earlier tradition; and that
provides a strong degree of control — as do the still fixed points already
noted. Nevertheless, the Fourth Evangelist presumably shows us how extensive could be the manipulation of such core tradition in the retelling of specific occasions.

(b) *The healing miracles of chs. 5 and 9*, unlike the healing of ch. 4, and
the feeding of the five thousand and the walking on the water in ch. 6, are not
closely paralleled by any specific healing miracles in the Synoptics. Nevertheless, they have typical force — ch. 5 as the healing of a paralyzed man on the
sabbath, and ch. 9 as the healing of a blind man also on the sabbath (9.14, 16).
As such they echo a number of stories of such healings of which there must
have been several recalled regarding or attributed to Jesus during his ministry. To that extent we can speak of stories rooted in the memory of Jesus' ministry.[41] But once again John's use of them shows tremendous creativity. For
John, the miracle of ch. 5 is a further example of Jesus' life-giving ministry
(4.46–5.47),[42] which is finely integrated into a theological exposition of the
Son's continuity with the Father. In providing the occasion for that discourse,
John has quickly shifted the focus of the dispute arising from the episode
away from the issue of sabbath law to that of christology. The same is even
more true of the John 9 miracle, where the fact that it took place on the sabbath has become almost incidental and soon forgotten. In addition, the exposition of J. L. Martyn is widely accepted today, that in these two chapters especially we see the Fourth Evangelist operating on two levels — telling a story
which functions both on the historical level (Jesus' ministry) and on the contemporary (John's time), the blind man in particular being an example of the
adherent to or beneficiary of the Johannine community who is now faced
with the choice between synagogue or church, a both-and solution no longer

41. So also Brown, *John*, p. 379.

42. C. H. Dodd, *The Interpretation of the Fourth Gospel* (Cambridge: Cambridge University, 1953) pp. 318-32.

being possible (9.22).[43] This too was evidently regarded as an acceptable way of retelling a story about Jesus.

(c) *The wine miracle at Cana and the raising of Lazarus.* Dodd includes these in his review, but recognizes the difficulties in so doing.[44] In the former case, since the Johannine motifs are pervasive, Dodd concludes that the pre-canonical form may have to be seen as a Christian symbolical adaptation of a non-Christian tale, though possibly of a parable (of Jesus) of a wedding feast. In the latter case, the best points of contact Dodd can offer are the two raisings of the dead in Luke and Matthew, the widow of Nain's son (Luke 7.11-17) and Jairus's daughter (Matt 9.18-26), and the otherwise surprising outburst of emotion on the part of Jesus in John 11.33 (cf. Mark 1.43; Matt 9.30). Apart from these details, once again the Johannine motifs overwhelm the parallels, and the pivotal position of the episode, as providing the trigger for Jesus' arrest (thus supplanting the Temple incident in the Synoptics), makes its omission (if historical) by the other Evangelists almost incredible.[45] What are we to make of this? — two episodes whose symbolic power in the Fourth Gospel surpasses that of most of the other miracles, and yet whose historical rootage in historical tradition is so slight. There would appear to be a danger here of Johannine elaboration becoming detached from its historical roots and of uncomfortable precedents being set. Perhaps the acceptability of these stories within the Johannine account depended on the fact that they were part of a whole whose overall grounding in historical tradition was much sounder than in these two passages themselves. In contrast, then, to most of the examples documented in §§3 and 4, it would probably be wisest to limit further re-use of them to their servicability in illustrating Johannine themes.

(d) *Elaborations of sayings of Jesus.* In the list of sayings in §2, we noted parallels to John 3.3, 5, 5.19-20a, 10.1-5 and 13.13-16. This suggests the further probability that these elements of common tradition have provided the basis on which the passages, within whose context these sayings are now found, were developed, the core round which these larger treatments were woven. In ch. 3 the radicalizing form of the earlier tradition (§4e) probably provided the source for the new birth dialogue of 3.1-10. In its radicalized form (new birth, not just reversion to childhood), it could also serve as a focal point of the

43. Martyn, *History.*

44. Dodd, *Historical Tradition,* pp. 223-32.

45. Brown, *John,* pp. 428-30, suggests a basic story of a raising of Lazarus of Bethany which may stem from early tradition, but whose positioning and elaboration is the work of the Evangelist. B. Lindars, "Rebuking the Spirit. A New Analysis of the Lazarus Story of John 11", *NTS* 38/1 (1992) pp. 89-104, conjectures that John's story retains traces of a tradition of an exorcism by Jesus (cf. particularly John 11.38, 41-44 with Mark 9.25-29).

much larger "life" motif, announced in the prologue (1.4, 12-13) and so prominent in chs. 4–6. So too the Father-Son imagery of 5.19-20a strongly evokes
the powerful Father-Son imagery of Matt 11.27 par. and the more widely
rooted tradition of Jesus' dependence in prayer on God as abba,[46] and may be
seen as the basis for the fuller exposition of the theme in 5.19-30 in classic Johannine fashion. In a similar way it is plausible to argue that the parable of
10.1-5 is itself an adaptation of the parable of the good shepherd (Matt 18.10-
14/Luke 15.4-7), given christological focus, and in this form able to serve as
the basis of the fuller shepherd/sheep discourse of 10.1-30. So too, given John's
freedom in developing earlier tradition, it is not hard to see 13.1-20 as an elaboration of the motif of lordship and service as illustrated by Jesus himself, as
the earlier tradition had already indicated (Mark 10.42-45/John 13.13-16). It is
not possible to reach a confident verdict that Jesus actually did wash his disciples' feet on the occasion of the last supper: the silence of the Synoptics on
such a powerfully inspirational action points in a different direction; as does
the essentially theological point at the heart of the episode (albeit a minor Johannine theme in just these terms — 13.10-11; 15.3; 1 John 1.7, 9). It would make
better sense of our data if we can assume that John had contrived a symboli-
cally typical expression of the character of Jesus' whole ministry, as reaching
its climax in his own self-giving on the cross (cf. again Mark 10.45). But if that
is the case, we have four further examples of how utterances and motifs well
rooted in the earliest memories of Jesus could be elaborated in subsequent usage in an extensive way, but one which proved quite acceptable to the Johannine community and (subsequently) to the Church at large.

(e) Further elaborations of the Jesus-tradition may be cited in the dia-
logues/discourses of John 4.7-26 and 6.25-58. The former cannot be tied to
any core saying from the earlier tradition (that we know of) with any confidence. That of course does not necessarily imply that there was no such saying, which the Synoptics simply neglected to use. If the material just reviewed
(§5d) is typical, it would seem that the Johannine re-use and re-telling of earlier tradition worked by elaborating earlier, briefer units of tradition into a
richer tapestry of teaching where the nuances of the earlier forms were explored and drawn out — typically by the technique of misunderstanding on
the part of Jesus' auditors providing the occasion for further elaboration. But
it may also be the case that John felt able to develop a whole episode and sequence of teaching on the basis of more fragmentary memories of a mission
in Samaria and the theme of Jesus' teaching and Spirit as replacing the old To-

---

46. See further my *Jesus*, ch. 2; also *Christology in the Making* (London: SCM/Philadel-
phia: Westminster, 1980, [2]1989) pp. 22-33.

rah and cult (cf. §5c).[47] In the case of the great bread of life discourse, the strongest points of contact with earlier tradition are those with the words of institution at the last supper, and their influence is only clear (to the extent that it is so) in the last few verses of the whole discourse. Whereas the whole, so far as it is a whole, is best seen as an exposition of the text, "He gave them bread from heaven to eat" (6.31),[48] which, as such, lacks clear connection with the earlier tradition. In other words, here too we should probably allow for a larger degree of creativity on the part of the Johannine tradition (than in the cases cited under §5d), and should probably draw a similar conclusion as in the cases reviewed in §5c. In view of §5d, it might be possible to formulate a rule of thumb (and one which John himself would probably have accepted): the more removed from the core/earlier Jesus-tradition any re-telling of the Jesus-tradition is, the less should it serve as the basis for further elaboration and the more strictly that re-telling should be read within its primary context (here John's Gospel).

6. Conclusions

It is as impossible to deny that the themes and dialogues of John's Gospel are rooted in earlier tradition, as it is to deny that John's formulation is an elaboration (often considerable) of that tradition. The historical rootage consists of geographical details, particular traditions, broad outline of events (particularly the passion narrative), individual sayings, specific themes or typical events;[49] and while our methodology inevitably depends on demonstration of Synoptic or Synoptic-like parallels, we cannot exclude the possibility that material lacking actual Synoptic parallel was also rooted in historical tradition neglected by the Synoptics. The elaboration seems to reflect the later situation confronting John and/or his community, and to consist principally of typical episodes used for their thematic value, midrashic or meditative elaboration of themes or sayings drawn from the earlier tradition, and all with a focus on the significance of Christ as the revealer of God, which is well in advance of the Synoptic tradition in its degree and consistency of development. The whole, however, is contained within the continuities of the traditioning process and held within the framework of the Gospel structure, as provided

47. In the Synoptics we could compare the birth narratives and the temptation narrative of Matt 4.1-11/Luke 4.1-13.

48. The classic study is P. Borgen, *Bread from Heaven* (Leiden: Brill, 1965).

49. How much is to be attributed specifically to "the beloved disciple" it is impossible now to say.

probably first for the Jesus tradition as a whole by Mark (driving forward to the climax of the passion narrative).

So far as the oral gospel tradition is concerned, we can draw the following conclusions.

(1) Most of the earliest historical tradition within John reveals a degree of variation which makes John's direct dependence on one or more of the Synoptics as such highly unlikely, and which indicates rather a diversity in the traditioning process from the beginning. This finding also highlights an important corollary: the diversity of the tradition need not imply a long sequence of transmission with many links in the chain; the diversity could be the result of each tradition-bearer drawing directly on the earliest forms of various traditions and retelling them with his/her own emphases.

(2) We can speak of a degree of fixity in such tradition — in the broad outline of the narrative or theme of the saying, and often too in particular points in the narrative. This suggests that there were fixed points in the oral tradition process, round which a story or the teaching drawn from such fixed points was constructed in the retelling. Since the fixed points are not necessarily of strong theological significance (e.g. most of the numbers in the feeding miracle), we may further deduce that such fixing of structural elements was simply part of the normal "technique" of oral tradition rather than theologically motivated.

(3) If John's own elaboration of such tradition is any guide, we also have to recognize a considerable degree of freedom permitted to the story-teller or teacher (tradition-passer-on). The extent of the freedom demonstrated by John appears somewhat alarming (and may have been so for many of the earliest Christians prior to Irenaeus's retrieval of the Gospel), but we may presume that in John's eyes it was always under control of the fixed points of the earlier tradition and held within the constraints of the Gospel itself (not least 1.14 and 19.34-35).[50] To that extent John's Gospel is probably best regarded as an example of how elaboration of the Jesus-tradition did (and might) happen, rather than as a basis for further elaboration.

---

50. See further my *Unity and Diversity in the New Testament* (London: SCM, 1977, [2]1990, [3]2006) §64.

CHAPTER 7

John's Gospel and the Oral Gospel Tradition

This paper is part of an ongoing attempt to make sense of the way in which the New Testament Gospels present the mission of Jesus. The starting point is the character of the Synoptic tradition: that each of the first three Gospels tells basically the same story, but with different details, groupings of episodes and teachings, different introductions and conclusions, and often different emphases. Yet it is clearly the same tradition, the same episodes, the same themes and substantive points in the teaching. These differences I have argued elsewhere are not best explained on the theory of literary dependency, in terms of a process best described as copying and editing. That thesis works well for some of the material, but certainly not for the whole body of shared tradition. The better solution I have argued is to recognize that for most of the time between Jesus' own mission and the writing of the earliest Gospel (probably Mark) the Jesus tradition was in oral form, circulating round the early churches, transmitted to new churches, used in regular instruction and worship in these churches.[1] The specialists in oral tradition are largely agreed that a common feature of oral tradition is 'the same yet different', retellings of the same story or teaching but with different details as the story-teller or teacher deemed appropriate in the act of delivery or performance. In the words of Eric Havelock, 'Variability and stability, conservatism and creativity, evanescence and unpredictability all mark the pattern of

---

1. My main thesis is developed in *Christianity in the Making*. Vol. 1. *Jesus Remembered* (Grand Rapids: Eerdmans, 2003); also *A New Perspective on Jesus: What the Quest for the Historical Jesus Missed* (Grand Rapids: Baker Academic/London: SPCK, 2005).

oral transmission' — 'oral principle of "variation within the same".[2] Or as Alan Dundes puts the same point: '"multiple existence" and "variation" [are] the two most salient characteristics of folklore'.[3] What I have always found exciting about this thesis of the Synoptic Gospel tradition as oral tradition is that it helps explain so well why such a high proportion of the Synoptic Jesus tradition has precisely this character of stability and diversity, of the same yet different.

So far as the current volume is concerned, as to the relation between memory and oral performance, I should at once note the three basic premises on which my thesis builds. First, that Jesus made a considerable *impact* on his disciples, an impact which is clear from the Jesus tradition of the Gospels, and which is expressed in greater or less degree in the tradition itself. From the impression made by Jesus, as expressed in the first place by the Synoptic tradition, we are able to discern a clear outline of the mission and person who made that impact. Second, that Jesus was remembered in somewhat diverse ways, as again expressed in 'the same yet different' character of the Synoptic tradition; the shared impact was expressed differently; the shared tradition took different forms in divergent tellings of the same material. Third, the differences of impact and tradition indicate that the remembered past of Jesus was not uniform or learned or repeated in parrot-fashion; the remembered tradition was also moulded tradition, adapted in some measure to the divergent interests of the teacher and community celebrating that memory. I should probably stress the fact that this thesis is not built primarily on theories of memory, but much more directly on the character of the Synoptic Jesus tradition itself. It is because the thesis explains so well the strange character of this Jesus tradition ('the same yet different') that I find it so persuasive.

John's Gospel, however, adds a further dimension or twist to the discussion, and precisely because the formula which so well describes the Synoptic tradition ('the same yet different') does not seem to fit John's Gospel in its relation to the other three New Testament Gospels — 'different' certainly, but in what sense or in what degree 'the same'? On any reckoning the contrast between the first three canonical Gospels and the fourth, the Gospel of John, is striking. It is often summed up and can be typified in the following terms:

---

2. Werner Kelber, *The Oral and the Written Gospel* (Philadelphia: Fortress, 1983) 33, 54; quoting E. A. Havelock, *Preface to Plato* (Cambridge, MA: Belknap Press of Harvard University, 1963) 92, 147, 184, *passim*.

3. *Holy Writ as Oral Lit: The Bible as Folklore* (Lanham: Rowman & Littlefield, 1999) 18-19.

Synoptics	John
Matthew and Luke begin with virgin conception/birth	Begins with incarnation of pre-existent Logos
Jesus goes to Jerusalem only for the last week of his mission; only one Passover mentioned	Jesus is active in Judea for a large part of his mission; mission extends over three Passovers
Jesus speaks little of himself — nothing quite like John's 'I am's'	Jesus speaks much of himself — notably the 'I am' statements
Jesus calls for faith in God	Jesus calls for faith in himself
The central theme of Jesus' preaching is the kingdom of God	The kingdom of God barely features in Jesus' speech
Jesus speaks of repentance and forgiveness quite often	Jesus never speaks of repentance and of forgiveness only in 20.23
Jesus speaks typically in aphorisms and parables	Jesus engages in lengthy dialogues and circuitous discussion
Jesus speaks only occasionally of eternal life	Jesus speaks regularly of eternal life[4]
Strong concern for the poor and sinners	Little concern for the poor and sinners[5]
Jesus is notable for his ministry of exorcism	No exorcisms

Older harmonizing explanations, keen to affirm that John's Gospel is as historical in its presentation as the Synoptics, tried to explain such differences in terms of the different audiences to whom Jesus spoke — for example, the Synoptics recalling Jesus' teaching to the crowds, John recalling Jesus' teaching to his disciples.[6] But as David Friedrich Strauss pointed out long ago,[7] the style of Jesus' speech in John's Gospel is consistent, whether Jesus is depicted as speaking to Nicodemus, or to the woman at the well, or to 'the Jews', or to

---

4. Mark 10.30 pars.; Matt. 25.46; John 3.15-16, 36; 4.14, 36; 5.24, 39; 6.27, 40, 47, 54, (68); 10.28; 12.25, 50; 17.2-3.

5. Texts like Matt.5.3/Luke 6.20; Matt. 11.5/Luke 7.22, and Mark 10.21, 12.42-43 ('the poor'), and Mark 2.15-17 pars. and Matt. 11.19/Luke 7.34 ('sinners') have been sufficient to indicate to most of the last two generations' treatments of the historical Jesus that these were strong concerns of Jesus. John 12.5-8 and 13.29, and 9.16, 24-25, 31 would never have given that impression.

6. Cf. e.g. those referred to in my 'Let John Be John', in P. Stuhlmacher, ed., *Das Evangelium und die Evangelien* (WUNT 28; Tübingen: Mohr Siebeck, 1983) 309-39 (here 314 n. 11); P. N. Anderson, *The Fourth Gospel and the Quest for Jesus* (London: T&T Clark, 2006) 61. More discriminating is C. L. Blomberg, 'The Historical Reliability of John', in R. T. Fortna & T. Thatcher, eds., *Jesus in the Johannine Tradition* (Louisville: Westminster John Knox, 2001) 71-82. The relation of history to theology in John is the main theme of P. N. Anderson, et al., eds., *John, Jesus and History*, Vol. 1: *Critical Appraisals of Critical Views* (Atlanta: SBL Symposium Series 44; 2007).

7. D. F. Strauss, *The Life Critically Examined* (ET 1846; Philadelphia: Fortress, 1972) 384-6.

his disciples. And the style is very similar to that of the Baptist, as indeed to that of 1 John. The inference is inescapable that the style is that of the *Evangelist* or of the Evangelist's tradition, rather than that of *Jesus*.[8]

Given this further dimension of the discussion about how Jesus was remembered by the first Christians, what are the consequences of bringing in John's Gospel for the case I have made for the Synoptic tradition as oral tradition? That is, to be more precise, if the Synoptic tradition provides good evidence of the impact made by Jesus, of the speech forms in which the earliest memories of Jesus were formulated by the immediate disciples of Jesus, and of the way (the groupings, ordering and emphases) in which the Jesus tradition was used and transmitted in the earliest churches, then how do we take best account of the different character of John's Gospel, and how does that different character affect the case for the oral tradition character of the Synoptics? Is John's Gospel not the product of oral tradition? Is John's Gospel also *remembering* Jesus? Does it indicate that the oral tradition thesis is inadequate to explain the way Jesus was remembered and the way the Jesus tradition was celebrated and passed on? The potential corollaries are of major significance for our understanding of how the Gospel tradition reached the state in which we still have it, for our understanding of the function of the Jesus tradition, and for our understanding of how and why Jesus was remembered.

1. The Gospel Format

The first thing which should be said is that *the differences between John's Gospel and the Synoptic Gospels should not be exaggerated.* John's Gospel is a *Gospel* in the sense and format of the other three canonical Gospels. That is to say, it begins its account of Jesus' mission with John the Baptist and climaxes with Jesus' passion and resurrection. It recognizes that there is a story to be told, with a clear beginning, a development charting the actions and teaching of Jesus with his disciples, and a climactic conclusion. Its very form defines this as 'Gospel', that John the Baptist is the beginning of the Gospel, that integral to the Gospel is the story of how Jesus both lived and taught his mission as witnessed by his disciples, and that the Gospel story drives towards the culmination of Jesus' death and resurrection.[9]

---

8. As Anderson recognizes (*Fourth Gospel*, 58-9). See further J. Verheyden, 'The De-Johannification of Jesus: The Revisionist Contribution of Some Nineteenth-Century German Scholarship', in Anderson et al., eds., *John, Jesus and History*, Vol. 1, 109-20.

9. The narrative and structural parallels are listed in my 'John and the Oral Gospel Tradition', in H. Wansbrough, ed., *Jesus and the Oral Gospel Tradition* (JSNTSup 64; Sheffield: JSOT, 1991) 351-70 (here 355-6), reprinted above 138-63. See also Anderson, *Fourth Gospel*, 129-30.

Now the evidence suggests that it was Paul, the earliest Christian writer known to us, who baptized the noun 'gospel' *(euangelion)* into Christian vocabulary,[10] Paul who made 'gospel' the term which summed up the earliest kerygmatic and catechetical tradition of the first Christians. In so doing, Paul was no doubt conscious of the wider usage of the term, particularly of the good news of the *pax Romana* established by Augustus.[11] But it is more likely that Paul was still more conscious of the Isaianic vision of one who would 'preach the good news' *(euangelizesthai),*[12] on which he himself drew in Rom. 10.15, and which had also memorably inspired Jesus' own mission.[13] The fact that the earliest of the four canonical Gospels (Mark) uses the same word in his opening sentence — 'The beginning of the *euangelion* of Jesus Christ . . .' (Mark 1.1) — is very striking. For he uses it in a way which equally suggests that the term was already shifting from the *content* of what he was about to narrate, to the character of the *narration* itself.[14] What he was writing was not simply conveying the gospel, but was Gospel itself. As in Paul's usage we see *euangelion* emerging as a Christian technical term for the message preached by apostles and evangelists, so with Mark's usage we see the emergence of the idea of the Gospel as a *written document.* Which also suggests that it was Mark, or the tradition on which he already drew, who framed the character of a 'Gospel', the definitive form of the Christian Gospel — that is, as we have already noted, as an account of Jesus' mission, beginning with John the Baptist and climaxing in his death and resurrection.

We should also note that at precisely this point John's Gospel also diverges from the other documents referred to and now commonly described as 'Gospel', the Gospel of Thomas, the Gospel of Philip, the Gospel of Judas, etc. Although they contain what purports to be teaching of Jesus, they have none of the characteristics which attracted the title 'gospel' (the good news of Jesus' death and resurrection) and which gave a 'Gospel' its definitive shape — an account beginning with the Baptist, a narrative within which Jesus' action and teaching were set, and which climaxed in Jesus' passion. *For*

10. No less than 60 out of the 76 occurrences of the term appear in the Pauline letters.

11. For bibliography see my *Beginning from Jerusalem* (Grand Rapids: Eerdmans, 2008) §29 at n. 120.

12. Particularly Isa. 40.9; 52.7; 60.6; 61.1.

13. Matt. 11.5/Luke 7.22; Luke 4.16-21; cf. Luke 6.20/Matt. 5.3. See further my *The Theology of Paul the Apostle* (Grand Rapids: Eerdmans, 1998) 164-9.

14. See particularly R. Guelich, 'The Gospel Genre', in P. Stuhlmacher, ed., *Das Evangelium und die Evangelien* (WUNT 28; Tübingen: Mohr Siebeck, 1983) 183-219 (here 204-16). See also R. A. Burridge, *What Are the Gospels? A Comparison with Graeco-Roman Biography* (Grand Rapids: Eerdmans, ²2004) 186-9.

*all the freedom it displays in the presentation of Jesus and despite all its differ-
ences from the Synoptics, John's Gospel is far closer to them than to the apocryphal Gospels.* From all this we may deduce that John's Gospel, or the Johannine tradition on which John's Gospel is based, stood well within the main
stream of tradition, which summed up the good news of Jesus as 'gospel' and
which followed Mark's definitive expression of a written Gospel. The apocryphal Gospels, in contrast, evidence a different way in which the influence
of Jesus was envisaged, a way that diverged, it would appear, increasingly
from mainstream Christianity, even a mainstream broad enough to include
John's Gospel.

The relevance of this to our question about the relation of John's Gospel to the oral Jesus tradition is fairly obvious. For Paul's formulation of the
story of Jesus as 'gospel' belongs to the first decade or two of Christianity's
existence. And the tradition on which Luke draws to formulate the preaching to the Gentile centurion Cornelius in Acts 10.34-43, already contains
what was to become the Markan pattern of Gospel — beginning with John
the Baptist, an account of his healing ministry (with a preceding reference
to preaching the good news of peace through Jesus), and the climax of his
death and resurrection.[15] Since Paul's formulation of the Christian message
as 'gospel' took place during the period while the Jesus tradition was still
predominantly in oral form, and since the Acts 10 tradition also harks back
to the period of oral tradition, we may infer that *the shaping of the Jesus tradition as 'gospel', and in the shape that Mark provided (or indicated), was already taking place during that period when the Jesus tradition was still being
told in oral form.* So long as we avoid the unjustified and misleading impression that the Jesus tradition existed orally only in fragmentary aphoristic forms or small collections of teaching material or of stories about Jesus,[16] then it becomes entirely plausible that the earliest tradents regularly
retold the Jesus tradition conscious of the Gospel shape of the material as a
whole and often providing mini-Gospel presentations, as are still evident in
the Acts 10 tradition, perhaps also in Mark 2.1–3.6, as well as in the passion
narrative.[17]

In short, the Gospel-shape of John's material already attests the influence of the oral Jesus tradition on John's Gospel and perhaps the direct de-

15. See further my *Beginning from Jerusalem* §21.3c.

16. One of the key mistakes made by the Jesus Seminar; see *Jesus Remembered*, 245-8.

17. C. H. Dodd, *Historical Tradition in the Fourth Gospel* (Cambridge: Cambridge University, 1963) suggested that the transitional passages and topographical notices in John were
'traditional data summarizing periods in the ministry of Jesus, with indications of the places
where they were spent' (243).

pendence of John's Gospel on such tradition.[18] What I am referring to will become clearer as we proceed.

2. The John the Baptist Tradition as the Beginning of the Gospel

Each of the Evangelists fills out the same Gospel framework in his own way. In so doing they provide many fascinating parallels — fascinating because they are parallel, versions of the same or similar tradition, but diverse in their detail and function within each Gospel. One of these is the common starting point — the John the Baptist tradition as the beginning of the Gospel, where I begin my closer examination of the shared and the distinctive traditions.[19]

The shared tradition is clear:

- that the mission of Jesus' immediate predecessor was characterized by a (once-only) baptism (Mark 1.4 pars.), that he was known as 'the Baptizer' or 'the Baptist',[20] and that he practised his mission of baptizing in the Jordan river (Mark 1.5, 9; Matt. 3.5-6, 13; Luke 3.3; John 1.28);
- clearly stated or implied is the success of the Baptist's mission in attracting so many to be baptized (Mark 1.5/Matt. 3.5; Luke 3.21; cf. John 1.19-25; 3.25);
- the quotation from Isa. 40.3 — the Baptist identified as 'the voice crying out in the wilderness; make straight the way of the Lord' (John 1.23; Mark 1.3; Matt.3.3/Luke 3.4);[21]
- the contrast made by the Baptist between his own status and that of the one to come — 'I am not worthy to untie the thong of his sandal' (John 1.27; Mark 1.7; Luke 3.16; Matt. 3.11);[22]

18. Anderson argues that Luke and Q were able to draw on Johannine oral tradition (*Fourth Gospel*, 102, 113-4, 117-9, 134-5). I would prefer to speak of a widespread shared oral Jesus tradition, before it gained its distinctive Markan, Matthean, Lukan and Johannine characteristics. See further R. Kysar, 'The Dehistoricizing of the Gospel of John', in Anderson et al., eds., *John, Jesus and History*, Vol. 1, 75-101 (here 89-92), who refers also to Barnabas Lindars and Raymond Brown, and who criticizes Anderson's thesis as entailing 'an enormous amount of speculation and conjecture' (92).

19. See also Dodd, *Historical Tradition*, 248-78.

20. *ho baptizōn* — Mark 6.14; cf. 1.4; *ho baptistēs* — Matt. 3.1; 11.11-12; etc.; Mark 6.25; 8.28; Luke 7.20, 33; 9.19); see further *Jesus Remembered*, 355-7.

21. Mark gives the quotation a headline role, combined with Ex. 23.20; Luke extends the quotation (Isa. 40.3-5, presumably to round it off with the reference to 'the salvation of God' (Luke 3.4-6); John abbreviates the Isa. 40.3 quotation, combining the last two lines in one (John 1.23).

22. The variations are typical of oral variation in retelling the same tradition: John uses

- the Baptist's contrast between his own mission of baptizing in water and the coming one's baptizing in Holy Spirit (John 1.26, 33; Matt. 3.11/Luke 3.16; Mark 1.8);[23]
- that Jesus was baptized by the Baptist is taken for granted, though John does not actually say so explicitly, whereas the event is described by the others (John 1.31; Mark 1.9 pars.);
- all four are clear that the central and climactic event of the encounter between the Baptist and Jesus is that the Holy Spirit descended 'like a dove' upon him (John 1.32-33; Mark 1.10 pars.);[24] this is the real beginning of the gospel (cf. Acts 10.38);
- the descent of the Spirit is tied in to Jesus' status as the Son of God — in the Synoptics by the declaration of the heavenly voice which accompanied the descent of the Spirit ('You are my son, the beloved one, with you I am well pleased' — Mark 1.11 pars.), in John by the Baptist's testimony that because he saw the Spirit descending and remaining on Jesus, therefore he could 'bear witness that this man is the Son of God' (John 1.34).

There can be little doubt that all four Evangelists were drawing on the same tradition — the memory of Jesus' first disciples that his mission emerged out of the successful mission of the Baptist and from what happened at the Jordan when Jesus was baptized by the Baptist, that is with the descent of the Holy Spirit on him, confirming his status as God's Son. Almost the only part of the Baptist's teaching recalled by all four Evangelists is the Baptist's contrast between his own baptizing in water and the coming one's baptizing in the Spirit, which strongly suggests that their consciousness of having been

---

axios ('worthy', while the others use *hikanos* ('qualified/competent'); in Matthew's version the Baptist says 'I am not qualified/competent to *carry* his sandals'; John has singular 'sandal', while the others have the plural ('sandals').

23. In Matthew the Baptist baptizes with water 'for/into repentance' (Matt. 3.11); Matthew/Luke have the Baptist predicting that the one to come will baptize in Holy Spirit *and fire* (Matt. 3.11/Luke 3.16), whereas Mark and John have the Baptist speaking only of baptizing in Holy Spirit (Mark 1.8; John 1.33); the Synoptics predict that the one to come 'will baptize in Holy Spirit', whereas John has it as a defining characteristic of the one to come — 'the one who baptizes in the Holy Spirit' (John 1.33).

24. Mark indicates that the Spirit descended 'into' Jesus (Mark 1.10), whereas Matthew/Luke describe the Spirit descending 'upon' Jesus (Matt. 3.16/Luke 3.22), and John emphasizes that 'the Spirit descended and remained on him' (John 1.33); Mark also gives the event an apocalyptic character — the heavens split *(schizomenous)*; Luke notes that the Spirit descended while Jesus was praying (Luke 3.21); and John has the Baptist admitting that he did not know him until the Spirit descended upon him (John 1.33).

given the Spirit was one of the self-defining characteristics of the early Christians across the range of churches represented by the four Gospels, a claim to being the beneficiaries of the promised baptism in Spirit predicted by the Baptist. Both emphases, that Jesus' mission began with the Spirit's descent on him after he had been baptized by the Baptist, and that the first Christians were those who were experiencing the Spirit directly for themselves, explain why the great body of earliest Christians had to begin their account of the Gospel with the preaching and mission of the Baptist. We can take it for granted that this memory and this basic story were integral to the oral tradition of the first disciples and churches from the first.

At the same time, an equally striking feature is the different emphases that have been drawn from the Baptist tradition. I note the most obvious of the distinctive features.

- For the Synoptics a central and defining feature of the Baptist's preaching and mission was his call for *repentance* (Matt. 3.2; Matt. 3.8/Luke 3.8); his baptism was 'a baptism of repentance' (Mark 1.4; Luke 3.3; Acts 13.24; 19.4; cf. Matt. 3.11); John, in contrast never uses the terms 'repent' and 'repentance'.
- Whereas Mark and Luke do not hesitate to describe the Baptist's baptism as a 'baptism of repentance for the forgiveness of sins' (Mark 1.4; Luke 3.3), Matthew speaks of the Baptist's baptism only as a baptism 'into repentance' and does not speak here of 'the forgiveness of sins' (Matt. 3.11);[25] whereas John again never uses the noun denoting 'forgiveness'.
- Both Matthew and Luke retain a strong account of the Baptist's judgmental preaching, an account which is so verbally identical that it could come only from a shared source, already in Greek and probably already written, usually described as Q tradition (Matt. 3.7-10, 12/Luke 3.7-9, 17). Luke also has a unique passage on the Baptist's ethical teaching (Luke 3.10-14).
- Mark in contrast has no note of judgment; the 'fire' which features so strongly in the Q version (Matt. 3.10-12/Luke 3.9, 16-17) is entirely lacking in Mark — the one to come will baptize in Holy Spirit, not in Holy Spirit and fire (Mark 1.8). This is usually explained by the fact that what was regarded as the fulfilment of the Baptist's prediction was only in terms of an endowing with the Spirit (classically expressed in the ac-

---

25. Matthew uniquely inserts the same phrase in Matt. 26.28 — 'This is my blood of the covenant which is poured out for many for the forgiveness of sins' — perhaps because Matthew wanted to link (or limit) the forgiveness of sins to Jesus' sacrificial death.

count of the day of Pentecost — Acts 2), so there was little need to recall the fuller preaching of the Baptist.

- Matthew reflects an obvious embarrassment in some Christian circles that Jesus had undergone a baptism 'of repentance', in that he has the Baptist protesting against the request that Jesus should receive the Baptist's baptism (Matt. 3.13-15).
- John in effect meets a similar challenge by focusing almost exclusively on the Baptist's role as a *witness* to Jesus (already signalled in John 1.6-8):[26]
  - the contrast between the Baptist and Jesus is heightened (already in 1.15; also 1.30, and elaborated in 3.27-36);
  - the Baptist makes a triple confession ('he confessed and did not deny it, but confessed' — 1.20) that he was not the Messiah, not even Elijah or the prophet (1.20-21);
  - he attests of Jesus that he is 'the Lamb of God who takes away the sin of the world' (1.29, 36), already foreshadowing Jesus' passion;
  - he emphasizes that the main, or indeed only purpose of his mission, was to reveal Jesus to Israel, his true status as the Son of God (1.31, 34).

It is fascinating, then, to see how the same basic tradition was and could be retold and elaborated, or curtailed, to bring out the different emphases that the Evangelists wanted brought out, or indeed, emphases which had already become familiar in the use made of the Baptist tradition in their churches or in the tradition on which they drew. Nothing tells against this already happening during the time when the Jesus tradition was almost entirely in oral mode. To be sure, John's use of the tradition suggests that he was consciously combating what he regarded as a too high evaluation of the Baptist.[27] Hence, we may deduce, the sustained downgrading of the Baptist in relation to Jesus: he was not the light but came only to testify to the light (1.6-7, 31); the Messiah always ranked before him (1.15, 30); he was not the Messiah, as he himself triply confessed (1.20; 3.28); he had to decrease while Jesus increased (3.30); he came from the earth, whereas Jesus came from above, from heaven (3.31). This we should note comes in typical Johannine language, so we can certainly speak of the Johannine elaboration of the earlier tradition, whether that elaboration is to be traced to the Evangelist himself or to the (elaborated) traditions on which he drew. But we should also note that *the distinctive Jo-*

26. The point was made very effectively by W. Wink, *John the Baptist in the Gospel Tradition* (SNTSMS 7; Cambridge: Cambridge University, 1968) 87-106.

27. This is an old hypothesis usually traced back to W. Baldensperger, *Der Prolog des vierten. Evangeliums: sein polemisch-apologetischer Zweck* (Tübingen: Mohr, 1898); see also e.g. R. E. Brown, *The Gospel according to John* (AB 29, 2 vols.; New York: Doubleday, 1966) lxviii-lxx.

hannine emphasis is rooted in the earlier tradition — of the Baptist speaking of the one to come as of a far higher status than his own ('I am not worthy to untie the thong of his sandals' — Mark 1.7 pars.).

The Johannine version of the Baptist tradition can thus be seen as a good example of a tradition deeply rooted in the memory of the first disciples, a tradition which was retold in different ways, all drawn from the earliest memories, some abbreviating the traditions selectively, presumably in order that the tradition might speak more meaningfully to the new audiences, some elaborating the traditions, but as an elaboration of early emphases rather than as an invention and insertion of entirely new emphases. *The elaboration created new material, but only to reinforce the earlier emphasis,* perhaps against a new challenging evaluation of the Baptist's mission. John's version of the Baptist tradition, therefore, illustrates both the fixity and core material in the Baptist tradition, and the way in which key elements in that tradition could be developed and retold in unexpected ways as the language and needs of the Johannine churches changed.

3. The Body of the Narrative

As already indicated each of the Evangelists fills out the same Gospel framework in his own way. It is easy to conclude from a superficial comparison of John's Gospel with the Synoptic Gospels that John's structure is wholly distinctive and different from the Synoptics. In fact, however, each Evangelist draws on shared tradition in his own way to make his own points.

Mark sets out a fast-moving tale, marked by his repeated use of the historic present and 'immediately'. He jumps straight from Jesus' anointing by the Spirit at Jordan and his forty-day period of temptation to Jesus' entry into Galilee subsequent to the Baptist's arrest (1.14). This already suggests that his intention was to focus more or less exclusively on Jesus' Galilean ministry (1.14-15); and the deliberate note that Jesus (in effect) only began his mission 'after John was arrested' (1.14) probably also indicates that he was aware that he was omitting the earlier period when Jesus' mission overlapped with the Baptist's.[28] It was one of Mark's ways of emphasizing the difference between Jesus and the Baptist. Mark also characterizes Jesus' preaching as summed up by reference to the kingdom of God (1.14-15), and emphasizes both Jesus' healing and exorcistic ministry, and Jesus' role as a teacher,[29] though he does

28. See below §4a.
29. 'Kingdom of God' — Mark 1.15; 4.11, 26, 30; 9.1, 47; 10.14, 15, 23, 24, 25; 12.34; 14.25; 'teacher' — Mark 4.38; 5.35; 9.17, 38; 10.17, 20, 35; 12.14, 19, 32; 13.1.

not draw on the tradition of Jesus' teaching as much as the others. The description of his Gospel as a passion narrative with an extended introduction[30] catches well the way Mark foreshadows the climax with hints and allusions from early on (2.20; 3.6), and with the thumping repetition of the passion predictions, of the suffering and resurrection of the Son of Man, in 8.31, 9.31 and 10.33-34. The slowness of Jesus' disciples to understand what Jesus was about[31] is also a reminder that Jesus' mission only makes full (Gospel) sense in the light of that climax.

Matthew and Luke both preface their accounts of Jesus' mission with birth narratives (Matt. 1–2/Luke 1–2), but otherwise use the same framework for the mission itself — following Mark in focussing on Jesus' Galilean mission, separated in time and region from the Baptist's mission (Matt. 4.12; Luke 4.14), emphasizing Jesus' message as focussing on the kingdom of God,[32] also his diverse ministry of miracle, and likewise building up to the climax of the passion narrative in Jerusalem. Matthew orders the insertion of a good deal more teaching material (Q) by presenting it in five blocks (starting with the Sermon on the Mount), probably as an echo and reflection of the five books of Moses.[33] Luke provides an elaborated version of Jesus' preaching in the synagogue of Nazareth as the 'lead story' which sets the tone for what is to follow (4.16-30), and organizes his fuller supply of Jesus tradition by setting a good deal of it in a much lengthier travel journey from Galilee to Jerusalem (9.51–19.28).[34]

John's treatment of the main sequence of Jesus' mission, however, is quite distinctive. I focus here on three aspects.

a) The Beginning of Jesus' Own Mission (John 1–3)

John seems to have been able to draw on tradition which the others had either set to one side or did not know about. He does not hesitate to include reference to a period prior to the Baptist's imprisonment (3.24), during which Je-

---

30. M. Kähler, *The So-called Historical Jesus and the Historic Biblical Christ* (1896; ET Philadelphia: Fortress, 1964) 80 n. 11.

31. See e.g. U. Schnelle, *The History and Theology of the New Testament Writings* (ET London: SCM, 1998) 212.

32. 'Kingdom' — Matthew and Luke have 9 references in common (Q), and a further 28 references distinctive of Matthew and a further 12 references distinctive of Luke.

33. A common view made more persuasive by the repeated conclusion to the collected sequence of Jesus' teaching, 'When Jesus finished these words' (7.28; 11.1; 13.53; 19.1; 26.1), though it leaves out ch. 23!

34. See particularly D. P. Moessner, *Lord of the Banquet: The Literary and Theological Significance of the Lukan Travel Narrative* (Minneapolis: Fortress, 1989).

sus' mission overlapped with the Baptist's (John 3.22-36) and was apparently of the same character as the Baptist's (3.22-26), though John takes care to deny that Jesus himself practised baptism (4.2).[35] This tradition almost certainly goes back to the first disciples, since it includes the detail that *some of Jesus' own key disciples had earlier been the Baptist's disciples* (1.35-42).[36] Neither detail nor emphasis was likely to have been invented given the degree of embarrassment indicated elsewhere in the Jesus tradition over the extent to which Jesus could be counted as himself a disciple of the Baptist.[37] Also to be noted is that the emphasis on the kingdom of God has gone — the only echo of Synoptic-type talk of the kingdom, curiously, coming during the overlap with the Baptist (3.5).[38] Since for John, the Baptist was such an effective witness of Jesus, the difference between them in style of mission did not need to be highlighted so much, or at least in the same way.

The outcome for our particular inquiry is that once again we see firm evidence of how the oral Jesus (and Baptist) tradition could be and was handled:

- by omitting a not unimportant aspect of the tradition in order to prevent any confusion between the two missions and to highlight the distinctiveness of Jesus' mission;
- or by focussing the retold tradition on the Baptist's witness-bearing to and inferior significance to that of Jesus.

The fact that the Synoptic tradition ignored or suppressed the overlap period, of course, makes it difficult for us to evaluate the Johannine tradition in the usual way (by comparing John's version with that of the Synoptics). But we can be sufficiently confident that *the Johannine tradition too goes back to the first disciples,* and indeed, in this case, *has retained a clearer memory of the overlap period than we could have deduced from the Synoptic tradition.* A simple uniform rule that the Synoptic tradition is always more reliable than John's is immediately ruled out.[39] John's version of the beginning of Jesus'

35. A. T. Lincoln, '"We Know That His Testimony Is True": Johannine Truth Claims and Historicity', in Anderson et al., eds., *John, Jesus and History,* Vol. 1, 179-97 suggests that there may be 'slightly fewer difficulties' with the hypothesis 'that the discussion of Jesus baptizing is the result of the creativity of the Fourth Evangelist or his tradition' (187-91).

36. See also Dodd, *Historical Tradition,* 279-87, 302-5.

37. Note again particularly Matt. 3.14-15.

38. Though we should not assume that the sequence John 2–3 is in chronological order; see below §4b.

39. On this point certainly Anderson's protest against the 'de-historicization of John' and the 'de-Johannification of Jesus' is valid (*Fourth Gospel,* 2).

mission is itself an example of how the memory of that overlap was handled in at least one strand of earliest Christianity or some churches.

b) The Frame of Jesus' Mission in John

The Synoptics frame the body of Jesus' mission in a consistent way. The first frame is given by the temptation of Jesus and the entry into mission in Galilee (Mark 1.12-15 pars.); Luke also brings forwards a filled-out version of Jesus' preaching in the synagogue of Nazareth to provide a window into the character of Jesus' mission which Luke wanted to highlight (Luke 4.16-30). At the other end, the mission is rounded off with the entry into Jerusalem and the cleansing of the Temple (Mark 11.1-17 pars.), which point forward to the arrest and accusations against Jesus in the hearing before Caiaphas (Mark 14.53-65 pars.) The implication is clear that it was Jesus' symbolic act against the Temple (11.12-14, 15-17) and what Jesus had said (or was reputed to have said) about the temple's destruction, which triggered the decision to act against Jesus and gave some substance to the (false) accusations levelled against Jesus (14.55-58).[40]

John's Gospel uses quite different brackets. In contrast to the Synoptics, John provides a double *opening bracket*:

- *The marriage at Cana* (John 2.1-11) — a tradition totally unknown to the Synoptics, though possibly illustrating the point made in the earlier tradition, about the wedding-like character of Jesus' mission (Mark 2.18-19 pars.), by telling it as a story rather than as formal teaching.[41] The symbolism is obvious: water intended for Jewish rites of purification (2.6) transformed into high quality wine (2.10), illustrating the transformation brought by Jesus' mission, quite probably once again as a way of making the same point as in Mark 2.21-22 pars.
- *The cleansing of the Temple* (2.14-22). Most probably this is John's version of the tradition shared by the Synoptics, but placed by them at the *end* of Jesus' mission. It is highly unlikely that there were two such episodes in Jesus' mission, one at the beginning and the other at the end:
  - It has precisely the same character — the sellers of animals and doves

---

40. See also *Jesus Remembered*, 769-70, 785-6.

41. Dodd notes that Jesus is recalled as telling several parables featuring wedding feasts (he refers to Matt. 22.1-14; 25.1-13, and Luke 12.35-36) and suggests that 'the traditional nucleus of this *pericope* may have been a parable' (*Historical Tradition*, 226-7). See also Lincoln, '"We Know That His Testimony Is True"', 191-5.

are expelled from the Temple precincts, and the tables of the money-changers are overturned, with some variation in detail as one would expect in an oral tradition.

– Jesus' rebuke is different — John 2.16, 'Stop making my Father's house a marketplace'; Mark 11.17 pars., 'You have made it a den of robbers' — but to similar effect.
– John even has Jesus saying, 'Destroy this temple, and in three days I will raise it up' (John 2.19), the very words which Mark and Matthew attribute to false testimony at Jesus' trial (Mark 14.58/Matt. 26.61). It is hard to avoid the conclusion that Jesus was remembered as saying something like this, and that while the way it was turned against Jesus at his trial amounted to false witness, Jesus did in fact predict the destruction of the temple (cf. Mark 13.2 pars.) and possibly/probably also spoke about its rebuilding (whatever he meant by that).[42] In which case, *John is a better witness to Jesus than the Synoptics, and shows how the oral memory of what Jesus had said was retained in the Jesus tradition, despite the way it was used against Jesus* (a similar conclusion can be drawn from Acts 6.14).[43] John's version also strengthens the probability that Jesus gave this teaching in the context of his cleansing of the temple, and that it was the combination of the two (the event and the teaching) which determined the temple authorities to take action against him.

The conclusion which follows most naturally is that John has elected to begin his account of Jesus' mission with this episode, because, together with the wedding at Cana, it *foreshadowed and epitomized the effect of Jesus' mission in relation to his native Judaism:* he would transform the Jewish purity ritual into new wine; he would replace the temple with his own body (John 2.21); the water he gave is far superior to the water of Jacob's well (4.12-14); as the bread of life from heaven he far transcends the bread which Moses gave (6.30-35); etc.[44] Somewhat as Luke moved Jesus' preaching in the synagogue at Nazareth to the forefront of his account, to indicate the character of what was to follow, so John felt free (evidently) to move the climactic cleansing of the temple likewise to set the scene and epitomize what was to follow.[45] This

42. See again discussion in *Jesus Remembered*, 630-3.
43. See further *Beginning from Jerusalem*, §24.2c.
44. See further, e.g., A. T. Lincoln, *The Gospel according to St John* (BNTC; London: Continuum, 2005) 76-8.
45. Anderson is the most recent to argue that Mark's chronology for the cleansing of the temple is wrong; it is John who got the placement of the temple incident right and thus was cor-

may seem an overbold move, but only if we assume that the Evangelists were bound to order their material in strict chronological order, an assumption which we have no reason to make and which runs counter to too much evidence to be followed without question.[46] That there was a substantive story to be told about Jesus is clear, but as such passages as the Sermon on the Mount in Matt. 5-7, the journey to Jerusalem in Luke 9-19, and the cleansing of the temple in John 2.14-22 also clearly show, *how the teaching and events of the Jesus tradition were ordered within that narrative of Jesus' mission was a matter of free choice in the different tellings of the oral Jesus tradition.*

If John felt free to shape the beginning of his account of Jesus' mission, he felt equally or more free in constructing the *closing bracket*, the event which sparked off the decision to do away with Jesus. In the Synoptics it was the symbolical 'cleansing of the Temple' which set off the final spiral of opposition to Jesus[47] and led directly to the arrest of Jesus made possible by Judas' betrayal (Mark 14.10-11 pars.). John, however, provides a quite different trigger. In John's Gospel, it is *the recalling of Lazarus from the dead* which is the immediate trigger to the final move against Jesus. The signs which Jesus had performed, climaxing in the recall of Lazarus to life, led the high priest himself to the conclusion it was better for one man to die than for the whole nation to be destroyed (John 11.47-53, 57). John reinforces the point by narrating how famous the raising of Lazarus became, and how threatening to the status quo the resulting support for Jesus and his message quickly became (12.9-11, 17-19).

Of this raising of Lazarus from the dead (11.1-44), none of the other Evangelists show any awareness.[48] One could conceive that the earlier tradition set that episode on one side, for fear that the authorities might act against Lazarus (cf. John 12.10). But the Synoptics were writing about forty or more years after the event. Would that still be a factor then, when the vicinity of Je-

---

recting Mark (*Fourth Gospel*, 32, 48, 67, 70-1, 111-2, 158-61). But the episodes of John 4–5 hardly presuppose or depend on the temple incident, and, if an early 'cleansing' evoked opposition such as Anderson sees in John 5.18, then the time interval between the 'cleansing' and Jesus' arrest is entirely surprising. See further John Painter's review of Anderson in *RBL* (http://www.bookreviews.org/bookdetail.asp?TitleId=5879). See also M. A. Matson, 'The Temple Incident: An Integral Element in the Fourth Gospel's Narrative', in Fortna & Thatcher, eds., *Jesus in the Johannine Tradition*, 145-53.

46. The words of Papias are regularly quoted on this point: that Mark 'wrote accurately all that he remembered, not, indeed, in order, of the things said or done by the Lord' (Eusebius, *HE* 3.39.15).

47. Mark 11.18/Luke 19.47-48; Mark 12.12 pars.; 14.1-2 pars.; cf. Matt. 21.15-16.

48. The character Lazarus appears only in John (John 11.1-44; 12.1-2, 9-10, 17). The only other Lazarus in the NT is the beggar by that name in Jesus' parable of the rich man and Lazarus (Luke 16.20-25).

rusalem had been devastated during the siege and conquest of Jerusalem, and its residents widely scattered? Moreover, the Johannine presentation seems to reflect the beliefs and concerns of the later Johannine churches: the sign of Lazarus' recall to life prefiguring Jesus' own resurrection (11.4-5, 23-27); the High Priest unwittingly confessing that Jesus died 'for the nation . . . and to gather into one the dispersed children of God' (11.51-52); many of the Jews believing in Jesus (12.11); the expanding influence of Jesus being counteracted by expelling from the synagogue of those who believed in Jesus (12.42); all this reflecting the high and distinctive Johannine christology (11.4, 25-26; 12.27-36, 44-50).

It is hard to avoid the conclusion that John removed the account of the cleansing of the Temple to provide a window through which the unfolding of Jesus' mission and revelation should be seen. And that he did so also to make room for his own version of the climax to Jesus' mission, the climax which triggered the decisive action against him. More has to be said about the raising of Lazarus, but it is best said in the context of John's account of Jesus' signs.

c) The Book of Signs

Equally striking is the way John has structured *Jesus' mission of healing* (John 3–12), what C. H. Dodd designated as 'the Book of Signs'.[49] John seems to work to a pattern of a characteristic miracle which highlights an aspect of Jesus' mission and its significance. That significance is typically brought out by *the often lengthy discourse or dialogue which is attached to the miracle*, before or after. The point is underlined by the term which John uses consistently for the miracles — 'sign',[50] a sign-ificant event which conveys a meaning far larger than the event itself. The most persistent themes are new life and light from darkness, as already signalled in the prologue (1.4-5, 7-9, 13):

- 2.1-11 — water to wine, first sign (2.11) — significance indicated by the clues (third day, 2.1; wedding; water of purification rites; a sign which revealed his glory, 2.11)
  - 3.1-21 — dialogue with Nicodemus on new birth (3.3-8, 15-16, 19-21)

49. C. H. Dodd, *The Interpretation of the Fourth Gospel* (Cambridge: Cambridge University, 1953).

50. John 2.11, 23; 3.2; 4.48, 54; 6.2, 14, 26, 30; 7.31; 9.16; 10.41; 11.47; 12.18, 37; 20.30. Despite traditions like Matt. 12.28/Luke 11.20 and Mark 3.27 pars., exorcisms did not function sufficiently as 'signs' for John; see also G. H. Twelftree, 'Exorcisms in the Fourth Gospel and the Synoptics', in Fortna & Thatcher, eds., *Jesus in the Johannine Tradition*, 135-43.

- 4.46-54 — saving a royal official's son from death — emphasis on life (4.50-53), second sign (4.54), though also a warning against a faith based solely on signs (4.48; cf. 2.23-25)
  - corollary to the water of life discourse with the Samaritan woman (4.7-26, especially 4.10, 14), and reaping the fruit for eternal life (4.35-36) already in Samaria (4.29-30, 39-43)
- 5.1-9 — healing of a paralyzed man — a more traditional format (healing on a Sabbath)
  - 5.10-47 — dialogue with 'the Jews' focusing on the christological significance of Jesus so acting on the Sabbath (the theme returned to in 10.11-39), but also on Jesus' working as indicating the life which is in the Son and granted by the Son (5.24-26, 40)
- 6.1-14 — feeding of five thousand, attached to the walking on water (6.16-21)
  - 6.25-65 — the great bread of life discourse (particularly 6.27, 33, 35, 40, 47, 48, 51, 53-54, 57-58, 63; rounded off by Peter's confession, 6.68)
- 9.1-7 — healing of a blind man
  - led into by preceding discussion begun with Jesus' promise of the light of life (8.12), and leading into extensive discourse on blindness and sight (9.8-41)
- 11.1-44 — recalling Lazarus from death — significance emphasized from the beginning (11.4)
  - discourse on eternal life despite and through death (particularly 11.23-26), prior to the miracle itself.

There are several curiosities in the Johannine tradition worth noting.

- No type of miracle is repeated. It appears to be the case that John has taken six characteristic miracles, perhaps even miracle types, in order to draw out the sign-ificance of each.
- For some reason he does not include one of Jesus' most characteristic healings (at least according to the Synoptic tradition) — that is, an exorcism. Similarly he nowhere speaks of 'unclean spirits', and the term 'demon' is limited to accusations against Jesus (7.20; 8.48-49, 52; 10.20-21).
- The listing of the first two signs as the 'first' and the 'second' (2.11; 4.54) suggests that John may have been able to draw on a sequence of signs, possibly already written down.[51]

---

51. R. T. Fortna, *The Gospel of Signs* (SNTSMS 11; Cambridge: Cambridge University, 1970); other bibliography in Schnelle, *History,* 494 n. 167 and critique 494-6 and n. 169.

- The fact that John has retained the close sequence between the feeding of the five thousand and the walking on water miracles (6.1-21; Mark 6.32-52 pars.), even though the accompanying discourse develops the significance only of the former, strongly suggests that these two miracles were already so firmly attached to each other in the various forms of the tradition,[52] that it would have raised more questions to omit the latter than it did to retain it as the undeveloped twin.
- The recalling of Lazarus from death (ch. 11) brings to a fitting climax the theme of life out of death so prominent in the earlier discourses (the new birth, water of life, renewed life, eternal life, bread of life, the light of life).

One of the questions which this raises is whether John draws the actual miracles which he relates from his tradition. Or does he provide a sequence of miracle types, (a) partly drawn from specific tradition (feeding of the five thousand, healing a child at a distance), (b) partly illustrating types of healing for which Jesus was famous (of paralysis and blindness), and (c) partly stories which express the richest significance of Jesus even if not actually rooted in specific events (water of Jewish purification into abundant and high quality wine, recalling Lazarus to life). (a) The first of these possibilities is already intriguing, since John's account of the healing of the royal official's son is so different from the parallel in Matthew and Luke,[53] and since virtually the only significant points of agreement between John and the Synoptics, on what is obviously the same tradition of the feeding of the five thousand, are the actual numbers (5,000, 200 denarii, 5 loaves and 2 fishes, 12 baskets of fragments).[54] Here is *important evidence of the degree to which the same memory and tradition could be diversely retold.* (b) The second of the possibilities suggests that John or his tradition had no qualms in telling the story of Jesus using *types* of his healing ministry rather than any particular instances.[55] (c) The third pos-

---

52. Matt. 14.13-33; Mark 6.32-52; Luke however omitted the walking on water (Luke 9.10-17).

53. The possibility that the healing of the royal official's son is a variation of Matthew's and Luke's account of the healing of the centurion's boy certainly cannot be excluded (see Dodd, *Historical Tradition*, 188-95; and my 'John and the Oral Gospel Tradition', 359-63 [above, 146-9]; also *Jesus Remembered*, 212-6).

54. See also 'John and the Oral Gospel Tradition', 363-5 (above 154-6). Anderson also concludes that the contacts between Mark and John have to be traced back to the oral stages of their tradition (*Fourth Gospel*, 29-30). In *Jesus Remembered*, 645-7, I also point out that John's report that the crowd wanted to 'take Jesus by force to make him king' (John 6.15) is very plausible as recalled historical data (understandably passed over by other tradents), not least because it helps explain the oddities of Mark's account at the same point.

55. Similarly Dodd, *Historical Tradition*, 174-88; see also my 'John and the Oral Gospel Tradition', 374 (above, 159-60).

sibility cannot be excluded, since it is so hard to locate both the water into wine miracle[56] and the recalling of Lazarus to life[57] within Jesus' mission, and since they so powerfully illustrate the effect of Jesus' mission. This could suggest that *John or his tradition felt free to document Jesus' mission with parabolic stories and not only actual remembered events.* Also it would fit with John's attribution of speeches/discourses to Jesus, as we shall see.[58] If this is the case, it would be quite wrong and a serious misunderstanding of John and his purpose to accuse him of deception. That is to say, the evidence of John's Gospel itself suggests that we should not assume that he saw his role as simply recalling memories of actual events of Jesus' mission, or simply reciting the earlier tradition, in the fashion of the Synoptics.[59] John may have concluded that to bring out the full significance of Jesus' mission he had to retell the tradition in bolder ways that brought out that significance more clearly.

d) The Judean Mission

One of the most striking differences between the Synoptics and John is that whereas the Synoptics focus on Jesus' mission in Galilee, the bulk of John's narrative focuses on Judea and Jerusalem — 2.13–3.36; 5.1-47; 7.10 onwards. It is not unlikely that Jesus did pay more visits or spend longer time in Judea and Jerusalem than the Synoptic tradition allows:[60]

- The early period of overlap between the missions of the Baptist and Jesus suggests early mission in Judea (cf. John 3).

---

56. The provision of 480-720 litres of wine would certainly be grotesque as a historical event; but as a symbolic parable it was very powerful. See also n. 41 above and Lincoln, '"We Know That His Testimony Is True"', 196-7.

57. If we assume that John knew one or more of the raisings from the dead miracles attributed to Jesus by the earlier tradition (Jairus' daughter — Mark 5.35-43 pars.; Luke 7.11-15), he presumably thought they were not climactic enough for his purpose. He may also have known the tradition that Jesus himself claimed to raise the dead (Matt. 11.5/Luke 7.22). So a parabolic story of Jesus raising a dead person was hardly unjustified especially when it could serve as such a fitting climax to his own retelling of Jesus' mission. See further the careful discussions of Dodd, *Historical Tradition*, 228-32; and Lincoln, *John*, 531-5.

58. See below §5.

59. Anderson's criticism that I claim Baur and Strauss are correct in disparaging John's Gospel as a historical source (*Fourth Gospel*, 2 n. 4) ignores what I actually say, that 'John's Gospel cannot be regarded as a source for the life and teaching of Jesus of the same order as the Synoptics' (*Jesus Remembered*, 166).

60. See also *Jesus Remembered*, 323-4.

- Luke records the close discipleship of Mary and Martha (Luke 10.38-42), and though he locates them in a village passed through on the journey to Jerusalem, John is clear that the village was Bethany, close to Jerusalem (John 11.1, 18; 12.1-8),[61] and John's geographical locations are generally reckoned to be evidence of firm historical rootage.[62]
- That Jesus had close disciples in Jerusalem or in the near environs is suggested by the (secret?) disciples who provided the donkey for his entry into Jerusalem (Mark 11.2-3 pars.) and the room for the last supper (Mark 14.12-16 pars.).

In that case, why did the Synoptic tradition ignore or set to one side Jesus' earlier Jerusalem visits? The fact that they deliberately excluded the overlap period with the Baptist is evidence enough that they felt free to do so. And perhaps Mark or the tradition on which he drew wanted to make the (final) visit to Jerusalem the climax of the Jesus story, and Matthew and Luke simply followed him (or their main stream of tradition) in doing so. Since the leadership of the earliest Jerusalem community of believers in Messiah Jesus were all Galileans, one could understand why the tradition which they began and taught focused on the Galilean mission.

John, of course, does not ignore the Galilean mission, even though Jesus' coming and going to Galilee in the early chapters of his Gospel does read rather awkwardly.[63] The two miracles included in that material are, as just noted, the closest to the Synoptic miracle tradition. But the likelihood grows throughout John's Gospel that John had a source for the mission of Jesus which was different from, or rather in addition to the remembrances of Peter — the figure indicated (and obscured) by the reference to him as 'the one whom Jesus loved' (13.23; 19.26; 21.7).[64] If that disciple is also referred to in 1.35-39, then he

61. Jesus lodged in Bethany during his last week (Mark 11.11-12 par.; 14.3 par.). The depiction of Martha and Mary in John 12.1-3 (Martha served; Mary focused attention on Jesus) echoes the similar presentation of Luke 10.39-42; on the fuller story (John 12.1-8) see Dodd, *Historical Tradition*, 162-73, and my 'John and the Oral Gospel Tradition', 365-7 (above 151-2).

62. E.g. John 1.28 (Bethany across the Jordan); 3.23 (Aenon near Salim); 5.2 (pool of Bethzatha); 11.54 (town called Ephraim). The topographical references in John are usually taken as well-rooted historical information (e.g. Anderson, *Fourth Gospel*, 3, 5).

63. John 2.1, 12, 13; 4.1-3, 43-46; 5.1; 6.1, 59; 7.1, 9, 10.

64. See particularly R. Bauckham, *Jesus and the Eyewitnesses: The Gospels as Eyewitness Testimony* (Grand Rapids: Eerdmans, 2006) 358-411; also 'The Fourth Gospel as the Testimony of the Beloved Disciple', in R. Bauckham & C. Mosser, eds., *The Gospel of John and Christian Theology* (Grand Rapids: Eerdmans, 2008) 120-39. M. Hengel, *The Johannine Question* (ET London: SCM, 1989), argues that the Fourth Evangelist had been a resident in Jerusalem, was an eyewitness of Jesus' death and a member of the earliest community, emigrated to Asia Minor in

would have been a good source for the overlap period between the Baptist's and Jesus' missions (including the recruitment of the Baptist's disciples to become followers of Jesus). Similarly if that disciple is also referred to in 18.15-16, then he had good contacts in Jerusalem (he was known to the high priest!). This suggests that this disciple could have known or cherished memories of Jesus' mission in Jerusalem on one or another of his brief visits to the capital, as also episodes and contacts (like Nicodemus and Joseph of Arimathea) which the other tradents largely ignored,[65] since the Galilean tradition was more familiar and so full in itself.[66] With only John's attestation for the Judean mission, and given the freedom with which the tradition he uses or draws upon has represented the memories of Jesus' overall mission, it is difficult to draw firm conclusions. But the most likely explanation is that *John has drawn on good memories of one or two/some visits to Jerusalem by Jesus, even if he has treated them in his own distinctive parabolic or symbolic terms.*

4. The Johannine Discourses of Jesus

So far I have concentrated primarily on the narrative tradition of John's Gospel. The other obvious area to examine is the teaching material in John. As already noted, this provides one of the most striking contrasts between John's Gospel and the Synoptics: whereas they depict Jesus as a sage typically teaching by means of *meshalim,* aphorisms and parables, John depicts Jesus engaged in lengthy back and forth discussions in various settings.

I have already noted elsewhere that in every chapter of John's Gospel there are particular sayings or part-sayings which echo Synoptic material or form different versions of the Synoptic tradition.[67] I remain convinced that

---

the early 60s and founded a school; he there wrote his Gospel in his old age, 'in which typical "Jewish Palestinian" reminiscences are combined with more "Hellenistic", "enthusiastic" and indeed even Pauline approaches into a great synthesis [in which] the christological doctrinal development of primitive Christianity reached its climax' (134). See also R. A. Culpepper, *John: The Son of Zebedee; The Life of a Legend* (Edinburgh: T&T Clark, 2000) ch. 3; T. Thatcher, 'The Legend of the Beloved Disciple', in Fortna & Thatcher, eds., *Jesus in the Johannine Tradition*, 91-9; Lincoln, '"We Know That His Testimony Is True"', 180-3.

65. Joseph is mentioned by all the Gospels at the end (Mark 15.43 pars.; John 19.38); but Nicodemus appears only in John (3.1-9; 7.50; 19.39).

66. Similarly with regard to any missioning in Samaria (John 4), whereas the Synoptics show why such mission might have been excluded (Matt. 10.5; Luke 9.52-54). O. Cullmann, *The Johannine Circle* (London: SCM, 1976) made much of John 4.38 at this point (47-9).

67. 'John and the Oral Gospel Tradition', 356-8 (above, 143-4), drawing particularly on Dodd's *Historical Tradition*. See also C. M. Tuckett, 'The Fourth Gospel and Q', and E. K. Broad-

John either did not know the Synoptic Gospels, or did not draw his versions from the Synoptic tradition as such.[68] Yet *the overlap with the Synoptic tradition at point after point indicates an independent awareness of the teaching which the early churches all remembered as Jesus' teaching. The lack of reworking by John at these points is both what allows us to recognize the parallel (the shared memory of the same teaching) and what enables us to say with confidence that John's discourses are rooted in the memories of what Jesus taught during his mission, in Galilee or in Judea.*

It is this rootage of the Johannine discourses, in tradition which echoes and parallels Synoptic tradition, which suggests the most plausible way to understand these discourses — viz. that they are discourses and themes which not only emerge out of and express the developed christology of John and the Johannine churches, but which express the reflection over some time on things Jesus said and taught, reflection in the light of the richer christology which Jesus' resurrection and exaltation had opened up to them.[69] This thesis finds support first of all in several examples:[70]

- Entry into the kingdom dependent on being born again/from above (John 3.3, 5) looks as though it is a sharper expression of the Matt. 18.3 tradition (entry into the kingdom dependent on becoming like children); these are the only kingdom references in John which come close to the Synoptic kingdom of God motif.[71]

---

head, 'The Fourth Gospel and the Synoptic Sayings Source', in Fortna & Thatcher, eds., *Jesus in Johannine Tradition,* 280-90 and 291-301 respectively. A much briefer sequence in Schnelle, *History,* 497-8. But about 70 verses in the Johannine discourses can be said to have Synoptic parallels. See also Anderson, *Fourth Gospel,* 52-3, 60-2, 131-2.

68. I suspect that those who conclude that John was dependent on one or another of the Synoptic Gospels — for details see D. M. Smith, *Johannine Christianity* (Columbia: University of South Carolina, 1984) chs. 6 and 7; also *John Among the Gospels: The Relationship in Twentieth-Century Research* (Minneapolis: Fortress, 1992) — are too much governed by a literary mindset, assuming that any close parallel can be (plausibly) explained only by literary dependence. On this point I follow Dodd and Smith and largely agree with Anderson (*Fourth Gospel,* 24, 28, 74-6).

69. Tom Thatcher, 'The Riddles of Jesus in the Johannine Dialogues', in Fortna & Thatcher, eds., *Jesus in Johannine Tradition,* 263-77, notes the substantial body of riddles in the Johannine dialogues. Since riddles are a widely attested oral form, he suggests that at least some of these sayings circulated orally in Johannine circles before the Fourth Gospel was written, and that some of the larger dialogues may also have circulated orally as riddling sessions (he refers particularly to John 8.12-58).

70. See also my 'John and the Oral Gospel Tradition', 369-73 (above 155-8) for brief treatment of John 2.18 and 6.30, 4.35-38, 44, 12.25, 13.20, 21, 38 and 20.23.

71. See also C. C. Caragounis, 'The Kingdom of God: Common and Distinct Elements

- Likening Jesus' presence to the presence of the bridegroom (John 3.29), as marking the difference between Jesus and the Baptist, echoing Mark 2.19 pars. (also Mark 2.21-22 pars.); I have already suggested influence from this motif on the account of the wedding at Cana (John 2.1-11).

- The great bread of life discourse (John 6.26-58) is most obviously to be understood as a reflection on Jesus' words at the last supper (Mark 14.22-25 pars.) bringing out not so much the Passover significance as the contrast with Moses and the manna of the wilderness.

- The good shepherd theme in John (John 10) most obviously takes up the memory of Jesus' use of the same imagery in his teaching.[72]

- John's principal theme of presenting Jesus as the incarnate Word who reveals God most fully (John 1.14-18) forms a consistent theme of Jesus' discourses:

  - Jesus' repeated talk of himself as *the Son* to God as Father is an obvious elaboration of the much more limited early memory of Jesus' praying to God as 'Abba', perhaps already elaborated in the Synoptic tradition;[73]

  - Similarly Jesus' repeated talk of his having been *sent* by the Father (John 4.34; 5.24, 30, 37; 6.38-39, 44; etc.) is an obvious elaboration of the memory of Jesus' occasional self-reference in similar terms;[74]

  - Similarly the elaboration of Jesus' undoubted talk of 'the Son of Man' by adding the thought of his *descent and ascent* (John 3.13; 6.62; cf. 1.51) and of his *being lifted up glorified* (3.14; 8.28; 12.23; 13.31).

  - The 'Amen, Amen' introductory formula so regularly used by John is obviously drawn from the tradition, well-known in the Synoptics, of Jesus' introducing a saying with 'Amen'.[75]

  - The noteworthy 'I am's of John's Gospel[76] are certainly formulations unknown to the earlier Synoptic tradition (what Evangelist could have omitted such sayings of Jesus?); but equally it is likely that the

---

Between John and the Synoptics', in Fortna & Thatcher, eds., *Jesus in the Johannine Tradition*, 125-34. Anderson observes that John has a number of 'king' references (*Fourth Gospel*, 54), but the point of comparison is with Jesus' preaching of the kingdom of God.

72. Matt. 18.12/Luke 15.4; Mark 6.34; Matt. 10.6; 15.24; Luke 12.32.

73. J. Jeremias, *The Prayers of Jesus* (London: SCM, 1967) 30, 36 noted the tremendous expansion of references to God as 'Father' in the words of Jesus within the Jesus tradition — Mark 3, Q 4, special Luke 4, special Matthew 31, John 100.

74. Mark 9.37 pars.; 12.6 pars.; Matt. 15.24; Luke 4.18; 10.16.

75. See further R. A. Culpepper, 'The Origin of the "Amen, Amen" Sayings in the Gospel of John', in Fortna & Thatcher, eds., *Jesus in the Johannine Tradition*, 253-62.

76. John 6.35, 41, 48, 51; 8.12, 24, 28, 58; 10.7, 9, 14; 11.25; 13.19; 14.6; 15.1, 5; 18.5-8.

> memory of some awe-inspiring assurances of Jesus (Mark 6.50 pars.; John 6.20) provided the stimulus for the uniquely Johannine forms.[77]

This data strongly suggests that *many if not most of the principal themes of the Johannine discourses are the fruit of lengthy meditation on particular sayings of Jesus or of characteristic features of what he said and of how he acted*. In other words, they exemplify not simply the passing on of Jesus tradition, but the way that tradition stimulated their understanding of Jesus in the light of what had happened subsequently.

John himself attests and justifies this very process.

- Twice he explicitly notes that Jesus' disciples did not understand what Jesus was saying or doing, but that they remembered and later understood in the light of Jesus' resurrection and glorification (2.22; 12.16; similarly 13.7; 14.20; 16.4). This makes precisely the point that the claims regarding Jesus were rooted in Jesus' own mission as illuminated by Easter. His immediate disciples already had a true knowledge of Jesus during his mission (6.69; 17.7-8), but they did not fully understand; their knowledge was still imperfect (8.28, 32; 10.6, 38; 13.28; 14.9).[78]
- To the same effect is the role ascribed to the Spirit/Paraclete. During Jesus' mission 'the Spirit was not yet', that is, presumably, not yet given (7.39). But when the Spirit came he would teach Jesus' disciples everything and remind them of all that Jesus had said to them (14.26); he would guide them into all truth and declare more of Jesus' truth that they were as yet unable to bear (16.12-13).[79] This is the same balance be-

---

77. Cf. Anderson, *Fourth Gospel*, 56-8.

78. See also T. Thatcher, 'Why John Wrote a Gospel: Memory and History in an Early Christian Community', in A. Kirk & T. Thatcher, eds., *Memory, Tradition, and Text: Uses of the Past in Early Christianity* (Semeia Studies 52; Atlanta: SBL, 2005) 79-97 (particularly 82-5); also *Why John Wrote a Gospel: Jesus — Memory — History* (Louisville: Westminster John Knox, 2006) 24-32.

79. In his review of Anderson's *Fourth Gospel* (n. 45 above), Painter observes: 'the historical tradition in John has been thoroughly shaped by deep theological reflection from a perspective that makes difficult the separation of the tradition from the later theological development. It is the degree to which this has happened in John that separates it from the Synoptics. That need not rule out continuity between the tradition and the interpretation, but it does not mean that the interpretation is in some sense already present in the tradition, even if it is rooted there and in some way grows out of it. The experience of the resurrection and the Spirit created Johannine interpretation that was not foreseen or foreseeable beforehand'. See further Painter, 'Memory Holds the Key: The Transformation of Memory in the Interface of History and Theology in John', in Anderson et al., eds., *Jesus, John and History*, Vol. 1, 229-45 (especially 238-45).

tween revelation already given and received, and fuller revelation still to come, a fuller revelation which makes the revelation already given clearer and enables it to be more fully grasped.[80]

In short, it is hard to doubt that *John's version of Jesus' teaching is an elaboration of aphorisms, parables, motifs and themes remembered as characteristic of Jesus' teaching, as attested in the Synoptic tradition.* At the same time, John's version was not pure invention, nor did it arise solely out of Easter faith. Rather it was elaboration of typical things that Jesus was remembered as saying. Unlike the later 'Gospels', John does not attribute the fuller insight into who Jesus was to secret teaching given to a few following Jesus' resurrection. Rather, he roots it in the Jesus tradition which he shared with the other churches (who knew mainly the Synoptic tradition) and which was itself rooted in the memory of Jesus' mission. This was the truth of Jesus for John — not a pedantic repetition of Synoptic-like tradition, but the significance of that tradition brought out by the extensive discourses which John or his tradition drew out of particular features of Jesus tradition as exemplified in the Synoptic tradition. To criticize John's procedure as inadmissible is to limit the task of the Evangelist to simply recording deeds and words of Jesus during his mission. But John evidently saw his task as something more — the task of drawing out the fuller meaning of what Jesus had said (and done) by presenting that fuller understanding as the Spirit both *reminding* Jesus' disciples of what Jesus had said and *leading them into the fuller understanding of the truth* made possible by Jesus' resurrection and ascension.

5. The Johannine Passion Narrative

The Johannine passion narrative shares the same structure as its Synoptic equivalents, each of them with their own distinctive features and characteristics, though once again John shows how varied at least some re-presentations of the final part of Jesus' mission could be.[81]

---

80. The dialectic of the Johannine conception of revelation here is summed up in the word *anangellō*, which John uses three times in 16.13-15, and which can have the force of 're-announce', 're-proclaim', but also denote the announcing of new information/revelation in 16.13. Arthur Dewey, 'The Eyewitness of History: Visionary Consciousness in the Fourth Gospel', in Fortna & Thatcher, eds., *Jesus in the Johannine Tradition*, 59-70, speaks of 'anticipatory memory' (65-7).

81. Dodd concludes his lengthy discussion of the passion narrative: 'there is cumulative evidence that the Johannine version represents (subject to some measure of "writing up" by the

- Like the others, John begins the final phase with Jesus' last meal with his disciples (John 13). Like the others
  - the meal is linked to the Passover (13.1);[82]
  - Jesus predicts his betrayal (13.18, 21; Mark 14.18 par.), causing confusion among his disciples (13.22-25; Mark 14.19 pars.);
  - the account emphasizes that the traitor eats from the same dish (13.26-27; Mark 14.20 pars.);
  - Peter protests his loyalty and Jesus predicts his denial — 'The cock will not crow until you deny me three times' (13.36-38; Mark 14.29-30 pars.).
- The shared tale recalls Jesus leading his disciples to the other side of the valley (18.1; Mark 14.32 pars.), Judas leading the arresting troop, and Jesus' arrest after some brief resistance in which 'the slave of the high priest' had his ear cut off (18.2-12; Mark 14.43-47 pars.)
- There follows the hearing before the High Priest Caiaphas (18.13-14; Mark 14.53 pars), with some cross-examination by Caiaphas (18.19-21; Mark 14.60-61 pars.).
- In all Gospel accounts Peter follows the arresting party, gains entry to the courtyard (18.15-16; Mark 14.54 pars.) and denies Jesus as predicted (18.17-18, 25-27; Mark 14.54, 66-72 pars.).
- In all four Gospels the case is transferred to Pilate (18.28; Mark 15.1 pars.), who begins by asking Jesus 'Are you the king of the Jews?' (18.33; Mark 15.2 pars.), but who finds no case against him (18.38; most specifically Luke 23.4).
- The release of one prisoner is offered to the crowd, on account of the feast, Jesus or Barabbas; the crowd choose Barabbas (18.39-40; Mark 15.6-11 pars.). To Pilate's query as to what should be done with the king of the Jews the crowd call for Jesus to be crucified (19.5-6, 15; Mark 15.13-14 pars.); Pilate gives way and hands Jesus over to be crucified (19.16; Mark 15.15 pars.).
- The flogging and mockery of Jesus (the crown of thorns, the purple robe, and the mock hailing of the 'King of the Jews') is a shared mem-

---

evangelist) an independent strain of the common oral tradition, differing from the strains of tradition underlying Mark (Matthew) and Luke, though controlled by the same general *schema* (*Historical Tradition*, 150). See also Schnelle, *History*, 500-502. For a recent attempt to reconstruct the pre-Johannine passion narrative see F. Scherlitt, *Der vorjohanneische Passionsbericht: Eine historisch-kritische und theologische Untersuchung zu Joh 2,13-22; 11,47–14,31 und 18,1–20,29* (BZNW 154; Berlin: de Gruyter, 2007).

82. Whether the meal itself was on Passover (Mark 14.12 pars.), or on the day of preparation for the Passover (John 19.14), remains unclear; see further *Jesus Remembered*, 771-3.

ory, though set at different points in the sequence of events (19.1-3; Mark 15.15-19 pars.).

- Jesus carries his own cross (19.17; Mark 15.21 pars.) to the place called Golgotha (19.17; Mark 15.22 pars.), where he is crucified with two others (19.18; Mark 15.24, 27 pars.).
- The inscription on the cross reads, 'The king of the Jews' (19.19; Mark 15.26 pars.).
- Jesus' clothes are divided by the casting of lots among the soldiers (19.23-25; Mark 15.24 pars.).
- Jesus asks for or is offered drink and drinks, and then yields up his life (19.28-30; Mark 15.36-37 pars.).
- Joseph of Arimathea asks Pilate for Jesus' body because it was the day of Preparation, and attends to his burial in a tomb (19.38-42; Mark 15.42-46 pars.).

The distinctive features of John's version are only in part as obvious as the distinctiveness of his earlier accounts. Yet even here there are various indications of the shared tradition on which John drew and which he elaborated in his own way.

- Surprisingly, John does not actually describe Jesus' last supper with his disciples, though we have already noted that 'the words of institution' seem to have been the basis for the extended meditation in 6.51-59.
- The focal point of the evening is presented as Jesus washing the disciples' feet (13.1-20) — an oddity if it was part of the shared memory, since it illustrated so well what Jesus was recalled as having said earlier, that he came not to be served but to serve (Mark 10.42-45 pars.), though that very parallel suggests that John told the story to illustrate what that very teaching could/should involve. The parallel between John 13.16 (cf. 15.20) and Matt. 10.24/Luke 6.40 ('the slave is not above/ greater than his master') points in the same direction. And the echo of Matt. 10.40/Luke 10.16 in John 13.20 ('he who receives me receives him who sent me') similarly suggests one of the roots of John's distinctive growth of tradition.
- The command to love one another (13.34-35) can presumably be seen as an extension of Jesus' more widely known teaching on love of one's neighbour (Mark 12.31 pars.).
- The most strikingly distinctive features of the Johannine passion narrative are the extended discourse which he attributes to Jesus at the close of the shared meal (John 14–16), and particularly Jesus' great prayer of

intercession for his disciples (John 17). These evidently have to be seen as extended meditations on the definitive significance of Jesus' revelation and on how the disciples could expect to prosper after Jesus' departure. Even in these chapters, however, there are various points at which the rootage in the early memories of Jesus is sufficiently clear.[83]

- The promises of the Paraclete Spirit (14.26; 15.26-27; 16.4-15) probably began with the elsewhere remembered assurance of Jesus that the Spirit would inspire what they should say (Mark 13.11 pars.).
- Jesus' assurance that his disciples are more than servants (15.14-15) echoes Jesus' teaching that whoever does the will of God is one of his family (Mark 3.35 pars.). Likewise, the promise of effective prayer in his name (15.16) echoes the similar promise of Mark 11.23-24 pars.
- Jesus' forewarning of the world's hatred (15.18-25) probably grows out of the same tradition as Matt. 10.24-25, 28/Luke 12.4.
- Even more clearly the warnings to expect persecution (16.1-4) echo several similar traditions in Mark 13.9, 12-13 pars./Matt. 10.17-18, 21-22.
- Even Jesus' great prayer for his disciples (ch. 17) owes its inspiration to the tradition of Jesus praying in the Garden of Gethsemane (Mark 14.32-42),[84] and though the Johannine prayer has nothing of the Angst of the Synoptic tradition, we should recall that the earlier prayer of John 12.27 does share a similar troubled quality (Mark 14.33-36 pars.), remembered also in Heb. 5.7.

• The exchange between Jesus and Pilate (18.33-38; 19.9-12, 19-22) is a fascinating elaboration of the 'King of the Jews' charge, even though it is unlike any other of Jesus' teaching on the kingdom of God.

• John has several distinctive utterances of Jesus from the cross (19.26-27, 28, 30), but so has Luke (Luke 23.34 v.l.; 23.43, 46). If the beloved disciple was one of John's sources, that would help explain John 19.26-27 (Jesus' mother being consigned to the care of the beloved disciple). The concern was evidently to express the spirit of Jesus as clearly as possible during his greatest suffering to death.

---

83. J. Beutler, 'Synoptic Jesus Tradition in the Johannine Farewell Discourse', in Fortna & Thatcher, eds., *Jesus in Johannine Tradition*, 165-73, boldly concludes 'that John 13-17 is pervaded by early Jesus tradition, mostly tradition of a synoptic character and perhaps even derived from the Synoptics themselves', though 'no single coherent discourse source can be uncovered. Rather, there has been creative use of the traditional material, forging it into a new form that expresses F(ourth)E(vangelist)'s peculiar view of Jesus . . .' (173).

84. Anderson suggests that John 17 is an 'embellished form' of the Lord's Prayer in Matt. 6/Luke 11 (*Fourth Gospel*, 55).

- John (or his backing group) make a point of vouchsafing some of his distinctive testimony — notably Jesus' side being pierced and the emission of blood and water: 'He who saw this has testified so that you also may believe. His testimony is true and he knows that he tells the truth' (19.35).
- John's version of the empty tomb tradition has a similar distinctiveness, though all agree on the timing of its discovery, and on the leading involvement of Mary Magdalene; Luke 24.12 also accords with John on Peter's involvement, and on his seeing the linen wrappings left behind from Jesus' body.
- Similarly John's account of Jesus' resurrection appearances looks as though it was dependent on another source, perhaps not known to or not used by the Synoptic tradition; the obvious tradent in this case would have been Mary Magdalene.
- The Thomas tradition (20.24-29) reminds readers of the NT of the much more extensive Thomas tradition in apocryphal writings and in the mission to India and suggests that John was able to draw on some or several source traditions no longer known to us.
- A final affidavit confirms that the Gospel had a first-hand source of substantial authority: 'This is the disciple (referring to the beloved disciple) who is testifying to these things and has written them, and we know that his testimony is true' (21.24).

The most plausible inference to draw from all this data is that *different members of the initial disciple group drew somewhat varying emphases from what was a shared stream of tradition, each with memories of the same period, events and teachings, but distinctively their own memories on individual details.*

6. Conclusion

John's Gospel cannot be and should not be simply paralleled to the other three Gospels. Although all four Gospels can be set in parallel, as in the Aland *Synopsis,* the first three Gospels are clearly parallel in a way and to a degree that is not true of John's Gospel; that is why Matthew, Mark and Luke can be referred to collectively as 'the Synoptic Gospels'. John's Gospel is not a synoptic Gospel.

The distinctiveness of John's portrayal of Jesus should not be diminished or ignored. The older attempt to harmonize all four Gospels should be recognized to be wrong-headed. John was evidently *not* attempting to do the same thing as the Synoptics. And though we should recognize that all Evangelists had theological axes to grind, *the briefest of comparisons is sufficient to show that the Synoptics were much more constrained by the forms of their tradition than ever John was.* The closeness of the Synoptic parallels cannot be explained otherwise. And contrariwise, it is equally impossible to make sense of John's Gospel on the assumption that he was attempting to do the same as the Synoptics.

We should not hesitate to draw the unavoidable corollary: that *to read and interpret John's Gospel as though he had been trying to do the same as the Synoptics is to misread and misinterpret his Gospel.* This remains the challenge for those who approach John's Gospel from a conservative perspective: by so doing, they may be missing and distorting John's message! The truth of Jesus, the story of his mission and its significance, were not expressed in only one way, as though the Gospel of Jesus Christ could be told only by strictly limiting the interpretation of the earliest Jesus tradition, the ways in which Jesus was remembered. It proved also acceptable (just!) that *the character and themes of Jesus' mission provided the basis for fuller and deeper reflection on what Jesus stood for and achieved* — still the Gospel of Jesus Christ.

At the same time, it is equally important to note that John clearly knew the same sort of tradition known to and used by the Synoptic Evangelists.

- He follows the same Gospel format in giving his account of Jesus' mission.
- He had sources of/access to earliest memories of close disciples of Jesus which filled out parts of Jesus' mission which the other Evangelists passed over, for understandable reasons — the overlap period between the Baptist and Jesus' earlier trips into Judea and Jerusalem being probably the most obvious.
- The indications that John had good sources of tradition (Baptist tradition, attempt to make Jesus king in Galilee, contacts in Jerusalem), of which we would not have known had John not retold them, suggest that other parts of John's Gospel are better rooted in historical tradition than we now can tell (the Synoptists did not include all the traditional material available to them); John 21.25 speaks for all the Gospels.
- John's use of the tradition of Jesus' miracles was selective, but the types of miracle he described and which he encompassed by profound discourse and teaching were mostly familiar as types of Jesus' healing ministry.
- Again and again the elaborate discourses and teaching give evidence of being rooted in Synoptic-like tradition or seem to be an elaboration of particular sayings/parables of Jesus known from the Synoptic tradition.

• John evidently knew the final passion of Jesus at first hand or from first-hand sources, a claim which is emphasized at 19.35 and 21.24 in particular; the beloved disciple and Mary Magdalene may be identified as such sources.

The most obvious way to explain and understand the distinctiveness of John's portrayal of Jesus is that John knew well the tradition which he shared with the Synoptics, and that *he wove his much more refined fabric from the same stuff as the Synoptics* — the product and expression of many years of reflection on the significance of what Jesus had taught and done and on the significance of the revelation he had brought and constituted in his life and mission.[85] While we should not understate the distinctiveness of John's Gospel, given the many echoes and parallels in John neither should we exaggerate the difference. *John in his own way was telling the same story as the other Evangelists.* That he chose to do so by elaborating that story in his own way should be acknowledged and properly appreciated. John's Gospel should be valued for what it is, not for what it is not.

In terms of the oral Jesus tradition, *John's Gospel shows just how diverse and varied the Jesus tradition could become in its various retellings.* In terms of memory, "remembering Jesus", John's Gospel shows clearly the degree to which the memory of Jesus could be, and was, informed by subsequent insight and conviction, and shaped to portray Jesus as the Johannine author(s) or communities now saw him or wanted to present him to their contemporaries. The elaboration which John provided made his version of the Jesus tradition controversial; he sailed near the edge of what was acceptable. To speak of John's Gospel as "the remembered Jesus" is bound to make a historian nervous — somewhat as a Shakespeare play performed in a twentieth-century setting might make Shakespearean scholars somewhat nervous (are aspects of the play which are tightly interrelated to the historical setting of the play given by Shakespeare being lost in the twentieth-century setting?). The facts that John retained the Gospel character, and that its rootage in the earlier oral tradition was clear, were presumably sufficient to ensure that John's Gospel would be recognized as one of the four Gospels to be designated as canonical. At one and the same time, however, John demonstrated that for the remembered Jesus to continue to be seen as relevant to subsequent generations, the way he was remembered would have to be adaptable if the same Jesus was to speak to these generations.

85. See also the conclusion to 'John and the Oral Gospel Tradition', 378-9 (above 162-3).

PART II

CHAPTER 8

On History, Memory and Eyewitnesses:
In Response to Bengt Holmberg and Samuel Byrskog

I am most grateful to Bengt Holmberg (BH) and Samuel Byrskog (SB) for the care they have taken in offering their critiques of my *Jesus Remembered (JR)*. The initial drafts of their critiques were prepared for the 'Historical Jesus' Seminar at the Bonn meeting of Studiorum Novi Testamenti Societas in July/ August 2003, although delay in the publication of *JR* meant that they had little enough time to read through the nearly 900 pages prior to that meeting. The Seminar was a challenging time for the author of *JR*, though I found it more enjoyable than I had anticipated: the testing and refining of one's insights and suggestions is one way to prove and improve such worth as they have. But the finished form of the BH/SB critiques, in the preceding two papers,[1] has given me further stimulus and opportunity to craft a more considered response. So I am happy to acknowledge once again my debt to them and appreciation for their remarks, both the positive commendations and the constructive criticisms. Hopefully they have helped me to clarify and to sharpen up some key features of the theses of *JR*, and so the dialogue may be of value to others interested in the quest of the historical Jesus.

It is a particular pleasure to have critiques from two Scandinavians, since, as SB reminds us (p. 461), interest in oral tradition has been a particularly Scandinavian preoccupation in biblical scholarship.

---

1. B. Holmberg, 'Questions of Method in James Dunn's *Jesus Remembered*', *Journal for the Study of the New Testament* 26 (2004) 445-57; S. Byrskog, 'A New Perspective on the Jesus Tradition: Reflections on James D. G. Dunn's *Jesus Remembered*', 459-71. I will include page references to these articles in the body of my text.

Some of the two critiques overlap, and certainly they are quite complementary, but BH has focused his critique more on a discussion of history, and SB more on memory, and it makes best sense to deal with them in sequence.

BH focuses on the tension in historiography between events and the remembering of them. He rightly recognizes that historiography inevitably involves at least some degree of 'fictionalizing' events recorded. By 'fictionalizing' I understand that events are witnessed and retold within frameworks of conceptualization and language (of both witness and historian), and that in recording or retelling the events it is natural to see and relate them as part of some narrative (p. 447). But BH also wants to insist that such recalling or reporting is not totally fiction; there is an event to be remembered, even if the remembering involves some degree of transmutation into the perspective and categories of both witness and historian. 'Refiguring memory is not the same as disfiguring it' (p. 447).

I accept all this and tried to make space for it in *JR* by my repeated emphasis that 'Jesus Remembered' is the *impression* Jesus made and left on his various disciples. My recognition that the impression would be different as different disciples witnessed events and heard teaching slightly differently[2] is a way of saying that the 'fictionalising' process would begin 'from day one'. I recognize in particular that the language and the life-stories of the individual witnesses would have been different, so that both the remembering and the ways in which and the narrative framework within which the remembering was expressed and the tradition retold would have been always at least subtly different and sometimes quite significantly different. But I already knew that, simply by looking at the differing wording, details, forms and sequencing of the Synoptic tradition.

My point here in *JR* is threefold. (1) That the impressions left by Jesus, still evident in the Jesus tradition, despite their fictionalizing diversity, overall demonstrate a consistency which strongly suggests that the impression was left by one and the same historical figure, Jesus.[3] (2) That from the contours of the impressions left we can gain a fairly clear idea of the character of the mission and person who left that impression. That is, from the impact left in the Jesus tradition we are able to discern what and who made that impact. But

---

2. *Jesus Remembered* (Grand Rapids: Eerdmans, 2003) 133-4, 241-2.

3. C. H. Dodd, *The Founder of Christianity* (London: Collins, 1971): 'The first three gospels offer a body of sayings on the whole so consistent, so coherent, and withal so distinctive in manner, style and content, that no reasonable critic should doubt, whatever reservations he may have about individual sayings, that we find here reflected the thought of a single, unique teacher' (21-2).

I still find it necessary to add (3) that we have to be content with these differing and somewhat fictionalized portrayals of Jesus. We cannot press through the tradition to some objective Jesus whom we can discern and evaluate independently of the diverse witness to him, that is, a Jesus disentangled from the differing perspectives of the tradition, with their differing 'fictions' stripped away.[4] As Bultmann reminded us in the case of 'myth', 'myth' is not an element within thought which can be extracted, but a way of thinking. So here, the problem for us is that the personalized impacts pervade the *whole* of an individual disciple's witness, because *ex hypothesi* it was the witness of one who had been *transformed* by that impact. Of course we can deduce a good deal about the Jesus who made these impacts (point 1). But our discerning of this Jesus will always be at least a little out of focus, as when two or three negatives of the same person are superimposed on one another.

BH is not happy with my pressing this point, even though it seems to me to follow directly from the observation that memory and historiography inevitably 'fictionalize' what is remembered to at least some extent. He wants to press behind the impact to the hard facts. Jesus was remembered as preaching about the kingdom because he preached about the kingdom (p. 448). Yes of course. But it is still important to emphasise that we only have access to that preaching through the memory of it, that is, through the particular memories which have been formed into Jesus tradition. We don't have any record of Jesus' preaching the kingdom of God from any other sources, so we do not know how selective that tradition has been — that is, whether some kingdom teaching was not so impact-ful, or not so impress-ive, and so has not been retained in the tradition. Had we only John's Gospel we would have had to conclude that the kingdom was *not* a major feature of Jesus' preaching. Even if we insist on the faithfulness of the first witnesses and of the Synoptic tradition, which I would want to do on my own account, as historians we still do not have a rounded, 360-degree picture of Jesus, only Jesus as he was remembered by his disciples.

Or in the case of miracles (p. 449), it is quite important to continue insisting that we today are not in a position to assert 'miracle' as though we had been able to investigate the event itself. What we can say is that something happened to a particular person ministered to by Jesus and witnessed by others, which was experienced and witnessed as a miracle (a lame man walking again, a blind man seeing). As historians we can say no more, but that much the historian has to say. If we hesitate to say 'miracle' of a healing claimed today at Lourdes or in a rally of some healing evangelist, because the claim has

---

4. *Jesus Remembered*, 125-32.

not been fully investigated by reputable and professional authorities, then we should certainly be that much more discreet in our evaluation of reports of miracles two millennia ago.

And BH's distinction of three different kinds of 'facts' in the case of the resurrection (pp. 451-3) still falls into the trap of yearning for some objectivity in a fact which dispenses with all interpretation. Of course if there was an empty tomb, then there was an empty tomb. But an empty tomb in Jerusalem 30 CE would be a 'datum', not a 'fact' in the definition I use. And the problem for the twenty-first-century historian or biblical scholar is that he is in the twenty-first century and not the first century. For him the empty tomb is *not* itself a datum. For him the only real data are the *reports* of an empty tomb. It is for him to interpret *that* data. And if he concludes that the tomb wherein Jesus was laid was in fact empty, then that is an *interpretation* of the data, a 'fact' as I use the term.[5]

In other words, I think BH is wrong in asserting that I was dealing with three different kinds of 'facts'. I was dealing only with two. For both the first two 'facts' (empty tomb, disciples seeing Jesus) are equally *interpretations* of the only important data available to us, that is, the reports of the first disciples and earliest Christians to that effect. My second kind of 'fact' runs the danger of straining the category 'fact'; I acknowledge that. For it is a way of saying that the *interpretations* of these *facts* (empty tomb, disciples seeing Jesus) can be regarded as a kind of fact too — a meta-fact that makes sense of all the data, including the interpretations put on the basic data of empty tomb and encounters with Jesus.[6] Part of that argument is that the very choice of 'resurrection' as the key category to describe what had happened to Jesus is so unexpected that the unexpectedness of the interpretation becomes an important key to our own interpretation of all the data. Tom Wright's *The Resurrection of the Son of God*[7] picks up the same point to good effect.

BH finally tackles me on the question of a 'grand narrative', arguing that 'grand narratives' are not 'a bad thing', and are indeed unavoidable in historical reconstruction (pp. 453-7). This, I take it, is simply BH pressing home his initial observation that memory and historiography fictionalize and narrativize the past. I can readily accept the basic thrust of this contention. To be sure, one could conclude that Jesus characteristically spoke of 'the kingdom of God' and used the phrase 'the son of man', and these elements of his

---

5. For the distinction between 'event', 'data' and 'fact' see my *Jesus Remembered*, 102-3, but also 107-9.

6. *Jesus Remembered*, 876-9.

7. London: SPCK, 2003.

message do not in themselves constitute a grand narrative. But I agree that they imply some kind of narrative and that for us to spell out their significance in the Jesus tradition inevitably involves us attempting to discern the narrative connecting the various references implied in the different ways Jesus used these phrases.

However, we should not so quickly downsize the postmodern critique of the grand narrative. For that constitutes a protest against the imposition of a single story seen with the eye of the beholder upon a much more diverse and fragmented spread of historical data — as, for example, the idea of scientific 'progress' which has dominated so much modernist thinking.[8] The problem being that the single grand narrative effectively brackets out a good deal of the data, privileges some of the data as more conducive to the story the historian wants to tell, and orders the selected data into a narrative sequence which validates the view put forward by the modern historian. I find that critique applicable to the 'lives of Jesus' of both Dominic Crossan and Tom Wright.[9] They have both bracketed out too much of the data due for consideration (the particularities of Jewish including Galilean culture; the variety of eschatological expectation in Second Temple Judaism). They have privileged some of the data (sapiential and non-apocalyptic Jesus tradition; any echoes of 'return from exile'). And they have imposed a grid on the whole (Mediterranean peasantry; 'return from exile') which fails to do adequate justice to the full range of data.

So I wholly accept that we cannot do history or study the historical Jesus without working with and within various narratives — of God and creation, of God and Israel, and so on. But I find it necessary to continue protesting against the imposition of a particular form of these grand narratives on the much richer and fuller picture of Jesus and his mission which emerges from the more diverse material of the Jesus tradition, the more diverse rememberings of Jesus.

SB queries whether the 'new perspective' I offer on Jesus is very new and then poses six 'points of debate'. It will be simplest to work through them one by one.

But first a comment on the 'new perspective' on Jesus. This was a phrase I introduced in the final chapter of *JR*, not intending to imply that I was at-

8. *Jesus Remembered*, 27-8, 93; I also appreciated the contribution of another Scandinavian on this subject — H. Moxnes, 'The Historical Jesus: From Master Narrative to Cultural Context', *BTB* 28 (1998) 135-49.

9. *Jesus Remembered*, 269, 396-8, 402, 470-7; in reference to J. D. Crossan, *The Historical Jesus: The Life of a Mediterranean Jewish Peasant* (San Francisco: Harper, 1991); N. T. Wright, *Jesus and the Victory of God* (London: SPCK, 1996).

tempting such a major shift in Jesus studies as E. P. Sanders brought about in Pauline studies.[10] But I still would like to claim that the combination of emphases of *JR* does amount to a 'new perspective'. In answer to SB's questions (p. 460): (1) It *is* important to assert that Jesus made an impact before Easter. So much twentieth-century discussion on the historical Jesus/Christ of faith issue has assumed that the faith impact evident in the Gospels is all and only Easter faith. My claim is precisely that the pre-Easter impact of Jesus is still evident in the content and forms of the Synoptic tradition. The degree to which Heinz Schürmann's famous article[11] has been marginalized reinforces the importance of the point to be made.

(2) It is also crucially important to my thesis that the impact was remembered. The point I have already made to BH bears repeating: the impact was a *transformative* impact.[12] What Jesus said (and did) changed the lives of these first disciples; it shaped them; it was truly bread of life for them; it became an integral part of their life-perspective. So of course they remembered it, as we today remember words and events which have helped make us what we are, the transformative moments (weddings, births, deaths, conversion, experiences of the holy, flashes of life-illuminating insights), the mantras and proverbs and principles by which we live. It is not 'ordinary' remembering that I have in mind, but the remembering of the transformative impact.

(3) Of course the claim that the earliest Jesus tradition was oral is not new. But as E. P. Sanders noted, 'The problem is that we do not know how to imagine the oral period'.[13] My criticism in *JR* is that previous attempts to envisage the oral period of the Jesus tradition have been inadequate or have been too quickly sidetracked. I have attempted what seems to me, in the light of the actual shape of the Synoptic tradition as it has come down to us, a more realistic envisaging of that period. The key point of my hypothesis is the connection of the first three points: that the transformative impact drew those thus impacted together (drawn together by the shared response they had

10. *Jesus Remembered*, 881. In fact, however, my attempt to articulate more clearly what I regard as the three major methodological emphases and contributions of *JR* is now published under the title *A New Perspective on Jesus* (Grand Rapids: Baker Academic, 2005).

11. H. Schürmann, 'Die vorösterlichen Anfänge der Logientradition: Versuch eines formgeschichtlichen Zugangs zum Leben Jesu', in H. Ristow & K. Matthiae, eds., *Der historische Jesus und der kerygmatische Christus* (Berlin: Evangelische, 1961) 342-70.

12. I could perhaps call in the supportive testimony of the younger Pliny, cited by SB (p. 470): 'what is affixed by delivery, expression, appearance and gesture of a speaker resides deeper in the soul'. Cf. the observation of David Tracy, that there is never an authentic disclosure of truth which is not also potentially transformative (*The Analogical Imagination: Christian Theology and the Culture of Pluralism* [New York: Crossroad, 1991] 77-78).

13. In E. P. Sanders & M. Davies, *Studying the Synoptic Gospels* (London: SCM, 1989) 141.

made and were continuing to make to Jesus), and that the mutual sharing of these shared experiences/rememberings was strictly speaking the origin of the Jesus tradition as such.

(4) Likewise the insistence that the oral Jesus tradition was performed and celebrated collectively is hardly new. The insight lay at the heart of the initial emergence of form criticism. But again that insight was too quickly lost to view as the focus turned to the communities/churches and the assumption was too readily granted that oral forms reflected more the faith and Sitz im Leben of these churches than the (pre-Easter) impact of Jesus' own mission.[14] The new element is the possibility given us by Kenneth Bailey of envisaging a realistic Sitz im Leben for the performance of the earliest tradition — a middle way between Bultmann's model of 'informal, uncontrolled tradition' and Gerhardsson's model of 'formal, controlled tradition'.[15]

In my view all that amounts to what can be justifiably called 'a new perspective on Jesus'. And there is after all an analogy with 'the new perspective on Paul'. For the latter emerged as a result of Sanders' advocacy of views on Palestinian Judaism which were not new but had hitherto fallen largely on deaf ears.[16] So too I am attempting to bring together and to sharpen insights which have not been sufficiently integrated before or which have been too much neglected.

But now to SB's six main 'points of debate' which I very much welcome; my hope is that such a debate will greatly clarify the whole situation, both the considerable hermeneutical issues at stake and what my contribution amounts to (if anything!).

My response to BH already covers much of what needs to be said on the first two points ('Intention and Impact', 'Remembering and Interpreting'). On the former, I accept that to the extent that I attempt to inquire into Jesus' own intention, the attempt seems to be at some odds with my insistence that we cannot get back to Jesus himself, only the remembered Jesus (p. 462). My point, once again, is simply that it is after all possible to discern the thrust and character of Jesus' message from the impact which it made. As the mark left by a seal on a parchment allows us to deduce the shape of the seal and what it was made of; as crime scene investigation officers can deduce the trajectory of a bullet from its points of entry and exit in the dead body; so the impression left by Jesus tells us quite a lot about Jesus — that is, about the Jesus-who-

---

14. *Jesus Remembered*, 127-8.

15. *Jesus Remembered*, 206, referring to K. E. Bailey, 'Informal Controlled Oral Tradition and the Synoptic Gospels', *Asia Journal of Theology* 5 (1991) 34-54 (here 35-40).

16. E. P. Sanders, *Paul and Palestinian Judaism* (London: SCM, 1997) 1-12, 33-59.

made-that-impact. Again I want to insist that it is the transformative impact made by the teaching of Jesus which in large part determined the modulation from impact to the tradition of that teaching and its resultant shape. It was evidently not an impact which made only a transient or minor effect, but an impact which transformed. Of course it is possible to imagine disciples not much 'switched on' to or by Jesus prior to Easter, or only later trying to recall teaching which became important to them in a subsequent stage of discipleship but only half remembered. What I see in the bulk of the Synoptic tradition, however, is the impact of the teaching which was experienced as transformative photosynthesized (as it were) into oral tradition. So to speak of an impact remembered could be misleading, as though they were two quite distinct processes. What I have in mind, rather, is an impact which transformed and continued to exercise its effect as the teaching became part of them, their *raison d'etre*, fundamentally constitutive of their new way of life. That's what I mean by 'remembering'.[17]

As for 'Remembering and Interpreting' (pp. 463-4), I readily admit that in *JR* I do not provide any theory of memory or of remembering or engage in discussion with those who have. This is principally because *my concern has always been to understand better why and how the Synoptic tradition came to take the shape which it still has,* with all its commonalities and differences, its verbal agreements and disagreements, etc. So my focus has been on traditioning processes, trying to understand better the transition from Jesus to written Gospel. And particularly in *JR* on the *beginnings* of that process: Jesus → disciples → oral tradition. To that extent the title I chose for the analysis, *Jesus Remembered,* left a hostage to fortune which I partly regret, but overall am glad about since it has resulted in this further, I hope clarificatory but also developing, debate.

As already indicated in my response to BH, I have no wish to deny an interpretative element in such remembering, or that any description of an event or recollection of a teaching involves something of interpretation. I deliberately try to avoid the trap of thinking we can easily distinguish a transformative experience from the conceptuality and language we use to de-

---

17. In private correspondence with Birger Gerhardsson I have illustrated the difference I perceive between my 'remembering' and his 'memorization' (see below n. 21) from a personal anecdote. As a primary school child, aged between 5 and 9, I learned my 'times table' by memorization. I owe the fact that I today instantly know $7 \times 8 = 56$ to the memorization exercises in which I participated more than 55 years ago. In the school's cloakroom there was a mirror, which bore the slogan, 'You get back what you give, so smile'. I remember that not because I memorized it. Rather, the slogan made such an impact on me that it became part of my philosophy of life ever since I first read it.

scribe it; on the contrary, I fully acknowledge an unavoidable element of interpretation in the conceptuality and language used. But again the key element for me is the transformative character of the impact made by Jesus. For if the transformative impact involved words (the words of Jesus himself), then in most cases the wording itself is part of the impact — the wording which made the greatest impact probably being the most stable element in the transformed remembering. Here again I have in mind, as part of my overall historical hypothesis, that it was the realization that the impact made on individuals was shared by others which drew disciple groups and then churches together; and that what gave them their continuing identity as disciples was that shared memory and the continuing sharing of these memories = the oral traditions which bound them together as one.

SB's second point merges into his third, on the collective and the individual. On this point I recognize the importance of the case made by Maurice Halbwachs and others on the creative character of 'social memory'.[18] I will want to follow this up in the second volume of my *Christianity in the Making*, where the formation of Christian communities will inevitably be a major concern including the continuing impact of the Jesus tradition. In *JR*, however, my principal focus was on the beginning of the process, where it may be more historically realistic to speak of disciple groups than of churches.

SB's main point of critique on this subject (pp. 464-7), however, is that I have not given enough weight to the role of the *individual* and that to speak of collective or corporate memory 'empties it of a distinctive meaning' (p. 464). I find this critique somewhat puzzling. For on the one hand, I have no desire to play down the role of individuals in the process. I may not have given them the emphasis and attention that SB thinks necessary, but I do emphasize the role of teachers, of 'apostolic custodians' and church-founding apostles; I stress not least the function of Jesus' disciples generating tradition by sharing their personal (eye-witness) experiences; and I envisage assemblies dependent on such individuals and 'senior disciples' telling again particular elements of the Jesus tradition.[19] But on the other hand, it is not really possible to speak of *tradition* except as community tradition.[20] Of course it is true that

18. M. Halbwachs, *On Collective Memory* (ed. L. A. Coser; Chicago: University of Chicago, 1992), incorporating 'The Social Frameworks of Memory' (1952); see also particularly J. Fentress & C. Wickham, *Social Memory* (Oxford: Blackwell, 1992).

19. *Jesus Remembered*, 176-81, 186, 239-40.

20. See further my 'Altering the Default Setting: Re-envisaging the Early Transmission of the Jesus Tradition', *NTS* 49 (2003) 139-75 (here 151-3; above, 54-6). As Fentress & Wickham observe, an individual's memory becomes 'social' when he/she talks about it, shares it with others (*Social Memory*, ix-x).

talk of a community remembering something from a past which no single member of the community experienced personally is an extended use of 're-membering'. But Christians accustomed to celebrate the Lord's Supper 'in re-membrance' of Jesus should have no problem with this extended usage. As a Jewish family celebrating the Passover 'remembers' the first Passover in first person ('we') terms, so a celebration of the living character of the tradition which bound the first churches together can quite adequately be spoken of as a 'remembering', without misleading or falsifying.

Again, I have no wish to deny the importance of eye-witnesses for Papias and Irenaeus (p. 466). But again I insist that my focus in *JR* is on the *beginnings* of the traditioning process, where shared memory and the sharing of these memories (retelling of the shared tradition) must have been fundamental to the process. Of course, I say again, such an emphasis in no way denies or downplays the initiating and continuing input of significant individuals from their per-sonal experience of and with Jesus: the shared memories were those of eye-witnesses! But the initial growth of Christianity would quickly have outpaced the capacity of the original disciples (not just the twelve) to maintain a presence at each new church. We can hardly envisage early churches wholly unable to draw upon the teaching and stories of Jesus unless and until an eye-witness was actually present. To hypothesize that communication of and reflection on the Jesus tradition was the sole preserve of those who had accompanied Jesus from the baptism of John onwards (Acts 1.21-22) is simply unrealistic, in terms both of Christianity's growth and of the enduring character of the Jesus tradition.[21]

As I indicated in my critique of SB in *JR*,[22] it is precisely his lack of at-

---

21. This was also where my questionings begin of the important alternative to Bultmann offered by Birger Gerhardsson, *Memory and Manuscript: Oral Tradition and Written Transmis-sion in Rabbinic Judaism and Early Christianity* (Lund: Gleerup, 1961, 1998). His suggestion of 'a fixed, distinct tradition from, and about, Jesus' (p. 335) taught by Jesus through memorization (p. 328), and thus passed on to the earliest churches, did not seem to me to take full enough ac-count of the flexibility of the tradition as it still appears in the Gospels, which I judge to reflect in part at least the many retellings of many different tradents; though I am happy to acknowl-edge at once that the flexibility which Gerhardsson insists is true also of his hypothesis (see his further contributions on the subject listed in *Jesus Remembered*, 197 n. 129) means that the two hypotheses (Bailey's 'informal, controlled tradition' and Gerhardsson's 'formal, controlled tradi-tion') draw much closer than initially seemed to be the case.

22. SB charges me with denying the importance of the insights of the oral history ap-proach (p. 463). I dispute that reading: in fact I draw on SB's insights at several points later in *JR*; my strictures at *Jesus Remembered*, 198-9 n. 138, 244 n. 284, were focused entirely on SB's failure to take any account of the oral tradition behind the Gospels — all of it, of course, derived more or less from eye-witness disciples (that is integral to my own thesis!), but all of it reflecting in greater or less degree an oral-traditioning process.

tention to the fact of a common shared oral tradition known and rehearsed in the early Christian communities which I see as a major weakness of his own treatment.[23] I simply do not believe that Peter, Mary of Magdala, etc. stored up many memories of Jesus' mission which were only jerked into remembrance by 'oral history' inquiries of a Luke or a Matthew. They had already fed these memories into the living tradition of the churches, as major contributory elements in the forming and shaping of that tradition. No doubt other memories were brought to the surface by inquiries of a Luke or a Matthew, but these would be supplementary to what was already known and performed in the various assemblies week by week. I guess the same was true of Papias and Irenaeus. Their high evaluation of the 'living voice' can hardly be taken as a denial that they knew the Gospel traditions or as suggesting that they in any way denigrated the information provided by the Gospels. After all, it is precisely Papias who tells us about the origins of both Mark's and Matthew's Gospels (Eusebius, *HE* 3.39.15-16),[24] and Irenaeus whose defence of the fourfold Gospel was decisive in determining the boundaries of the canonical Gospels (Irenaeus, *Haer.* 3.11.11).[25]

I see no difficulty, then, in merging the insights of oral tradition as community tradition and recognition of the importance of individual eyewitnesses in providing, contributing to and in at least some measure helping to control the interpretation given to that tradition. Church-founding apos-

---

23. S. Byrskog, *Story as History — History as Story: The Gospel Tradition in the Context of Ancient Oral History* (WUNT 123; Tübingen: Mohr Siebeck, 2000). Fentress & Wickham also observe that oral historians prefer 'to treat memory as a set of documents that happen to be in people's heads rather than in the Public Records Office', and warn against 'a danger of reification' (*Social Memory*, 1-8 [here 2]). The concern is similar to mine on the dangers of objectifying historical 'facts' and of treating oral tradition as equivalent to sequential edition(s) of a literary text.

24. Mark wrote his Gospel as an account/reminder [*hypomnēma*] of the teaching Peter had given verbally (*HE* 2.15.1-2).

25. R. Bauckham, 'The Eyewitnesses and the Gospel Tradition', *JSHJ* 1 (2003) 28-60 (also cited by SB n. 11), deduces quite fairly from Papias that 'oral traditions of the words and deeds of Jesus were attached to specific named eyewitnesses'; but then he draws the further inference that 'this speaks decisively against the old form-critical assumption' that eyewitness origins of the Gospel traditions would have been 'lost in the anonymity of collective transmission' (35; see the whole section, 31-44). He has apparently forgotten that the Synoptic tradition is *not* attributed to named individuals, and that sayings of Jesus echoed or alluded to in Paul, James, 1 Peter, Didache, etc. are *not* even attributed to Jesus (*Jesus Remembered*, 182-3). Papias presumably regarded 'the living voice' as supplementary to the known Gospel tradition, and of course preferable (a living voice), especially by the time of Papias, to a now written tradition. It is not entirely helpful to thus play off the still 'living voice' of individual eyewitnesses against oral tradition becoming written Gospel; not an either-or but a both-and.

tles would have provided a foundational layer of tradition for the churches they founded; Paul no doubt was following an already established practice in this (e.g. 1 Cor. 11.2, 23; Col. 2.6-7; 1 Thess. 4.1). Original disciples of Jesus would of course have contributed crucial recollection and witness in local assemblies to which they belonged. Visits of apostles and highly respected disciples would have been major events in the lives of further-flung Palestinian congregations.[26] Nor need the group settings for the celebration, transmission, reflection on, and elaboration of the oral tradition be always envisaged in liturgical or worship terms. Small catechetical groups, what we today would call study groups, friends meeting over a meal, strategy or planning groups, etc. — the occasions on which teachers rehearsed elements of the oral tradition would have been many and diverse. C. F. D. Moule, in a too much neglected work, provided a good survey of such factors.[27] The interplay of individual and community must have had all the complexity of group dynamics. I press the argument perhaps more than necessary, since the issues are so important — and since it spills over into SB's fourth point of debate.

The second part of SB's fourth point is his criticism of my failure to clarify the role of the Evangelists (pp. 467-8). Here again I find somewhat surprising SB's apparent inability to envisage how the Evangelists presumably interacted with the communities whose tradition must have made up the bulk of their Gospels. What is the problem? Is it so hard to envisage an author/Evangelist familiar with tradition because he was part of a congregation which knew and celebrated that tradition — including the input from original disciples, local teachers and visiting apostles? We should hardly envisage Evangelists starting with a *tabula rasa* and having to gather material for their Gospels 'from scratch', by discovering it all for the first time through personal encounters/interviews with participants in events 50 years earlier, should we? That each did so to some extent at least is entirely feasible; one thinks particularly of some of the so-called M and L material in Matthew and Luke. But to sug-

26. Acts 9.32-43 presumably gives us some inkling of the sort of thing I have in mind. Worth noting is that Luke can represent Peter's sermon to the God-fearing Cornelius beginning, 'You know the message he [God] sent to the people of Israel, preaching peace by Jesus Christ . . .' (10.36).

27. C. F. D. Moule, *The Birth of the New Testament* (London: Black, [3]1981). This was why I hesitated to define oral tradition simply in terms of 'transmission' (SB, p. 462; *Jesus Remembered*, 203). I certainly do not want to imply (nor did I do so) that 'there was no such thing as — or only a minimum of — actual transmission of the Jesus tradition' (SB, p. 470). I find the inference almost ludicrous! Of course the traditioning process included transmission; transmission was certainly a major part of the task of apostles and teachers. But we should not ignore the implication given us in the Synoptic tradition itself, that this was material much mulled over and rehearsed in the very early Christian assemblies.

gest that this was the chief means of gathering Jesus tradition, or the way in which the bulk of the Jesus tradition was gathered by Matthew and Luke is unrealistic in my view. Above all it ignores the larger amount of shared material common to the three Synoptics, which, if I am correct, is much more readily explained in terms of oral tradition shared across churches, rather than as, say, Matthew working in solitary authorial isolation drawing his material exclusively from written documents (Mark and Q).[28]

I have already dealt with the main thrust of SB's fifth point (pp. 468-70) in my response to BH. To reiterate briefly. I have no wish to deny at least a degree of selectivity and creativity in the process of remembering Jesus. But that does not affect my two main arguments, regarding (a) the transformative impact of Jesus on his first disciples, (b) as evidenced in the character of the Jesus tradition in its enduring forms. For example, in *JR* I note that the Galilean and non-passion character of so much of the Q material is best explained as a reflection of the Galilean and pre-passion mission of Jesus.[29] Again, the parable of the two houses (Matt. 7.24-27/Luke 6.47-49) makes much better sense as a memory of the emphasis Jesus put on his teaching; it is less likely that a post-Easter formulation would envisage the 'sure foundation' only in terms of Jesus' pre-Easter teaching. Or again, the Q cluster of discipleship sayings (Matt. 8.19-22/Luke 9.57-62) is best explained as drawn from a pre-Easter tradition, in contrast to the Markan group (Mark 8.34-38 pars.), heavily marked as they are (in contrast) by the lead saying on 'taking the cross' (8.34 pars.).

Finally, I readily accept that in *JR* I have not given sufficient attention to the rhetoric of oral performance. This again is principally due to the tightness of my focus on the beginning of the process of oral traditioning and on the crucial character of the transformative impact of Jesus' mission — crucial as enabling us both to discern the clear outlines of the one who made the impact (my main concern), but also to appreciate better the way in which the transformative impact translated or mapped into the stabilities of the oral tradition. I will have to devote further attention to the latter aspect in volume 2 of *Christianity in the Making*, at which time it will be essential to pay closer attention to the rhetoric of the traditioning process, particularly as Christianity and its tradition began to spread more widely through the Hellenistic world. But I was never in doubt that performance of oral tradition must have involved rhetorical technique, and took it more for granted than was probably wise. For me it was subsumed within the recognition of the flexibility and variability of the tradition-in-performance, which I hope I have emphasized sufficiently.

28. See further my 'Altering the Default Setting', particularly 170-2 (above, 74-76).
29. *Jesus Remembered*, 159 n. 95.

At the same time, however, I would not want that acknowledgment to detract from my other main emphasis as I envisage the traditioning process: that is, the emphasis also on the stabilities of what were probably judged key elements within individual traditions. Here I repeat, my central concern has always been to make best sense of the character of the Jesus tradition as we still have it in the Synoptic Gospels. Central to my attempt to offer a 'new perspective' on Jesus is the conviction that the best explanation is to be found in the transformative impact of Jesus' mission as from the beginning verbalized by the first disciples in the oral tradition, rehearsed by them and others in and through the early disciple groups and earliest churches, and subsequently taken up in fresh (now) literary performance by the Evangelists.

CHAPTER 9

Eyewitnesses and the Oral Jesus Tradition: In Dialogue with Birger Gerhardsson and Richard Bauckham

In *Jesus Remembered*[1] I attempted to penetrate the darkness of the period when the only (or almost the only) information about Jesus' Galilean mission and teaching was in oral form. The attempt was necessitated by the fact that research into the Synoptic tradition had become too dependent on and skewed by a literary mindset which could conceive the functioning of the Jesus tradition and its transmission only in terms of original versions (pure forms, earliest editions), of copying sources conceived as written documents, and of subsequent forms of the tradition produced by deliberate editing of the earlier written material.[2]

The attempt began from a clearly observable fact: (1) that the Synoptic tradition of Jesus' mission provides *a remarkably consistent and coherent portrayal of Jesus*. Even allowing for all the diversity of the individual compilations and emphases, as of course we must do, the Jesus portrayed is recognizably the same.[3] It has always been a primary concern of my study of the Gospel tradi-

---

1. *Christianity in the Making*: Vol. 1. *Jesus Remembered* (Grand Rapids: Eerdmans, 2003). I should perhaps also refer to my briefer *A New Perspective on Jesus: What the Quest for the Historical Jesus Missed* (Grand Rapids: Baker Academic, 2005).

2. See further my 'Altering the Default Setting: Re-envisaging the Early Transmission of the Jesus Tradition', *NTS* 49 (2003) 139-75, reproduced as an appendix (with texts in English) in the *New Perspective* volume (above, 41-84).

3. C. H. Dodd, *The Founder of Christianity* (London: Collins, 1971) expressed it well: 'The first three gospels offer a body of sayings on the whole so consistent, so coherent, and withal so distinctive in manner, style and content, that no reasonable critic should doubt, whatever reservations he may have about individual sayings, that we find here reflected the thought of a single, unique teacher' (pp. 21-22).

tions to understand how and why the Synoptic tradition takes the form that it does — what is clearly the same teaching given in varied terms and combinations, what are clearly the same events narrated in varied detail and with differing emphases.

To this initial fact I add the *a priori* probability as the heart of my oral Jesus tradition thesis: (2) that Jesus was a figure whose mission, in its character and its teaching, made a considerable *impact* on his immediate followers; (3) that this impact was expressed more or less from the first by his disciples in stories about Jesus and in forms of his teaching which were integral to the disciples' own identity as disciples and to their preaching and teaching both before Jesus' death and after his resurrection; and (4) that when individuals joined the new sect by baptism 'in the name of Jesus', (soon) accepting the name 'Christian', they would naturally have wanted to know about this Jesus by whose name they were being identified.[4]

My thesis (5) is that we can best see the link between the fact of (1) and the probabilities of (2)-(4) in the oral celebration, reflection on and transmission of what Jesus did and said, that is in the pattern of *same yet different* which is characteristic of oral tradition and its repeated performance. This suggests in turn (6) that the Synoptic tradition, which has precisely that character, already took that character in the oral period and more or less from the first. Here I should perhaps also point out that my concern, in what was intended to be the first volume of a three-volume analysis of the beginnings of Christianity, was primarily with the *earliest* stage of the traditioning process, with the transition (as we might say) from the impact made by Jesus to the oral tradition which conveyed that impact and which began to take form as an integral feature of the earliest beginnings of the movement which became Christianity. Although I see in the character of the Synoptic tradition as it still is clear evidence of the way the Jesus tradition functioned from the first, I had no intention of discussing the subsequent use and function of the Jesus tradition or its transition to written forms and the written Gospels. That will more naturally be a subject for treatment in the subsequent volumes.

The thesis has been subjected to a good deal of critique, all of it personally helpful in clarifying issues and in clarifying my own thinking. I have al-

---

4. For me it is hard to avoid the inference that this was a or principal reason for Paul spending so much time with Peter on his first visit to Jerusalem following his conversion (Gal. 1.18) — 'to get to know' Peter precisely in his role of leading disciple of Jesus and therefore primary source of stories about and teaching of Jesus; see further my *Galatians* (BNTC; London: Black, 1993), pp. 73-4.

ready responded to several of these critiques,[5] and in another context have taken further the discussion, neglected in *Jesus Remembered,* on social memory.[6] Two of the main criticisms have been that I have not given sufficient weight either to *the teaching process* by which the oral tradition was transmitted[7] or to the *eyewitness* character of the Jesus tradition.[8] Since I share much of the motivation and concern of both the principal critics, Birger Gerhardsson and Richard Bauckham, I welcome the opportunity to clarify the issues which have emerged between us and, hopefully, to take the discussion of this important subject forward. Bauckham's is a large monograph on the theme covering many aspects of the subject,[9] but Gerhardsson's essay is primarily a critique of *Jesus Remembered,* so I will begin with it.

It was Gerhardsson who stimulated the interest I already had in the Gospel tradition as oral tradition when he invited me to join a valuable international seminar on the subject, whose discussions extended across several years.[10] And his work on the Gospel tradition from the perspective of oral rabbinic tradition has been an invaluable correction to the alternative models of the early form critics.[11] I regret that in my response to Gerhardsson I over-reacted to his emphasis on *memorization* as the principal characteristic of earliest Christian teaching (how they learned from and about Jesus), without

5. 'On History, Memory and Eyewitnesses: In Response to Bengt Holmberg and Samuel Byrskog', *JSNT* 26 (2004) 473-87 (above, 199-212); 'On Faith and History, and Living Tradition: In Response to Robert Morgan and Andrew Gregory', *ExpTim* 116 (2004-5) 13-19.

6. 'Social Memory and the Oral Jesus Tradition', in S. C. Barton, L. T. Stuckenbruck & B. G. Wold, eds., *Memory in the Bible and Antiquity* (WUNT 212; Tübingen: Mohr Siebeck, 2007), pp. 179-94 (below, 230-47). See also A. Kirk & T. Thatcher, eds., *Memory, Tradition, and Text: Uses of the Past in Early Christianity* (SBLSS 52; Atlanta: SBL, 2005); S. Byrskog, 'A New Quest for the *Sitz im Leben*: Social Memory, the Jesus Tradition and the Gospel of Matthew', *NTS* 52 (2006) 319-36.

7. Particularly B. Gerhardsson, 'The Secret of the Transmission of the Unwritten Jesus Tradition', *NTS* 51 (2005) 1-18.

8. R. Bauckham, *Jesus and the Eyewitnesses: The Gospels as Eyewitness Testimony* (Grand Rapids: Eerdmans, 2006), building particularly on S. Byrskog, *Story as History — History as Story* (WUNT 123; Tübingen: Mohr Siebeck, 2000).

9. I will here focus only on his critique of *Jesus Remembered;* other matters, especially Bauckham's treatment of John's Gospel, will provide an agenda for discussion on another occasion.

10. See H. Wansbrough, ed., *Jesus and the Oral Gospel Tradition* (JSNTSup 64; Sheffield Academic, 1991).

11. B. Gerhardsson, *Memory and Manuscript: Oral Tradition and Written Transmission in Rabbinic Judaism and Early Christianity* (Lund: Gleerup, 1961, 1998); *Tradition and Transmission in Early Christianity* (Lund: Gleerup, 1964); and most recently *The Reliability of the Gospel Tradition* (Peabody: Hendrickson, 2001), which includes two other earlier studies.

taking sufficient account of the degree to which his model also allows for the variation which is still evident in the Synoptic tradition.[12] I also accept Bauckham's shrewd observation that I may have allowed myself to follow Kenneth Bailey[13] too closely in setting Bultmann and Gerhardsson in sharp antithesis — between informal, uncontrolled tradition (Bultmann) on the one hand, and formal, controlled tradition (Gerhardsson) on the other — in order to make more room between them for Bailey's own thesis of informal, controlled tradition.[14] In the event, the difference (as with Bauckham)[15] becomes more one of the relative weight to be given to the 'formal' and 'informal' of the different formulations. Since we all want to affirm the 'reliability' of the Gospel tradition (to use Gerhardsson's term) the difference does not amount to very much.[16]

Gerhardsson's *NTS* essay, unfortunately, bears the marks of these differences of emphasis, so I hope in this response to continue rebuilding some of the bridges which link our concerns and our work.

On two of Gerhardsson's initial points of criticism I agree, that Jesus was pre-eminently a teacher, and hardly to be categorized merely as 'a popular teller of tales who captivated disciples and throngs with variable performances'.[17] Nor was he simply passing on the wisdom of others.[18] I am not sure if this is a criticism directed at me, since I nowhere present Jesus in such terms. On the contrary, central to my thesis regarding the Jesus tradition is the claim that Jesus made a huge impact on his disciples by his mission and teaching, and that it is this impact which is imprinted on the Jesus tradition,

---

12. 'Secret', pp. 15-16, where he observes that he had developed the point about the flexibility of memorized text/tradition too little in *Memory,* but did so in several of his later studies. I hope that subsequent exchanges with Gerhardsson have already clarified and softened the point of disagreement.

13. K. E. Bailey, 'Informal Controlled Oral Tradition and the Synoptic Gospels', *Asia Journal of Theology* 5 (1991) 34-54; also my *Jesus Remembered,* pp. 205-9. It should be evident from my critique of W. H. Kelber, *The Oral and the Written Gospel* (Philadelphia: Fortress, 1983) in *Jesus Remembered,* pp. 199-204, that although I found Kelber's interest in 'the oral gospel' stimulating (as also his continuing interest in the subject), it was Bailey's model which has been for me the primary inspiration (*pace* Gerhardsson, 'Secret', p. 6).

14. *Eyewitnesses,* p. 251.

15. Like Gerhardsson, Bauckham operates with an understanding of 'memorization' which includes the sort of variation and the extent of variation still visible in the Synoptic tradition (*Eyewitnesses,* pp. 285-7).

16. Gerhardsson ('Secret', p. 17) makes a claim for the 'relative uniformity' of the Jesus traditions similar to my own (above at n. 3).

17. I am not sure whom Gerhardsson thinks he is criticizing when he returns to the point in 'Secret', p. 9. The same confusion is evident in the final summary on p. 17.

18. 'Secret', p. 7.

in that the tradition was both itself an expression of that impact and transmitted that impact to others. The talk of 'variable performances' must refer to the way the Jesus tradition was used, in celebration, teaching and worship, though I also regard it as entirely likely that Jesus did repeat and vary his teaching on the same subjects, and that such variation is wholly in character with oral teaching and transmission.

Gerhardsson seizes on my term 'impact' — wholly understandably, since I make so much of it. But he plays it off against his own emphasis on Jesus' teaching: I did not describe Jesus' teaching methods; and 'it is presumably rather difficult to explain what an *impact* is'.[19] There is a valid point here. I did not go into Jesus' teaching methods in any detail as teaching methods; when I treated Jesus as teacher my focus was on what Jesus taught.[20] But I use the term 'impact' because it is a fuller term than 'teaching'; it includes the impression made by what Jesus did as well as the teaching he gave. The Synoptic tradition is not made up solely of teaching; it includes narratives as well. The term 'impact' I continue to regard as helpful because it describes the *effect* Jesus had on his disciples, by his life and actions as well as by his teaching. But also because the term describes the effect of his teaching, not simply as 'firm texts' taught and learned, but as *life-shaping lessons* learned both from Jesus' explicit teaching and from the way in which Jesus lived out his teaching. So 'impact' and 'teaching' should not be played off against each other.[21]

A further criticism is that I do not think the Jesus tradition was passed on 'in the form of texts' — tradition, yes, 'but not one of firm texts'. 'Dunn believes neither in firm texts nor in proper acts of transmission'.[22] I find this criticism somewhat puzzling. My concern from the first, as already indicated, is to make sense of the variability of what are stories of the same events and the same teaching. If Gerhardsson wants to classify this variable tradition as 'firm texts', then I am a little surprised, since the variability seems to be somewhat other than the firmness of 'firm texts'. If however the emphasis is on the

---

19. 'Secret', p. 8. I have in mind what Gerhardsson himself observes: 'Nobody can have had a greater interest than Jesus' disciples and adherents in his person, his actions, his teachings, and his destiny; and nobody can have had a greater reason for preserving the legacy from him' (p. 14).

20. *Jesus Remembered*, p. 177, chs. 12-14.

21. As Gerhardsson is in danger of doing ('Secret', p. 9). Prior to Gerhardsson's article, in private correspondence with him I had attempted to elaborate the distinction between 'impact' and 'memorization', and repeat the point in *New Perspective*, pp. 44-5 n. 31.

22. 'Secret', pp. 7-8. He also criticizes me for avoiding talk of Jesus' 'sayings' and preferring 'the softer expression Jesus' "teaching"' (p. 8). I am not sure quite what he is after here; for me the term 'teaching' is the stronger.

fact that the variable texts convey what is in substance the same teaching, the same narrative, then we are at one, though I continue to have reservations as to whether these traditions are most helpfully classified as 'firm texts'. I think I see what he means by 'proper acts of transmission' — presumably thinking of teachers and what has more traditionally been designated as catechetical tradition. For my own part I also emphasize the role of teachers, with the obvious implication that they *taught* the tradition for whose retention and transmission they would have had a primary responsibility in the early Christian communities. I would have hoped that it was more obvious than evidently it is that when I speak of 'performances' of the Jesus tradition within early Christian communities I of course include the specific role and function of the teachers of the community.[23] True, I may not emphasize Paul's use of the technical terms for tradition and tradition transmission as much as I might have done.[24] But that was because my primary concern was with the tradition as it has actually come down to us. Assuming the Jesus tradition had much the same form and character for Paul as it still has in the Synoptics, the Synoptic tradition can then be said to represent the tradition which he received and its variability the manner in which he transmitted it. And presumably Paul and the teachers narrated stories about Jesus as well as passed on teaching; how else can we envisage the narrative tradition of the Gospels being used and conveyed among the churches?[25]

It is true that I did not deal with the Jesus tradition by classifying it into different types, like the early form critics.[26] It was more to the point in developing my thesis to be able to highlight how much of the tradition, not only narrative but also the sayings material, was marked by considerable variation in detail, variations which it was more sensible to attribute to the variability of the oral traditioning process than to literary pasting and redaction.[27] At the same time I made a specific point of noting that many of the narratives have a constant core element, usually focused in a dialogue with Jesus or a saying of

23. It is true that we have little evidence of 'celebrations and other performances following Bailey's rural model' as customary in the earliest churches ('Secret', p. 17), though I think it a fair assumption that the Jesus tradition was not simply 'taught' but 'celebrated' in different ways (reflection, worship, the delight of story-telling) in the earliest gatherings of believers in Messiah Jesus — as probably reflected in passages like 1 Cor. 14.26 and Col. 3.16.

24. 'Secret', p. 9.

25. This in response to Gerhardsson's observation that 'nowhere in the NT sources do I get the impression that they [the teachers] were popular narrators' ('Secret', p. 10).

26. 'Dunn has not studied the interesting differences between types of text in the synoptic gospels' ('Secret', p. 13).

27. See *Jesus Remembered*, pp. 210-38; 'Altering the Default Setting', pp. 160-70 = *New Perspective*, pp. 106-20 (above, 63-74).

Jesus.[28] So far as the sayings material was concerned, it was necessary to focus on such variations in what were evidently recollections of the same teaching of Jesus in order to make the case for an oral rather than a literary-type process of transmission. But of course I could assume the point which Bailey had made in distinguishing the inflexibility in poems and proverbs, from the relative flexibility of parables and traditions important for the identity of the community, and from the total flexibility of jokes and casual news.[29] And the stability and sameness of the sayings tradition was and remains central to my whole thesis: that it attests the degree of close similarity in the impact Jesus made and that such a unanimity of the diverse impacts assuredly indicates what it was which Jesus had actually said or taught on one or several occasions.

I was surprised, then, that Gerhardsson associates my understanding of community tradition with Durkheim's ideas about the creativity of the collective and the early form critics' arguments that many elements in the gospels are community creations.[30] I have addressed the theories of social memory, associated particularly with Maurice Halbwachs, elsewhere.[31] Here I should perhaps just say that I find the comment rather astonishing, since it is precisely the concern of my thesis in *Jesus Remembered* to affirm the *stability* of the tradition, that the tradition retains and continues to convey the impact made by Jesus on his first disciples. It was in effect one of my main concerns, to refute the social memory theorists and the early form critics whom Gerhardsson detects lurking behind *Jesus Remembered*.

The principal ground of Gerhardsson's critique, however, focuses on the issue of 'orality'. He begins by criticising a model of oral tradition which is 'supposed to exist here, there, and everywhere in the world' or is drawn from a twentieth-century Arab peasant culture (Bailey), instead of a model anchored in the 'concrete historical milieu' of Jesus' own times (referring presumably to the rabbinic model).[32] That critique, I think, hardly does justice to a thesis based on the character of oral tradition in a good many communities of the recent past and the present (not just folk stories from ancient Greece and Yugoslavia or twentieth-century Arab peasants), as demonstrated by various anthropologists and specialists in oral tradition.[33] What drew me to Bailey's model (I first met him thirty years ago) is the way the examples Bailey gives

---

28. *Jesus Remembered*, pp. 210-24.
29. *Jesus Remembered*, pp. 206-7.
30. 'Secret', pp. 8-9.
31. See above n. 6.
32. 'Secret', pp. 6-7.
33. Bauckham (*Eyewitnesses*, pp. 271-4) draws very helpfully on some of the same material, particularly J. Vansina, *Oral Tradition as History* (Madison: University of Wisconsin, 1985).

parallel the Synoptic tradition and the degree to which the model he offers helps to explain the Synoptic tradition's character as 'the same yet different'.

Gerhardsson seems to think of 'verbosity (wordiness with many repetitions)' as characteristic of oral narration and contrasts this with the 'laconicism and brevity' of Jesus' sayings;[34] but it is the character of the Jesus tradition as it still is in the Synoptic tradition (and always was), in its character as the same despite differences, that we are trying to explain. He insists on taking the model of orality ('tellers of Dunn's orality type') from the 'folkloristic type' made familiar by A. B. Lord, and drawn on by Kelber.[35] With this he contrasts the 'didactic, tersely and carefully formulated' Jesus material.[36] Here again the conception of orality with which he works is different from the model suggested by Bailey, who makes a point of noting that in the communities to which he refers, proverbs and aphorisms retain a much more fixed and stable form than popular tales of little importance for the life and identity of the community. It is precisely the Bailey model that I follow; 'folkloristic' orality extends across several generations, a quite different situation from that envisaged for the Jesus tradition as it appears in the Synoptic Gospels.[37]

The most astonishing element in Gerhardsson's critique, for me, is his refusal to accept that 'the Israel of NT times can be characterized as an oral society'.[38] It is true, of course, that Israel understood itself in terms of its sacred scriptures — Torah, Prophets and Writings. But how many Torah scrolls were available for public consultation, let alone private ownership? And how many could read such Torah scrolls as they had access to? The most authoritative estimates of literacy levels in first-century Israel put them at no higher than 10%, or lower.[39] Given the centrality of these scriptures to Israel's iden-

---

34. 'Secret', p. 11; Gerhardsson seems to be focusing on the sayings material and generalizing from it to make his contrast with 'popular narration'.

35. Dunn's 'is a forceful variation of the folkloristic orality approach' ('Secret', p. 17).

36. 'Secret', p. 12; similarly the penultimate summary point: 'The gospel *material* cannot have been narrative material with the character of orality' (p. 18). But apart from anything else, that is to ignore the fact that so much of the gospel tradition is narrative.

37. Bauckham builds on Vansina's discussion of oral tradition in noting that 'oral *history*' is the more appropriate term to describe the process of retaining and recording memories within the lifetime of the individuals who heard the person and witnessed the events, whereas 'oral *tradition*' has customarily been used to denote the transmission of tradition across the generations; Bauckham's whole treatment on the theme (*Eyewitnesses,* chs. 10-13) has many valuable insights.

38. 'Secret', pp. 14, 17.

39. See particularly C. Hezser, *Jewish Literacy in Roman Palestine* (Tübingen: Mohr Siebeck, 2001).

tity we should probably allow for higher percentages in cities and larger villages. But most of those who had such skills would be priests, scribes and rabbis; the prominence of a class of 'scribes' in the Gospel tradition is a reminder that the majority of Israelites would have had to depend on such professionals for reading and writing important documents. And I agree that it is certainly unwise to assume that 'leading representatives of the gospel tradition were illiterate',[40] even when Acts 4.13 is taken into account.[41] Nevertheless, it is a much more probably historical scenario to assume that the great majority of Galilee and Judea knew their scriptures only by *hearing* them read and taught, and that the large majority of the first disciples similarly learned by hearing rather than reading. I simply question whether such a society can be denied the epithet 'oral'. The description does not dispute the centrality of Torah and other written texts with the authority of scripture to Jewish (and earliest Christian) communities. It simply recognizes that by far the most predominant way of passing on teaching and tradition and information in and to these communities was by oral communication, that is, in an oral culture.

Gerhardsson is evidently reacting against an understanding of 'orality' which he associates with the retelling of stories, and which he identifies as a 'folkloristic approach' and attributes to me. Thus in his final summary he writes, 'nor is it easy to produce any evidence showing that Jesus or his disciples and other leading adherents were *tellers* of the orality type'.[42] Of course he cannot and would not deny that Jesus gave his teaching orally, or that his disciples and the earliest tradents passed on their accounts of Jesus and of his teaching orally. Since his own major work was precisely on the oral transmission of the Jesus tradition he can hardly dismiss the term 'orality' so completely or confine its reference to a specific folkloristic telling of ancient sagas as he seems to want to do.[43] Nor do I infer that he wants to regard the early oral Jesus tradition as already having the character of written text ('firm texts' in that sense), since he thinks that his own thesis regarding the oral transmis-

---

40. 'Secret', p. 14.

41. Recent commentators on the letter of James, for example, do not think that the quality of Greek and rhetoric need be counted against the view that the letter was written by a Christian leader of the first generation from Jerusalem.

42. 'Secret', pp. 17-18.

43. I presume this is what he means when he claims finally that 'the orality model, a variable telling of *one and the same kind* during the whole traditioning process, cannot explain the clear differences between different text types within the gospel tradition' ('Secret', p. 18; my emphasis). On the contrary, the value of envisaging the early transmission of the Synoptic tradition in oral terms is that it provides an explanation precisely for the range and character of the differences still evident in the Synoptic tradition.

sion of the Jesus tradition is fully able to explain the variableness still evident in the Synoptic tradition. Gerhardsson seems, unfortunately, to have something of a blind spot here, since by denigrating the concept of 'orality' so completely and without qualification he runs the danger of undermining his own thesis.

In the end, I confess to leaving Gerhardsson's essay feeling rather baffled and wondering what it is we are arguing about since we seem to have such similar concerns and since our views of the origin and early transmission of the Jesus tradition seem to be so close in substance if not in terminology.

Richard Bauckham's volume is in large part — the only part I interact with here — a critique of an argument introduced by the early form critics which has become a too unquestioned assumption of most study of the Gospel traditions since then: 'that the traditions about Jesus, his acts and his words, passed through a long process of oral tradition in the early Christian communities and reached the writers of the Gospels only at a late stage of this process.[44] . . . [the assumption] that, whatever the form in which the eyewitnesses of the history of Jesus first told their stories or repeated Jesus' teachings, a long process of anonymous transmission in the communities intervened between their testimony and the writings of the Gospels. . . . [the assumption that] however conservative or creative the tradition may have been, the eyewitnesses from whom it originated appear to have nothing significantly to do with it once they have set it going'. Bauckham's counter-thesis is that 'the period between the "historical" Jesus and the Gospels was actually spanned, not by anonymous community transmission, but by the continuing presence and testimony of the eyewitnesses, who remained the authoritative sources of their traditions until their deaths. . . . Gospel traditions did not, for the most part, circulate anonymously but in the name of the eyewitnesses to whom they were due'.[45]

> It is the contention of this book that, in the period up to the writing of the Gospels, gospel traditions were connected with named and known eyewitnesses, people who had heard the teaching of Jesus from his lips and committed it to memory, people who had witnessed the events of his ministry, death, and resurrection and themselves had formulated the stories about these events that they told. These eyewitnesses did not merely set going a process of oral transmission that soon went its own way with-

44. See further *Eyewitnesses*, pp. 241-6.
45. *Eyewitnesses*, pp. 6, 8.

out reference to them. They remained throughout their lifetimes the sources and . . . the authoritative guarantors of the stories they continued to tell.[46]

I agree in fact with much of this criticism. A characteristic expression of the prevailing 'assumption' is the deduction (from the fact that the NT letter-writers show little interest in attributing echoes of Jesus tradition to Jesus) that early churches' anonymous Jesus tradition was part of a larger resource of catechetical and paraenetic material from which the Evangelists subsequently drew in composing their Gospels. The consequence being that the Synoptic tradition contains a largely indiscriminate mixture of material, some of it stemming from Jesus, some of it from elsewhere — hence requiring, of course, modern attempts to disentangle genuine Jesus material from material which did not stem from Jesus.[47] Bauckham, however includes me among those whom he critiques,[48] so a response is called for, by way partly of clarification and partly in the hope of helping to take the debate on the subject forward. I make a number of points.

(1) In *Jesus Remembered* I did not wish to play down the role of the first disciples and apostles, as Bauckham suggests,[49] though I confess I did not give them so much prominence.[50] It is my own view that the first disciples continued to preach and teach. I fully accept one of Bauckham's main arguments, that the early churches would have wanted to hear first-hand accounts of Jesus from those who had been with him during his mission. And though I also agree that the Jerusalem leadership would have provided a primary reference point for these traditions (as, I strongly believe, Gal. 1.18 attests), I am less sure that they were able to exercise a very extensive monitoring role ('controlled tradition') as the new movement spread more widely.[51]

---

46. *Eyewitnesses*, p. 93.

47. The argument is most recently restated by J. Schröter, 'Anfänge der Jesusüberliefe-rung: Überlieferungsgeschichtliche Beobachtungen zu einem Bereich urchristlicher Theologie-geschichte', *NTS* 50 (2004) 53-76.

48. *Eyewitnesses*, p. 34 n. 71, ch. 12.

49. In *Jesus Remembered* I refer to 'first disciples' and 'teachers' quite frequently (in ch. 8 particularly).

50. I have attempted to rectify some of that in subsequent discussion — directly with Byrskog (n. 5 above) and in the essay in n. 6 above. It is perhaps worth noting that I have also been criticized for giving too much weight to the role of the first disciples and apostles, by Schröter in particular, in discussion arising out of his 'Anfänge' (n. 47 above), in 'Kontroverse: Der erinnerte Jesus als Begründer des Christentums?', *Zeitschrift für Neues Testament* 20.10 (2007) 46-61.

51. Bauckham echoes the argument of Gerhardsson's *Reliability*, though he thinks Ger-

(2) In *Jesus Remembered*, however, I thought it important to recognize that the first disciples could not provide an authoritative check on the use made of the Jesus tradition in more than a few churches. Apart from anything else, as soon as the number of congregations grew beyond about 100, there would not have been enough 'first disciples' around to instruct all the new communities and to continue in attendance at their gatherings during the time they received their basic foundation training.[52] Within twenty-five to thirty years little churches (house churches, apartment congregations, tenement groups) had spread widely through the north-eastern quadrant of the Mediterranean — and more widely elsewhere, but of that expansion we know too little. Not just in the city centres established by Paul in particular, but spreading from these centres, through Asia, Macedonia and Achaia,[53] and no doubt elsewhere. The point is that many of these churches at their foundation received their stock of Jesus tradition at second or third hand; Epaphras as the church-founder of the Lycus valley churches (Colossae, Laodicea, Hierapolis) is a good illustrative example (Col. 1.7; 4.12-13).[54]

(3) For me in *Jesus Remembered* the important point which needed to be made is that the process of oral tradition, both transmission and ongoing celebration and use, retained throughout that process *more or less the character and substance of its earliest telling and use* (by the first disciples). Even when eyewitnesses were not present, in the foundation and establishment of the church, the Jesus tradition retained the same character and substance which we still see in the Synoptic tradition to this day. So I slightly react

---

hardsson's focus on (just) the Twelve is excessive (*Eyewitnesses*, pp. 94, 299). He criticizes me for focusing 'on the early transmission of Jesus tradition in Palestinian Jewish villages, ignoring the Jerusalem church' (p. 298). My model did focus on village communities, partly because the model includes a process of Jesus tradition which began before Easter, and partly because it also includes the growth of earliest Christianity beyond Jerusalem, as also very soon beyond Palestine.

52. In responding to a first draft of this section of the paper, Richard refers to the more than 500 of 1 Cor. 15.6 ('many of the 500 of 1 Cor 15 must surely have been eyewitnesses of some events in the ministry of Jesus as well as of that resurrection appearance'). It is more likely, in my view, that the majority of the 500 were recruited during the post-Easter preaching. Many of them, no doubt, like the 'all the apostles' of the subsequent resurrection appearance (15.7), had a role in establishing and growing new churches, but most of them would have depended on instruction from the original disciples as to the large bulk of the Jesus tradition.

53. 'The assemblies' (plural) of Galatia (1 Cor. 16.1), Asia (16.19), Macedonia (2 Cor. 8.1) and Achaia (Rom. 15.26; 2 Cor. 9.2).

54. Richard responds: 'People travelled a lot between the churches [a claim I strongly agree with]. Travelling teachers who had received their Jesus traditions from eyewitnesses would visit many churches.' 'When Epaphras first taught the Colossians, for example, about Jesus, I guess he'd have said: "These are the traditions Paul received from the apostles in Jerusalem, who saw and heard Jesus".'

against part of the opening quotation from Bauckham,[55] because my point is precisely that 'the form in which the eyewitnesses of the history of Jesus first told their stories or repeated Jesus' teachings' had enduring significance — not, let me be clear on this, in fixing a precise combination of material or sequence of words, to be repeated rote-like by subsequent teachers, but in establishing the form and substance of a story or teaching which remained stable,[56] and often a core element of a story and key-note terms which did remain more or less fixed, in the varied retellings of the tradition thereafter, that is, in the manner still evident in the Synoptic tradition.[57] My concern was not to emphasize the fact of community transmission (certainly not in contrast to the continued teaching role of those who had been earliest disciples), but to observe that even if or when the tradition that has come down to us came through communities without explicit attribution, *that tradition could be and was assumed to retain the character and substance and variability of the tradition as first articulated by the earliest disciples*, 'whose memories already had a degree of stability that severely limited the degree to which they were changed by further interpretative insight.'[58]

(4) Bauckham, of course, is concerned primarily with the tradition which the Evangelists actually incorporated in their Gospels.[59] His argument is that there are sufficient indicators in the Synoptic tradition both that the Jesus tradition originated with eye-witnesses and that implicit in the Synoptic tradition is the claim that this tradition was authenticated by the eye-witnesses. Now there is certainly something in this. I agree that at least sev-

---

55. '... whatever the form in which the eyewitnesses of the history of Jesus first told their stories or repeated Jesus' teachings, a long process of anonymous transmission in the communities intervened between their testimony and the writings of the Gospels'.

56. Bauckham's preferred term is 'gist' (*Eyewitnesses* particularly pp. 333-4).

57. In insisting on the importance of the eyewitness 'source' (*Eyewitnesses*, p. 292), Bauckham may be in danger of lapsing into the literary fallacy of assuming that there was an original version of any story or teaching, so that variations from the original were by definition of lesser value than and a corruption of the original. The same danger is evident in his response: 'Especially importantly, many Jewish Christians from everywhere would have visited Jerusalem and heard the Jerusalem apostles themselves recite their official version of the traditions'. The idea of an 'official version' is close to that of an 'original version', and carries an even stronger implication that any divergence from the 'official version' was less 'official'. A major concern of mine has been to emphasise that integral to the Jesus tradition from the beginning was its diversity and variance of detail and emphasis, and that this should be recognized as simply the character of the oral Jesus tradition and not be regarded as a negative feature. Variation is not degeneration. See further 'Altering', pp. 172-3 = *New Perspective*, p. 123.

58. I quote the last clauses from Bauckham, *Eyewitnesses*, p. 355.

59. I should perhaps repeat that my concern in *Jesus Remembered* was primarily with the beginning of the process, not the later stages.

eral of the stories included in the Synoptic tradition can and probably should be referred back to those actually involved in the episode narrated.[60] But Bauckham's case is illustrated most clearly by the narrative tradition.[61] And the arguments about anonymity have always focused primarily on the sayings or teaching tradition. Here it is much harder for Bauckham to make his case,[62] especially when we have to reckon with the Q material behind Matthew and Luke, where no attempt seems to be made to identify particular earwitnesses as the authority for attributing this teaching to Jesus.[63] Although it is certainly plausible that Matthew and Luke, familiar as they were with the Q traditions, made a point of checking out each item they used in composing their Gospels with Peter and the others, their seemingly straightforward dependence on the unattributed traditions of Q leaves the issue in some doubt. My alternative proposal is that both Matthew and Luke could be confident that the Q material, however it came to them (but much of it probably familiar from regular usage in their congregations), was in character and substance ('gist') teaching that had originated with Jesus himself, and passed on initially (and repeatedly) by Jesus' first disciples.

(5) My primary concern in *Jesus Remembered* was to understand how

60. *Eyewitnesses*, ch. 3. The obvious examples are Bartimaeus, Simon of Cyrene and the women at Jesus' tomb. I made similar suggestions myself in *Jesus Remembered*, pp. 643, 774 n. 55 and 832-4. I remain puzzled, however, as does Bauckham, at what may be deduced from the fact that Matthew changes the name of the taxcollector called by Jesus from Levi to Matthew (*Eyewitnesses*, pp. 108-12): if Levi was the one personally involved, why the change to Matthew? or if Matthew was the eyewitness, then why does Mark have him as Levi?

61. In interesting contrast to Gerhardsson who focuses on the sayings tradition (the *meshalim*).

62. In our correspondence Richard refers me to *Jesus and the Eyewitnesses*, chs. 5–7, where he argues 'that the list of the Twelve in all three Synoptics functions to claim the general authority of the Twelve for much of their traditions', and claims 'that Mark, Luke (and John) use the "inclusio of eyewitness testimony" to indicate the major eyewitnesses behind their Gospels'.

63. The claim made by Luke in the prologue to his Gospel (Luke 1.1-4) is naturally critical for Bauckham's argument (*Eyewitnesses*, pp. 116-24). I have no particular wish to question its bearing on Luke's own use of the Jesus tradition. But how far can Luke's claim be applied to the pre-Lukan oral tradition? And does it imply that Luke checked the Q tradition, or that he was able to 'follow through' (*parakoloutheō*) everything carefully from the first' (see BDAG 767) because he knew he could take it for granted that the Q material had derived from eyewitnesses ('just as they were handed on to us by those who from the beginning were eyewitnesses and servants of the word')? In response to P. Barnett, *The Birth of Christianity: The First Twenty Years* (Grand Rapids: Eerdmans, 2005) and his somewhat dismissive critique (p. 117 n. 27), it should be noted that the key term (at this point), *diēgēsis*, simply refers to 'an orderly description of facts, events or words' and can refer to other than a *written* narrative (BDAG, p. 245); see further J. A. Fitzmyer, *Luke I–IX* (AB 28; New York: Doubleday, 1981), p. 292.

the Synoptic tradition came to its present form, which, for all its variation and diversity, provides such a remarkably consistent and coherent portrayal of Jesus. My thesis, that Jesus made a major impact on his first disciples which is imprinted in the stories they told about Jesus and the teaching they passed on from Jesus, helps explain that consistent and coherent portrayal. For it indicates a mechanism (the process of oral tradition) whereby that initial impact has been permanently retained in and transmitted through the oral tradition which became the Synoptic tradition. The strength of this thesis, in relation to Bauckham's, is that even if we have to allow that much of the tradition was transmitted without explicit attribution to first disciples (eye-witnesses), the tradition nevertheless had imprinted upon it the character of the impression made by Jesus on his first disciples.[64] I am as eager as Bauckham that the role of eye-witnesses in formulating the Jesus tradition be fully recognized, but if he wants *the eye-witnesses themselves* to bridge the gap between initial formulation and transcription in written Gospels, he may be pressing his case beyond the evidence as it has come down to us.[65] An alternative thesis which recognizes the degree of anonymity that seems to be indicated in the transmission and use of the Jesus tradition, but which can also affirm that such anonymous tradition has nevertheless retained the character and substance of the tradition as initially articulated by the first witnesses, is surely to be welcomed by those who share Bauckham's legitimate concerns.

(6) A minor, but significant grumble is the way Bauckham uses the Papias tradition.[66] Papias certainly affirms the importance he attributed to eyewitness testimony. But he did so in antithesis to 'information from books', not to 'a lengthy chain of oral tradition'. It is certainly true that for Papias the 'living voice' is 'first-hand information', and *not* oral tradition, as many scholars have supposed. But the contrast Papias makes is between first-hand information and information from books; oral tradition is not in view here. To draw from Papias' statement an inference that Papias distrusted oral tradition is at best tendentious. Rather we should infer, in my view, that what Papias knew about these earlier days he knew through the oral tradition of the com-

---

64. Here I welcome Bauckham's helpful analysis of what makes eyewitness *memory* so reliable (*Eyewitnesses,* ch. 13; in reference to 'remembering Jesus', particularly pp. 341-2).

65. 'Dunn cannot take seriously a role for the eyewitnesses once their testimony had been absorbed into the oral tradition. . . . The alternative . . . is that the traditions as transmitted in the churches *explicitly* acknowledged their sources in the eyewitnesses and the authority of the eyewitnesses for their reliability' (*Eyewitnesses,* p. 292; my emphasis). But it is precisely the 'explicit' acknowledgment of eyewitness sources which is lacking (or has to be deduced — but is it then 'explicit'?) in the Q and Synoptic tradition.

66. Particularly *Eyewitnesses,* ch. 2.

munities.[67] It was entirely natural and understandable that he should cherish the opportunity provided by occasional visits from eye-witnesses or disciples with first-hand experience and information from the first generation — not necessarily because they told him something he had never heard before but because they confirmed what he already knew through the oral tradition. It is the contrast which Bauckham drives between the eyewitness accounts and the oral tradition (never in view in Papias' statement) which is uncalled for.[68] What person who was an eager and well-instructed disciple would not cherish the opportunity to hear even familiar stories and teaching from such highly regarded disciples of his Lord? Just as anyone today might well want to hear the first-hand account of an encounter with some great historic figure, even though the story itself is well known.

My larger concern here is that the more the emphasis is placed on eyewitness testimony, as a controlling as well as an initiating force in the tradition, the more we actually denigrate the value of the oral tradition. But to how many churches could Bartimaeus, say, have told his first-hand story? And did that mean that the story of Bartimaeus was devalued or distrusted when told in his absence? Bauckham may not want to draw that conclusion, but the thrust of his argument, set up as a contrast between eyewitness testimony and unattributed oral tradition, is in that direction. My own thesis is an attempt to affirm that the quality of the eyewitness testimony was substantially retained through the process which resulted in the Synoptic tradition, whether it was 'authenticated' throughout by eyewitnesses or not.[69]

67. Bauckham justifiably argues that Papias was referring in this statement to an earlier period (c. 90 CE) (*Eyewitnesses*, pp. 16-19).

68. Repeated in *Eyewitnesses*, p. 294, though he goes on to note: 'There is no reason, then, why the tradition Papias knew from local transmission should have been any less closely connected with named eyewitnesses than those he collected from his visitors'. Bauckham's concern is to highlight the difference between oral history and oral tradition. My point is slightly different: that given the beginning of the traditioning process in the eyewitness testimony of the first disciples, the character they gave it in their various retellings and reusings was essentially the same as the character it retained in subsequent retellings and reusings, so that whether the Synoptic tradition (as we now have it) was drawn directly from eyewitnesses themselves or from the subsequent retellings and reusings in one or more churches, the essential character remained the same.

69. Bauckham comes very close to my own position when he observes that 'there is no reason to postulate that the oral traditions once varied to a much greater extent than they do in the extant versions in the Gospels. . . . We may reasonably suppose that the extent of variation we can observe in the extant records (the canonical Gospels along with the early extracanonical material) is the same — no greater or less — as the extent to which the traditions varied in oral performance. . . . Matthew and Luke varied their Markan written source in the same kinds of ways they would have done had they been performing oral tradition' (*Eyewitnesses*, pp. 285-6; also pp. 309 and 473).

The extent of disagreement (or difference in emphasis) I have with Bauckham can be summed up by reference to his chapter on 'Anonymous Tradition or Eyewitness Testimony?'[70] He sums up his thesis in effect under four points (the numbering is my own):

1. the traditions were originated and formulated by named eyewitnesses,
2. in whose name they were transmitted
3. and who remained the living and active guarantors of the tradition.
4. In local Christian communities which did not include eyewitnesses among their members, there would probably be recognized teachers who functioned as authorized tradents of the traditions they had received from the eyewitnesses either directly or through very few (authorized) intermediaries.[71]

I can correspondingly sum up my response to Bauckham's most valuable monograph by echoing point 1 whole-heartedly, and by affirming that point 3 has much to be said in its favour. Points 2 and 4, however, are more problematic. I do not see much evidence for the view that the Jesus tradition was transmitted in the name of the original eyewitnesses (2). And although I agree in principle with point 4, I also note that many of the small churches outside the main centres of Asia, Macedonia, Achaia and elsewhere must have been at several removes from the eyewitnesses, so that the 'reliability' of their knowledge of Jesus' mission and teaching would have been dependent on the reliability of the oral tradition with which the founding evangelist (Epaphras, etc.) provided for them. It was the concern of *Jesus Remembered* to demonstrate how that 'reliability' would have been maintained and secured.

I close by expressing again my appreciation for the writings of Gerhardsson and Bauckham, and the hope that the above response will help clarify any misunderstandings, will identify issues which require further examination and discussion and will advance our mutual appreciation both of how the Jesus tradition was handed down and of the extent to which it still provides a reliable testimony to Jesus' mission and teaching.

70. *Eyewitnesses,* ch. 12.
71. *Eyewitnesses,* p. 290.

CHAPTER 10

Social Memory and the Oral Jesus Tradition

1. Introduction

My interest in this topic stems from my 'historical Jesus' study, *Jesus Remembered*.[1] The volume is the long-term outworking of a concern which has fascinated and motivated my work on the Gospels ever since I first handled a Gospel Synopsis. That concern has been *to understand and explain why it is that the Synoptic Jesus tradition takes the form that it does.* Any Synopsis makes it repeatedly clear that the traditions are traditions of the same event and the same teaching. Yet, at the same time, the traditions are diverse and divergent, often very markedly so. What does this two-fold phenomenon — traditions *the same yet different* — tell us about the way the Jesus tradition was used? What does it tell us about the concerns of the first Christians and Evangelists in recording the Jesus tradition in just this way? Does this two-fold phenomenon indicate a lack of interest in matters of historicity or historical detail of what Jesus said and did? Or does it simply indicate the way in which they recalled Jesus' teachings and doings, a way natural to first-century Jews of no great education, even if strange to those trained in the Western intellectual traditions of historiography?

My interest, therefore, was principally in the initial formation and early shape of the Jesus tradition. My thesis starts from the entirely probable hypothesis that the tradition was initially formed and shaped as *oral* tradi-

1. J. D. G. Dunn, *Christianity in the Making.* Vol. 1: *Jesus Remembered* (Grand Rapids: Eerdmans, 2003); also *A New Perspective on Jesus* (Grand Rapids: Baker Academic, 2005).

tion.[2] My thesis is that we have good grounds for deducing that many if not most of the individual traditions were given an initial form and shape which endured to a remarkable degree through the oral period, and indeed through the transition into the written Synoptic tradition. In that sense I take up the motivating concerns of the early form critics, before the practice of form criticism went off at a tangent to focus more on the character of the communities which maintained the tradition.

The title I chose for the work, however, invited the inference that I was primarily interested in the way in which Jesus was *remembered,* and invited the consequent criticism that I provide no theory of remembering, of how memory functions, in support of the thesis.[3] That is quite true, and a fair criticism so far as it goes. It is true that I stress a concern on the part of Jesus' first disciples to remember him. But what the criticism may miss is one of the key features of my thesis: that *the oral Jesus tradition is the primary way in which Jesus was remembered.* So again, I insist, my study of *Jesus Remembered* is primarily a study of the Jesus tradition — an attempt to understand it better and to make best sense of its twofold character of 'same yet different'.

Nevertheless, that said, I recognize that in a volume entitled *Jesus Remembered,* of course a thesis is involved regarding how memory operated in first-century Palestine and in the earliest Christian groups and congregations. It follows inevitably that I have to pay attention to contemporary theories of memory, and where they run counter to my thesis it is incumbent on me to explain my thesis more carefully and to defend it where necessary. In fact, the contemporary 'social memory' school has tended to follow the same path as form criticism, and is characterised by an emphasis on the *creative,* rather than the *retentive* function of memory. That emphasis alone constitutes a challenge to a thesis whose contrasting emphasis is on the retentiveness of the form and substance of the Jesus tradition. So I need to offer some further thoughts and reflections on the subject of how Jesus was remembered.

2. How Does Memory Function?

Attempts to shed light on how memory functioned in first-century Palestine regularly seem to assume that modern experience of remembering is a suffi-

2. See further my 'Altering the Default Setting: Re-envisaging the Early Transmission of the Jesus Tradition', *NTS* 49 (2003) 139-75 (above, 41-79).

3. I have already responded to criticisms by Bengt Holmberg and by Samuel Byrskog in 'On History, Memory and Eyewitnesses: In Response to Bengt Holmberg and Samuel Byrskog', *JSNT* 26 (2004) 473-87 (above, 199-212).

cient guide. It should not require much consideration to appreciate how un-sound that assumption may be, even if it could be accepted on physiological grounds that the human constitution and basic brain function have remained the same over two millennia. Consider, however, some of the distinctions and differences which must be borne in mind.

One basic error is to assume that all remembering is individual and ca-sual in character, or that casual recall typifies all remembering. For example, in his discussion of the subject Dominic Crossan seems to assume as a model something more of the order of the serendipitous remembering of a college reunion across a twenty-year gap.[4] So fragmentary and 'flash-bulb' memories become the norm. But does that give us any guidance in relation to a group memory which was important to the group and which was rehearsed in the group on several or many occasions across the twenty years? The challenge is posed most succinctly by Pierre Nora in his observation that memory 're-mains in permanent evolution, open to the dialectic of remembering and for-getting, unconscious of its successive deformations, vulnerable to manipula-tion and appropriation, susceptible to being long dormant and periodically revived'.[5] But still we have to ask how applicable is that insight, drawn from the twentieth century, to the arguably very different context of largely illiter-ate groups functioning in a first-century oral culture, whose theoretical and practical knowledge depended on what the elder or sage had stored in his memory.

Robert McIver conducted experiments with groups of students in which a joke, an aphorism and a poem were read twice to the groups, and their recall was then tested immediately, a week later and again three months later.[6] The results are interesting, not least in the confirmation that 'long-term memory in humans tends to be for the gist or meaning, rather than for the verbatim words'.[7] But the basic question arises once again: whether such an experiment, conducted in a society where memory has been long accus-tomed to relying on literary texts, is any kind of guide to how an oral society functioned.

Samuel Byrskog with good cause has drawn attention to the role of the

4. J. D. Crossan, *The Birth of Christianity* (San Francisco: Harper, 1998) 49-93.

5. P. Nora, 'Between Memory and History: Les Lieux de memoire', *Representations* 26 (1989).

6. R. McIver & M. Carroll, 'Experiments to Determine Distinguishing Characteristics of Orally Transmitted Material when Compared to Material Transmitted by Literary Means, and Their Potential Implications for the Synoptic Problem', *JBL* 121 (2002) 667-87.

7. 'Memory, Orality, and the Historical Jesus', a paper delivered to the Historical Jesus Seminar at the meeting of Studiorum Novi Testamenti Societas in Barcelona, 2004.

eye-witness in determining the shape and substance of the Jesus tradition.[8] The model he draws on, however, is that of oral history. Typical of oral history projects in UK today are recent attempts to record memories of the London blitz, while those who have these memories are still alive. So the typical task of the oral historian is to jog and restimulate memories which may have been dormant for years or even decades before they disappear for good. And the model invites the historian to imagine Luke, say, going from individual to individual — Mary, mother of Jesus, Mary Magdalene, and so on — in the hope of reactivating memories which had been inactive during an equivalent span of years or decades. But what does this model say in regard to Jesus tradition which may have been formulated during Jesus' own mission and must have been in fairly constant circulation ever since?

The main challenge to my thesis, however, comes from theories of what is variously entitled 'collective memory', or 'social memory', or 'cultural memory'. The first is associated particularly with the name of Maurice Halbwachs.[9] The challenge is posed by the observation of Lewis Coser in his Introduction to the English version of Halbwachs' work: 'collective memory is not a given but rather a socially constructed notion'; 'for Halbwachs, the past is a social construction mainly, if not wholly, shaped by the concerns of the present'.[10] In Halbwachs' own words, 'collective memory reconstructs its various recollections to accord with contemporary ideas and preoccupations'.[11] The importance of such observations is that they move beyond remembering as a purely individual act and remembering as a purely casual act. Integral to theories of social memory is that it is *social* memory, and that it is a remembering which is *important* for the identity and character of a social group. This brings us much nearer to the kind of remembering that we must suppose for the first Christian groups or communities. And the challenge is that such group remembering is selective and creative in accordance with its self-understanding and the image it wants to portray of itself. As James Fentress and Chris Wickham argue:

> Unless a society possesses means to freeze the memory of the past, the natural tendency of social memory is to suppress what is not meaningful or intuitively satisfying in the collective memories of the past, and inter-

---

8. S. Byrskog, *Story as History — History as Story: The Gospel Tradition in the Context of Ancient Oral History* (WUNT 123; Tübingen: Mohr Siebeck, 2000).

9. M. Halbwachs, *On Collective Memory* (Chicago: University of Chicago, 1992).

10. L. A. Coser, 'Introduction' to Halbwachs, *On Collective Memory*, 22, 25.

11. *On Collective Memory*, 224.

polate or substitute what seems more appropriate or more in keeping with their particular conception of the world.[12]

To similar effect the more recent definition of 'cultural memorization' offered by M. Bal, J. Crewe and L. Spitzer, 'as an activity occurring in the present, in which the past is continuously modified and redescribed even as it continues to shape the future'.[13]

The most obvious illustration of a society shaping and being shaped by its collective or cultural memory is the museum: the selection of some items and omission or neglect of others, the ways in which the items are displayed and the narrative thread linking them, explicitly or implicitly, all express a deliberate effort on the part of the curators of the museum and their sponsors to create a certain image of the past. And even if the desire on their part is to be as objective as possible and to allow the 'facts' or artefacts to speak for themselves as far as possible, as in the various Holocaust museums opened over the last twenty years, the reality is still a past viewed from the present, and serving to promote the values of the present and not merely to remember the past.

In such cases, of course, the time scale is usually much more extended than the generation or two between Jesus and the Synoptic Gospels. The writing of Halbwachs most relevant to our concerns is his 'The Legendary Topography of the Gospels in the Holy Land'.[14] As the title suggests, Halbwachs' interest in the subject had been sparked by his observation that sacred sites typically 'commemorate not facts certified by contemporary witnesses but rather beliefs born perhaps not far from these places and . . . are based more on dogma than on actual testimony'.[15] One needs only to recall Queen Helena's grand tour of the Holy Land in the fourth century identifying the sites of Jesus' ministry to see the force of Halbwachs' observation.[16] However, it is an insufficient answer to Halbwachs to point out that the time scale within which *Jesus Remembered* operates is much shorter, within one or two generations, rather than the time scale within which legends become established.[17] For Halbwachs envisages the process as operative from the beginning: that

12. J. Fentress & C. Wickham, *Social Memory* (Oxford: Blackwell, 1992) 58-9.

13. M. Bal, J. Crewe & L. Spitzer, eds., *Acts of Memory: Cultural Recall in the Present* (Hanover, NH: Dartmouth College, 1999) vii.

14. The English edition includes only the Conclusion — *On Collective Memory*, 193-235.

15. *On Collective Memory*, 199.

16. See further *On Collective Memory*, 202-25, 229-30, 233 — 'the case of a collective memory that attempts after the fact to localize its recollections on an almost untouched earth where it does not find any traditions' (212).

17. Halbwachs recognizes that, for example, traditions locating the upper room, the Cenacle, in its current position are late (*On Collective Memory*, 220).

the beliefs regarding Jesus were established early on, but that in order for these beliefs to become settled in the memory of the group they had to be presented 'in the concrete form of an event, or a personality, or of a locality'; that is, the belief was prior, the location and the particulars were secondary.[18] He also recognizes the influence of oral and local traditions but argues that at the end of the first century or beginning of the second the traditions of discourses and miracles were given specific locations 'in a more or less arbitrary manner'.[19]

Despite the validity of Halbwachs' observations regarding the Constantinian and Crusader periods, his attempt to push the process back to the earliest years is much less sound. It is true that the early form critics concluded that chronology and location were usually not part of the original forms and usually constituted evidence of subsequent redaction. But the passion narratives, on which Halbwachs concentrates much of his attention, are among the exceptions so far as recollection of time and place is concerned. And such observations do not really affect the substance of the teaching recalled or of the event attested. More important from my own perspective, Halbwachs makes no real attempt to discuss the dynamics of oral tradition or to engage with the idea that the earliest churches lived by and kept alive the initial memories of Jesus by regular repetition and celebration of their (oral) tradition.

Somewhat analogously, Fentress and Wickham reflect on the mediaeval Song of Roland and observe that if it is regarded as a record of real events, 'then we conclude only that memory is indeed a weak and fragile faculty'. But they continue,

> If we look at it as a story, however, we are forced to come to a very different conclusion. The memory of the story is as tenacious and stable as the memory of the actual events of Roncevaux is fragile. . . . The process of conceptualization, which so often disqualifies social memory as an empirical source, is also a process that ensures the stability of a set of collectively held ideas, and enables these ideas to be diffused and transmitted. Social memory is not stable as information; it is stable, rather, at the level of shared meanings and remembered images.[20]

They also note that in social memory facts 'are lost whenever, in a new external context, old information is no longer meaningful; or, alternatively, because they do not fit into the new internal context designed to hold the infor-

---

18. *On Collective Memory*, 200-201.
19. *On Collective Memory*, 205, 210-11.
20. *Social Memory*, 59.

mation'.[21] Such distinctions are potentially valuable. They raise several possibilities in regard to the Jesus tradition: in particular, that while mere facts (e.g. time and location) might have been neglected and forgotten in regard to events and teachings of Jesus, *significant* facts were more likely to have been retained;[22] and where Jesus tradition continues to reflect the context of a Galilean milieu, even when the tradition was being remembered in a Jerusalem or diaspora context, it is more likely than not that the tradition took its enduring shape in that Galilean context and was retained in that form despite its lack of 'fit' with the context of cities like Antioch and Ephesus.[23]

Jan Assmann agrees with Halbwachs that memory is constituted by means of social frameworks of memory, and that the identity and continuity of a community depend upon its constant revitalization of its constitutive memories.[24] In addition, he has made a helpful distinction between 'communicative memory' and 'cultural memory'. 'Communicative memory (kommunikative Gedächtnis)' can be used of communities still close to their origins, a period characterized by face-to-face circulation of foundational memories.[25] These memories are biographically vested in those who experienced originating events; it is the time of 'eyewitnesses and living memory (Augenzeugenschaft und lebendigen Erinnerung)'.[26] The outer limit of 'communicative memory' is the passing of those able to claim living contact with the original generation, hence three to four generations, that is, eighty to one hundred years.[27] On this theory, communicative memory cannot sustain group-constitutive remembrances beyond the three to four generations who can claim living contact with the generation of origins.[28] Assmann argues that the limitations of communicative memory force themselves upon a community as a crisis at approximately the 40-year threshold, the point at which it becomes apparent that the original generation of living carriers of memory is dying.[29] It

21. *Social Memory,* 73.

22. I allude here to the debate sparked by M. Kähler, *The So-called Historical Jesus and the Historic Biblical Christ* (1892), ET ed. C. E. Braaten (Philadelphia: Fortress, 1964) and developed in my *Jesus Remembered,* 125-34.

23. I develop the point in *A New Perspective on Jesus* ch. 1 #2.

24. J. Assmann, *Das kulturelle Gedächtnis. Schrift, Erinnerung und politische Identität in frühen Hochkulturen* (Munich: C. H. Beck, 1992, ²1997) 30, 132-3.

25. *Das kulturelle Gedächtnis,* 50-6. In this paragraph I drew on the unpublished paper by Alan Kirk, 'Introduction to Social Memory'.

26. *Das kulturelle Gedächtnis* 32; also *Religion und kulturelles Gedächtnis. Zehn Studien* (Munich: C. H. Beck, 2000) 88.

27. *Das kulturelle Gedächtnis,* 56; *Religion,* 37-8.

28. *Das kulturelle Gedächtnis,* 50.

29. *Das kulturelle Gedächtnis,* 11; *Religion,* 29.

is at this threshold that the community, if it is not to disappear with its memory, must turn self-consciously toward more enduring forms of 'cultural memory (kulturelle Gedächtnis)'.[30] In oral societies, foundational stories as well as associated social norms are cast in genres oriented towards oral transmission. As cultivated and performed by cultural specialists, these continually integrate the present of a society with its past.[31]

It is probably unnecessary to delve further into the various versions of social or cultural memory. Enough has been said to indicate that the line of research opened up by Halbwachs does raise the question, as to whether such theories of social memory require a revision of my thesis in *Jesus Remembered* of the way Jesus was remembered and on the historical value of what was 'remembered'. Or whether, alternatively, Assmann's distinction of 'communicative memory' from 'cultural memory' may be more relevant, given the limited time span in view in the period in which the Synoptic tradition was formed.

3. The Key Features of Oral Tradition/Remembering in My Thesis

3.1. Jesus the Teacher

I begin with a point which I did not develop much in *Jesus Remembered*. This is the fact that Jesus was commonly recognized, both by his contemporaries and his disciples, as a teacher.[32] The very term implies a deliberate and structured impartation of knowledge and wisdom, and a concern on the part of both teacher and taught that the teaching be remembered and become part of the disciples' repertoire and resource in the practice of their discipleship. In an oral society remembering would be the primary means by which the individual disciple could retain and be able to draw upon the teaching in future. As Philip Alexander observes, 'It is hardly an exaggeration to say that for the ordinary educated person what was not in the memory was not readily accessible'.[33]

The other side of the same coin is that memorisation and constant repetition was the principal technique in all education practice of the time. So *any*

---

30. *Das kulturelle Gedächtnis*, 218-21; *Religion*, 53-4.
31. *Das kulturelle Gedächtnis*, 49-50; *Religion*, 136-7.
32. Details in *Jesus Remembered*, 176-7.
33. P. S. Alexander, 'Orality in Pharisaic-Rabbinic Judaism at the Turn of the Eras', in H. Wansbrough, ed., *Jesus and the Oral Gospel Tradition* (JSNTSup 64; Sheffield: JSOT, 1991) 159-84 (here 160).

idea that Jesus gave particular teachings to his disciples on only one occasion and only as a sequence of unrepeated statements has to be seriously questioned. A teacher would typically check whether his teachings were being remembered by requiring his pupils to repeat them back to him, and might well drill them in what he regarded as the most important axioms, maxims and rules he was endeavouring to inculcate. These of course are points already familiar in the discussion of the Jesus tradition from the work of Birger Gerhardsson and Rainer Riesner in particular.[34]

The relevance of this aspect to our discussion is obvious. Here is a different kind of remembering from that which has been mentioned above. What is envisaged is not a casual recall across several decades of something once heard and little thought about since. Nor is it the case of a later generation choosing what that generation should 'remember' about its past. What is in view is a deliberate instruction intended to be retained for its value in discipleship. What is in view is a deliberate attempt to implant firmly and rootedly matters of importance in the memory of individuals motivated to listen, to absorb and to live accordingly. That is not to deny Pierre Nora's observations above about the deformation and manipulation active in the process of remembering. But it quite properly demands that the evaluation of the remembering of the Jesus tradition not be conducted solely from the perspective of a second (or subsequent) generation trying to remember. Equally, and arguably more important is the *initiating* of memory, the process of *inputting* memory, the *beginning* of the remembering of what Jesus said and taught.

Relevant at this point is recognition of the extent to which the Jesus tradition is designed for easy remembering. Prominent features are various kinds of parallelism, alliteration, assonance and paronomasia,[35] all of which can be justly regarded as aids to remembering. Notable also in the Jesus tradition of the Synoptics is the high proportion of the tradition which takes the form of aphorisms and parables. For such teaching material, we could say

---

34. B. Gerhardsson, *Memory and Manuscript: Oral Tradition and Written Transmission in Rabbinic Judaism and Early Christianity* (Lund: Gleerup, 1961); R. Riesner, *Jesus als Lehrer* (WUNT 2.7; Tübingen: Mohr Siebeck, 1981).

35. C. F. Burney, *The Poetry of Our Lord* (Oxford: Clarendon, 1925); T. W. Manson, *The Teaching of Jesus* (Cambridge: Cambridge University, 1931) 50-6; M. Black, *An Aramaic Approach to the Gospels and Acts* (Oxford: Clarendon, [3]1967) 160-85; J. Jeremias, *New Testament Theology*. Vol. 1: *The Proclamation of Jesus* (London: SCM, 1971) 3-29; R. Riesner, *Jesus als Lehrer*, 392-404. Riesner estimates 'about 80 per cent of the separate saying units are formulated in some kind of *parallelismus membrorum*' — 'Jesus as Preacher and Teacher', in H. Wanbrough, ed., *Jesus and the Oral Gospel Tradition* (Sheffield: Sheffield Academic, 1991) 185-210 (here 202). See also D. C. Rubin, *Memory in Oral Traditions* (Oxford: Oxford University, 1995) 75-88.

quite fairly, was well designed, and probably intentionally so by Jesus, for ease of remembering. Kenneth Bailey, for example, notes the publication in Jerusalem in 1985 of two volumes of some 6,000 proverbs, over 4,000 of which are popular and colloquial in nature and were collected orally. He comments: 'We are here observing a community that can create (over the centuries) and sustain in current usage up to 6,000 wisdom sayings'.[36] From which can be deduced, as Bailey suggests, that the wisdom teaching of Jesus would probably have been an effective mode of teaching and provided not simply a prominent but also a remarkably stable element in the varied memories of Jesus' teaching.

3.2. The Impact of Jesus

In *Jesus Remembered* I chose to focus attention on the *impact* made by Jesus on his disciples rather than on the mode of teaching and learning. I did this for three principal reasons.

One was that the focus on teaching explains only part of the Jesus tradition. There is also the narrative tradition, the accounts of what Jesus did and of what happened to him. Now an interesting and somewhat neglected feature of the Jesus tradition is the fact that the narrative tradition manifests the same character of 'same yet different' as the sayings tradition. The range of difference, from closely parallel to quite divergent, is much the same in both the sayings and the narrative tradition.[37] This suggests that the same factors were at work in both the sayings and the narrative tradition. But whereas it can be argued that the sayings tradition is the result of Jesus' deliberate pedagogical instruction, the same can hardly be claimed for the narrative tradition. That is to say, the narrative tradition is at best the result of eye-witnesses recording what they witnessed. It is *the impression made by Jesus* which is the decisive factor at the beginning of the narrative traditions, not any teaching that he demanded them to hear and retain. This raises the question whether it would not be wiser to look at the sayings tradition in the same way — that is, as the result of the impression made by Jesus and by his particular teachings.

I followed that logic and envisaged the Jesus tradition as the evidence of the *impact* made by Jesus.[38] Here were disciples whose lives had been trans-

---

36. K. E. Bailey, 'Informal Controlled Oral Tradition and the Synoptic Gospels', *Asia Journal of Theology* 5 (1991) 34-54 (here 41).

37. See e.g. *Jesus Remembered*, 210-38.

38. *Jesus Remembered*, 129-34, 239-42, 327-9; *New Perspective on Jesus*, ch. 1 #2.

formed by Jesus, who had responded to Jesus' call to follow him and abandoned livelihoods and even families in order to live out their discipleship. This was no casual, dilettante affair, where they remembered Jesus as one today might remember a great parliamentarian or actor. Jesus' words meant life for them, his life-style was a model for their own living. Of course they remembered what he said and did. The impact of Jesus' sayings and doings was such that they shaped their lives as lives of discipleship. What they witnessed entered into them and became part of them. I believe this insight provides a key to one of the conundrums regarding the Jesus tradition — that is, why Jesus' teaching is so seldom attributed explicitly to Jesus by Paul and the other letter-writers of earliest Christianity.[39] Part of the answer, I suggest, is precisely that the Jesus tradition was not 'memorised' as 'teaching of Jesus'; rather it was absorbed into the consciousness and life-manual of the first churches to become a resource on which they could draw almost instinctively and without having to engage in an act of 'remembering' what Jesus taught.

Secondly, it seems to me that the characterisation of that process in terms of *memorisation* is inadequate to describe the *impact* made by Jesus. May I illustrate what I see to be the difference from my own learning experience. When I think of memorisation I recall the way I was taught the multiplication tables as a child. I recall too the way I learned the paradigms of irregular Greek verbs as a young teenager. The only reason I today know, and know automatically, without thinking, that seven times eight equals 56 ($7 \times 8 = 56$) is that it was drilled into me all these years ago. In a similar way I can recall the aorist passive of most irregular Greek verbs simply by repeating in my head, rote-like, the appropriate paradigm. But I also recall different learning experiences from the same periods. I recall a slogan across the bottom of a mirror on the wall of the cloak-room of my primary school. It said, 'You get back what you give, so smile'. As soon as I saw it, that slogan seemed to me to make perfect sense and to provide a very healthy attitude to life. It became part of me, an expression of my own life philosophy from that day on. I did not memorise it. Rather, it made such an impact on me that I could not forget it! And later, when I began to learn Greek, I was early on introduced to the famous epigram from Delphi, *'Gnōthi s'auton'*, 'Know thyself'. That too made a huge impact on me; to be wholly honest about oneself seemed to be such a sensible rule for living that I made it my own from that first encounter. Again I did not have to remember it. Rather, it became part of my own life philosophy, a resource on which I drew, a goad which pricked my conscience when I began to relapse into self-deceptive self-regard. It seems to me that the distinction between

39. See further *Jesus Remembered*, 181-4.

memorisation and impact deserves more attention than it has received — not a great distinction, but a significant one nonetheless. It was a distinction which initially I perceived instinctively rather than in a thought-through way. So I am grateful for exchanges with Birger Gerhardsson which have helped me to clarify and develop my thoughts on the subject.[40]

Thirdly, what seemed to me initially at a more conscious level to be unsatisfactory about Gerhardsson's model of memorisation was that it did not seem best suited to explain the content and forms of the Jesus tradition as it has come down to us in the Synoptics. Memorisation, particularly when it is understood in terms of learning by means of constant repetition, of drilling pupils till they remember the teaching accurately, would seem to imply a greater agreement in word and detail than we find in the Synoptics. But the Synoptic tradition displays quite a wide range of diversity — that is, no great evidence of a concern to recall a memorised text, no great concern to reproduce the teaching of the Master just as he gave it, no real evidence of a desire to pass down the tradition with verbal faithfulness. Gerhardsson is the first to insist that the model he evokes from what we know of the transmission of rabbinic tradition fully allows for the flexibility that is so evident in the Jesus tradition.[41] And I do not particularly wish to dispute with him on that; hence my giving first place in this section to 'Jesus the teacher'. It is simply that a process summed up in the term 'memorisation' does not do sufficient justice to the evident flexibility of the Jesus tradition. Perhaps a combination of 'memorisation' and 'impact', such as I am attempting to articulate now, will meet both strengths and weaknesses of both models.

In short, the emphasis on the impact made by Jesus suggests that what informed the Jesus tradition and what the Jesus tradition retained was not *mere* facts about Jesus' mission, but the facts about Jesus, his teachings and doings, which had struck home to those who heard what he said and witnessed how he acted, the facts that were *significant* for these first disciples. It is the impact which Jesus actually made which has left its clear impression on the Jesus tradition, not 'historical facts' that the would-be objective historian might want to uncover.[42] Consequently, the observation of Fentress and Wickham, that 'we have no way of knowing, *a priori*, where, in oral tradition, historical facts are likely to lie', does not disqualify use of the Synoptic tradi-

---

40. In private correspondence.

41. His 1961 work was refined in a succession of further publications: *Tradition and Transmission in Early Christianity* (Lund: Gleerup, 1964); *The Origins of the Gospel Traditions* (Philadelphia: Fortress, 1979); *The Gospel Tradition* (Lund: Gleerup, 1986); the last two are reprinted in *The Reliability of the Gospel Tradition* (Peabody, MA: Hendrickson, 2001).

42. See again *Jesus Remembered*, 125-33, 882-4.

tion in the quest of the historical Jesus. For the quest is, or should be, aimed to uncover not 'historical facts' as such, but the Jesus whose impact is still evident in the Jesus tradition.

3.3. *The Beginning of the Oral Tradition*

Integral to my thesis is the claim that *the impact made by Jesus would have found expression almost immediately in spoken exchanges between and among the first disciples.* At this point it is necessary to insist once more that the remembering of the disciples was not an individual and isolated affair, and that consequently models of how memory works, based on examples of individual remembering, are less than relevant to the consideration of how Jesus was remembered. Still less relevant are models of individuals being asked to recall events or things heard several months or years earlier, items of memory on which they might never have reflected during the intervening years.

Quite different is the hypothesis that such a life-changing impact would typically have been the subject of conversation and witness-bearing wherever there was a group (or groups) of disciples who had been similarly impacted by Jesus' mission. Such recounting of events in which they had been involved or witnessed, such rehearsing of teaching which had become of life-directive force was the beginning of the oral tradition, *the first articulation of Jesus tradition.* In the sharing of such memories the oral tradition would begin to take its shape. Where memories of particular teachings and events were common, and agreed as to theme and substance, we may infer the emergence of the forms in which these elements began to be circulated.

I have in mind here, naturally, in the first instance the inner group of twelve disciples. I envisage such a dynamic under way as they reflected on what they had seen and heard while Jesus was still with them. But there were other disciples and followers, who did not literally follow Jesus, and I envisage the same sort of sharing and group dynamic forming oral tradition. I also see no reason to doubt that this process went on before as well as after Easter. Moreover, if indeed Jesus did send out the twelve in mission, then there must have been agreement between Jesus and these disciples on the message they should preach and the life-style they should follow.[43] That would necessarily have involved an agreed range of oral tradition, though once again, more as bearing witness to what had become of central importance to them, and not necessarily as a script learned and repeated.

43. Cf. Riesner, *Jesus als Lehrer*, 453-75, 500-501.

Complementary would have been the continuing role of the first disciples/apostles, and as the movement began to spread after the first Easter, the continuing role of the wider group of eye-witness disciples.[44] Whether settled in one or another specific church or travelling between churches, their role in drawing together such articulated memories and in shaping the forms and content of the Jesus tradition would have been substantial.

This tradition would have been crucial for the earliest groups of disciples, for their identity and *raison d'etre*. They would need such tradition to explain why they had become such a group, both to themselves and to those outside the group. Such tradition would have been their very life-blood. And as they became more explicitly religious groups, some at least of the tradition would take on the force, but also the stability of ritual and liturgy. What we have to envisage here, therefore, is *the formative force* of such impactful tradition. Certainly we have to recognize the strength of the social memory theorists: that groups tailor their tradition to fit the image of themselves which they wish to project. But first we have to recognize that such tradition begins by tailoring the groups which cherish it. The more important a tradition is in defining and explaining the identity of a group, the more the group will be determined by the tradition rather than vice-versa.[45]

All this is speculative, of course. But it is a priori plausible in terms of group formation. And, for me more important, it is consistent with the character of the Jesus tradition as it has come down to us in the Synoptic tradition, that is, as 'the same yet different'. For, on the one hand, there we see shared memories articulated in particular forms, that is, memories of the same events and of the same or repeated teaching. And there, on the other hand, we see these same memories in diverse forms, whose diversity we may attribute in part at least to the fact that Jesus' mission impacted different disciples differently, and in part at least also to the fact that different groups, even if under the guidance of 'the teaching of the apostles', would have formulated the shared memories in different terms and with different emphases. I see the Je-

---

44. I regard Byrskog's thesis in *Story as History* as complementary, not contradictory to my own.

45. I distance myself at this point from the criticism of Gerhardsson and Riesner by W. H. Kelber, 'The Case of the Gospels: Memory's Desire and the Limits of Historical Criticism', *Oral Tradition* 17 (2002) 55-86, that in the work of Gerhardsson and Riesner the concept of memory 'has been reduced strictly to its retentive, reproductive, and preservative function. . . . In other words, memory acts as the stalwart of stability, safeguarding an unchanging tradition and thus guaranteeing the historical reliability of the gospels' (62). But recognition of the creative element of social memory should not be seen as a denial of the retentive potential of a tradition like the Jesus tradition.

sus tradition as already shaped by these forces well before we need to take into consideration, as we do, the deliberately redactive work of subsequent Evangelists.

3.4. Performing Oral Tradition

The final strand in my thesis focuses on what we know about the way oral tradition was rehearsed and performed in oral communities within an oral culture. In the twenty or so years which most accept must have intervened prior to the first extensive writing down of the Jesus tradition,[46] communities would have had to depend on such tradition being rehearsed and expounded to them orally. Since, in any case, only a small minority would have had even basic literary skills of reading and writing,[47] community knowledge of Jesus tradition would have depended on teachers or elders or apostles skilled in the amassing and retention and retelling of extensive amounts of the tradition. They had no media, newspapers, radios or television to inform them. They had no books, reference works or encyclopaedias to consult. They were dependent on the regular gatherings of the community for their knowledge and understanding of what their Lord and Master had done and taught.

Studies of oral tradition have taught us that a key characteristic of oral communication is the same feature of 'the same yet different'. The same story or teaching is repeated. But consistently the retelling varies from time to time and from setting to setting. The same aphorism or parable is retold, but the words and particulars are different. In oral performance there is no original version,[48] only a storyline retold in diverse and divergent versions, only a teaching the same in substance but diverse in detail.

This must surely provide at least some part of the explanation for the continuing character of the Synoptic tradition — the same yet different. Where that explanation fits so well the character of the Gospel material it seems unnecessary and misguided to attribute all the differences to the work of literary redaction, thirty to fifty years after the Jesus tradition began to take

---

46. Even allowing for a(n initial) written version of Q as early as 50.

47. Recent estimates are of less than 10% literacy in the Roman Empire under the principate, falling to perhaps as low as 3% literacy in Roman Palestine; see particularly W. V. Harris, *Ancient Literacy* (Cambridge, MA: Harvard University, 1989); M. Bar-Ilan, 'Illiteracy in the Land of Israel in the First Centuries CE', in S. Fishbane & S. Schoenfeld, *Essays in the Social Scientific Study of Judaism and Jewish Society* (Hoboken, NJ: Ktav, 1992) 46-61; C. Hezser, *Jewish Literacy in Roman Palestine* (Tübingen: Mohr Siebeck, 2001).

48. See further 'Altering the Default Setting', 153-4 (above, 56-7).

shape as tradition, that is, as oral tradition. The two explanations are not anti-thetical, of course. But to deny knowledge of the development of the Jesus tra-dition at the oral stage, because we know too little about that stage, and to at-tribute all the development and variation to the later literary stage of the tradition is a counsel of despair. There is in fact nothing to debar the thesis that the Jesus tradition took its characteristically 'same yet different' forms more or less from the beginning. Originating events in the life of Jesus, origi-nating teaching given by Jesus, we may confidently assume in most cases. But original *versions* of these events and teachings, as though only the 'original' version should be regarded as historically authentic, is simply to confess in-ability to envisage the process of oral performance and transmission of the Je-sus tradition.

Moreover, the community dimension in the process of remembering Je-sus should caution us against too easy inferences that individuals could readily introduce distortions to the tradition. A congregation made up of people whose identity was given in large part by their deposit of Jesus tradi-tion would not take kindly to major divergences in the content of the tradi-tion by individual performers.[49] Their knowledge of the Jesus tradition would enable them to appreciate the variations introduced on various occasions, variations such as we find in the Synoptic tradition.[50] But any attempt to cre-ate a significantly different memory would be likely to meet with protest, not least from the teachers and elders of the congregation to whom the preserva-tion and maintenance of the tradition was principally entrusted.

Here again the enduring form of the Synoptic tradition is a reliable guide whose implicit testimony on this point is insufficiently appreciated. For here we have three different, indeed at points divergent versions of the Jesus tradition. And yet a remarkably coherent and cohesive portrayal, or memory of Jesus emerges.[51] Here, I suggest, is sufficient evidence that the oral traditioning processes represented in and extended as late as the composition of the Synoptic Gospels were sufficient to maintain the 'same yet different' character of the tradition and to retain the diverse nature of the early

---

49. Bailey develops his concept of 'informal controlled oral tradition' on this basis (see particularly his 'Informal Controlled Tradition', 42-5).

50. See Bailey's illustration in 'Informal Controlled Tradition', 47-8, and J. M. Foley's con-cept of 'metonymic reference' referred to in 'Altering the Default Setting', 151-2 (above, 54).

51. The mature assessment of C. H. Dodd in his last great work, *The Founder of Christian-ity* (London: Collins, 1971), still deserves repetition: 'The first three gospels offer a body of say-ings on the whole so consistent, so coherent, and withal so distinctive in manner, style and con-tent, that no reasonable critic should doubt, whatever reservations he may have about individual sayings, that we find here reflected the thought of a single, unique teacher' (21-2).

churches' remembering within limited bounds. We know that there were streams of the same tradition which did diverge very markedly from the Synoptic format, notably of course the Gospel of Thomas. But the *restraint* of the Synoptic 'same yet different' suggests both that Thomas-type divergences were later and that they were marginalized by the churches whose Jesus tradition was of the Synoptic type.

All this indicates that a straightforward application of social memory theory to the early phase of the Jesus tradition, or even to the first two generations of Christian remembering of Jesus, would be unwise. Certainly its appropriateness can be asserted to explain the character of the Jesus of Thomas, or even the Word become flesh of John.[52] And even if in regard to the Synoptics one can readily argue that, for example, the law-affirming Jesus of Matthew reflects the concerns of Matthew or of the Matthean community, even so the larger consistency and coherence of the Synoptic tradition remains a clear reminder of the constraints which operated to maintain the impact and character of the original remembering of Jesus as first articulated in the beginnings of the Jesus tradition. The more the character of Jesus tradition became valued as sacred word, the more we have to recognize that the congregations' remembering of Jesus was predominantly marked by the subordination of the congregation to the word rather than the subordination of the word to the congregation.

Conclusion

According to D. Ben-Amos and L. Weissberg, 'Tradition is finally nothing but deformed memory'.[53] That seems to me to overemphasise the *creative* character of remembering as a whole. More to the point here, however, the dictum fails to take account of the considerations marshalled above:

- of how tradition functions in an oral society;
- of how repeated instruction can shape a life and become the life-blood of a community;
- of how tradition can serve as the actively continuing expression of a transforming encounter with the one remembered;

52. To extend the discussion to John's version of the Jesus tradition would extend the scope of the paper far too much.

53. D. Ben-Amos & L. Weissberg, *Cultural Memory and the Construction of Identity* (Detroit: Wayne State University, 1999) 15, adding 'more organized perhaps, and seemingly more "objective"'.

- of how regular performance in quasi-liturgical contexts can sustain the substance and overall shape of what and who is remembered.

These are the features I continue to find as hallmarks of the Jesus tradition in its character of 'the same yet different'. And these continue to persuade me that the Jesus tradition preserved in the Synoptic Gospels has been much more *retentive* than the various theories of social or cultural memory would seem to suggest.

CHAPTER 11

Kenneth Bailey's Theory of Oral Tradition: Critiquing Theodore Weeden's Critique

I am grateful for the opportunity to continue the dialogue with Ted Weeden (TW) which we have maintained off the record for some seven years. The thesis of Kenneth Bailey (KB) which TW critiques[1] has in my view considerable potential to explain the character of the Synoptic Gospel tradition. Consequently one might have expected it to attract a good deal of attention and to have been subjected to rigorous examination and critique. Unfortunately KB's presentation of his thesis appeared in not so prominent journals and did not attract the attention it deserved.[2] Not only so, but the thesis itself was less than scientifically rigorous in presentation and largely anecdotal and impressionistic in character, so it could be safely ignored by those content with older paradigms of research into the Jesus tradition. TW however has been one of all too few scholars who have recognized the potential importance of the KB hypothesis and that it deserved careful evaluation if it was to carry any weight. So I repeat my gratitude for this opportunity to carry forward our earlier e-mail and seminar discussion of TW's developing critique of the KB thesis.

I should just add, by way of preliminaries, that I first heard KB on the subject more than thirty years ago. As one who had always been fascinated by the character of the Synoptic tradition — teaching substantially the same but

1. T. J. Weeden, 'Kenneth Bailey's Theory of Oral Tradition: A Theory Contested by Its Evidence', *Journal for the Study of the Historical Jesus* 7 (2009) 3-43.
2. K. E. Bailey, 'Informal Controlled Oral Tradition and the Synoptic Gospels', *AJT* 5 (1991) 34-54 = *Themelios* 20.2 (1995) 4-11; also 'Middle Eastern Oral Tradition and the Synoptic Gospels', *ExpTim* 106 (1995) 363-7.

diverse in detail and grouping, narratives evidently of the same events yet often very different in introduction, length, particular wording and conclusion — I found that KB's anecdotes (including those to which TW refers) provided a plausible explanation which I had never heard or considered earlier. This, I should perhaps emphasize, is what most attracted me to the KB thesis: that it *provided such a good explanation of the character of the Synoptic tradition*, a character which is so clearly evident in the Synoptic tradition as we still have it — the same yet different, firm in substance yet variant in detail. When I returned to the subject in the preparation of my *Jesus Remembered* volume, that earlier impression was reinforced by a growing dissatisfaction with the predominant attempt to resolve the 'Synoptic problem' more or less entirely in literary terms of copying and editing written sources — what I refer to summarily as 'the literary mindset'.[3]

For all that KB is vulnerable to critique, his model of tradition processing in village communities still opens up a window into the earliest stage of the development of the Gospel tradition. No other model promises quite so much. The Homeric sagas and the more contemporary Yugoslavian parallels investigated by Milman Parry and Albert Lord[4] are too remote from first-century Palestine; the Jesus tradition hardly fits the character of generations-old sagas. Birger Gerhardsson's model of rabbinic teaching and tradition is much closer and works to a substantial extent, but presupposes a more formal and even regimented process.[5] KB's model provided at least an important complement — a complement, not necessarily a substitute or alternative. It allows for the situations where tradition was not only brought formally by apostles or teachers, but was also celebrated, drawn and reflected upon and

---

3. 'Jesus in Oral Memory: The Initial Stages of the Jesus Tradition', in D. Donnelly, ed., *Jesus: A Colloquium in the Holy Land* (New York: Continuum, 2001) 84-145; *Christianity in the Making*, Vol. I: *Jesus Remembered* (Grand Rapids: Eerdmans, 2003); 'Altering the Default Setting: Re-envisaging the Early Transmission of the Jesus Tradition', *New Testament Studies* 49 (2003) 139-75 (above, 41-79); *A New Perspective on Jesus: What the Quest for the Historical Jesus Missed* (Grand Rapids: Baker Academic/London: SPCK, 2005).

4. See particularly A. B. Lord, *The Singer of Tales* (Cambridge, MA: Harvard University, 1978).

5. B. Gerhardsson, *Memory and Manuscript: Oral Tradition and Written Transmission in Rabbinic Judaism and Early Christianity* (Lund: Gleerup, 1961); refined in a succession of further publications: *Tradition and Transmission in Early Christianity* (Lund: Gleerup, 1964); *The Origins of the Gospel Traditions* (Philadelphia: Fortress, 1979); *The Gospel Tradition* (Lund: Gleerup, 1986); the last two are reprinted in *The Reliability of the Gospel Tradition* (Peabody, MA: Hendrickson, 2001). Gerhardsson critiques my *Jesus Remembered* in B. Gerhardsson, 'The Secret of the Transmission of the Unwritten Jesus Tradition', *NTS* 51 (2005) 1-18; I respond in 'Eyewitnesses and the Oral Jesus Tradition', *JSHJ* 6 (2008) 85-105, particularly 88-96 (above, 215-22).

performed when groups of disciples gathered together in mutual support.[6] There is, of course, an obvious question as to whether the experience of Christian communities in twentieth-century Egypt or Lebanon can serve as evidence for first-century, pre-Islamic Palestine.[7] But I never thought this need be a fatal flaw in the KB thesis; the social habits and modes of passing on tradition in Middle Eastern villages I suspect have differed very little over the centuries, just as pre-radio, pre-TV and pre-internet village communities the world over have tended to retain very conservative patterns of social life and values. Above all, I repeat, the most weighty factor for me was that the KB model helped explain the enduring character of the Synoptic Jesus tradition more effectively than any other I had hitherto encountered.

Before turning to the TW critique of KB's 'theory of oral tradition', it may be helpful for me to summarize both KB's thesis as I have understood it (at some points different from TW's view of it, as we shall see), and how the KB model has helped me formulate my own thesis about how the Jesus tradition was formulated, how Jesus was remembered.

KB's thesis is of a tradition prized by village communities and regularly drawn upon in evening gatherings of the community by community leaders or those held in respect by the community. He notes that there would be varied 'flexibility' in the retelling and performing of the tradition: no flexibility with poems and proverbs; some flexibility with episodes important for the history of the communities; 'total flexibility' with material irrelevant to the identity of the community.[8] This recognition of the varied flexibility of the traditions retold also determines the character of the 'informal control' exercised in regard to the retelling of the tradition. The less flexible the tradition, the more careful the control, in that any departure from the inflexible or less flexible element in the tradition would occasion protest or rebuke from leaders of the community.

As already indicated, my own drawing on KB's thesis begins from a clearly observable fact: (1) that the Synoptic tradition of Jesus' mission provides a remarkably consistent and coherent portrayal of Jesus; even allowing for all the diversity of the individual compilations and emphases, as of course we must do, the Jesus portrayed is recognizably the same. To this I add the *a priori* probability: (2) that Jesus was a figure whose mission, in its character

---

6. See also my response to R. Bauckham, *Jesus and the Eyewitnesses: The Gospels as Eyewitness Testimony* (Grand Rapids: Eerdmans, 2006) in 'Eyewitnesses and the Oral Jesus Tradition', 96-105 (above, 222-29).

7. This was one of Gerhardsson's criticisms, 'Secret', 6-7.

8. 'Informal Controlled Oral Tradition', 42-45.

and its teaching, made a considerable impact on his immediate followers; (3) that this impact was expressed more or less from the first by his disciples in stories about Jesus and in forms of his teaching which were integral to the disciples' own preaching and teaching both before Jesus' death and after his resurrection; and (4) that when individuals joined the new sect by baptism 'in the name of Jesus', (soon) accepting the name 'Christian', they would naturally have wanted to know about this Jesus by whose name they were now being identified.

My thesis (5) is that we can best see the link between the fact of (1) and the assumptions of (2)-(4) in the oral celebration and transmission of what Jesus did and said, that is in the pattern of same yet different which is characteristic of oral tradition and its repeated performance. This suggests in turn (6) that the Synoptic tradition, which has precisely that character, already took that character in the oral period and more or less from the first.

However, TW's critique of KB's 'theory' may seem to undermine my attempt thus to build on it. So I turn to TW's critique. Overall I find it rather disappointing. TW's lack of sympathy with KB comes through consistently and he seems more determined to do the thesis down than to interact sympathetically with what KB was evidently drawing from many years of personal experience. A *Sprache*-criticism can often miss the more penetrating *Sache*-critique. A Broadway level of critique might entirely miss the point when applied to the local village's annual theatrical production. A high literary critique of the village sermon might be entirely fair as a literary critique, and still miss the preacher's message and fail to appreciate its appropriateness. Given that KB has *not* presented his thesis as an exercise in PhD writing, any critique has to bear that in mind. Are personal experiences stretching over several decades to be dismissed simply because they are recorded with an anecdotal casualness that the scientific mind abhors? How much knowledge, not to say wisdom, would be lost to humanity if that were to be the rule!

For the most part I follow TW's order of dealing with the KB thesis, but I start with what TW evidently regards as the principal weakness.

1. The *Haflat Samar*

I am impressed by TW's careful examination of what *'haflat samar'* can properly refer to,[9] but am less impressed by his unwillingness to consider the like-

---

9. TW consulted several native Middle Easterners and Arabist scholars and reports his findings: that *haflat samar* denotes a party, attended purely for entertainment; 'an occasion

lihood that KB has in mind a usage familiar among and perhaps distinctive to the Christian communities to which KB refers. After all, it is entirely possible to know German well and yet fail to appreciate the peculiarities of Südlich Deutsch. For the first half of the twentieth century BBC English was the standard form of English for the broadcast media in UK. Only in the second half of the twentieth century did it become recognized and accepted that Birmingham or Newcastle English were also public English. Or should UK English object to American English with its un-English(!) usages like 'pavement' and 'gas'? We recall that until the end of the nineteenth century, NT Greek was regarded as an oddity, since it compared so poorly with the literary Greek of the first century. But the sands produced many copies of everyday letters and examples of 'vulgar' speech of the time, and we soon realized that NT Greek was not unique or so distinctive.

The point I make, of course, is that KB is really reporting the usage which, we can fairly assume, was/is common among the Christian church gatherings with which he had enjoyed considerable experience. Was the way these churches understood the gatherings as *haflat samar* distinctive to them — perhaps a deviation from more literary speech, as many regional accents and usages are a deviation from a more sophisticated formality? I don't know the answer to that question. But what I find disappointing in TW's critique is that he does not seem to have considered this possibility. He sounds rather like a member of the Académie Française insisting that only properly controlled usage, strictly derived from the classical precedents, can be considered permissible French usage.

What I found most interesting in TW's findings was that his consultants speak so regularly of the *haflat samar* as an evening gathering which consisted of talking together, discoursing, telling old familiar stories, etc. This seems to me very consistent with KB's characterisation of the *haflat samar* tradition with which he was familiar. TW's correspondents seem to emphasize the 'party' dimension — an aspect of which KB is clearly well aware.[10] However, it would be entirely understandable if the 'party' dimension was less prominent in the language and customs of the Christian village communities. TW also emphasizes that the element of 'preservation' is not part of the *haflat samar* culture with which his consultants were familiar. But he does not ask

---

when people gather together at night to hear stories about historical events or personages, with the emphasis being placed upon telling such stories for entertainment or amusement. . . . The story tellers at a *haflat samar* are there to entertain, not to assure the accurate transmission of the traditions of the particular oral culture' ('Kenneth Bailey's Theory of Oral Tradition', 38-42).

10. 'Middle Eastern Oral Tradition', 364.

whether such a concern might have become more prominent for small Christian village communities, sensing a need to define themselves and their distinctive features within a predominantly non-Christian culture — somewhat as we may well imagine was the case also for the earliest Christian communities in the middle of the first century.

Here not least I regret an opportunity lost. TW's critique could have been so much more effective and persuasive if he had approached KB's thesis with a degree of empathy and readiness to hear KB's testimony (based on long experience) whatever the anecdotal inadequacies and unusual usages.

2. The Urinating Episode[11]

Let us assume that the two accounts (by KB and by Rena Hogg) refer to the same episode, as does TW. Also that Rena Hogg covers some embarrassment by referring to Hogg being urinated upon as 'vile water poured on his head'.

An initial point should be noted: that KB tells/repeats a *story*; Rena Hogg refers to an *incident* (and does not tell it as a story). So quite how Rena Hogg's reference would be filled out in story form is not at all clear. In terms of the tradition process we are comparing apples and oranges, not two kinds of apple/versions of the same story. Consequently it is inappropriate to compare KB's conclusion to his version of the story with Rena Hogg's failure to draw any conclusion from her reference. The point common to both is the shamefully embarrassing indignity to which Hogg was subjected. That is the only point that Rena Hogg's reference makes. KB's story version of the episode provides a context and conclusion — presumably a typical or characteristic version of the story still retold in the Christian communities which KB visited.

TW's fault-finding criticism misses the point, in at least three ways. (1) He ignores the fact that Rena Hogg does not tell the story of the episode

---

11. TW contrasts the story heard by KB regarding an experience of the Scottish missionary John Hogg, in which Hogg was urinated on by a village guard (sent by the mayor) above him while he was preaching, with his daughter's (Rena Hogg) reference to what appears to be the same incident in her biography of her father. In Rena Hogg's reference 'vile water was poured on his (John Hogg's) head through a gap in the ceiling' — TW suspects that talk of someone urinating on her father's head would have been offensive to Rena Hogg, hence the 'more delicate euphemism, "vile water"'. But more significant for him is that Rena Hogg makes no mention of the conclusion to the story as heard by KB — that the mayor was so ashamed that he joined the infant church and became one of its leaders ('Kenneth Bailey's Theory of Oral Tradition', 9-12).

but simply refers to it.[12] Despite this, TW tries to depict Rena Hogg as telling a story (Rena Hogg's version) with a 'conclusion' which does not match KB's. But Rena Hogg's reference does not have a 'conclusion'. (2) TW assumes that the 'punch line' of the story is the successful conclusion of the (KB) story, whereas the key point which unites the two accounts (the KB story and the Rena Hogg reference) is the shameful indignity to which Hogg was subjected. TW seems to draw his idea of a 'punch line' from the punch line joke which climaxes in such a punch line, so essential if the joke is to 'work' well. But my understanding of the KB thesis is more in terms of the stable core at the heart of a story than of a punch line at its end.

(3) TW's initial criticism (Rena Hogg's description of the urinating incident 'does not exactly match the way in which Bailey describes the event') gives the game away, since it ignores the character of oral tradition. In an oral culture oral tradition is not evaluated in terms of versions which 'exactly match' each other. On the contrary, such a judgment evidences what I call the literary mindset, which thinks in terms of an *original* version, and which judges all subsequent versions by comparison with the 'original', deducing that all variation from that version is less 'authentic' (since it is not 'original'). But in oral tradition the story is told in different ways and with different details — the *same* story! *The ideal of a pure original, capable of being reconstructed from the less than satisfactory later versions, has been one of the most misleading working assumptions in Gospel and Quest of the Historical Jesus research for about one hundred years.* However, TW seems to think that there is some original version of the story of Hogg's disgraceful embarrassment, and that KB's version is open to criticism because it does not 'exactly match' what he assumes to have been the original. He misses the point that in an oral culture the same episode can be narrated or referred to in different ways without any implication that one is more authentic/accurate than the others. This again is where reference to the Synoptic Gospel tradition would have been helpful, since the kind of variation we find between different versions and different applications drawn from particular episodes is not dissimilar to the variations between KB's story and Rena Hogg's reference.

---

12. '. . . on one occasion vile water was poured on his head through a gap in the ceiling of a room from which his audience had been forcibly ejected' ('Kenneth Bailey's Theory of Oral Tradition', 10).

3. The Robber Band Episode[13]

This is the most substantial of TW's criticisms of KB. But once again there is more to be said for KB than TW allows.

For one thing, KB is illustrating the character of oral tradition, how the stories about Hogg were circulated — that is, had been circulating in the late nineteenth and early twentieth centuries and were still being told decades later when KB was personally present. In this case we can speak properly of a Rena Hogg version of the story. And what immediately grasps the attention is the very close parallels between the two versions (KB's and Rena Hogg's). Indeed, the 'synoptic' presentation which TW provides,[14] is strikingly similar to the synoptic parallels which typify a Synopsis of the first three Gospels.

Here I have been disappointed once again with TW's critique. He finds fault with the facts that whereas Rena Hogg talks of the robbers being 'converted', KB speaks only of them being 'convicted', and that the two versions differ in the detail of the outcome. Is TW forgetting that many Synoptic Gospel parallels have similar variation of detail/wording and outcome? So when Luke tells the story of the centurion's servant in order to highlight the theme of 'unworthiness/worthiness', whereas Matthew tells the same story in order to emphasize the theme of 'faith' (Matt. 8.5-13/Luke 7.1-10), is one or the other wrong or inaccurate or an unfaithful tradent? No, of course not; they simply tell the same story differently, to bring home somewhat different lessons for their readers/audiences — both lessons drawn quite fittingly from the same story.

Once again TW seems to be falling into the trap of assuming that there can be only one 'original', 'historically authentic' and 'faithfully transmitted' version of any story or episode. He thereby shows that he has not even begun to appreciate the character of oral tradition with its defining character as 'the

13. Both KB and Rena Hogg tell the story of John Hogg accosted by a robber band at night. In both versions Hogg surrendered his gold watch and money, but referred the robbers to another treasure which he had. Hogg then withdrew a small book from his pocket (Scriptures) and entranced the robbers by reading from it. The consequence was that the robber band were convicted (KB)/converted (Rena Hogg), were anxious to return the stolen items, and resolved to abandon their life of robbery. Hogg refused to take back the money, and thereafter supported them financially. Only Rena Hogg identifies the robbers as Copts and Moslems and claims that they became respected members of the Church ('Kenneth Bailey's Theory of Oral Tradition', 12-16). TW goes on to point out that Rena Hogg herself 'reports the story as an example "to show how fact and fancy mingle in . . . lore" about her father'; 'the story has many versions'; she saw a 'danger that the message of his (her father's) life may be lost under a tangled mass of fact and fiction' (16-20).

14. 'Kenneth Bailey's Theory of Oral Tradition', 14-15.

same yet different'. TW again gives the game away when he speaks not only of 'the original story' but also of 'an orally fixed version of the story'.[15] But KB repeatedly makes the point that in the oral tradition he is describing there is a range of fixity and flexibility; the 'fixity' may be (only) a proverb, or the substance of the story, or the core element in the story, but otherwise the detail may be very diverse — as we see consistently in the Jesus tradition. Here again TW's reference to the 'punch line' of a story betrays a failure to appreciate the character of oral tradition. He uses the phrase consistently of the *conclusion* to a story. But in the Synoptic tradition the reference is as often or more often to the focal point of the story — for example, in the word for word agreement in the exchange between the centurion and Jesus (Matt. 8.8-10/ Luke 7.6-9), or the word for word agreement in the exchange between the risen Jesus and the persecuting Saul in the different tellings of their encounter on the road to Damascus (Acts 9.4-6; 22.7-10; 26.14-16). The 'punch-line' in the robber band episode is the more powerful effect of Bible stories than that of greed and robbery. The views of Rena Hogg and KB show how the story was being told with varying detail and conclusion.

Rena Hogg's own misgivings and questions about the story as she (and KB) heard it raise important questions about the story as told and the correlation between the story and the event which gave rise to the story. TW is justified in drawing attention to the issues here and provides an appropriate warning against reading historical events too quickly from the stories to which the events gave rise. What I would have liked to see is a careful inquiry into how quickly the story assumed the shape that it has in both Rena Hogg's and KB's versions. By way of some comparison, I suspect that a number of the miracle stories regarding Jesus took their continuing shape very early indeed. In *Jesus Remembered* I suggest the likelihood that many of the healing stories and perhaps deliverance from danger (e.g. the storm on the lake) were *experienced as miracles* in that the 'miracle' was not a later addition or revision of some non-miraculous 'original' version.[16] So I find myself asking of the Rena Hogg and KB versions in this case whether those who survived such a dangerous experience through the night had been so conscious of the divine protection which had saved them, that *from the first* the story was told as attesting the power of a biblical story to restrain potential evil and to evoke faith even among likely thieves. I do not know the answer to the question thus posed. Just as I do not know what 'literally' happened in many of the healings and deliverances for which Jesus was responsible. If the telling of the stilling of the

15. 'Kenneth Bailey's Theory of Oral Tradition', 18.
16. *Jesus Remembered*, 688-9.

storm in terms of a divine theophany goes back to the earliest telling of the story, then no matter how far we penetrate 'behind' the story we will still end up with what was experienced as a miraculous deliverance.

The point for KB, I take it, is that this was the way the story had been told for several decades, so that the story illustrates how the memory of John Hogg had been established during his ministry in Egypt and how it was still being preserved, by retelling the same story.

4. The Eight Non-Hogg Anecdotes

I am not in a position to answer the various questions that TW raises in response to KB's several examples of how the model of 'informal controlled tradition' worked, though his resolute scepticism simply underlines the fact that TW seems unable to read KB's testimony with any degree of sympathy.[17] But on several of the instances covered, the scepticism becomes uncritically censorious. Four call for particular comment

(2) In his comment on *the* zajali *monk,*[18] the second of the eight anecdotes, TW again shows that he operates on the assumption that in the case of a historical account there will be an 'original' tradition which alone will be 'historically authentic'. What a strange view of history writing or of how historians draw on earliest tradition! Once again TW misses the point that oral tradition typically produces *variant* versions of the *same* events (as in the Synoptic Gospel tradition). To insist that only one of these can properly be described as 'original' or 'authentic' simply betrays a literary mindset which thinks in terms of first or original editions and can only evaluate subsequent editions by comparing/contrasting them with the 'original'.

Similarly I have to ask whether TW appreciates the point about *ad libing*. Parry and Lord observed long ago that the singer or saga teller would operate as an *ad lib* performer, as he drew spontaneously on a variety of possible adjectives or descriptive phrases to refer to characters in the tale being told. But the tales were substantially the same. To say it again, the point is that oral tradition is characterized by the combination of fixity and variety, the same yet different. KB seems to be referring to the equivalent in his reference to the history of the Maronite Church.

17. 'Kenneth Bailey's Theory of Oral Tradition', 21-32.

18. TW follows KB in noting that a *zajali* is one who possesses the required skills to create a *zajal,* a form of village poetry, and argues that a *zajali's* 'ability to create stanza *ad lib*' (quoting KB's own words) militates against KB's claim that such *zajal* poems count as witness to accurate transmission of oral tradition ('Kenneth Bailey's Theory of Oral Tradition', 22-3).

(6) The story of *Bailey's preaching*[19] is one which I recall KB telling me in the 1970s. What struck me then — and still does — is the point KB was making, that the oral tradition was being framed in front of his eyes. The story of KB's visit and sermon would be retold during the evening gatherings, and the main point, the primary thrust of the sermon, would be recalled and repeated. What KB experienced and what was so fascinating (for KB and for me) is that even before he had finished his sermon that principal message and its primary thrust were being agreed on by leaders (elders) of the community. Those agreed formulations were being 'fixed'. They would form the core element in the oral tradition, which would retain that degree of fixity in the future retellings of the story.

So TW again betrays his unreadiness to hear what KB is saying. Of course the stories were not of *haflat samar* gatherings as such. But the point is still obvious: that the formulation being established and agreed on would form the core and fixed elements in future retellings in the *haflat samar*. Such retellings would allow a degree of diversity, but if the formulations established at the time of the event were missed or changed, then it is clearly implied that members of the gathering would be likely to object. So KB's account does feed directly into his thesis about informal controlled tradition.

I should just add that TW's concern about 'accuracy' again misses the point. What was of primary importance was the message the congregation was actually receiving, not that it was 'accurate'. TW is all the while asking about historicity, whereas KB is describing the formation of tradition. I personally do not want to hold the two aspects very far apart, but regrettably TW is all the time missing KB's concern to describe how oral tradition has worked in the Christian communities of southern Egypt. First appreciate how the tradition, the tradition process works, then we can turn to the question of historical concern and historical value.

(7) *The Ibrahim Dagher parable.* TW's critique of the Ibrahim Dagher

---

19. KB recounts that regularly when telling a new story during his own preaching an elder would interrupt and ask the congregation if they had heard what KB had just said, and then the elder would repeat 'a line or two of the story including the punch line'. The people would then follow the lead of the elder and turn to people next to them and repeat 'the central thrust of the story twice or thrice to each other. They wanted to retell the story that week across the village and they had to learn it on the spot'. KB comments that 'Through such incidents it was possible to observe *informal controlled* oral tradition functioning at close range, and watch it solidify and orally record information for transmission'. TW objects that such an account cannot provide evidence of informal *controlled* oral tradition, since the description is of a sermon, not of any subsequent retelling of the story in a *haflat samar,* and hardly gave assurance that the story would be 'retold *accurately*' ('Kenneth Bailey's Theory of Oral Tradition', 25-6).

(ID) story[20] I found to be more frustrating than any other. The story is that ID took a familiar parable (the camel and the tent)[21] and altered the ending: the story did not end with the camel taking over the tent and expelling the Bedouin (the normal ending); but with the camel jerking his neck up, striking the tent top, and causing the tent to collapse.[22] TW is critical because ID changed the end of the parable, without occasioning protest (so no 'informal control').[23] But again TW misses the point. The parable was well known — I have been familiar with it for many decades myself. The point is that it was also well known to ID's audience, including the standard end to the parable. ID gained his effect because he knew what the audience would expect. It was precisely because he could assume that common knowledge and the expectation of the audience for the traditional ending that his modification of the parable could be so effective. And the powerful reshaping of the parable became itself a memorable event to be preserved in the oral tradition.[24] KB's account makes its point not because it illustrates a tradition being controlled, but because by varying the familiar tradition, by departing from the traditionally expected end, ID's retelling of the parable was all the more effective. It was effective because it modified the well-known parable tradition.

We should note that the story is about the modification of a *parable*. The parable itself was not an account of an event in the history of the Christian community; the *modification* of the parable *was* such an event, and it is that event which was important in the history of the community, and so was remembered in the community's tradition. TW is entirely justified in drawing the parallel with Jesus' parable in Matt. 22. Both Matthew and ID show how a parable can be retold in a way that makes it all the more immediately relevant to the changing situation of the community. But that simply underlines again the character of oral tradition in using the parable form. It says

20. 'Kenneth Bailey's Theory of Oral Tradition', 26-9.

21. The parable is of a camel trying to get inside a Bedouin's tent, and ends with the camel driving the Bedouin from the tent.

22. ID clearly intended his audience to understand that the Bedouin symbolized the Lebanese and the camel referred to the Palestinians.

23. ID 'failed to observe a principal canon of informed controlled oral tradition, as Bailey represents it. Dagher changed the parable's "inviolable" punch line' ('Kenneth Bailey's Theory of Oral Tradition', 27). TW sees a parallel in Matthew's revision of the Q parable of the Great Supper (Matt. 22.1-10) 'to fit the kerygmatic requirements of his church's own existential "present"', both Matthew's and ID's revisions illustrating that an oral tradition could be thus reshaped without provoking challenge and question ('informal control') from the audience (28).

24. ID's variant ending expressed the Lebanese fear that their welcome to the exiled Palestinians might break down Lebanon's social and political structures and bring the whole country crashing down about their ears.

nothing about who first told the parable and reminds us that the parable form is very adaptable and that evaluations using terms like 'original' and 'authentic' (implying that only one form is original and authentic and all other forms are not original and inauthentic) are entirely inappropriate.

This is a good example of what John Foley refers to as the 'metonymic reference' character of much oral performance.[25] The oral performer is able to assume that his audience is already familiar with a much richer and broader range of traditional material on which to draw. He will deliberately trigger allusions and cross references by phrases and images used. He will not need to elaborate every point, because in many cases the point will already be familiar. ID was effective in his reworking of the parable of the camel and the tent precisely because the metonymic reference was so well known — the customary version of the parable. He was effective because his ending was at such odds with the familiar and expected customary ending.

So KB's account is relevant to his 'informal control' model in two ways. (1) The particular re-telling of the parable was so effective because it could assume the normal constraints of informal control — the audience's knowledge of the traditional form of the parable. (2) ID's redrafting of the familiar parable made such a powerful impact that the retelling of the story — that is, not the retelling of the parable, but ID's revision of it — became a fixed item in the history of the Lebanese Christians. The 'inviolable' punch line here which ID's retelling gave to the parable was inviolable because his retelling was so dramatic ('like a mental hand-grenade') and so became the punch line of the story as it was subsequently retold over the following twenty years.

(8) *The tragic death at a wedding.*[26] I am almost as disappointed with TW's critique[27] of the account of another of KB's stories which made a huge impact on me when I first heard it in the 1970s. The point I took from KB's initial telling, which is still the point of KB's subsequent retellings on which TW draws, is that the local community within which the tragedy occurred

25. J. M. Foley, *Immanent Art: From Structure to Meaning in Traditional Oral Epic* (Bloomington, IN: Indiana University, 1991) chs. 1 and 2 (particularly 6-13 and 42-5); he is drawing on the language of H. R. Jauss and W. Iser. The argument is developed in *The Singer of Tales in Performance* (Bloomington, IN: Indiana University, 1995) chs. 1-3.

26. 'As Bailey tells the story, in the celebration which followed the wedding, Hanna, a friend of Burus, the groom, was joining others in firing rifles as a traditional part of the festivities. Hanna's rifle failed to fire, whereupon, in lowering his rifle, it discharged, killing Burus. In order to protect the hapless Hanna from being charged with murder, the villagers told the police when they arrived that "[a] camel stepped on him [Burus]". . . . Henceforth they [the villagers] told the story of the groom's death in this way: "Hanna fired the gun. The gun did not go off. He lowered the gun. The gun fired [passive]"' ('Kenneth Bailey's Theory of Oral Tradition', 29).

27. 'Kenneth Bailey's Theory of Oral Tradition', 29-32.

quickly resolved that the death was an accident, and not deliberate. This conclusion was enshrined in what became the official or standard telling of the episode, using the passive form at the key point in the story — 'the gun fired', *not* 'Hanna fired the gun' — referring to firing of the fatal bullet. In terms of informal controlled tradition, this would be the crucial element. Anyone who retold the story *not* using the passive would be subject to correction in subsequent *haflat samar* gatherings.

That for me was the principal element in KB's story. I recall KB telling me that he heard the story in different versions — from the ferryman across the river, from the donkey boy on the lengthy subsequent journey, and from the headman in the village itself. What was so striking was that each retelling, sometimes briefer, sometimes lengthy, sometimes less formal, sometimes more formal, was built round the same key phrases, making it clear in each case that the death had been an accident and not a murder that was being recalled. The parallel example of the three Lukan retellings of Paul's conversion (Acts 9, 22, 26) immediately struck me — the core of the exchange between Jesus and Saul being unchanged (fixed), whereas the rest of the detail could be very varied.[28]

TW goes on about 'the inviolate punch line' of KB's account.[29] I am not at all clear what he has in mind. What was clear to me when I first heard KB telling the story, and in his subsequent written versions, is that the *core* of the account was the passive formulation of the fatal shooting ('the gun fired', not 'Hanna fired the gun'). That was the 'inviolate' (but I don't recall KB using the term) element in the telling, the formulation round which an acceptable performance of the story would be built and on which its acceptability (informal controlled tradition) would depend. In wholly ignoring the multiple retellings of the story which KB heard, with the core element consistently fixed, TW seems to me to have missed the key point in the retellings.

Despite more conciliatory closing comments on the story, TW can only see 'falsification' and 'fictionalization' at play, the 'rule of preventive censorship' as a rejection of 'the historically authentic version of the story'. That judgment comes across to me as at best curmudgeonly. As I hear the story, there is no falsification, only an account of how the community perceived what had happened, an account of how Burus's death had come about. There is no

---

28. *Jesus Remembered*, 210-2.

29. 'The inviolate punch line . . . has been altered. . . . the oral tradition of that historic episode was immediately falsified and fictionalized in its transmission to the police. . . . The community to a person rejected the *historically authentic* version of the speech-event . . . and concocted and sanctioned yet another punch line for acceptable reciting of the story within the community' ('Kenneth Bailey's Theory of Oral Tradition', 29, 31).

'fictionalization', no attempt to narrate a story of a camel stepping on Burus, only an account of how the formulation served, without any deceit intended or achieved, to articulate the communal opinion that Burus's death was a tragic accident. The fact that we know as much as all this is evidence of the *historical* character of the story; here is how what could have become a very dangerous crisis for community relations was resolved. For TW to deduce that the agreed account was *not* accurate, a misleading account of what actually happened, a 'corruption of the oral tradition' is simply perverse. The story as KB heard it and retold it made no secret of the fact that the gun which killed Burus was in the hands of Hanna when the fatal shot was fired. It simply makes the point that despite that being the case, Hanna was not guilty of murder. I see no historical inaccuracy here. This was how the community's oral tradition of the event was formulated; theirs was no corruption of some more accurate original version. TW allows his antipathy against KB's thesis and story telling to spill over in misrepresentation and unjustifiably antagonistic criticism.

The main thrust of TW's critique comes to clearest expression in the section with which TW sums up his critique.[30] It is a version of the well-established 'social memory' thesis — that a community's oral tradition is subservient to the community's social identity, serving to give expression to that social identity rather than to retain accounts of the history of that community as it happened; historical memory is a permeable expression of how the community sees itself and wants to be seen.[31] There is, of course, a good deal of sound insight in this basic thesis. The most obvious example of how a community adapts its recalled history to serve the image it wishes to portray of itself is, of course, the local museum, with its inevitably high degree of selectivity. In the Synoptic Gospels we have illustrations of how the Jesus tradition regarding the law was interpreted/told differently in communities for whom the law was still of central importance (Matthew) from the way it was retold in communities for whom the Torah was of less immediate importance (Mark). So I am

---

30. 'Kenneth Bailey's Theory of Oral Tradition', 32-7. TW draws particularly on Jan Vansina, *Oral Tradition as History* (Madison: University of Wisconsin, 1985).

31. See particularly M. Halbwachs, *On Collective Memory* (Chicago: University of Chicago, 1992); J. Fentress & C. Wickham, *Social Memory* (Oxford: Blackwell, 1992); J. Assmann, *Das kulturelle Gedächtnis. Schrift, Erinnerung und politische Identität in frühen Hochkulturen* (Munich: C. H. Beck, 1992, [2]1997); A. Kirk & T. Thatcher, eds., *Memory, Tradition, and Text: Uses of the Past in Early Christianity* (Semeia Studies 52; Atlanta: Society of Biblical Literature, 2005). I engage with some of the issues in 'Social Memory and the Oral Jesus Tradition', in S. C. Barton, L. T. Stuckenbruck & B. G. Wold, eds., *Memory in the Bible and Antiquity* (The Fifth Durham-Tübingen Research Symposium, Durham, September 2004; WUNT 212; Tübingen: Mohr Siebeck, 2007) 179-94 (above, 230-47).

very open to the recognition of where Jesus tradition was being told in a way that reinforced the social identity of different earliest Christian groups.

Where I think TW is on much less firm ground is in his critique of KB on this point. (1) TW continues to assume that there was or could have been an 'uncorrupted', 'original' account of the 'historical facts'. He seems to have no appreciation of the character of historical study, still assuming that beneath the layers of tradition there is some objective historical artefact which we today can recover, untouched and unaffected by the witnesses who first saw the event and initially spoke of it. That has never been a realistic conceptualization of the historical method. At best we can get back no further than the testimony of original eyewitnesses and, in law-court fashion, have to make what sense and deduction we can in regard to what it was these witnesses actually saw and heard.

So, when he sets up a KB story in contrast to or even opposition to the 'uncorrupted original account' of the event being narrated, TW is operating in cloud-cuckoo-land at considerable remove from the realities which KB narrates.

(2) TW is justifiably critical of the story of the robber band, but he continues to miss the point about the Ibrahim Dagher story and about the wedding death story. In the former (the ID story), the shared tradition was a parable; the parable itself was not part of the history of the community. The *historically* relevant element was ID's *retelling* of the parable to make a point of considerable political and social implication for the community. That was why the story of ID's retelling of the parable was so important for the community and was remembered so faithfully by the community. It was *not* that the community's social identity caused a familiar parable to be reformulated. The story was of the historical event of ID actually reformulating the familiar parable and making a considerable impact by his variation from the familiar form. It was the actual historical impact of ID's retelling of the parable which is preserved in the story. In attempting to switch the issue to ID's departure from an 'authentic'/'original' version of the parable, TW entirely misses the point.

(3) Similarly with the death at the wedding story. Does TW imply that a more 'historically accurate and authentic' telling of the story would have been a statement that Hanna killed Burus? Is the version which was agreed by all, including the investigating police, that the death was a tragic accident for which Hanna was not responsible ('the gun fired') historically inaccurate and inauthentic? Here is TW in a wholly different culture and context making a severe judgment on the event recalled and on those involved. That I regard as irresponsible. A more sympathetic listening to the story would hear it as a historically factual account of what happened, incorporating the almost immediate judgment of those involved in the event that it was an accident. KB is

right: this is a good example of how the story that was to be told regarding the incident was formulated and its *fixed* element established. In contrast, TW's suspicion and fault-finding does little or no justice either to the story itself or to the community who formulated it or to the authorities who accepted it.

One other point calls for comment. It is that TW has focused his critique more or less exclusively on *narrative* tradition. But when the parallel with the Jesus tradition is so much to the fore, the result is strangely deficient. For most of the last century or so the main focus has been on the teaching or sayings tradition in the Gospels. KB's thesis relates as much to the sayings/ teaching tradition as to the narrative tradition, not least since the subject matter of the evening gatherings could be as much if not more focused on what Jesus taught as on what Jesus did. From my perspective here again the Synoptic tradition well illustrates how what was explicitly understood and remembered as the teaching of Jesus could be and was differently grouped, elaborated, and interpreted, not as something different from or a departure from the 'original and (solely) authentic' version of the teaching, but precisely as the way in which the remembered teaching was performed in the regular gatherings of the earliest churches. The fact that TW has nothing to say on this whole dimension of the Jesus tradition and of the relevance of KB's thesis to our understanding of how the Jesus tradition was remembered and performed, is, I think, a major weakness in his critique.

So I return to my starting point. I wholly agree that the support which KB produces for his thesis is anecdotal. Like TW I regret that the thesis has not been subjected to critical scholarly testing in the field. With the spread of radio and TV to the village communities in Egypt and Lebanon, such testing may no longer be possible; the centuries-old character of oral memory, communication and elaboration might well already be irretrievable. So there is much to regret here.

At the same time, however, the original fascination and impact of the KB thesis remain, in that it helps explain, and explain better than an exclusively literary model, the enduring character of the Synoptic Jesus tradition — again and again the same event being narrated, the same teaching being passed on, but with diverse detail and differing emphases, in different groupings, sometimes compressed, sometimes extended. I am less interested in the history of the Christian communities of Egypt and Lebanon, but the stories which KB tells about these communities and the way they remembered and performed their traditions, have opened for me a window into how the Synoptic tradition took its present shape, a window I am very loath to shut without much more effective critique than TW has offered. Regrettably, TW's critique is methodologically much weaker than the thesis he critiques.

PART III

CHAPTER 12

Remembering Jesus:
How the Quest of the Historical Jesus Lost Its Way

Jesus Remembered[1] was the product and climax of some thirty years' engagement with what is almost universally known as 'the Quest of the Historical Jesus'. During the course of the research for the book itself I became increasingly dissatisfied with three key methodological presuppositions which have determined the course of the Quest, all three of them more or less from its inception. In reaction I found it necessary to engage in the Quest from a different starting point, with a different perspective on the source material, and with a different objective in analysing that material. These three protests and proposals are somewhat scattered and easily missed or lost to view in the scope and detail of the volume (900 pages!). In this essay I will attempt to bring them to clearer view, though it will be understood that the relative brevity of the essay permits neither the detail nor the nuance of the larger volume.[2] Nevertheless, the attempt to focus more sharply on the three protests and proposals may help to make the methodological issues clearer and to highlight their importance. Each of my protests is double-barrelled. My proposals do not fall into such a neat repeating pattern.

---

1. J. D. G. Dunn, *Christianity in the Making*. Vol. 1: *Jesus Remembered* (Grand Rapids: Eerdmans, 2003).

2. I give a fuller account in the three lectures published as *A New Perspective on Jesus: What the Quest for the Historical Jesus Missed* (Grand Rapids: Baker Academic/London: SPCK, 2005).

Protest One

My first protest is directed in the first place against the assumption that 'the Christ of faith' is a perversion of 'the historical Jesus'; that *faith is something which prevents a clear historical view of Jesus.* The objective of the first phase of the Quest was to find the *man* behind the *dogma,* the *historical* Jesus, the *real* Jesus. The assumption was that the real Jesus must have been *different* from the Christ of faith. The real Jesus was obscured by layers of faith and dogma, hidden behind the Christ of the creeds, the God-man, the second person of the Trinity, the Pantocrator, like an original masterpiece obscured by layers of later 'improvements' and centuries of pollution. The Quest was motivated by the conviction that these layers of dogma could be stripped away to reveal a more human Jesus, a Jesus more believable by 'modern man'.

The first to pose the antithesis between the historical Jesus and the Christ of faith in these terms was D. F. Strauss[3] in his sharp critique of Schleiermacher's *Life of Jesus.*[4] Schleiermacher's lectures had been based primarily on John's Gospel, particularly the discourses of Jesus in that Gospel, and had been delivered thirty-two years earlier, prior to Strauss's own *Life of Jesus* in which Strauss had seriously questioned the historical value of the Johannine discourses.[5] So Strauss's reaction to the publication of Schleiermacher's lectures was predictable.

> Schleiermacher's Christology is a last attempt to make the churchly Christ acceptable to the modern world. . . . Schleiermacher's Christ is as little a real man as is the Christ of the church.
>
> The illusion . . . that Jesus could have been a man in the full sense and still as a single person stand above the whole of humanity, is the chain which still blocks the harbour of Christian theology against the open sea of rational science.
>
> The ideal of the dogmatic Christ on the one hand and the historical Jesus of Nazareth on the other are separated forever.[6]

3. D. F. Strauss, *The Christ of Faith and the Jesus of History* (1865; ET Philadelphia: Fortress, 1977).

4. F. D. E. Schleiermacher, *The Life of Jesus* (1864; ET Philadelphia: Fortress, 1975).

5. D. F. Strauss, *The Life of Jesus Critically Examined* (1835-36, [4]1846; ET 1846, Philadelphia: Fortress, 1972) 365-86. The decisive consideration for Strauss was the fact that the style of speech in the Gospel was everywhere the same, whether that of the Baptist, or of Jesus, or of the Evangelist himself, pointing to the conclusion that the style, both of speech and thought, was that of the Evangelist (385).

6. Strauss, *Christ of Faith,* 4, 5, 169.

Strauss, then, marks the beginning of the devaluation of the historical value of John's Gospel which has been a principal feature of the Quest for well over a century. And the critical determinant was that John's Gospel expressed so clearly the developed *faith* of the early church: John presents the Christ of faith rather than the Jesus of history.

If Strauss insisted that John should be placed on the faith side of the history/faith divide, the later-nineteenth-century Liberals were equally insistent that Paul should be placed on the same side. According to Adolf Harnack, Jesus had preached a simple gospel centred on the fatherhood of God, the infinite value of the human soul, and the importance of love. It was Paul who had turned the religion *of* Jesus into a religion *about* Jesus. It was Paul who had transformed the simple moralizing message of Jesus into a religion requiring redemption by bloody sacrifice.[7] Here again it was faith, the faith already of the first Christians, which had begun to obscure the clearer outlines of the historical Jesus.

The late-nineteenth-century Liberals were not worried about dating so early the beginning of the process whereby faith had progressively obscured the lineaments of the historical Jesus. For they were confident that in the Synoptic Gospels, in Mark in particular, they still had direct access to the mind (messianic consciousness) and message of Jesus himself. William Wrede punctured that confidence in a rebuttal which largely determined the attitude of critical scholarship to the Synoptic Gospels for the rest of the twentieth century. He argued that the motif of 'the messianic secret', so integral to Mark's Gospel, was clear evidence of a later, faith, perspective on Jesus; for example, the designation of Jesus as 'Son of God' by demoniacs already expressed *Christian faith* in Jesus.[8]

In short, then, faith pervaded the NT writings and their presentation of Jesus. No single Gospel could be set over against the others as more historical and less theological. This critical perspective thus established a century ago has continued to dominate the way the Gospels are approached and the use made of them in the quest of the historical Jesus. Subsequent to Wrede, Bultmann simply abandoned the quest (at least for the life and personality of Jesus)[9] and focused attention on the kerygmatic Christ. To be sure, his disciples insisted that faith too was interested in the historical Jesus, but could never quite manage to cut a through way round the roadblock of faith. It was not simply that the writers of the NT expressed their faith in and through

---

7. A. Harnack, *What Is Christianity?* (1900; ET London: Williams & Norgate, 1901).

8. W. Wrede, *The Messianic Secret* (1901; ET Cambridge: Clarke, 1971).

9. R. Bultmann, *Jesus and the Word* (1926; ET New York: Scribners, 1935) 8.

their writings. It was more the case that the Easter message, Easter faith, had so transformed their apprehension of Jesus that everything they said about Jesus expressed that faith. As Gunther Bornkamm, the classic expression of the so-called 'second quest of the historical Jesus', put it:

> We possess no single word of Jesus and no single story of Jesus, no matter how incontestably genuine they may be, which do not embody at the same time the confession of the believing congregation, or at least are embedded therein.
>
> In every layer, therefore, and in each individual part, the tradition is witness of the reality of his history and the reality of his resurrection. Our task, then, is to seek the history *in* the Kerygma of the Gospels, and in this history to seek the Kerygma.
>
> Nothing could be more mistaken than to trace the origin of the Gospels and the traditions collected therein to a historical interest apart from faith. . . . Rather these Gospels voice the confession: Jesus the Christ, the unity of the earthly Jesus and the Christ of faith.[10]

If the second questers tried to retrieve the situation, the latest phase of the Quest as represented by the Jesus Seminar marks a reversion to the simplifications of the Liberal quest, compounded by the radical scepticism of Wrede and Bultmann. For Robert Funk, the leading spokesman of the Seminar, the task is as it was 150 years ago: to rescue Jesus from Christianity, to free the historical Jesus from the prisons in which faith has incarcerated him.[11] The method is straightforward: whatever resonates with early Christian faith can be discarded.[12] The desired result is a Jesus amenable to questers' values and prejudices.[13]

In short, then, throughout the history of the quest of the historical Jesus, leading participants have all accepted as a methodological given the twofold proposition: that Christian (post-Easter) faith pervades all our chief sources for the life and mission of Jesus; and that this faith prevents the present-day quester from seeing Jesus as he was, or even as he was seen by his disciples pre-Easter. It is against this twofold proposition that I direct my first protest.

10. G. Bornkamm, *Jesus of Nazareth* (1956; ET London: Hodder & Stoughton, 1960) 14, 21, 23.

11. R. W. Funk, *Honest to Jesus* (San Francisco: HarperSanFrancisco, 1996) 300.

12. R. W. Funk & R. W. Hoover, *The Five Gospels: The Search for the Authentic Words of Jesus* (New York: Macmillan, 1993); see e.g. the references to the Jesus Seminar in the Author Index of *Jesus Remembered*, 959.

13. More extensive criticism in *Jesus Remembered*, 58-65.

Proposal 1

In direct contrast to this deeply rooted suspicion of faith as a barrier to and perversion of any historical perspective on Jesus, my proposal is that *the quest should start from the recognition that Jesus evoked faith from the outset of his mission* and that *this faith is the surest indication of the historical reality and effect of his mission.*

One thing we can be sure about: that Jesus made an *impact* in and through his mission. There were people who became his disciples; this we can be sure of, since otherwise no one would have remembered this Jesus or have wanted to do so, and he would have quickly disappeared in the soon gathering mists of history. The fact that Jesus made disciples is generally recognized. What has not been given sufficient recognition or weight, however, is the effect of this impact. These disciples encountered Jesus as a life-transforming experience: they followed him; they left their families; they gave up their livelihoods. Why? Because they had believed Jesus and what he said and taught. Because they believed in Jesus. They entrusted their lives and futures to him. Such a response cannot be denied the characterisation 'faith'. Their discipleship was a faith commitment, already before Easter. Of course it was not yet Easter faith. And Easter faith transformed the pre-Easter faith. But the faith of discipleship was still faith.

The point is obvious. The earliest faith of the first Christians is not a hindrance or barrier to our perceiving the reality of what Jesus did and said and the effect he had. On the contrary, the impact thus made by Jesus is itself the evidence needed by those who want to appreciate the character and effectiveness of Jesus' mission. But what of the challenge posed by Bornkamm? Has that evidence been diluted or overlaid by the subsequent post-Easter faith? To some extent the answer must be Yes. But the second part of my first proposal is that *the original impact of Jesus' mission on his first disciples is, nevertheless, still clearly evident in the tradition preserved by the Synoptic Gospels.*

Here I draw particularly on a neglected article by Heinz Schürmann to the effect that the beginnings of the sayings tradition in the Gospels must lie in the pre-Easter circle of disciples, and thus, as Schürmann added, with Jesus himself.[14] The claim can easily be documented. Consider only the Sermon on the Mount (Matt. 5-7) or the parallel material in the Lukan Sermon on the Plain (Luke 6.17-49): the beatitudes, the call to love the enemy and not retali-

---

14. H. Schürmann, 'Die vorösterlichen Anfänge der Logientradition: Versuch eines formgeschichtlichen Zugangs zum Leben Jesu', in H. Ristow & K. Matthiae, eds., *Der historische Jesus und der kerygmatische Christus* (Berlin: Evangelische, 1961) 342-70.

ate, the demand to give to those who beg from you, the warning against judging others, about the speck in someone else's eye and the log in one's own, the tree known by its fruits, the parable of the wise man and foolish man. Which of these shows traces of post-Easter embellishment or perspective? Arguably one or two, but not the bulk of them. Of course, within the present Gospels they are retold within a Gospel context, that is, as part of a story climaxing in Jesus' death and resurrection (Bornkamm's chief point). My point, however, is that their form and content show no signs of being originated or shaped by post-Easter faith. Who, for example, in a post-Easter context would have deemed it sufficient to challenge disciples to build their lives on Jesus' teaching (Matt. 7.24-27/Luke 6.47-49) rather than on Jesus Christ himself (as in 1 Cor. 3.11)? In other words, here we have *material which had been given its still enduring content and shape prior to the rise of Easter faith.*

The difference between the two perspectives, the one against which I protest and the one I propose, is well illustrated by their different responses to the hypothetical Q document. Two features of this document are generally agreed among Q specialists. One is that the traditions generally assigned to this document have a marked Galilean character, as indicated by the story of the centurion's servant (Matt. 8.5-13/Luke 7.1-10) and the woes on Chorazin and Bethsaida (Matt. 11.21-24/Luke 10.13-15), and illustrated by the characteristically agrarian setting of many of the traditions, assuming the daily reality of debt, day labourers, absentee landlords, and the like. The other is the lack of a passion narrative, such a prominent motif in all four canonical Gospels. From one perspective the explanation of these features is obvious. Assuming that the character of the Q document tells more about its own provenance and the faith of its compilers than about Jesus, the features point to communities/churches in Galilee which did not know the passion narrative or were even opposed to a gospel which climaxed in the crucifixion of Jesus, as in Mark.[15] From my perspective the more obvious explanation for these features is that *the Q material first emerged in Galilee and was given its lasting shape there prior to Jesus' death in Jerusalem.* That is to say, it expresses the impact made by Jesus during his Galilean mission and before the shadow of the cross began to fall heavily upon either his mission or the memory of his teaching.

The third part of my first proposal is the straightforward corollary that *we can discern Jesus from the impression he left on/in the Jesus tradition.* Here I wish to take up in my own terms the protest made against the nineteenth-century Quest by Martin Kähler. His protest is embodied in the

---

15. See particularly J. Kloppenborg Verbin, *Excavating Q: The History and Setting of the Sayings Gospel* (Minneapolis: Fortress, 2000) chs. 4 and 5.

title of his famous essay, *Der sogenannte historische Jesus und der geschicht-liche, biblische Christus.*[16] Kähler's point was that 'the historical Jesus' was a creation of the questers. The Gospels themselves do not give enough infor-mation to write the sort of Life of Jesus to which the nineteenth-century questers aspired. Lacking that information, they had to fill in the gaps from another source, a fifth gospel — themselves, their own values and aspira-tions. Hence the '*so-called* historical Jesus'. In Kähler's view the Gospels give access only to the *geschichtliche Christus,* the 'historic Christ', that is, Jesus recognized in and by his historical significance.

It is at this point that I part company with Kähler, since by the 'historic Christ' he meant the preached Christ, that is, Christ seen in his post-Easter significance, the crucified and risen Christ seen through the eyes of post-Easter faith. But his protest can be reformulated to express the outcome of my first proposal. That is to say, if we take seriously the undeniable fact that Jesus made an impact on his first disciples, and that that impact is still clearly rec-ognizable in the content and form of the traditions by which Jesus' teaching and practice were remembered, then two things follow.

One is Kähler's point that *we cannot realistically expect to find a Jesus different from the Jesus of the Jesus tradition.* Welcome as it would be for a his-torian, we simply do not have any other substantive sources for Jesus' mis-sion.[17] We have no firsthand testimony from Caiaphas or from Pilate. We do not know how Jesus impacted others. What we *do* know is how he impacted his *disciples.* If we want to strip away all faith from the traditions as part of our critical analysis of these traditions, we condemn ourselves to impotence and failure; for nothing will be left. If we want to find a Jesus who did not inspire faith, or who inspired it differently, we chase a will-o'-the-wisp. But if we take seriously the evidence of the faith-creating impact of Jesus it becomes a means to our even now being able to discern the effect of Jesus' mission and during his mission.

The other is that *by means of and through this impact we can discern the one who made the impact.* As one can discern the shape of the seal from the mark it leaves upon the paper, so we can discern the shape of Jesus' mission from the impression he left on his first disciples. Not the 'historical Jesus', as though he was some objective artefact which we could prise from the tradi-tions and from whom we could then brush off the dirt (faith) of the interven-ing ages. But the '*historic Jesus*', the one who left the impact still evident in the

16. M. Kähler, *The So-Called Historical Jesus and the Historic Biblical Christ* (Leipzig: A. Deichert, 1892; ET Philadelphia: Fortress, 1964).

17. Further details and discussion in my *Jesus Remembered,* #7.

Gospels, the one who transformed fishermen and taxcollectors into disciples. For historians who want to understand better the ways in which and the reasons why Christianity emerged, what more could be desired as outcome for 'the quest of the historical Jesus'?[18]

Protest 2

My second protest is against a twofold assumption which has been more pervasively determinative of the findings of the Quest than is usually appreciated. The first assumption is that *the only way to understand both the relation of the traditions in the Synoptic Gospels and the earliest transmission of the Jesus tradition is in literary terms*. My protest is against the assumption that the processing of the tradition of Jesus' teaching and activities from its first hearers to the written Gospels has to be conceived almost entirely, or even exclusively as a process of copying and editing earlier written documents.

This should be plain to anyone who is familiar with the history of the Quest. Inextricably interwoven with that history is the progress of Gospel criticism. The two have gone hand in hand, often to the disadvantage of both. An obvious first step in the Quest was to ascertain what were the sources for the information about Jesus provided by the Gospels. Source criticism was conceived for the most part, and in effect almost exclusively in terms of written documents. The relations between the Synoptic Gospels, which obviously overlap to a considerable extent in the material they use, were most readily conceived in terms of Evangelists using each others' Gospels or a common written source now lost. A Synopsis demonstrated that one Evangelist must have been dependent on another, by copying or abbreviating, or expanding, or otherwise editing his source. The dominant solution to the Synoptic problem was and still is the 'two *document* hypothesis' — Mark as the earliest Gospel, Matthew and Luke drawing on Mark and on a sayings source (Q).[19] B. H. Streeter's authoritative treatment of the Synoptic problem cautioned against studying the Synoptic Problem 'merely as a problem of literary criticism', but in the event resolved the question of Matthew's

18. My exchanges with Bob Morgan on faith and history may help carry forward the discussion here: Robert Morgan, 'James Dunn's *Jesus Remembered*', *ExpTim* 116 (2004-5) 1-6, and 'Christian Faith and Historical Jesus Research: A Reply to James Dunn', *ExpTim* 116 (2004-5) 217-23; with my own responses — 'On Faith and History, and Living Tradition', *ExpTim* 116 (2004-5) 13-16, and 286-7.

19. See e.g. W. G. Kümmel, *The New Testament: The History of the Investigation of Its Problems* (ET Nashville: Abingdon, 1972) 146-51; Kloppenborg Verbin, *Excavating Q*, 295-309.

and Luke's additional material in terms of two further writings (M and L) — hence the 'four *document* hypothesis'.[20]

The main alternatives offered to the dominant two document hypothesis have been those of William Farmer[21] and Michael Goulder.[22] Both continue to exemplify a modern mind-set which can conceptualize the history of the Jesus tradition only in terms of copying or editing an earlier written source. And the re-emergence of interest in the Q source in the last twenty years has likewise operated entirely from the working hypothesis that Q was a document written in Greek. The most influential analysis of Q, by John Kloppenborg, has even found it possible to stratify the hypothetical Q document into three layers or editions, Q^1, Q^2 and Q^3.[23] In short, the challenge of tracing the tradition history of the Gospel materials, and thus of finding the earliest or most original information for any historical account of Jesus' mission, has been conceived purely as a problem of literary dependency and resolved in the same terms.

The second assumption which I wish to protest against is the assumption that *oral tradition functioned like written tradition;* or that *it is no longer possible to say anything about the oral phase of the Gospel tradition;* or that *only written tradition is reliable.* It is not entirely true that the literary paradigm for analysing the Jesus tradition has completely dominated the analysis of the history of that tradition. Voices were raised early on in favour of recognizing an oral period for the tradition, even oral sources for the Gospels. And form-criticism emerged in the 1920s as an attempt to penetrate behind the written sources into the oral period.[24] The trouble was that the most influential exponent of form-criticism, Rudolf Bultmann, assumed that oral and written tradition were transmitted in the same way. He conceived the whole tradition about Jesus as 'composed of a series of layers'.[25] The conception was of each layer being constructed on the basis of the preceding layer — a conception no different in effect from that of successive editions of a document. But is such a way of conceptualizing oral tradition and transmission realistic? Bultmann apparently never saw the need to ask such a question.

---

20. B. H. Streeter, *The Four Gospels: A Study of Origins* (London: Macmillan, 1924) ch. 9 (quotation from 229).

21. W. Farmer, *The Synoptic Problem* (New York: Macmillan, 1964).

22. M. Goulder, *Luke: A New Paradigm* (2 vols; JSNTSup 20; Sheffield: Sheffield Academic, 1989) in his attempt to dispense with Q (particularly vol. I, ch. 2).

23. J. Kloppenborg, *The Formation of Q* (Philadelphia: Fortress, 1987). For critique see my *Jesus Remembered,* 147-60.

24. E.g. R. Bultmann (with K. Kundsin), *Form Criticism* (1934; ET New York: Harper Torchbook, 1962) 1.

25. Bultmann, *Jesus and the Word,* 12-13.

Others have assumed that oral tradition and transmission would have been so fluid, and anyway are now lost behind the relative fixity of the written traditions of the Gospels, that it is no longer possible to reconstruct any tradition in its oral phase and not worth the trouble to try.[26] Since it is actually technically possible to explain *every* divergence in the Synoptic tradition in terms of *literary* editing, then what need have we of any further hypothesis? Others take the modern standpoint that oral material is unreliable and only written material is reliable. Consequently it becomes important for them to argue that the writing down of Jesus' teaching began very early, even already during his mission.[27] Matthew, the taxcollector, is the most obvious candidate for the role of a literary disciple (one who could read and write), who, conceivably, could have taken notes during Jesus' preaching and teaching sessions. What has obviously not been sufficiently appreciated is the fact that in the ancient world the prejudice was reversed: written material was not trusted, because it could be so easily lost, or destroyed, or corrupted in the copying; much preferable was it to have the teaching or story firmly lodged in one's own mind, retaining the living voice of the teacher.[28]

The consequences of these assumptions are extensive and of a seriousness too rarely recognized. For if there was an 'oral period' at the beginning of the history of the Jesus tradition, lasting, say, for about twenty years, and if it is not possible to penetrate into that period with confidence, and if oral tradition is inherently unstable and unreliable, then the quest of the historical Jesus is confronted with *a yawning and unbridgeable gulf* between the tradition as we still have it and the Jesus to whom it bears witness. Here and there we may find some sayings or a motif which reaches out some way over the gulf, but the questers who rely on them to inch back towards 'the historical Jesus' are likely to suffer a severe attack of critical vertigo, and the chances of establishing a firm link on the other side of the gulf become ever more tenuous the further they try to reach back.

26. See particularly B. W. Henaut, *Oral Tradition and the Gospels: The Problem of Mark 4* (JSNTSup 82; Sheffield: JSOT, 1993).

27. See particularly A. Millard, *Reading and Writing in the Time of Jesus* (BS 69; Sheffield: Sheffield Academic, 2000) 223-9; also E. E. Ellis, *The Making of the New Testament Documents* (Leiden: Brill, 1999) 24, 32, 352.

28. L. Alexander, 'The Living Voice: Scepticism Towards the Written Word in Early Christian and in Greco-Roman Texts', in D. J. A. Clines, S. E. Fowl, & S. E. Porter, eds., *The Bible in Three Dimensions* (Sheffield: Sheffield Academic Press, 1990) 221-47. Contrast P. Barnett, *The Birth of Christianity: The First Twenty Years* (Grand Rapids: Eerdmans, 2005) who assumes that unless the earliest Jesus tradition was in *writing*, it is lost to us; in total antithesis to my thesis, Barnett regards a study 'based on the culture of orality' as effectively closing off 'any pathway to the actual teaching of Jesus' (136).

This is the burden of my second protest against the traditional assumptions which have governed the quest of the historical Jesus. The literary mind-set of the nineteenth to twenty-first centuries has conditioned the very way in which we conceptualize the processes by which the Jesus tradition first emerged and was initially transmitted. We think in a box of literary dependency, of copying and editing. And we are the more confident of the results of our analysis of that tradition because they are so containable within the box. But the box is one constructed by the fifteenth-century invention of printing and it prevents us from seeing outside of its containment. We shut out the reality of what an oral society must have been like, and have failed to think through the character of the traditioning process in an oral society. We think that the results of reconceptualizing the processes of oral transmission would be destructive of our grasp of the tradition's 'authenticity' because of orality's inherent instability. And the outcome is that we cut ourselves off from the Jesus we want to rediscover and hear again afresh in his own terms.

Proposal 2

In direct contrast to the blinkeredness of the literary paradigm, I affirm, first, *the necessity of taking the oral phase of the history of the Jesus tradition with all seriousness.* And second, in direct response to any resignation before the difficulty of gaining real access to the tradition in its oral phase, I maintain that it *is* in fact *possible to envisage the oral phase of the Jesus tradition.*

First, it is necessary that we *do* make an attempt to envisage the way an oral society functions, not least in regard to the traditions it regards as important. For first-century Palestine certainly was an oral rather than a literary culture. Those who have inquired most closely into the subject tell us that literacy in Palestine at the time of Jesus would probably have been less than 10%.[29] And

---

29. Recent estimates are of less than 10% literacy in the Roman Empire under the principate, falling to perhaps as low as 3% literacy in Roman Palestine; see particularly W. V. Harris, *Ancient Literacy* (Cambridge, MA: Harvard University, 1989); M. Bar-Ilan, 'Illiteracy in the Land of Israel in the First Centuries CE', in S. Fishbane & S. Schoenfeld, *Essays in the Social Scientific Study of Judaism and Jewish Society* (Hoboken, NJ: Ktav, 1992) 46-61; C. Hezser, *Jewish Literacy in Roman Palestine* (Tübingen: Mohr Siebeck, 2001). Birger Gerhardsson refuses to accept that 'the Israel of NT times can be characterized as an oral society' ('The Secret of the Transmission of the Unwritten Jesus Tradition', *NTS* 51 [2005] 1-18 [here 14, 17]); but a society where the Torah was known almost entirely by being heard and taught, and where the initial accounts of Jesus were passed on almost exclusively by word of mouth is not yet to be described as a 'literate society'.

even if we can argue that a Jewish society would have prized the skills of reading and writing more highly than others, the increase in percentage may not have been very great. The reason why we read so much about 'scribes' in Palestine, as well as more widely in the ancient world, is that literary skills were the prerogatives of a relatively small group of professionals. We have to assume, therefore, that the great majority of Jesus' first disciples would have been functionally illiterate.[30] And even allowing for the possibility that one or two of Jesus' immediate disciples were able to read and write (Matthew) and may even have kept notes of Jesus' teaching, it remains *overwhelmingly probable that the earliest transmission of the Jesus tradition was by word of mouth.*

Second, the extensive study of oral communities and of how oral tradition functions has been greatly advanced over the latter decades of the twentieth century. Classic treatments of Yugoslavian epics, of folklore and of oral tradition for example in Africa,[31] have given us a clearer idea of what it must have meant to live in a community where information, knowledge and wisdom were all or mostly retained within an oral framework of memory and tradition in and on behalf of the community. I found Kenneth Bailey's accounts of his more than thirty years' experience of the oral culture of Middle East village life particularly insightful.[32] From this material I deduce five important characteristics of oral tradition and oral transmission.[33]

(1) *Oral performance is different from reading a text.* The reader can pause in the reading for reflection, can turn back to check something, can look forward to anticipate the outcome. The reader can take the book away and read it again. The editor can take the literary manuscript and make changes to the text, and so on. Nothing of this is possible for the hearer of an

---

30. Kloppenborg Verbin properly reminds us that '"literacy" itself admits of various levels: signature-literacy; the ability to read simple contracts, invoices and receipts; full reading literacy; the ability to take dictation; and scribal literacy — the ability to compose' (*Excavating Q,* 167).

31. Particularly A. B. Lord, *The Singer of Tales* (Cambridge: Harvard University, 1978); J. M. Foley, *Immanent Art: From Structure to Meaning in Traditional Oral Epic* (Bloomington, IN: Indiana University, 1991); J. Vansina, *Oral Tradition as History* (Madison: University of Wisconsin, 1985); I. Okpewho, *African Oral Literature: Backgrounds, Character and Continuity* (Bloomington: Indiana University, 1992); A. Dundes, *Holy Writ as Oral Lit: The Bible as Folklore* (Lanham: Rowman & Littlefield, 1999).

32. K. E. Bailey, 'Informal Controlled Oral Tradition and the Synoptic Gospels', *Asia Journal of Theology* 5 (1991) 34-54; also 'Middle Eastern Oral Tradition and the Synoptic Gospels', *ExpTim* 106 (1995) 363-7.

33. I draw here on my 'Altering the Default Setting: Re-Envisaging the Early Transmission of the Jesus Tradition', *NTS* 49 (2003) 139-75 (here 150-5), reprinted in *A New Perspective on Jesus,* 79-125 (above, 41-79).

oral tradition being retold. The hearing is an event, not a thing; the individual hearer cannot press a pause button or put the performance into reverse. It is evanescent, past and gone, and cannot be taken away for later perusal, or returned to for checking. It is not a written text which can be revised or edited. This very basic fact at once compels us to adopt a very different attitude towards the Jesus tradition in its pre-literary state. What was happening to the tradition in that important phase of its history? Was every performance different in content and character from its predecessors? Did changes occur then which significantly altered or randomly transformed the tradition prior to its being written down? At the very least, recognition of the oral phase of the traditioning process should cause us to look twice at explanations of differences between the Synoptic traditions which rely exclusively on a literary model.

(2) We can assume a *communal dimension* for oral tradition. Contemporary literary criticism inclines us to think of an individual author writing with a view to being read by an individual reader — hence such terms as 'implied reader' and 'reader response'. We can think without effort of the sole reader at a desk or curled up on a sofa having a one-to-one encounter with the text. But oral tradition is characteristically community tradition. This was recognized by the pioneers of form-criticism in the 1920s but its significance was lost to sight by those locked into the literary mind-set. Here Bailey's anecdotal accounts are helpful, as he envisages village communities gathering of an evening to share news and to recall and celebrate tradition that was important to them — what he calls the *haflat samar*. So present-day attempts to envisage the earliest disciple groups need to remember that there would have been no newspapers, no radio or television or cinema screen to provide a focal point for the gathering, and in most cases no scrolls of Torah or prophet to be read or consulted, but only the shared memories of what Jesus had said and done and shared experiences of their discipleship. Furthermore, as the community's tradition, it was not the property of any individual, to modify or develop at will. Where the tradition was important to the community, to its identity, there would be a natural concern to maintain the community-determining character of the tradition through all its varied performances.[34]

(3) At the same time it is also important to note that an oral community designates or recognizes *particular individuals* to bear the main responsibility

34. Although I entitle my study of Jesus *Jesus Remembered*, my interest here and in that volume is in the way the *tradition* of Jesus emerged, not in theories of 'collective or social memory'. For interaction with Bengt Holmberg and Samuel Byrskog on the latter subject I may refer to my response to their critiques of *Jesus Remembered* in 'On History, Memory and Eyewitnesses', *JSNT* 26 (2004) 473-87 (see above, 199-212).

(on behalf of the community) to retain and recite the community tradition as appropriate on occasions when the community come together. In the absence of dictionaries or encyclopedias, the bard, or apostle, or elder, or teacher would serve as the community's resource, the storage cistern for the community's reserves of story and wisdom built up and handed down over the years.[35] Luke almost certainly has this sort of thing in mind when he refers to 'the apostles' teaching' in Acts 2.42. And the prominence of teachers (e.g. Acts 13.1; Rom. 12.7; 1 Cor. 12.28-29; Gal. 6.6; Jas 3.1) and of tradition (e.g. Phil. 4.9; Col. 2.6-8; 1 Thess. 4.1; 2 Thess. 3.6) in the earliest communities points clearly in the same direction. For the 'tradition' would be the particular responsibility of the 'teachers', and since it was the Jesus tradition which really marked out the assemblies of the first disciples, a large part of that responsibility must have included the rehearsal and performance of the Jesus tradition at such assemblies.[36]

(4) In the performance of oral tradition we find *a characteristic combination of stability and diversity, of fixity and flexibility.* In the words of E. A. Havelock, 'Variability and stability, conservatism and creativity, evanescence and unpredictability all mark the pattern of oral transmission' — the 'oral principle of "variation within the same"'.[37] There is the same story, or the story of the same event; it is the same teaching, in substance at least; but the telling of the story, or the repeating of the teaching may be very diverse, the diversity determined by such factors as the circumstances of the occasion, or by the desire of the teacher to bring out a particular emphasis or point. A modern parallel is the punch-line joke — itself as near as we may be able to come to modern experience of oral tradition. The build-up to the punch line can be wholly diverse, but if the joke is to 'work', the punch line has to be 'word-perfect' and delivered with due attention to the timing. And this is what we find repeatedly in the Synoptic tradition of Jesus' mission: the same

35. E.g. E. A. Havelock, *The Muse Learns to Write: Reflections on Orality and Literacy from Antiquity to the Present* (New Haven: Yale University, 1986) speaks of an oral 'encyclopedia' of social habit and custom-law and convention (57-8).

36. R. Bauckham, *Jesus and the Eyewitnesses: The Gospels as Eyewitness Testimony* (Grand Rapids: Eerdmans, 2006), building particularly on S. Byrskog, *Story as History — History as Story* (WUNT 123; Tübingen: Mohr Siebeck, 2000), gives particular weight to the (apostolic) eyewitnesses and criticizes me for maintaining the tradition of anonymous tradents in anonymous communities (particularly ch. 12). My point, however, was that the nature of the oral traditioning process, as evidenced by the Synoptic tradition, was such that the passing on of the tradition, by whoever (first disciple, visiting apostle, local teacher), has clearly retained the same character and substance.

37. W. H. Kelber, *The Oral and the Written Gospel* (Philadelphia: Fortress, 1983) 33, 54; quoting E. A. Havelock, *Preface to Plato* (Cambridge, MA: Harvard University, 1963) 92, 147, 184, *passim.*

story, but told differently, and often with inconsequential difference of detail; the same teaching, but often in different wording and set in different contexts. It is this feature of the Synoptic tradition which has always intrigued me about the Jesus tradition, and I have found no better explanation for it than in terms of performance variation, 'variation within the same'.[38]

(5) A final important characteristic of orally performed tradition is that there is *no original version,* equivalent to an original edition of a written text. That there was an *originating* event in the mission of Jesus, or a particular teaching which he gave, I have no doubt, at least in most cases. But the witnesses would have seen and heard differently; the event or words would have impacted them differently. And their reporting or sharing of that impact would have been different. So there probably would not have been a single original version of any specific tradition; original/originating *event* is not to be confused with original *report* of the event. And if Jesus had given the same teaching or parable more than once, and in different terms (one thinks, for example, of the parable of the talents/pounds — Matt. 25.14-30/Luke 19.11-27), then there may never have been a single original/originating form of words. The immediate corollary has extensive repercussions. For it at once indicates that the search for an original version, as though that alone was 'authentic' or 'historical', is misguided. Likewise, diverse forms of particular traditions are in principle not a problem, they do not constitute a 'contradiction', they are not proof that the tradition has (been) developed away from 'the true'. On the contrary, they probably represent well the ways in which the Jesus tradition was performed in disciple groups and churches, and *from the first.*

What I envisage, then, for the beginning of the Jesus tradition, is that those whose lives were transformed by the impact of Jesus' mission, who became disciples, including those who did not literally follow Jesus, would have shared their experiences when they came together, talking among themselves. In such gatherings the impact made by what Jesus did and said would have been put into words, and the oral tradition of these doings and teachings would thus begin to take shape — essentially the shape which it still has in its enduring form. As already noted above, the enduring forms of so much of Jesus' teaching still bear the stamp of his Galilean mission, prior to the climax in Jerusalem. That stamp must have been given to it in such disciple gatherings, no doubt with the chief disciples (the twelve) having a prominent say in the basic shaping of the tradition. And no doubt the performance tradition after Jesus' departure would have become more varied. But if I am right, the

---

38. Examples in my 'Altering the Default Setting', 160-9 (above, 63-8), and throughout *Jesus Remembered.*

tradition was varied from the first, and the variations which have been preserved in the now-written texts seem again and again to be no different in kind from the variations which we can safely hypothesize as characteristic of the performance tradition from the first.

In other words, it *is* possible to penetrate back into the oral period of the Jesus tradition. For the bridge being pushed over the gulf does not come only from one side. The impact made by Jesus on the disciples, and expressed more or less from the beginning in oral tradition, means that the bridge can in effect be constructed from the other side as well. So long as we do not allow ourselves to be enticed and misled by the will-o'-the-wisp of an 'original version', and are content with recognizing a clear but diverse impression made by Jesus still evident in the tradition as we now have it, then we can be much more confident than before of gaining a clear sight of the one who made that impression.

Protest 3

My third protest is against the working assumption that *the Quest must look for a Jesus who was distinctive or different from his environment.* Not only would 'the historical Jesus', it was assumed, be different from 'the Christ of faith', but he must also and nevertheless have stood out from his fellows. Now, I do not wish to play down the distinctiveness of Jesus. That Jesus made a distinctive impact is my own first proposal, an impact attested in the content and character of the Jesus tradition itself. But the assumption to which I object here is that only if Jesus can be *distinguished from his context* is he worthy of our attention (he cannot surely have been just another Jewish teacher); only if his message was different from that of other teachers can we be sure we have the authentic voice of Jesus (and not just the accumulated wisdom of Jewish sages).

This assumption has in part been a sad corollary to Christianity's long and disgraceful history of antisemitism. Until recently, Christian biblical scholarship simply reflected that anti-Jewish tendency, by consistently downplaying or denigrating the continuity between Jesus and his native Judaism. As Susannah Heschel observes, liberal theologians painted 'as negative a picture as possible of first-century Judaism' in order 'to elevate Jesus as a unique religious figure who stood in sharp opposition to his Jewish surroundings'.[39]

39. S. Heschel, *Abraham Geiger and the Jewish Jesus* (Chicago: University of Chicago, 1998), here 9, 21. See also H. Moxnes, 'Jesus the Jew: Dilemmas of Interpretation', in I. Dunder-

A classic example is Ernest Renan, who wrote: 'Fundamentally there was nothing Jewish about Jesus'; after visiting Jerusalem, Jesus 'appears no more as a Jewish reformer, but as a destroyer of Judaism. . . . Jesus was no longer a Jew'.[40] And Albrecht Ritschl drew a line in the sand, which was not decisively questioned for most of the twentieth century, when he pronounced that Jesus' 'renunciation of Judaism and its law . . . became a sharp dividing line between his teachings and those of the Jews'.[41] The neo-Liberal quest of the last two decades has not been so brash in its anti-Judaism. But a guiding presumption that Jesus was not, could not have been influenced by Jewish apocalyptic thought, and a tendency to align him more with Hellenistic Cynic critique of establishment ethos and religiosity, produced not a greatly different result — a Jesus more recognizable by (and acceptable to) those concerned to find a non-particularist philosophy and life-style.[42]

My own much used example of the dismaying trend to distance Jesus from his Jewish context is the word *Spätjudentum;* this was a common way of referring to the Judaism of Jesus' time well into the second half of the twentieth century, and it still occurs in some German textbooks. Why should late Second Temple Judaism be described as 'late Judaism'? It is not simply that the term is ridiculous, in view of Judaism's continuing history; if first-century Judaism is '*late* Judaism', what on earth do we call twentieth- or twenty-first-century Judaism?! But the issue is much more serious than a verbal *faux pas*. For the term actually encapsulates Christianity's historic denigration of Judaism. It expresses the theological view that Judaism's function was solely to prepare for the coming of Christ, of Christianity. As soon as Christ came, Judaism's role was complete. As soon as Christianity was established, Judaism was finished. Hence *late* Judaism, for from that perspective first-century Judaism was the *last* Judaism! The protest at this point is long overdue.

A second working assumption follows. If first-century Judaism was so marked by false religiosity, legalism and hypocrisy, if it was merely preparatory for the climactic revelation which came through Jesus, then the Jesus whom the Quest should be looking for would be different from that; he would stand out against his environment. Hence the concern of the quest, as renewed in the 1950s, to find a *distinctive* Jesus. This working assumption

berg et al., eds., *Fair Play: Diversity and Conflicts in Early Christianity,* H. Räisänen FS (Leiden: Brill, 2002) 83-103.

40. Heschel, *Abraham Geiger,* 156-7.

41. Heschel, *Abraham Geiger,* 123.

42. Notably B. L. Mack, *A Myth of Innocence: Mark and Christian Origins* (Philadelphia: Fortress, 1988), and J. D. Crossan, *The Historical Jesus: The Life of a Mediterranean Jewish Peasant* (San Francisco: Harper, 1991).

came to particular expression in *the criterion of dissimilarity*.[43] To be recognized as a saying which derived from Jesus, the saying had to show itself dissimilar from first-century Judaism; the logic being that a saying which expressed concerns typical of Judaism might have been derived from Judaism; the assumption being that to be recognizable at all, Jesus had to be distinctive. In consequence the Quest majored on finding particular sayings which could not be attributed either to Judaism or to the later church(es), and which therefore stood out as different, or which would have been too embarrassing for Jew or Christian to attribute to Jesus had he himself not uttered it.[44]

Hence the typical concern of the second questers to find some saying which would meet this criterion and which could serve as the sure base on which to build a convincing reconstruction of the historical Jesus. Since the kingdom of God and son of man motifs are so well embedded in the Jesus tradition, a typical objective in the second half of the twentieth century was to find which saying was most secure, and to build out from that. Good examples from the post-Bultmannian generation were the assumption of H. E. Tödt and Ferdinand Hahn that Luke 12.8-9 was the most secure of the Son of Man sayings,[45] Werner Kümmel's argument that Mark 9.1 clearly indicated Jesus' expectation that the coming of the kingdom was imminent,[46] and Heinz Schürmann's conclusion that the Lord's prayer for the kingdom to come (Matt. 6.10/Luke 11.2) is the surest way into Jesus' understanding of the kingdom.[47] But the whole attempt was wrong-headed in that a single saying or motif could never provide a sufficiently substantial base on which to build a substantive reconstruction of Jesus' message. It was like building an inverted pyramid, with a resultant and unavoidable tendency for the construction to topple over at the first probing of the base. Or to change the metaphor, the claims and counter-claims regarding different sayings were al-

---

43. Classically defined by N. Perrin, *Rediscovering the Teaching of Jesus* (London: SCM, 1967) 39.

44. The criterion of embarrassment has been given some prominence by J. P. Meier, *The Marginal Jew: Rethinking the Historical Jesus*, Vol. 1 (New York: Doubleday, 1991) 168-71.

45. H. E. Tödt, *The Son of Man in the Synoptic Tradition* (1963; ET London: SCM, 1965) 42, 55-60; F. Hahn, *Christologische Hoheitstitel: Ihre Geschichte im frühen Christentum* (Göttingen: Vandenhoeck & Ruprecht, 1963, ⁵1995) 24-6, 32-42, 457-8. A. Vögtle, *Die 'Gretchenfrage' des Menschensohnproblems* (QD 152; Freiburg: Herder, 1994) continued to regard Luke 12.8-9 as the key to unlocking the problem of 'the Son of Man'.

46. W. G. Kümmel, 'Eschatological Expectation in the Proclamation of Jesus', in J. M. Robinson, ed., *The Future of Our Religious Past*, R. Bultmann FS (ET London: SCM, 1971) 29-48 (here 39-41).

47. H. Schürmann, *Gottes Reich — Jesu Geschick. Jesu ureigener Tod im Licht seiner Basileia-Verkündigung* (Freiburg: Herder, 1983) 135, 144.

ways liable to lead the Quest into a quagmire from which it would be difficult to extricate itself.[48]

Proposal 3

Once again in direct contrast, my proposal is that the quest of the historical
Jesus should come at the task from a different angle.

In the first place *we should look first of all for the Jewish Jesus rather than
the non-Jewish Jesus*. This does not mean that we should make the opposite assumption that Jesus' mission was wholly in conformity with the Judaism of his
day. Controversies with at least some Pharisees are a prominent theme in the Jesus tradition, and Jesus was crucified with at least the acquiescence of the Jewish authorities. But against that we must recall that Jesus was brought up as a pious Jew in Galilee, reciting the Shema, observing the Sabbath, attending the
synagogue, respecting the Torah. The *a priori* that Jesus belonged within Judaism is a more secure starting point for any quester than the assumption that he
must have differed from Judaism. On this point I am wholly at one with what I
regard as the main thrust of the so-called 'third quest of the historical Jesus', as
illustrated, for example, by the work of E. P. Sanders, James Charlesworth and
N. T. Wright.[49] The old question, 'Was Jesus the last Jew or the first Christian?',
speaks not only of the traditional Christian denigration of Judaism ('the *last*
Jew'), but also forces the question into an unnatural polarization which is neither historical nor helpful in the Quest. The points of continuity are as important as the points of discontinuity, and their importance for Christian self-
understanding as well as for Jewish/Christian relations should not be ignored.

In the second place, we would be much wiser to seek out the *characteristic* Jesus, rather than the distinctive Jesus.[50] The logic here is straightforward: any material within the Gospels which is characteristic through and
across the Gospels is likely to reflect characteristic features of Jesus' own mission. It is, of course, quite possible that particular elements within the Jesus
tradition, or particular stylistic features reflect the way the tradition was performed and retold by some highly influential apostle or teacher. But motifs,

48. I echo a comment to the same effect of E. P. Sanders, *Jesus and Judaism* (London:
SCM, 1985) 131.

49. Sanders, *Jesus and Judaism*; J. H. Charlesworth, *Jesus within Judaism: New Light from
Exciting Archaeological Discoveries* (New York: Doubleday, 1988); N. T. Wright, *Jesus and the
Victory of God* (London: SPCK, 1996).

50. I here follow the advice of L. E. Keck, *A Future for the Historical Jesus* (Nashville:
Abingdon, 1971) 33.

emphases and stylistic features which run throughout the tradition in the various branches which have come down to us or which we can still discern are most obviously to be attributed to a single originating or shaping force. And the only real candidate for that role is Jesus himself. Here my proposal obviously ties back into the first two, since what we are obviously talking about is the characteristic impact made by Jesus on those who initially formulated and began to pass on the tradition of Jesus' mission.

It is not at all difficult to nominate the features of the characteristic Jesus as reflected in the characteristic motifs of the Jesus tradition.

- Characteristic forms, best exemplified by parables and aphoristic sayings, most probably reflect Jesus' own style;

   Whatever else he did, he was a parabolist, a teacher of wisdom. It would be flying in the face of all historical probability to doubt that Jesus spoke in parables or in *meshalim*. Focus on these features of the Jesus tradition has been particularly prominent in recent years, but I have no doubt that Birger Gerhardsson and David Aune[51] are better guides on these features than the more prominent members of the Jesus Seminar.[52]
- Characteristic (and distinctive) idioms, such as 'Amen' and 'son of man', most likely reflect Jesus' own speech mannerisms.

   There is no reason whatsoever to doubt that the distinctive use of 'Amen' to introduce his own teaching, rather than to affirm assent with someone else's words recalls a distinctive feature of Jesus' teaching.[53] Likewise the phrase 'the son of man' is so distinctive of Jesus' speech that it beggars belief to argue, as some have, that the whole idiom was retrojected into the Jesus tradition — and that, *ex hypothesi*, by a community which otherwise shows no evident interest in the term![54] That Jesus himself drew upon Dan. 7.13-14 is not so self-evident, but still makes best sense of the overall data.[55]

51. See e.g. the essays by D. E. Aune, 'Oral Traditions and the Aphorisms of Jesus', and B. Gerhardsson, 'Illuminating the Kingdom: Narrative Meshalim in the Synoptic Gospels', in *Jesus and the Oral Gospel Tradition*, ed. H. Wansbrough (JSNTSup 64; Sheffield: JSOT, 1991) 211-65 and 266-309; also B. Gerhardsson, *The Reliability of the Gospel Tradition* (Peabody: Hendrickson, 2001). On Jesus' parables see K. R. Snodgrass, *Stories with Intent: A Comprehensive Guide to the Parables of Jesus* (Grand Rapids: Eerdmans, 2008).

52. See above nn. 11-13, 42.

53. In *Jesus Remembered*, 700-701, I refer especially to J. Jeremias, *The Prayers of Jesus* (London: SCM, 1967) 112-5, including his note that Jesus' use of 'Amen' was 'without analogy in the whole of Jewish literature and in the rest of the New Testament' (112).

54. See *Jesus Remembered*, §16.3-5, particularly 737-9.

55. *Jesus Remembered*, 747-54, 760.

- The most characteristic feature of the Jesus tradition's record of Jesus' preaching, 'the kingdom of God', almost certainly reflects one of the most characteristic emphases of Jesus' own preaching.

  The attempt to play off one emphasis in the kingdom of God tradition against the other, the kingdom as already present and the kingdom as yet to come, flies in the face of the deep-rootedness of *both* emphases in the Jesus tradition,[56] and tells us more about modern impatience with emphases which we find hard to reconcile than proper respect for characteristic features of the Jesus tradition.

- Equally characteristic of Jesus' ministry was his success as an exorcist.

  As with other characteristic features of Jesus' mission his reputation as a successful exorcist is beyond dispute. Exorcisms are the largest single category of Jesus' healing ministry in the Synoptic Gospels; his fame as an exorcist and 'doer of extraordinary deeds' is attested within both Christian and non-Christian sources (e.g. Mark 1.32-34, 39; 3.10-11; Josephus, *Ant.* 18.63); as a successful exorcist his name was widely regarded as one to conjure with by other exorcists (e.g. Mark 9.38; Origen, *contra Celsum* 1.25; PGM 4.1233, 3020); and, not least, Jesus himself was recalled as referring to his exorcistic ministry and drawing out its significance (Mark 3.22-29; Matt. 12.22-30/Luke 11.14-15, 17-23).[57]

- Nor should we ignore the fact that Jesus' mission was characteristically Galilean in location and as reflected in the details of his parables and ethical teaching.

  Although John's Gospel suggests more contact with Jerusalem than the Synoptics allow, the latter's focus on Galilee assuredly indicates that Galilee was the predominant locus for his mission, rather than that there were Galilean communities which preserved the memory of Jesus independently of Jerusalem.[58] Both aspects are confirmed by the fact that the early Christian leadership appears to have been exclusively Galilean rather than Judean.

Of course, recognition that a characteristic theme in the Synoptic tradition is best seen as reflecting a characteristic theme of Jesus' mission does not mean that every element in that theme is an unelaborated memory of Jesus' teaching and activity. A characteristic motif is likely to have been extended in

56. See *Jesus Remembered*, ch. 12, §§12.4-6.

57. Fuller details in *Jesus Remembered*, 670-1.

58. The recent attempt to reconstruct a history of Christianity's beginnings by setting the Acts of the Apostles to one side, by R. Cameron and M. P. Miller, eds., *Redescribing Christian Origins* (Atlanta: SBL, 2004), has proved a failure.

the retellings of the tradition, precisely because it was characteristic. The historical value of a *characteristic feature* of the Jesus tradition will not depend on the historicity of *particular* sayings or narratives. At the same time, the fact that a particular saying or action attributed to Jesus belongs to a characteristic feature of the tradition of Jesus' mission increases the probability that the particular item does record something that Jesus said or did. That is to say, the burden of proof shifts against those who insist on approaching every element of the Jesus tradition with a systematic scepticism. Nor, contrariwise, does my proposal imply that we can be wholly confident of the detail of what Jesus said or did in any specific teaching or event. Bearing in mind my earlier proposals, it is important to remember that what we see of Jesus, we can see only through the eyes of diverse witnesses, and that what we hear of Jesus we can hear only with the ears of assemblies who listened to such retellings and recitals of the Jesus tradition.

Nevertheless, the point of my proposal is that *the characteristic emphases and motifs of the Jesus tradition give us a broad, clear and compelling picture of the characteristic Jesus.*[59] A Jesus who called Israel to repentance and disciples to faith, one through whose ministry the blessings of God's final reign were experienced, one who was heard as speaking for God and with the authority of God, and one who antagonized the priestly authorities and was crucified by the Romans. I could go on, but hopefully enough has already been said to indicate how extensive is the portrayal of Jesus which results, a portrayal which sits firmly within the diversity of first-century Judaism, which has clear outlines and emphases, and which goes a long way to explaining how the impact of Jesus and his mission set in motion a movement whose impetus has never waned.

In conclusion, not least of value in approaching the Jesus tradition in the ways I have advocated is that we thereby gain much more of a sense of that tradition as living tradition. The memory of what Jesus said and did as formulated in the Jesus tradition was not regarded as a kind of sacred relic, to be shut up in some reliquary or encased in perspex to be venerated and carried in procession before reverent assemblies. It was their life-blood, their living breath. It enabled them to re-experience the remembered Jesus, to hear him afresh and to witness for themselves what he had said and done. It was living because they lived by it and it enabled them to live lives of discipleship.

59. C. H. Dodd, *The Founder of Christianity* (London: Collins, 1971) expressed my point well: 'The first three gospels offer a body of sayings on the whole so consistent, so coherent, and withal so distinctive in manner, style and content, that no reasonable critic should doubt, whatever reservations he may have about individual sayings, that we find here reflected the thought of a single, unique teacher' (21-2).

The classic examples, which exemplify the difference between the old way of questing for Jesus and the way advocated above, are the Lord's Prayer and the words of the Last Supper. Typical of the traditional Quest is to treat these as written texts, to assume that they were known only as written texts, to separate away as much as possible of the faith which preserved these texts, to inquire after their (written) sources and the redaction which has brought them to their present shape, and to look for the distinctive features of each by setting it over against the typical features of Jewish prayer and Passover tradition. But to assume that Matthew or Luke only knew the text because they had access to a written text (Q or Mark), and had not known the words until they read them in written form, simply attests a blinkeredness of historical imagination on the part of those who cannot extricate themselves from the literary mind-set. It is much more plausible that these words were known *because they were used regularly* within the gatherings of Jesus' disciples from earliest days, more or less from the first as part of the embryonic liturgy by which the first churches called to memory and re-enacted two of the most important elements of the heritage passed down from Jesus. Rather than to be regarded as cadavers suitable only for clinical dissection, the differing traditions and the developing traditions, as attested not least in the manuscript tradition of these texts, should have been seen as evidence of traditions much used and much beloved, whose development still bears witness to the symbiotic relation between the living tradition and the living church. The fact that precisely these texts, the Lord's Prayer and the words of institution of the Lord's Supper, the Eucharist, continue to develop, with differing forms familiar in the various liturgies of Christian worship now current, and still with their origins in the Jesus tradition clearly recalled, simply confirms that the tradition can retain its living character without losing its roots down through many generations.

This suggests in turn that those who still experience the Jesus tradition as living tradition may well be best placed to appreciate the initial stages of the traditioning process, that it is the ear of faith which is likely to hear the Gospels most effectively, and that the living quality of the Jesus tradition is most likely to be experienced by those who in effect sit with these early assemblies in sharing their memories of Jesus and in seeking to live by them.[60]

60. For further discussion of oral tradition in relation to the historical Jesus, see J. D. G. Dunn, "Social Memory and the Oral Jesus Tradition," in *Memory in the Bible and Antiquity* (ed. S. C. Barton, L. T. Stuckenbruck, and B. G. Wold; WUNT 212; Tübingen: Mohr Siebeck, 2007), 179-94; idem, "Eyewitnesses and the Oral Jesus Tradition," *JSHJ* 6 (2008) 85-105; idem, "Kenneth Bailey's Theory of Oral Tradition: Critiquing Theodore Weeden's Critique," *JSHJ* 7 (2009) 44-62 (in response to T. J. Weeden, "Kenneth Bailey's Theory of Oral Tradition: A Theory Contested by Its Evidence," *JSHJ* 7 [2009] 3-43). All three are reprinted above.

CHAPTER 13

Between Jesus and the Gospels

It should always be remembered that Second Temple Judaism was predominantly an oral society. That is to say, the great majority of the people were technically illiterate. Reading and writing were predominantly the preserve of the nobility, of priests and scribes. This is why, for example, 'scribes' are such a prominent group within the Gospel narratives: the great majority of people depended on someone who was technically literate to write contracts and letters on their behalf. The society was, of course, also a Torah-centred society. People generally knew the Torah and lived their lives in accord with its precepts. But their knowledge of the Torah did not come from personal copies which each had, as would be the case today. Nor did their knowledge come from their own personal reading of the Torah. For the great majority, Torah knowledge came from hearing it read to them by the minority who could read, Sabbath by Sabbath in the synagogue.

All this would be true also of the group round Jesus, his disciples. It is certainly quite likely that a disciple such as Matthew, the toll-collector, could read and write. But the only other profession or trade that we hear of in connection with the other close disciples of Jesus was fishing. And if Jesus' disciples were typical of the peasants, tradesmen and fishermen of Galilee, we can safely assume that the great majority of the disciples were functionally illiterate. We cannot exclude the possibility that Jesus himself was illiterate, or only semi-literate, though the very little evidence we have on the subject probably points to a more positive answer. On the other hand, no one has ever argued seriously that Jesus himself wrote anything or that Christian traditions about Jesus stem from his own pen.

The main points which immediately follow are twofold. First, Jesus' teaching was given *orally;* it began orally. And second, we can safely assume that the news about Jesus was initially passed around *orally.* The stories about Jesus would no doubt have been the subject of many a conversation in bazaars and around campfires. The disciples of Jesus no doubt spoke about what they had seen Jesus do, and about his teaching. This would have been the beginning of the Jesus tradition. It would be celebrated and meditated on in groups of his followers in oral terms. It would be passed on to the curious, to inquirers and to new disciples in oral terms. We can certainly assume that the period between Jesus and the Gospels was filled with such tradition. The alternative is too improbable even to contemplate: that those who followed Jesus during his mission kept all that they had seen and heard to themselves. Or that it was only when the Gospel writers began to look for stories about the past that all this material was dug out, from the fading memories of older first disciples. The probability is much the other way: that much at least, if not the bulk of the Jesus tradition, of the stories about Jesus and the main themes of his preaching and teaching, was being spoken about and celebrated, was the subject of much instruction, discussion and occasion for worship through the early years of the messianic sect of the Nazarene. This is not to deny that some of the Jesus tradition would have been put into writing quite early. But the probability is that in an oral society, the bulk of the Jesus tradition would have been oral tradition. If the period between Jesus and the Gospels is filled with material which was subsequently to go into the Gospels, that material would have been predominantly in oral form.

How does this insight help us to understand the period between Jesus and the Gospels? How does it help us to understand the character of the Gospels? Here we need to look more closely at the Gospels themselves — and particularly at the first three Gospels within the New Testament — Matthew, Mark and Luke. These we recall are regularly referred to as the Synoptic Gospels — from the Greek, *synopsis,* indicating that they can be read together. This is because the Gospels have a considerable amount of material in parallel. When these three Gospels are set down side by side they are telling the same stories and recording the same teaching. Let me illustrate with a sequence of passages in the three Synoptic Gospels, where the parallels are clear.

Episode	Matthew	Mark	Luke
Jesus rejected at Nazareth	13.53-58	6.1-6a	
The sending of the twelve		6.6b-13	9.1-6
Herod thinks Jesus is John raised	14.1-2	6.14-16	9.7-9
The death of John the Baptist	14.3-12	6.17-29	

Episode	Matthew	Mark	Luke
The return of the twelve and the feeding of the 5,000	14.13-21	6.30-44	9.10-17
The walking on the water	14.22-33	6.45-52	
Healings at Gennesaret	14.34-36	6.53-56	
What defiles a person	15.1-20	7.1-23	
The Syrophoenician woman	15.21-28	7.24-30	
Healing many sick people	15.29-31	7.31-37	
The feeding of the 4,000	15.32-39	8.1-10	
Pharisees seek a sign	16.1-4	8.11-13	
The yeast of Pharisees and Herod	16.5-12	8.14-21	
The blind man of Bethsaida		8.22-26	
The confession at Caesarea Philippi and first passion prediction	16.13-23	8.27-33	9.18-22
The conditions of discipleship	16.24-28	8.34–9.1	9.23-27
The transfiguration	17.1-8	9.2-8	9.28-36
The coming of Elijah	17.9-13	9.9-13	
The healing of the epileptic boy	17.14-21	9.14-29	9.37-43a
The second passion prediction	17.22-23	9.30-32	9.43b-45
The Temple tax	17.24-27		
The dispute about greatness	18.1-5	9.33-37	9.46-48

So it is evident why the first three New Testament Gospels are called the Synoptic Gospels — because they run in parallel for so much of their content. And yet — and this is the fascinating bit — they regularly have the same subjects, but treat them differently. This feature poses a question which has troubled or held the attention of Gospel specialists for centuries. Why are the Synoptic Gospels as they are? Why are they so *similar* and yet so *different*? Why are the *same* events narrated so *diversely*? Why are Jesus' teachings so differently formulated and grouped, often or usually the same message but presented with *different words* and in *different contexts?* The Synoptic Gospels are obviously interrelated; there is a manifest interdependence between the traditions which they variously reproduce. How best to explain this, and the differences between them?

The dominant answer to this question regarding the relationship of the Synoptic Gospels has been determined by the fact that there are many passages which are more or less word for word the same in two or all three of the Synoptics. These passages most obviously demonstrate a close *literary* interdependence — one Evangelist copying a written source available to him. The large consensus among New Testament scholars is, first, that of the three Gospels, Mark is the earliest, and was used by both Matthew and Luke. And secondly that Matthew and Luke were also able to draw on a second source, mainly of Jesus' teaching, and conveniently known as Q (from the German, Quelle = source).

However, there are an *equal* number of passages, where the subject is more or less the same, yet the wording and/or structure is noticeably *different*. This feature has not been given so much attention. The tendency has been to work from the identical and near-identical passages to deduce an *overall* literary interdependence, and then to adjust the thesis of literary interdependence to accommodate the other evidence, or to leave aside the very differing passages as problems to be solved some time in the future. In no case have the divergent passages been allowed to put a question mark against the primary thesis of literary interdependence. That thesis is too well rooted in the phenomenon of identical or near-identical passages for it to be called in question by the differing passages.

This way of treating the Synoptic problem however became increasingly unsatisfactory for me. Should not our understanding of the relationship between the Synoptic Gospels be determined by the *divergences* as well as the *similarities* between them? Are not the *differences* between the Synoptic Gospels as important as the *similarities*? Why should we base our theses concerning the interrelationships of the Synoptics only on *one* set of characteristic features? If we do not give the differences as prominent attention as we do the similarities, are we not in danger of failing to appreciate the full or real character of the Jesus tradition and the way the Evangelists handled it? Such questions as these have led me to give more attention to the oral character of the early Jesus tradition and to question whether the hypothesis of literary interdependence tells the whole story.[1]

I

I begin, then, by drawing attention to the character of the interrelationships between the Synoptics, and the diversity of these relationships.

First, *the cases of identical or near-identical wording.* I give two examples from the triple tradition — on the cost of discipleship (Mark 8.34-37 pars.) and the parable of the fig tree (Mark 13.28-32 pars.); and two from the non-Markan parallel material in Luke and Matthew, usually designated as Q — the

1. In what follows I draw on my *Jesus Remembered* (Grand Rapids: Eerdmans, 2003) particularly #8; also *A New Perspective on Jesus* (Grand Rapids: Baker Academic, 2005) 79-125.

preaching of John the Baptist (Matt. 3.7-10/Luke 3.7-9), and the parable of the returning evil spirits (Matt. 12.43-45/Luke 11.24-26). In each case I have underlined the verbal agreement.

(1) The Cost of Discipleship (Mark 8.34-37 pars.):

Matthew 16.24-26	Mark 8.34-37	Luke 9.23-25
²⁴Then Jesus told his disciples, 'If any man would come after me, let him deny himself and take up his cross and follow me. ²⁵For whoever would save his life will lose it, and whoever loses his life for my sake will find it. ²⁶For what will it profit a man, if he gains the whole world and forfeits his life? Or what shall a man give in return for his life?'	³⁴ And he called to him the multitude with his disciples, and said to them, 'If any man would come after me, let him deny himself and take up his cross and follow me. ³⁵For whoever would save his life will lose it; and whoever loses his life for my sake and the gospel's will save it. ³⁶For what does it profit a man, to gain the whole world and forfeit his life? ³⁷For what can a man give in return for his life?'	²³And he said to all, 'If any man would come after me, let him deny himself and take up his cross daily and follow me. ²⁴For whoever would save his life will lose it; and whoever loses his life for my sake, he will save it. ²⁵For what does it profit a man if he gains the whole world and loses or forfeits himself?'

(2) The Parable of the Fig Tree (Mark 13.28-32 pars.):

Matthew 24.32-36	Mark 13.28-32	Luke 21.29-33
³²'From the fig tree learn its lesson: as soon as its branch becomes tender and puts forth its leaves, you know that summer is near. ³³So also, when you see all these things, you know that he is near, at the very gates. ³⁴Truly, I say to you, this generation will not pass away till all these things take place. ³⁵Heaven and earth will pass away, but my words will not pass away. ³⁶But of that day and hour no one knows, not even the angels of heaven, nor the Son, but the Father only.'	²⁸'From the fig tree learn its lesson: as soon as its branch becomes tender and puts forth its leaves, you know that summer is near. ²⁹So also, when you see these things taking place, you know that he is near, at the very gates. ³⁰Truly, I say to you, this generation will not pass away before all these things take place. ³¹Heaven and earth will pass away, but my words will not pass away. ³²But of that day or that hour no one knows, not even the angels in heaven, nor the Son, but only the Father.'	²⁹And he told them a parable: 'Look at the fig tree, and all the trees; ³⁰as soon as they come out in leaf, you see for yourselves and know that the summer is already near. ³¹So also, when you see these things taking place, you know that the kingdom of God is near. ³²Truly, I say to you, this generation will not pass away till all has taken place. ³³Heaven and earth will pass away, but my words will not pass away.'

(3) *The Preaching of John the Baptist (Matt. 3.7-10/Luke 3.7-9):*

Matthew 3.7-10	Luke 3.7-9
⁷But when he saw many of the Pharisees and Sadducees coming for baptism, he said to them, 'You brood of vipers! Who warned you to flee from the wrath to come? ⁸Bear fruit that befits repentance, ⁹and do not presume to say to yourselves, "We have Abraham as our father"; for I tell you, God is able from these stones to raise up children to Abraham. ¹⁰Even now the axe is laid to the root of the trees; every tree therefore that does not bear good fruit is cut down and thrown into the fire.'	⁷He said therefore to the multitudes that came out to be baptized by him, 'You brood of vipers! Who warned you to flee from the wrath to come? ⁸Bear fruits that befit repentance, and do not begin to say to yourselves, "We have Abraham as our father"; for I tell you, God is able from these stones to raise up children to Abraham. ⁹Even now the axe is laid to the root of the trees; every tree therefore that does not bear good fruit is cut down and thrown into the fire.'

(4) *The Parable of the Returning Evil Spirits (Matt. 12.43-45/Luke 11.24-26):*

Matthew 12.43-45	Luke 11.24-26
⁴³When the unclean spirit has gone out of a man, he passes through waterless places seeking rest, but he finds none. ⁴⁴Then he says, 'I will return to my house from which I came'. And when he comes he finds it empty, swept, and put in order. ⁴⁵Then he goes and brings with him seven other spirits more evil than himself, and they enter and dwell there; and the last state of that man becomes worse than the first. So shall it be also with this evil generation.	²⁴When the unclean spirit has gone out of a man, he passes through waterless places seeking rest; and finding none he says, 'I will return to my house from which I came'. ²⁵And when he comes he finds it swept and put in order. ²⁶Then he goes and brings seven other spirits more evil than himself, and they enter and dwell there; and the last state of that man becomes worse than the first.

In these cases we can see the force of the standard two-source theory for the origin of the Synoptic Gospels. Much the most obvious explanation for that degree of agreement between different documents is that one is copying from another, or both are copying from the same source. It will not do, for example, to argue that Matthew and Luke drew their non-Markan material from an Aramaic source, each making *his own* translation into Greek. That in such a case they would have ended up with more or less identical Greek for their independent translations is almost impossible to envisage. Much the more obvious solution is either that Matthew copied Luke, or Luke copied Matthew, or the source they drew on was already in Greek. Here the case for a Q document already in Greek becomes very strong.[2] Equally clear is the basic

2. See particularly J. Kloppenborg Verbin, *Excavating Q: The History and Setting of the Sayings Gospel* (Minneapolis: Fortress, 2000).

case for Matthew's and Luke's dependence on Mark (or alternatively for some other literary dependence of one Synoptic Evangelist on the written Gospel of another Evangelist).

Here I have given only four examples. But I could have given many more, for example of the close agreement between Mark and Matthew in particular which can hardly be explained by other than literary dependence.[3] B. H. Streeter, for example, in the classic English language presentation of the two-document hypothesis, made much of the claim that 90% of Mark's subject matter reappears in Matthew 'in language very largely identical with that of Mark'.[4] Similarly, the support for the Q hypothesis from Matthew and Luke is clear from a good many more examples than the two given above.[5] So *the case for literary interdependence has a strong foundation.* For my own part I am strongly convinced of Markan priority, and have no problem with asserting some form of the Q written document hypothesis. My question, however, is whether *all* the evidence has been taken into account, and whether the *other* data should be sidelined either in making the case for literary interdependence or in regarding the case for literary interdependence as the whole story or the sole story, the only story.

II

Second, then, I draw your attention to the Synoptic material where there is *not* close verbal agreement, and in *a number of cases hardly any verbal agreement even though the subject matter is evidently the same.* Once again I give only a few examples, three from passages where Markan priority is usually inferred — the Syrophoenician woman (Mark 7.24-30/Matt. 15.21-28), the epileptic boy (Mark 9.14-27 pars.), and the dispute about greatness (Mark 9.33-37 pars.); and five from passages usually identified as Q tradition — Jesus' teach-

---

3. Mark 1.16-20/Matt. 4.18-22; Mark 2.18-22/Matt. 9.14-17/Luke 5.33-39; Mark 8.1-10/Matt. 15.32-39; Mark 8.31–9.1/Matt. 16.21-28/Luke 9.22-27; Mark 10.13-16/Matt. 19.13-15/Luke 18.15-17; Mark 10.32-34/Matt. 20.17-19/Luke 18.31-34; Mark 11.27-33/Matt. 21.23-27/Luke 20.1-8; Mark 13.3-32/Matt. 24.3-36/Luke 21.7-33. A similar degree of literary interdependence, but arguably with significant Matthean editing, is evident in Mark 2.23–3.6/Matt. 12.1-14; Mark 6.45-52/Matt. 14.22-33; and Mark 8.27-30/Matt. 16.13-20.

4. B. H. Streeter, *The Four Gospels: A Study of Origins* (London: Macmillan, 1924) 151, 159.

5. Matt. 3.7-10, 12/Luke 3.7-9, 17; Matt. 6.24/Luke 16.13; Matt. 6.25-33/Luke 12.22-31; Matt. 7.1-5/Luke 6.37-42; Matt. 7.7-11/Luke 11.9-13; Matt. 8.19-22/Luke 9.57b-60a; Matt. 11.2-11, 16-19/Luke 7.18-19, 22-28, 31-35; Matt. 11.21-27/Luke 10.12-15, 21-22; Matt. 12.39-45/Luke 11.29-32, 24-26; Matt. 13.33/Luke 13.20-21; Matt. 24.45-51/Luke 12.42-46.

ing on turning the other cheek (Matt. 5.39b-42/Luke 6.29-30), on the narrow way (Matt. 7.13-14/Luke 13.24), on dividing families (Matt. 10.34-38/Luke 12.51-53 and 14.26-27), on forgiving sins seven times (Matt. 18.15, 21-22/Luke 17.3-4), and the parable of the wedding feast/great banquet (Matt. 22.1-14/Luke 14.16-24). Once again the underlining indicates the extent of the verbal agreement.

(5) *The Syrophoenician Woman (Mark 7.24-30 par.):*

Matthew 15.21-28	Mark 7.24-30
[21]Jesus left that place and went off to the district of <u>Tyre</u> and Sidon. [22]Just then a Canaanite <u>woman</u> from that region came out and started shouting, 'Have mercy on me, lord, son of David; my <u>daughter</u> is tormented by a demon'. [23]But he did not answer her at all. And his disciples came and urged him, saying, 'Send her away, for she keeps shouting after us'. [24]He answered, 'I was sent only to the lost sheep of the house of Israel'. [25]But she came and knelt before him, saying, 'Lord, help me'. [26]He answered, <u>'It is not fair to take the children's food and throw it to the dogs</u>'. [27]She said, <u>'Certainly, lord</u>, for also <u>the dogs</u> <u>eat from the crumbs</u> that fall from their masters' <u>table</u>'. [28]Then Jesus answered her, 'Woman, great is your faith! Let it be done for you as you wish'. And her daughter was healed from that hour.	[24]From there he set out and went away to the region of <u>Tyre</u>. He entered a house and did not want anyone to know he was there. Yet he could not escape notice, [25]but a <u>woman</u> whose little <u>daughter</u> had an unclean spirit immediately heard about him, and she came and bowed down at his feet. [26]Now the woman was a Gentile, of Syrophoenician origin. She begged him to cast the demon out of her daughter. [27]He said to her, 'Let the children be fed first, for <u>it is not fair to take the children's food and throw it to the dogs</u>'. [28]But she answered him, <u>'Certainly, lord,</u> and <u>the dogs</u> under the <u>table</u> <u>eat from the crumbs</u> of the children'. [29]So he said to her, 'For saying that, you may go, the demon has left your daughter'. [30]So she went to her home, and found the child lying on the bed, and the demon gone.

(6) *The Epileptic Boy (Mark 9.14-27 pars.):*

Matthew 17.14-18	Mark 9.14-27	Luke 9.37-42
[14]And when they <u>came</u> to the crowd, a <u>man</u> came up to him and	[14]And when they <u>came</u> to the disciples, they saw a great <u>crowd</u> about them, and scribes arguing with them. [15]And immediately all the crowd, when they saw him, were greatly amazed, and ran up to him and greeted him. [16]And he asked them, 'What are you discussing with them?' [17]And	[37]On the next day, when they had <u>come</u> down from the mountain, a great <u>crowd</u> met him. [38]And behold, <u>a man</u> from <u>the</u>

Matthew 17.14-18	Mark 9.14-27	Luke 9.37-42
kneeling before him said, ¹⁵'Lord, have mercy on <u>my son</u>,	one of <u>the crowd</u> answered him, '<u>Teacher</u>, I brought <u>my son</u>	<u>crowd</u> cried, '<u>Teacher</u>, I beg you to look upon <u>my son</u>, for he is my only
for he is an epileptic and he suffers terribly; for often he falls into the fire, and often into the water. ¹⁶And I brought him to <u>your</u> <u>disciples, and</u> they could <u>not</u> heal him.' ¹⁷And Jesus answered, 'O faithless and perverse generation, how long am I to be with you? How long am I to put up with you? Bring him here to me.'	to you, for he has a dumb <u>spirit</u>; ¹⁸and wherever it grabs <u>him</u>, it dashes him down; and he foams and grinds his teeth and becomes rigid; and I asked <u>your</u> <u>disciples</u> to cast it out, <u>and</u> they were <u>not</u> able.' ¹⁹And he answered them, '<u>O faithless</u> <u>generation, how long</u> <u>am I to be with you? How long</u> <u>am I</u> <u>to put up with you? Bring</u> <u>him</u> to me.' ²⁰And they brought the boy to him; and when the spirit saw him, immediately it <u>convulsed</u> the boy, and he fell on the ground and rolled about, foaming at the mouth.	child; ³⁹and behold, a <u>spirit</u> seizes <u>him</u>, and he suddenly cries out; it convulses him till he foams, and shatters him, and will hardly leave him. ⁴⁰And I begged <u>your disciples</u> to cast it out, <u>and</u> they could <u>not</u>.' ⁴¹Jesus <u>answered</u>, '<u>O faithless and</u> <u>perverse generation, how long</u> <u>am I to be with you</u> and <u>to put up with you</u>? Lead your son here.' ⁴²While he was coming, the demon tore him and <u>convulsed</u> him.
	. . . . ²⁵And when Jesus saw that a crowd came running together,	
¹⁸And Jesus <u>rebuked</u> him,	he <u>rebuked</u> the unclean spirit, saying to it, 'You dumb and deaf spirit, I command you, come out of him, and never enter him again.' ²⁶And after crying out and convulsing him	But Jesus <u>rebuked</u> the unclean spirit,
and the demon <u>came out</u> of him,	terribly, it <u>came out</u>, and the boy was like a corpse; so that most of them said, 'He is dead.'	and healed the boy, and gave him back to his father. ⁴³And
and the boy was cured from that hour.	²⁷But Jesus took him by the hand and lifted him up, and he arose.	all were astonished at the majesty of God.

(7) The Dispute about Greatness (Mark 9.33-37 pars.):

Matthew 18.1-5	Mark 9.33-37	Luke 9.46-48
	³³Then they came to Capernaum; and when he was in the house he asked them, 'What were you arguing about on the way?' ³⁴But they were silent,	
¹At that time the disciples came to Jesus and asked, '<u>Who</u> is <u>greater</u> in the kingdom of	for on the way they had argued with one another about <u>who</u> was <u>greater</u>. ³⁵He sat down, called	⁴⁶An argument arose among them as to <u>who</u> of them was <u>greater</u>.

Matthew 18.1-5	Mark 9.33-37	Luke 9.46-48
heaven?'	the twelve, and said to them, 'Whoever wants to be first must be last of all and servant of all'.	
²He called <u>a little child,</u> <u>and put it</u> among them, ³and said, 'Truly I tell you, unless you turn and become like little children, you will never enter the kingdom of heaven. ⁴Whoever humbles himself like this little child is greater in the kingdom of heaven. 5 And whoever <u>welcomes one</u> such <u>little child in my name</u> <u>welcomes me</u>'.	³⁶Then he took <u>a little child</u> <u>and put it</u> among them; and taking it in his arms, he said to them,	⁴⁷But Jesus, aware of their inner thoughts, took <u>a little child</u> <u>and put it</u> by his side, ⁴⁸and said to them,
	³⁷'<u>Whoever welcomes one</u> of such <u>little children</u> <u>in my name</u> <u>welcomes me, and whoever</u> <u>welcomes me welcomes</u> not me but <u>the one who sent me</u>'.	'<u>Whoever welcomes</u> this <u>little child in my name</u> <u>welcomes me, and whoever</u> <u>welcomes me welcomes</u> <u>the one who sent me</u>; for he who is lesser among all of you, that one is great'.

(8) Turning the Other Cheek (Matt. 5.39b-42/Luke 6.29-30):

Matthew 5.39b-42	Luke 6.29-30
³⁹ᵇBut whoever hits you on your right <u>cheek</u>, turn to him <u>the other also</u>; ⁴⁰and to the one who wants to sue you and take your <u>tunic</u>, let him have your <u>cloak also</u>; ⁴¹and whoever forces you to go one mile, go with him a second. ⁴²<u>Give to</u> the one <u>who asks you</u>, and do not turn away the one who wants to borrow from you.	²⁹To the one who strikes you on the <u>cheek</u>, offer <u>the other also</u>; and from the one who takes away your <u>cloak</u> do not withhold your <u>tunic also</u>. ³⁰<u>Give to</u> everyone <u>who asks you</u>; and from the one who takes what is yours, do not ask for them back.

(9) The Narrow Way (Matt. 7.13-14/Luke 13.24):

Matthew 7.13-14	Luke 13.24
¹³<u>Enter through the narrow</u> gate; for the gate is wide and the road is easy that leads to destruction, and there are <u>many</u> who <u>enter</u> through it. ¹⁴For the gate is narrow and the road is hard that leads to life, and there are few who find it.	²⁴Strive to <u>enter through the narrow</u> door; for <u>many</u>, I tell you, will try to <u>enter</u> and will not be able.

(10) Dividing Families (Matt. 10.34-38/Luke 12.51-53 and 14.26-27):

Matthew 10.34-38	Luke 12.51-53; 14.26-27
³⁴Do not think that I came to bring peace to the earth; I came not to bring peace, but a sword. ³⁵For I came to set a man against his father, and a daughter against her mother, and a daughter-in-law against her mother-in-law; ³⁶and a man's foes will be members of his own household. ³⁷Whoever loves father or mother more than me is not worthy of me; and whoever loves son or daughter more than me is not worthy of me; ³⁸and he who does not take up his cross and follow after me is not worthy of me.	¹².⁵¹Do you consider that I am here to give peace on the earth? No, I tell you, but rather division! ⁵²From now on five in one household will be divided; three against two and two against three ⁵³they will be divided, father against son and son against father, mother against daughter and daughter against mother, mother-in-law against her daughter-in-law and daughter-in-law against mother-in-law. ¹⁴.²⁶Whoever comes to me and does not hate his father and mother, and wife and children, and brothers and sisters, yes, and even his own life, cannot be my disciple. ²⁷Whoever does not carry his own cross and come after me cannot be my disciple.

(11) Forgiving Sins Seven Times (Matt. 18.15, 21-22/Luke 17.3-4):

Matthew 18.15, 21-22	Luke 17.3-4
¹⁵'If your brother sins against you, go and point out the fault when you and he are alone. If he listens to you, you have regained your brother'. ²¹Then Peter came and said to him, 'Lord, if my brother sins against me, how often should I forgive him? As many as seven times?' ²²Jesus said to him, 'I tell you, not seven times, but seventy-seven times'.	³Be on your guard! If your brother sins, rebuke him, and if he repents, forgive him. ⁴And if the someone sins against you seven times a day, and turns back to you seven times and says, 'I repent', you must forgive him.

(12) The Parable of the Wedding Feast/Great Banquet (Matt. 22.1-14/Luke 14.16-24):

Matthew 22.1-14	Luke 14.15-24
¹Once more Jesus spoke to them in parables, saying: ²"The kingdom of heaven may be compared to a king who gave a wedding banquet	¹⁵One of the dinner guests, on hearing this, said to him, 'Blessed is anyone who will eat bread in the kingdom of God!' ¹⁶Then Jesus said to him, 'A certain person gave a great dinner and

Matthew 22.1-14	Luke 14.15-24
for his son. ³He sent his slaves to call those who had been invited to the wedding banquet, but they would not come. ⁴Again he sent other slaves, saying, "Tell those who have been invited: Look, I have prepared my dinner, my oxen and my fat calves have been slaughtered, and everything is ready; come to the wedding banquet". ⁵But they made light of it and went away, one to his farm, another to his business, ⁶while the rest seized his slaves, mistreated them, and killed them. ⁷The king was angered. He sent his troops, destroyed those murderers, and burned their city. ⁸Then he said to his slaves, "The wedding is ready, but those invited were not worthy. ⁹Go therefore into the streets, and invite everyone you find to the wedding banquet." ¹⁰Those slaves went out into the streets and gathered all whom they found, both good and bad; so the wedding hall was filled with guests. ¹¹But when the king came in to see the guests, he noticed a man there who was not wearing a wedding robe, ¹²and he said to him, "Friend, how did you get in here without a wedding robe?" And he was speechless. ¹³Then the king said to the attendants, "Bind him hand and foot, and throw him into the outer darkness, where there will be weeping and gnashing of teeth". ¹⁴For many are called, but few are chosen.'	invited many. ¹⁷At the time for the dinner he sent his slave to say to those who had been invited, "Come; for it is now ready". ¹⁸But they all alike began to make excuses. The first said to him, "I have bought a farm, and I must go out and see it; please accept my regrets". ¹⁹Another said, "I have bought five yoke of oxen, and I am going to try them out; please accept my regrets". ²⁰Another said, "I have married a wife, and therefore I cannot come". ²¹So the slave returned and reported this to his master. Then the owner of the house became angry and said to his slave, "Go out at once into the roads and lanes of the town and bring in the poor, the crippled, the blind, and the lame". ²²And the slave said, "Sir, what you ordered has been done, and there is still room". ²³Then the master said to the slave, "Go out into the roads and lanes, and compel them to come in, so that my house may be full. ²⁴For I tell you, none of those who were invited will taste my dinner".'

What is striking about all these examples is *the lack of verbal agreement* — typically less than 40%, and more like 20% or less in some cases.[6] And yet in each case the story being told or the teaching passed on is clearly *the same*; the parables have *the same* image, structure and message. Why the divergence? Why the variation? Here the argument for literary interdependence is hard to make. If Mark was the only source for Matthew's and Luke's

6. See also the summary of R. Morgenthaler, *Statistische Synopse* (Zürich and Stuttgart: Gotthelf, 1971) in Kloppenborg's *Excavating Q,* 63.

Gospels, why did they alter Mark in what seems to be often a rather cavalier or casual manner? In some instances a case can be made for Matthean or Lukan redaction of Mark. But overall many if not most of the variations are inconsequential; *there are no obvious reasons why Matthew or Luke should have departed from their sole source text,* presumably, on the literary hypothesis, their sole authoritative text. Similarly with the non-Markan agreements in Matthew and Luke, the 'Q' material. While it is true that more than 13% of the pericopes common to them are more than 80% in verbal agreement, it is also true that the verbal agreement in over a third of the common material is less than 40%. The latter evidence covers *nearly three times as much material* as the former, and yet it is passed over and largely ignored when the thesis of literary interdependence is developed into the two-source theory. But why would Matthew or Luke make such arbitrary alterations to their Q source if they were so dependent on the hypothesized Q document for the textual tradition in the first place? If the close verbal interdependence of many Synoptic parallel passages counts as strong evidence *for* literary interdependence, then should not the more extensive *disagreements* between parallel Synoptic texts be counted *against* the thesis or assumption of literary interdependence?

I repeat, I am very open to the possibility of a later Evangelist redacting his source — for example, with the majority I would consider it more likely that Matthew has modified Mark in each of the two following cases, rather than vice-versa.[7]

Matthew 13.58	Mark 6.5
And he *did not do many* <u>deed</u>s <u>of power there,</u> because of <u>their unbelief.</u>	And he *could do no* <u>deed of power there,</u> except that he laid his hands on a few sick people and cured them. And he was amazed at <u>their unbelief.</u>

Matthew 19.16-17	Mark 10.17-18
Then someone came to him and said, '<u>Teacher, what</u> *good deed* <u>must I do to</u> have <u>eternal life?</u>' And he <u>said to him, '*Why do*</u> <u>*you*</u> ask *me about what is* <u>*good?*</u> There is only one who is good.'	A man ran up and knelt before him, and asked him, '*Good* <u>Teacher, what</u> <u>must I do to</u> inherit eternal life?' Jesus <u>said to him, '*Why do*</u> <u>*you*</u> *call me* <u>*good?*</u> No one is good but God alone.'

7. See the full data collected by J. C. Hawkins, *Horae Synopticae: Contributions to the Study of the Synoptic Problem* (Oxford: Clarendon, 1898, 2nd ed. 1909) 117-25.

In these cases, however, it is evident that Matthew was taking care to remain as close as possible to his source (Mark), even while significantly altering the sense. These examples illustrate Matthew's *respect for his text and unwillingness to depart from it* more than was absolutely necessary to prevent his audiences drawing the wrong conclusion from the Markan original. But what we encounter in most cases of the diverging Synoptic tradition is *inconsequential* variation. If redaction is the only plausible or recognizable explanation, then we have to infer a *casualness* and *arbitrariness* in the redaction which can only imply a *lack* of respect for the authoritative original.

It was such reflection which led me to look for other or complementary explanations. If the degree of similarity and difference is explainable only in part by the thesis of literary interdependence, then ought we not to look for an alternative or complementary explanation for the other part of the same data of Synoptic interrelationship?

III

As indicated at the beginning of this chapter, an obvious area to look for such an alternative or complementary explanation lies in *the* oral *character of the earliest Jesus tradition*. This has been recognized in principle by not a few Gospel specialists, that there must have been a period before the writing of the Gospels (or their written sources) when the Jesus tradition, or at least the bulk of it, would have circulated and been used only in *oral form*. Unfortunately, when the major investigation into and debate on the sources of the Gospels was being undertaken there was too little appreciation of the character of oral transmission. Streeter, for example, cautioned against studying the Synoptic Problem 'merely as a problem of literary criticism'. Likewise he fully recognized the need to look beyond the two sources of Mark and Q to explain the composition of the Synoptic Gospels. Ironically, however, it is he who is particularly recalled for his promotion of 'a four *document* hypothesis'.[8] The oral period of transmission was not really examined or any real recognition given to the possibility that oral tradition and transmission might have different characteristics from the literary models which were being assumed in the focus on literary interdependence.

A more hopeful development was the emergence of Formgeschichte, or form criticism, as an attempt to reach behind the written Gospels to the oral forms of the tradition which the Evangelists put into writing. For Rudolf

---

8. Streeter, *Four Gospels*, ch. 9 (quotations from 229).

Bultmann, indeed, the purpose of form criticism was 'to study the history of the oral tradition behind the gospels'.[9] Hence his focus on identifying the forms on which the Evangelists were able to draw — apophthegms, dominical sayings, miracle stories, etc.[10] However Bultmann's attempt to illuminate the oral period of the Jesus tradition suffered from two major weaknesses.

First, he assumed that certain '*laws of style*' determined the transmission of the forms. These laws, apparently drawn from some acquaintance with studies in folklore elsewhere,[11] included the further assumptions of an original '*pure*' form, of a natural progression in the course of transmission from purity and simplicity towards greater complexity, and of a development in the tradition determined by form rather than content. But the so-called laws were neither drawn from what was known of folklore at the time,[12] nor were they validated by the character of the tradition in the Gospels themselves.[13]

Second, and more significant was Bultmann's assumption of a *literary* model to explain the process of transmission. This becomes most evident in his conceptualisation of the whole tradition about Jesus as 'composed of a series of layers'.[14] The imagined process is one where each layer is laid or builds upon another. Bultmann made such play with it because, apart from anything else, he was confident that he could strip off later (Hellenistic) layers to expose the earlier (Palestinian) layers.[15] The image itself, however, is drawn from the *literary* process of *editing*, where each successive edition (layer) is an edited version (for Bultmann, an elaborated and expanded version) of the previous edition (layer). But is such a conceptualisation really appropriate to a process of oral retellings of traditional material? Bultmann never really ad-

---

9. R. Bultmann (with K. Kundsin), *Form Criticism* (1934; ET New York: Harper Torchbook, 1962) 1.

10. R. Bultmann, *The History of the Synoptic Tradition* (1921; ET Oxford: Blackwell, 1963).

11. *History*, 6-7.

12. J. Schröter, *Erinnerung an Jesu Worte: Studien zur Rezeption der Logienüberlieferung in Markus, Q und Thomas* (WMANT 76; Neukirchen-Vluyn: Neukirchener, 1997): 'The "pure form" represents a mixture of linguistic and history of language categories, which is to be assigned to an out of date conception of language development' (59; also 141-2). See also G. Strecker, 'Schriftlichkeit oder Mündlichkeit der synoptischen Tradition?', in F. van Segbroeck, et al., eds., *The Four Gospels 1992, Festschrift Frans Neirynck* (Leuven: Leuven University, 1992) 159-72 (here 161-2, with other bibliography in n. 6).

13. See particularly E. P. Sanders, *The Tendencies of the Synoptic Tradition* (SNTSMS 9; Cambridge: Cambridge University, 1969): 'There are no hard and fast laws of the development of the Synoptic tradition. On all counts the tradition developed in opposite directions. It became both longer and shorter, both more and less detailed, and both more and less Semitic . . .' (272). And further W. H. Kelber, *The Oral and the Written Gospel* (Philadelphia: Fortress, 1983) 2-8.

14. R. Bultmann, *Jesus and the Word* (1926; ET New York: Scribners, 1935) 12-13.

15. *Jesus and the Word*, 12-13.

dressed the question, despite its obvious relevance. He simply assumed that the transmission of oral tradition was no different in character from the transmission of already written tradition.

Since Bultmann much more attention has been paid to the character of oral tradition and its transmission. I mention what I regard as the most illuminating for us. First, investigation into the early oral, pre-literary period in Greek culture, and the recognition both that Homer was recited orally for a lengthy period before being written down, and that the written text indicates the character of the oral recitations.[16] Second, Birger Gerhardsson's investigation of the oral procedures for preserving and transmitting rabbinical tradition within the most immediate context for the early Jesus tradition.[17] Third, there has been some very fruitful and illuminating research into oral communities in Africa.[18] And fourth, the impressionistic and anecdotal accounts by Kenneth Bailey of thirty years experience of oral communities in the villages of Egypt and Lebanon.[19] If the latter two seem remote from first-century Palestine, it should be noted that such village life, in both Africa and the Middle East, is likely to have been largely conservative and unchanging in the ways in which the communities operated as oral societies.

The most striking feature to emerge, and emerge consistently, from these different examples is the characteristic combination of *fixity* and *flexibility*, of *stability* and *diversity*, of *the same yet different*. In oral tradition there is characteristically a *tale* to be told, but told using different words to highlight different aspects in different tellings. In oral tradition there is characteristically a *teaching* to be treasured, but it is formulated variously depending on the emphases the different teachers want to bring out.[20] Oral tradition is oral memory; its

16. E. A. Havelock, *Preface to Plato* (Cambridge, MA: Harvard University, 1963); A. B. Lord, *The Singer of Tales* (Cambridge, MA: Harvard University, 1978).

17. B. Gerhardsson, *Memory and Manuscript: Oral Tradition and Written Transmission in Rabbinic Judaism and Early Christianity* (Lund: Gleerup, 1961, 1998).

18. I refer particularly to J. Vansina, *Oral Tradition as History* (Madison: University of Wisconsin, 1985), a revision of his earlier *Oral Tradition: A Study in Historical Methodology* (London: Routledge & Kegan Paul, 1965); R. Finnegan, *Oral Literature in Africa* (Oxford: Clarendon, 1970); and I. Okpewho, *African Oral Literature: Backgrounds, Character and Continuity* (Bloomington: Indiana University, 1992).

19. K. E. Bailey, 'Informal Controlled Oral Tradition and the Synoptic Gospels', *Asia Journal of Theology* 5 (1991) 34-54; also 'Middle Eastern Oral Tradition and the Synoptic Gospels', *ExpTim* 106 (1995) 363-7.

20. Gerhardsson makes the same point in regard to rabbinic tradition, not so clearly in his early work, but certainly latterly — most recently *The Reliability of the Gospel Tradition* (Peabody: Hendrickson, 2001), which includes two other earlier studies. I regret that I did not recognize this sufficiently in *Jesus Remembered*, 197-8.

primary function is to preserve and recall what is of importance from the past. Tradition, more or less by definition, embodies the concern for continuity with the past, a past drawn upon but also enlivened that it might illuminate the present and future. In the words of Eric Havelock, 'Variability and stability, conservatism and creativity, evanescence and unpredictability all mark the pattern of oral transmission' — the 'oral principle of "variation within the same"'.[21] Or as Alan Dundes puts the same point: '"multiple existence" and "variation" [are] the two most salient characteristics of folklore'.[22]

What excited me when I learned about this characteristic feature of oral transmission was that *it spoke immediately to the character of the Synoptic tradition.* For the character of the Synoptic tradition, the character which had intrigued me from the first, is well caught in the phrase 'the same yet different' — the same story told, but with different introduction and conclusion and different wording, the same teaching but differently worded and differently grouped. It was this Synoptic material, illustrated above, which could now be made sense of in terms of oral tradition. *That material was oral tradition,* its diversity frozen in the differing versions of the Synoptic Gospels. The model of literary interdependence could explain well the Synoptic passages where there was close verbal agreement. But the literary model made little sense of the passages where the verbal agreement was less than 40%, sometimes much less. Whereas the model of *oral* tradition seemed to meet the case precisely. The obvious conclusion to be drawn is that *large sections of the Synoptic tradition are the varying oral tradition put into writing.*

IV

Two important points emerge from this attempt to reappreciate the oral Jesus tradition, and with several equally important corollaries. They are important, I believe, for our understanding of the early Jesus tradition, its oral character, the use made of it, its early circulation and its transcription in writing in due course.

The first major point underlines the difference between the model of literary interdependence and oral interdependence. The oral tradition model subverts the idea of an *'original'* version. With minds attuned to the literary para-

---

21. Kelber, *Oral,* 33, 54; quoting E. A. Havelock, *Preface to Plato,* 92, 147, 184, *passim.*
22. *Holy Writ as Oral Lit: The Bible as Folklore* (Lanham: Rowman & Littlefield, 1999) 18-19.

digm, we envisage an original form, a first edition, from which all subsequent editions can at least in principle be traced by form and redaction criticism. We envisage tradition-history as an archaeological tell where we in principle can dig through the layers of literary strata to uncover the original layer, the 'pure form' of Bultmann's conceptualization of *Formgeschichte*. But in *oral* tradition each performance is not related to its predecessors or successors in that way. In oral tradition, as Albert Lord particularly observed, *each* performance is, properly speaking, an 'original'.[23]

The point as it applies to the Jesus tradition is *not* that there was no originating impulse which gave birth to the tradition. On the contrary, in at least many cases we can be wholly confident that there were things which Jesus said and did which made an *impact,* and a *lasting* impact on his disciples.[24] But, properly speaking, the *tradition* of the event is not the *event* itself. And the *tradition* of the saying is not the *saying* itself. The tradition is at best the *witness* of the event, and as there were presumably several witnesses, so there may well have been several traditions, or versions of the tradition, *from the first.* Of an originating *event* we can speak; but we should certainly hesitate before speaking of an original *tradition* of the event. The same is true even of a saying of Jesus. The tradition of the saying attests the impact made by the saying on one or more of the original audience. But it may well have been heard slightly differently by others of that audience, and so told and re-told in different versions *from the first.* Moreover if, as Werner Kelber points out, Jesus himself used his most effective parables and aphorisms on more than one occasion, the ideal of a single original, a single authentic version reduces once again more to the figment of a literary-moulded mind-set.[25] And who can doubt that Jesus did indeed teach the same message in different ways and words on many occasions — what good teacher ever teaches what is important to him on only one occasion? Which, then, of the various versions of the same teaching was the 'original' version?

23. 'In a sense each performance is "an" original, if not "the" original. The truth of the matter is that our concept of "the original", of "the song", simply makes no sense in oral tradition' (Lord, *Singer,* 100-101). R. Finnegan, *Oral Poetry: Its Nature, Significance and Social Context* (Cambridge: Cambridge University, 1977) also glosses Lord — 'There is no correct text, no idea that one version is more "authentic" than another: each performance is a unique and original creation with its own validity' (65) — and credits Lord with bringing this point home most convincingly (79).

24. As I have noted several times in these essays, this has been one of my presuppositions, as in *Jesus Remembered* where I emphasize the importance of recognizing that Jesus' mission must have made a considerable impact on his disciples.

25. 'Each oral performance is an irreducibly unique creation'; if Jesus said something more than once there is no 'original' (*Oral,* 29; also 59, 62).

From this first point several corollaries immediately follow. First, that we should regard the diversity within the Synoptic tradition much more positively than often has been the case in the past. The *differences* between the Synoptic Gospels within particular pericopes and collections of teaching are *not a problem*. The differences do not indicate 'mistakes' or 'errors' or 'contradictions'. They indicate simply *the different ways that Jesus was remembered and the fact that the Jesus tradition was handled and presented in different contexts.*

A second corollary is that we should not think of *only one* of the differing versions as the original and as having primary authenticity. We should not think of the alternative versions as less authentic, or as corruptions (for devious theological reasons) of the 'original'. We should rather regard them all as 'authentic', as the original actions and teaching of Jesus continued to exert their power on succeeding disciples.

Third, it also follows that the tradition of Jesus' teachings and doings was not regarded as fixed and frozen. It was not like a sacred relic paraded round for devout followers to venerate — 'Ah! This is what Jesus said on August 10, in the year 28; we must reverence and preserve it just as he gave it'. On the contrary, it was *living tradition,* tradition which they celebrated, tradition by which they lived and in the light of which they worshipped. This, I believe, is already evident in the way the Jesus tradition has been absorbed into the ethical teaching of Paul and James, so that it has become an integral part of their own paraenesis without any sense that particular exhortations would only be authoritative if explicitly attributed to Jesus.[26]

Fourth, all this gives us a fresh slant on the concept of the Evangelists' editing of earlier tradition. For in the event, editing was only a more extended example of the variety integral to the whole circulation, use and transmission of the Jesus tradition. If apostles and teachers had no qualms in repeating stories about Jesus and teaching of Jesus in their own words, neither, it is evident, did they have any qualms about interpreting some teaching of Jesus in a way which brought out its relevance more forcibly to their own situation[27] or any qualms about drawing a conclusion from their account of one of Jesus' miracles which again showed its relevance to their own hearers.[28] The impact of Jesus' mission thus continued to exercise direct influence on the first generation embryonic Christian churches.

26. I have argued this point in regard to Paul on several occasions — particularly *The Theology of Paul the Apostle* (Grand Rapids: Eerdmans, 1998) 649-58.

27. Good examples in 1 Cor. 7.10-15 and 9.14-18.

28. As in Matt. 14.33 (cf. Mark 6.52).

The second major point which emerges regards in particular the *transition* from *oral* Jesus tradition to *written* Jesus tradition. Regrettably Werner Kelber, who did so much to bring home to us the importance of understanding the oral character of the early Jesus tradition, headed off in a very misleading direction. He argued, in effect, that the oral tradition was itself the only authentic tradition and that the transcription of the oral tradition into writing was a kind of 'fall' from grace, the death of the living (oral) word.[29] But even though recognition of the character of oral tradition liberates us from a mind-set too rigidly controlled by our literary heritage, it would be a mistake to regard the scribalization of the oral Jesus tradition as changing its character altogether. Here I only have time to make three points.

First, I have no doubt that some at least of the Jesus tradition was transcribed at an early stage. It is not that written material would be regarded as more reliable than oral. Such a view is once again an expression of the literary mindset; we ourselves have become so reliant on written records that the ability to absorb quickly into the memory and to retain even information of first importance to us is much less efficient than in oral societies. In contrast, prior to the reliability of the printing press, written texts were generally regarded as *less* reliable than what the memory retained for itself. Writing would have become a factor when distance was involved, in the same way that letters could serve as a substitute for personal presence. Such writing, however, evidently did not rigidify or imprison the Jesus tradition. Here again we should learn from the Synoptic tradition. The diversity between the Synoptic Gospels again shows that the Evangelists did not regard it as essential that they should convey forms made fixed and rigid by writing. Even though Matthew and Luke evidently knew and used at least one written source (Mark), they did not merely copy what Mark had written, but gave their own version even of the traditions which Mark conveyed. In other words, *the flexibility of the oral transmission period carried over into the written forms of the tradition.*

One of the major failings of the attempts to resolve the Synoptic problem in exclusively literary terms was the inference (not usually consciously formulated) that when Matthew or Luke received their copies of Mark's Gospel that was the first time that each had encountered the stories and teaching contained in Mark. But such a scenario is hardly credible. Much or most of the Jesus tradition enscribed by Mark must have been widely circulating and well known in the Christian communities in Syria and beyond. In at least many cases where Matthew and Mark diverge on the same tradition, the most

---

29. Kelber, *Oral and the Written Gospel*, ch. 5.

obvious explanation is that Matthew knew an (oral) version of that tradition different from the Markan version, and that Matthew preferred in these cases to transcribe the other version, which perhaps he knew better. In other words, we probably see in such data evidence of Jesus tradition both oral and written circulating at the same time and among the same churches. Initially the written was essentially a transcription of one version of the oral, or was itself a scribal presentation of Jesus tradition sharing the same characteristics (the same but different) as typical oral presentations.

Second, all this means that the understanding of Q has to be revised. The non-Markan material common to Matthew and Luke should not simply be grouped together on the assumption that it all comes from a single document. As I noted earlier, there is certainly evidence that some of the Q material had been put into writing. But beyond that the evidence will not support the hypothesis of a single written document. Beyond the passages of near-identical wording, the diversity is such that another explanation is much more likely: namely, that such diversity exemplifies the varied sequence or sequences of oral tradition, as used by apostles and teachers in the various Christian assemblies, the varied sequences representative of the typical repertoires such as many Christian teachers drew from the community store of tradition for which they were particularly responsible. The fact that the Q hypothesis finds it necessary to envisage different versions or different editions of Q simply underlines the myopic character of the literary mindset at this point. That Matthew and Luke had access to much more material than Mark is clear. That some of it was already in writing is highly probable. But that they also knew the Jesus tradition as living oral tradition, with the sort of diversity which we still find in the Synoptic tradition, is equally probable. The attempt to recover a Q document is in many ways admirable.[30] But it has prevented us from recognizing that well into the second half of the first century the Jesus tradition was still well known in oral mode. And by assuming the fixity of written sources the attempt to recover a written Q has lost sight of the living character of the Jesus tradition.

Third, we should not make the mistake of thinking that there was a single transition from oral to written, as though the writing down of the Jesus tradition made an end to the oral tradition, or brought the flexible character of the Jesus tradition to an end. On the contrary, it is evident from the echoes and uses made of the Jesus tradition, for example in James, 1 Peter and the Apostolic Fathers, that they knew versions of the Jesus tradition alluded to

---

30. See particularly J. M. Robinson, P. Hoffmann, and J. S. Kloppenborg, *The Critical Edition of Q: Synopsis* (Leuven: Peeters, 2000).

which were different from the versions used by the Gospels.[31] To use such echoes and allusions of Jesus tradition only as evidence in the debates as to whether there was a Q document or whether the canonical Evangelists were already known is once again to lose sight of how widely the Jesus tradition was known in oral form and of its degree of variability. In other words, the oral forms of Jesus tradition continued alongside the written versions into the second century. And here again, as Richard Bauckham has demonstrated with regard to James, the way they drew on the Jesus tradition again evidences the flexibility of the tradition, as they adapted it to the needs which they were addressing.[32]

Moreover, textual critics like David Parker and Eldon Epp have been pointing out for some time that the transition to written forms did not kill the flexibility of the tradition.[33] For just as we have seen the inadequacy of thinking in terms of a single original version of items of the Jesus tradition, so these textual critics have moved away from assuming a single original text, alone authentic, with all the variations the result of textual corruption, of scribal error and mistake. On the contrary, what we have in the textual tradition is evidence of different versions of these texts, the different versions which were the NT writings for different churches, often reflecting the differing concerns and needs of their differing communities. In other words, the textual tradition itself attests the continuing flexibility of (in this case) the Jesus tradition.

To sum up, then. How should we envisage the period between Jesus and the Gospels? Not, assuredly, by a great empty space, with Jesus at one end, and stories about Jesus and teaching attributed to Jesus suddenly created more or less out of nothing for some reason at the other end. If Jesus proved to be an influential figure, as I assume, then the space was filled by people influenced by him. If Jesus said memorable and controversial things, then, assuredly, the memory of such sayings filled part of that space. If Jesus did remarkable and controversial things, then memory of such events no doubt filled part of the space too. These memories of Jesus would be in the form of oral tradition. These memories would be shared, they would be circulated, they would be interpreted, they would be elaborated, but initially almost entirely in oral

31. H. Köster, *Synoptische Überlieferung bei den apostolischen Vätern* (Berlin: Akademie, 1957).

32. Bauckham, *James: Wisdom of James, Disciple of Jesus the Sage* (London: Routledge, 1999).

33. D. C. Parker, *The Living Text of the Gospels* (Cambridge: Cambridge University, 1997); E. J. Epp, 'The Multivalence of the Term "Original Text" in New Testament Textual Criticism', *HTR* 92 (1999) 245-81.

forms. The first disciples, apostles and teachers, would tell stories about Jesus in the gatherings of the first believers in Jesus. They would introduce the stories and draw conclusions from the stories of relevance to their own situations. They would recall and repeat his teachings, grouping them in different combinations, drawing out different lessons for different circumstances, for the benefit of followers whose only access to that tradition was through those responsible for maintaining and preserving the oral tradition. It was not like the rote-learning or memorization of sacred texts. Rather it was living tradition, narratives which made their own life story meaningful, teachings by which they lived their own lives. Elsewhere in the New Testament there is little or no effort made to remember it as Jesus tradition as such. Rather in letters of Paul and James, for example, it has been absorbed into the life-blood of their own ethical teaching.

Why do I find such a portrayal of the gap between Jesus and the Gospels so appealing? For the simple reason that it explains so well the character and content of the Synoptic Gospels themselves. It shows how Jesus was remembered during that period between Jesus and the Gospels — the same yet different. It shows why Jesus was remembered during that period. It exemplifies the ways in which the memories of Jesus, his actions and his teachings, were formulated and used and passed on. It shows that the impact of Jesus was not dissipated or covered over by subsequent beliefs and dogmas about Jesus. It shows how the Jesus who made an impact during his mission continued to make an impact on those who had never seen him in the flesh through the tradition which embodied the character of his mission so clearly.

CHAPTER 14

The History of the Tradition (New Testament)

§1 Introduction

The New Testament (NT) is made up of twenty-seven documents of varying lengths and types. Their range is somewhat similar to that of the 'Old' Testament (OT):

> four Gospels, as primary in character for the NT as the five books of Moses for the OT;
>
> a book of history (but only one in the NT);
>
> a sequence of letters interpreting the primary traditions (the gospel) somewhat as the prophets interpreted the Torah;
>
> and an apocalypse (the Apocalypse of John = Revelation) equivalent to the OT's Daniel.

The most glaring lack of parallel is the absence of Psalms in the NT (but psalms and hymns do appear in various other NT books) and the absence of Wisdom writings (though James could qualify as such).

On this point the NT is more closely parallel to the OT than it is to the Apocrypha, or to the Dead Sea Scrolls (DSS), or to the Pseudepigrapha. The point highlights an important feature of the NT — what might be called the tension between continuity and discontinuity in the NT's relation to earlier Jewish writings, including the writings which were already regarded as 'scripture'. On the one hand, the NT can properly be classified as the literary product of what at least began as a Jewish sect (the Nazarenes). The indebtedness of its writings to the OT in particular can be documented on page after page. C. H. Dodd subtitled his study of the use of the OT in the NT, 'The Substructure of New Testament Theology'. At the same time, however, the NT writings do not appear simply as a supplement to the OT (like much of the Apocrypha) or simply as interpretation of the OT (like many of the DSS), or simply as a rewriting of the OT (like several pseudepigrapha). In its present 'shape' the NT is more like the OT itself, more a complement than a supplement, as we might say, more, indeed, like an alternative collection gathered round its own primary traditions.

For the task of clarifying how these documents and the NT took their historic and present shape, the more important difference between OT and NT is the time span covered by the process. In the case of the OT, the time span from the earliest traditions to the last of the OT writings (Daniel), and to a widely recognized Hebrew Bible (OT canon; cf. Sir. prologue), covered a millenium or more. In contrast, in the case of the NT, the time span from Jesus' first utterance to the latest of the NT writings (2 Peter?) was probably less than a century, and the NT canon was more or less finalised within a further three hundred years (see e.g. Kümmel, *Introduction* Part Two). Consequently it is relatively easier in the case of the NT to trace the history of the tradition which now constitutes the NT documents and the NT itself.

Given the importance of Jesus himself for the NT and of the Gospels within the NT it will be necessary to spend most time on what is usually described as the history of the Jesus tradition — that is, the traditions of teaching from Jesus and stories about Jesus which now make up the Gospels. But the rest of the NT is also tradition and it will be important to trace out its history too.

§2 The Gospels

§2.1. *From Jesus to Tradition*

The NT begins with Jesus. It was the impact of his ministry or mission, of his teaching and life, which forms the beginning of the history of the tradition which now makes up the Gospels. We can readily imagine these earliest traditions. They would be quite diverse. At one end they would consist of the reports and rumours regarding things Jesus said and did which circulated round Galilee and Judea and perhaps more widely. Typically they would consist of versions of stories he told (parables), of memorable sayings and teachings (e.g. proverbs), of striking acts of healing (particularly exorcisms). From the present character of the tradition (particularly the Synoptic Gospels) we can be sure that the main emphasis of his preaching (on the kingdom of God) would have been known, and the controversial nature of his dealings with those popularly regarded as 'sinners'. Reports and tales, we may speculate confidently, would be told and retold in market place, round camp fires, in homes and places of assembly. The semi-novellistic presentation by Gerd Theissen of *The Shadow of the Galilean* gives as good a 'feel' for this process as we are likely to be able to reconstruct now.

It is important to recognize at once that the traditions which come down to us attest and reflect the impact made by Jesus from the first. We do not have traditions which have come down through Herod or Pilate, through Pharisees or Sadducees (with possible but uncertain and minimal exceptions in Josephus, *Antiquities* 18.63, and Babylonian Talmud, *Sanhedrin* 43a). We do not have traditions preserved by dispassionate or uninvolved spectators who happened to hear or see something which accidentally lodged in the memory. We only have those traditions which made sufficient impact on audiences for them to be remembered and passed on. That is to say, their effect is already indicated in the very fact of their preservation and retelling, and is already embodied to some extent at least in the form in which they were retold and passed on. Alternatively expressed, we today have access to these sayings and events only because they became 'tradition'.

The corollaries to this insight are important. For it means, first, that the ideal sometimes maintained by scholars, that it should be possible to hear and encounter the historical Jesus as a disinterested spectator might have done in the year 30 or so, is wholly unrealistic. The preaching of Jesus does not come to us because he wrote it down or as a taperecorder or videorecorder might have preserved it. It comes to us only because it made the impact it did on the witnesses and only as it was experienced and remembered by them. In other words, the hearing (and witnessing) was what Paul calls faith-creating hearing (Rom. 10.14, 17), hearing with faith (Gal. 3.2, 5). Those who did not have 'ears to hear' (Matt. 11.15; 13.9; 13.43) heard and saw nothing of major or lasting significance. So they remembered nothing of importance (for them), they formulated no continuing tradition, and so we have no access to 'the historical Jesus' through them. The tradition we have is faith-tradition, disciple-tradition, and we have it because what was seen and heard created that faith and made disciples of those who thus heard, disciples through whom the tradition was remembered and passed on. This is not to say, of course, that what Jesus did and said had a uniform impact on his first disciples or that there was a uniform attempt to recall and pass on these remembrances of Jesus; the diversity of tradition in the Gospels no doubt reflects in some measure at least the diversity of impact which Jesus had on those who can be called 'disciples'. Nonetheless, the basic point remains: the Gospels are disciple-tradition.

The other corollary worth noting at this point is that Jesus must have said and done far more than has been recorded in the Gospels. Even for a three-year ministry, on the usual reckoning, it could hardly be otherwise (Mark's Gospel can easily be read in a single evening). This also means that not everything Jesus said and did was memorable, which is also to say, not everything Jesus said and did was remembered. The thought may be surprising or even offensive to some — that anything Jesus said or did might be considered not worth remembering. But the thought quickly degenerates into a false piety. It was the things Jesus did and said and which created faith which were remembered and they were remembered precisely because of their faith-creating power. To look outside that circle of witness on the assumption that there must be other faith-creating nuggets to be discovered is simply to fail to realise that the Gospel tradition is locked into and dependent on the circle of faith from the first. The point has been given weight at the end of the nineteenth century by Martin Kähler, and now again, a century later by Luke Johnson.

That is not so say that the Gospels themselves exhausted the complete stock of remembered tradition of what Jesus did and said. There are several sayings of Jesus preserved outside the Gospels which seem to belong to that same first circle (see e.g. Hofius). We may assume that the Evangelists were selective even among the traditions available to them. But the number of these individual sayings are few and, if anything, strengthen the view that the Synoptic writers in particular provide a full and thorough representation of the traditions as remembered from the first.

§2.2. Remembering Communities

The forming and passing on of the Jesus tradition was not the work of individuals as such. The impact made by Jesus was lasting because it was disciple-making. Which is also to say it was community-forming. The individuals influenced by Jesus were drawn together by their shared experience and by their shared discipleship. And that which bonded them together included, not least, the impressions and remembrances which they shared and which continued to motivate them as disciples. We can deduce this from a number of factors.

For one thing, sociology has made us aware that in group formation, foundation tradition plays a critical role in determining the identity and boundaries of the group. The members of the group have to be able to explain, to themselves as well as to others, what it is that constitutes them a distinctive group. In this case the foundation tradition would certainly include the shared remembrances of what Jesus did and said.

This is confirmed by the evidence we have of the first names given to the groups of Jesus' disciples. Early on they evidently thought of themselves simply as 'the disciples' (Acts 6.1, 2, 7; etc.) or as followers of 'the way' (Acts 9.2; etc.) — that is, disciples of *Jesus*, followers of the way *indicated by him* (cf. 4.13; 18.25-26). By others they were known as 'the sect of the Nazarenes' (Acts 24.5, 14; 28.22); that is, they were identified by their association with Jesus of Nazareth, the prophet/teacher/messiah from Nazareth (cf. 4.10). Subsequently the name 'Christians' emerged in Greek at Antioch — a group designated by their belief in Jesus as Messiah/Christ. In each case that which marked the first believers out was their relation to and belief in Jesus. Such a group would be bound to explain and define themselves by reference to Jesus — that is, by using the traditions regarding Jesus.

For another, group dynamic would ensure that some within the group assumed or were charged with the responsibility to remember and rehearse these traditions for strangers, newcomers and celebrations of the group. In villages it would be typically the older members, the elders. In the assemblies of disciples of Jesus we soon hear of just such 'teaching' (Acts 2.42) and of 'teachers' (Acts 13.1; Gal. 6.6; James 3.1) whose responsibility it must have been to tend to the teaching.

Of course, the process of group formation really got under way only after Jesus' death and resurrection. This climax of Jesus' ministry seems to have made more impact than his earlier ministry, at least on the central core of disciples. And very soon the conversion-effecting impact was that of the message *about* Jesus rather than that *of* Jesus himself; the tradition became the point of impact rather than its effect, or, alternatively expressed, the tradition of Jesus' teaching and life, death and resurrection, mediated the impact which Jesus himself had formerly made directly.

At the same time the process presumably already got under way at least to some extent during Jesus' ministry. Jesus early on is remembered as having taught his disciples a prayer (the Lord's Prayer) to function as the badge of their discipleship, that is, no doubt, to be said by them together (Luke 11.1-4). Prominent in the impact of Jesus was his own attitude to the teachings and traditions of the past — particularly his ability to cut through secondary issues to the heart of the matter (e.g. Matt. 5.21-30; Mark 2.23–3.5; 7.5-13) — an attitude to revered text and tradition and prioritising in teaching and action which his disciples presumably sought to follow in their discipleship more or less from the first. And Matthew can even include a code of church discipline already within the Jesus tradition (Matt. 18). Most of the sayings tradition preserved in Q (a source which most agree was used by Matthew and Luke) could have been taught and passed on without reference to Jesus' death and resurrection, and so may already have been gathered before these final events. And at one or two points we catch tantalising glimpses of active groups who were not part of the main stream of discipleship (Mark 9.38-41; Acts 19.1-7) and who had a patchy or fragmentary knowledge of the much larger shared deposit of foundation tradition.

This raises a further intriguing question: whether the impact made by Jesus was much more diverse than is reflected in our Gospels; whether, that is, there were, more or less from the beginning, other groups/churches which remembered different aspects of Jesus' ministry, or remembered solely Jesus the teacher (and not Jesus the crucified and risen). The issue has been raised in recent years by the discovery and subsequent reflection on the significance of the Gospel of Thomas. We will return to the issue below; suffice it to say here that the amount of reliable or authentic Jesus tradition outside the canonical Gospels (that is, tradition which begins from the hearing and witnessing of what Jesus said and did) seems to be very limited (see again Hofius and further Tuckett's 'Introduction to the Gospels'). And anyway, our primary task is to trace the history of the tradition which came to form the NT.

§2.3. Oral Tradition — the How

One of the important insights about the early tradition is that it was not conceived as something fixed — a memory of something Jesus said which had to preserved and paraded in a precious casket, as it were, reverenced as said by Jesus at such and such a time and place, a memory of something he did which had to be retold in just this and not that way. All the evidence we have indicates otherwise. The most immediate evidence is that of the Gospels themselves, particularly the three Gospels which share so much of the same material (the Synoptics). Of course they preserve the tradition in a later, written form. But the forms of the tradition reflect earlier usage, and the way in which the tradition was handled at the written stage may not have been so different from the oral use.

This oral usage can be illustrated in a number of points. First, most of the traditions of Jesus' sayings and actions do not display any concern to remember time and place of saying or doing — one of the preliminary insights behind the development of 'form criticism' (see below §§2.4, 5.4). And if they now give the impression of chronological and geographical sequence, that is usually because of the editorial work of the Evangelists in so sequencing them. In other words, the stories were retold because their point and continuing value was independent of original time or place (e.g. Mark 2.18, 23; 3.31; 4.21; etc.). We should add that such a conclusion says nothing for or against the historical value of these traditions; it simply observes how the traditions were remembered.

Second, similar traditions were put together, presumably for ease of remembering and retelling. For example, Mark 4 and Matt. 13 look as though they are the end products of quite a process of gathering together parables of Jesus, including some reflection on their significance. A sequence of Jesus' sayings about his exorcisms has been brought together, it would appear in overlapping collections (Mark 3.22-30; Luke 11.14-26). Similarly with a number of sayings about discipleship (Matt. 8.19-22/Luke 9.57-62). And a group of miracle stories round the lake of Galilee seems to lie behind Mark's sequence in Mark 4.35–5.43 and 6.30-56. Again, this is not to imply any casualness in the remembering process, but the manner and priorities in the process — the continuing benefit of these remembered words and deeds for the communities of faith.

Third, we can see how readily stories about Jesus could be told in different versions. We may compare, for example, Mark 2.23-28 with Matt. 12.1-8 and Luke 6.1-5, and Mark 5.21-43 with Matt. 9.18-26 and Luke 8.40-56. Material could be and was added or subtracted, expanded or curtailed. There was evidently a sense that the substance and value of the story did not depend on it being told and retold with slavish or pedantic accuracy. More generally, E. P. Sanders has shown that the detail of tradition evidently 'developed' both by elaboration and by abbreviation.

Fourth, not surprisingly, stories about Jesus could be told from different angles, to bring out different points for the attentive assemblies. The best example is the story of Jesus' encounter with the centurion and healing of his boy (Matt. 8.5-13; Luke 7.1-10). Behind the two versions is evidently a shared memory of a single event. The heart of the shared memory is the actual encounter between Jesus and the centurion, the dialogue between them, where, noticeably, the words are in close agreement (Matt. 8.8-10/Luke 7.6b-9). But both Evangelists seem to have taken a theme from the common core and elaborated it to bring out their respective points: Luke emphasises the centurion's humility (so in his account the centurion does not come personally — Luke 7.2-6a); and Matthew focuses on the centurion's faith (so he climaxes his account by attaching a saying of Jesus from elsewhere — Matt. 8.11-12/Luke 13.28-30). Here again we observe the same combination of respect for the tradition's substance and core, together with a certain freedom in reusing the tradition.

All this tells us something about the tradition and about the remembering. The tradition was a living tradition, of contemporary value, not an attempt simply to recall a heroic figure now dead and gone. Likewise the remembering was a means not so much of recalling the past as of bringing the tradition into the present. If we are to appreciate the history of the Jesus tradition it is vital that this character of it as living tradition be properly grasped. Too much ink has been wasted in debate about the Jesus tradition in posing as sharp opposites, either a scrupulous fidelity to historical facts and details, or a complete freedom to create and elaborate. The evidence of the Synoptic Gospels, illustrated above, is that the transmission of early Christian tradition was neither, but was rather a combination of respect and adaptation, a genuine concern to recall the teaching and example of Jesus blended with a concern that the tradition should continue to speak to the developing churches and changing situations of the time.

Much of this is borne out by the researches of Kenneth Bailey into oral tradition processes among the mountain villages in Lebanon in the middle of the twentieth century — as close as we are likely to get to the tradition-culture in the villages of upper Galilee, closer, at any rate, than the oral epics of Yugoslavia and Greece, on which Albert Lord built his not dissimilar conclusions regarding oral tradition. Bailey observed the same phenomena as described above — stories of memorable visitors or incidents, told often in different versions, but characteristically with the core of the story fixed, the substance and point of the story constant, while the supportive details could be elaborated or abbreviated as circumstances allowed or necessitated. It is the same kind of popular/formal, or semi-popular/semi-formal transmission of tradition which seems to be reflected in the tradition which makes up the Synoptic Gospels.

§2.4. Oral Tradition — the Why

The other side of the same process is the purpose to which these traditions were put. Here too we can gain a fairly clear idea of why the traditions were retained and retold.

In terms of the history of Gospel research we have now reached the phase at which the Synoptic tradition was analysed into different 'forms' (hence 'form-criticism') (especially Bultmann, *History*). This research recognized the living character of the tradition by envisaging tradition moulded to the situations for which it was being re-used ('Sitz-im-Leben' = 'life-setting') and by observing and arguing that much of the tradition took what might be called 'standard forms'. The working assumption was that in order for the tradition to be used in the churches it would naturally fall into the forms characteristic for different kinds of material. The clearest examples are miracle stories (trouble signalled, decisive word or act indicated, result described), pronouncement stories (climaxing in a memorable saying of Jesus), and the epigrammatic character of wisdom sayings. Unfortunately, however, the concept of the 'form' itself became too much the focus of debate, the conception of tradition-formation and tradition-transmission became too stereotyped and formalised (the 'laws' of transmission), and the appreciation of the living character of the process, of the malleability of the forms from the first was largely lost to sight.

More valuable was the attempt of C. F. D. Moule to turn the question round and to focus on the different contexts in which and purposes for which the tradition was maintained and used. For example, we need not doubt that worship was at the heart of the early Christian assemblies. Nor can we doubt that tradition deriving directly from the remembered Jesus was very much at the heart of that worship. We need only think of the Lord's Prayer, whose slightly differing versions (Matt. 6.9-13; Luke 11.2-4) tells the same story of tradition cherished, but cherished by the using, and adapted in the using to be the more useful. Jesus' own example of praying to God as 'Abba, Father' was evidently also cherished, as the preservation of the Aramaic term into Greek-speaking worship, as a prayer betokening sonship shared with Jesus, surely indicates (Rom. 8.15-17; Gal. 4.6-7). Similarly with the words of institution of the Last/Lord's Supper (cf. Mark 14.22-25 with Luke 22.17-20), whose regular usage in the earliest churches is confirmed by Paul in 1 Cor. 11.23-26. Many have deduced from the fact that the passion narrative is a continuous block of material, that it was put together for liturgical purposes, presumably to be recited afresh at each anniversary of Jesus' passion.

A second obvious case would be material for teaching within the assemblies of the believers and for catechizing inquirers or new converts. The clearest example here is probably the Sermon on the Mount (Matt. 5-7). The fact that most of the parallel material in Luke is scattered throughout Luke, strongly suggests that the Sermon has been put together as a teaching device, to gather appropriate teaching material from the remembered words of Jesus, and to frame it in a way that made it the more easily rememberable by those taught in turn. Once again this is not to say that the account of Jesus sitting down on the mountain and teaching (Matt. 5.1-2) is a later creation. No doubt Jesus quite often sat on a Galilean hillside to teach. It is simply to recognize that the early Christian teachers grouped and edited the Jesus tradition not so much in accord with any particular remembered where and when of Jesus speaking (as though that was the primary consideration) but in accord with the most effective remembrance and usage of the tradition.

The 'little apocalypse' of Mark 13 probably came to Mark as the end product of a text of Jesus tradition much used by assemblies when they came to reflect soberly on the end to come. And we can easily envisage many a story about Jesus or sequence of Jesus' teaching providing means of edification and cause for pause at the breakings of bread alluded to in Acts (2.42, 46) and the Lord's suppers and other gatherings for worship indicated in 1 Cor. 11–14.

If evangelistic preaching usually focused on the death and resurrection of Jesus (as both Acts and the Pauline letters imply — e.g. Acts 2.23-36; 4.2; 17.18; 1 Cor. 15.1-11; 2 Cor. 5.18-21; Gal. 3.1), apologetic in a Jewish context probably drew more immediately on the tradition of Jesus' words and actions itself. This is clearly suggested by the block of tradition used by Mark in 2.1–3.6, a collection of some five controversy stories, in which Jesus' authority to act in ways judged by many to be controversial is asserted. Since they touch on such matters as healing, eating with sinners, fasting and how to conduct oneself on the sabbath, we can easily see that they would have provided important precedents for the earliest Jewish believers. In other words, Mark 2.1–3.6 looks as though it was put together to provide early Jewish believers with arguments to counter the criticisms they may have received by following the teaching and life-style of Jesus as remembered in the tradition.

§2.5. New Tradition?

Thus far we have spoken only of tradition as the remembrances of Jesus' first disciples. But many assume that much if not most of the tradition in the Synoptics is the work of the post-Easter churches. Rudolf Bultmann (*History*) and Ernst Käsemann ('Is the Gospel Objective?' 60), for example, argued that traditions quite different from the original remembrances poured into the Jesus tradition from the wider Hellenistic world and from Christian prophets active in the early Christian assemblies. The counter attempt, by Birger Gerhardsson in particular, to argue for a greater fixity in the tradition from (later) rabbinic methods of rote learning and memorizing, has not proved an adequate response. For one thing, the evidence illustrated above on how the Synoptic Gospels handle the tradition, and the relative freedom with which they have done so, hardly bears witness to fixed tradition passed on by memorizing. Bailey's 'middle way' of 'informal controlled oral tradition' makes better sense of all the evidence. And for another, the basic scenario of prophets functioning in assemblies (as well as teachers) and speaking in the name of Jesus, possibly even in an 'I' form (speaking in Jesus' words), cannot be completely dismissed out of hand. Prophets and prophesying are certainly attested in Acts (11.27; 13.1; 15.32; 21.9-10) and Paul (Rom. 12.6; 1 Cor. 11.4-5; 12.28-29; 14.29-32; 1 Thess. 5.20), and a text like Matt. 18.20, which seems to presuppose a later setting of established 'churches', has all the appearance of a prophetic saying received as a saying of Jesus himself.

What has been forgotten, however, as Dunn, 'Prophetic "I"-Sayings' has pointed out, is that the heritage of prophecy made both Jew and Christian highly sensitive to the danger of false prophecy. In the OT we need think simply of the classic cases of Micaiah ben Imlah in 1 Kings 22.1-40 and of Jeremiah in Jer. 28. And Paul was alert to the danger from the first, as his repeated reminder that prophecies must be tested and evaluated indicates (1 Cor. 12.10), whether by the recognized prophets in particular (1 Cor. 14.29), or by the congregation as a whole (1 Thess. 5.19-22). There had also been much reflection on effective tests for false prophecy. One of the most effective within the assembly of Israel presumably was the appeal to what we might call the foundation tradition:

> 'If prophets . . . appear among you and promise you omens or portents . . . and they say, "Let us follow other gods" (whom you have not known) "and let us serve them", you must not heed the words of these prophets . . . ; for the Lord your God is testing you, to know whether you indeed love the Lord your God with all your heart and soul' (Deut. 13.1-3).

In other words, a prophet might make an accurate prediction, but if that prophet counselled departure from Israel's foundation confession, in Deuteronomy classically summed up in the *Shema* (Deut. 6.4), he was to be judged a false prophet.

Paul follows the same pattern: the prophet who fails to acknowledge the primary confession, 'Jesus is Lord', is a false prophet (1 Cor. 12.3). And 1 John subsequently indicates the same sure test: the prophet who denies that Jesus Christ has come in the flesh is false (1 John 4.1-3). Given the depth of this experience of false prophecy in Jewish scripture, confirmed early on in the Pauline assemblies, it is unlikely that the reappearance of prophecy as a living experience of the earliest assemblies would have caught these assemblies unprepared for the problem of false prophecy. As soon as prophets began to speak in 'I' terms in the assemblies there would almost certainly have been those who asked whether the prophecy was indeed from God. In those circumstances what test would they use to decide on the authenticity of the inspired words?

One of the most obvious answers is, the foundation tradition on which their assembly was built (Gerhardsson, *Gospel Tradition*, speaks of 'inner tradition'). In other words, these assemblies almost certainly did not gather tradition indiscrminately from all quarters. They had their core material, the remembered words and actions of Jesus which had first drawn them together, or, in the case of later assemblies, the tradition which had first converted them and brought them together as 'church'. This would be their foundation tradition, the yardstick remembrances which they would particularly cherish, and which they would almost certainly use when the issue of true or false prophecy came up. The measure would be clear: if the teaching accorded with the primary tradition it would be acceptable; but if not, the teaching or prophecy would probably have been rejected.

This provides a useful rule of thumb for those today concerned as to whether and how much new (post-Easter) tradition has crept (or flooded) into the Jesus tradition. Where there is teaching which clarifies or explains previous tradition, that is the sort of supplementation or elaboration of the earlier tradition which would prove acceptable. One of the best/most plausible examples is Mark 13.10. But where there is material in the Synoptic tradition which is distinctively different from other early tradition, it must be judged unlikely that that material was later added; for it is just such material, even if produced by prophet or teacher, which would most likely have been deemed to be at odds with the already accepted and revered tradition. For example, a distinctive self-reference like 'the Son of Man', or distinctive emphasis in regard to the kingdom of God (either its presence or its imminent approach), is almost certainly part of the original Jesus tradition; for it would be just such a new tradition which would have been judged to fail the test of foundation tradition.

A nice in-between example is the birth narratives of Matthew and Luke (Matt. 1–2; Luke 1–2). Interestingly enough, we observe the same story-telling features in these chapters. For both accounts focus on a central core: Jesus' birth was such that, from the beginning, he was both Son of David and Son of God (Matt. 1.20, 23; Luke 1.32, 35). But beyond that they are completely diverse with hardly any other common features. These stories cannot be strictly described as foundation tradition. But they attest an interest in the life as well as teaching of Jesus, which could evidently not be resolved without some account of his birth; this is frequently the case with figures early on recognized to have historic or epochal significance, like Alexander the Great. In this case the accounts as they emerged, whether in much briefer or in their present form, were deemed to be consistent with and an acceptable elaboration of the primary tradition of Jesus' ministry, death and resurrection.

§2.6. From Aramaic to Greek

In any attempt to trace the history of the Gospels tradition the next phase has to be the transition from Aramaic to Greek, when tradition which initially circulated in Aramaic (the language which all assume was the principal language of Jesus) was put into Greek (the principal lingua franca of the Eastern Mediterranean world). We do not know when this happened, but we can assume that it must have begun to take place quite quickly. For the traditions about Jesus would undoubtedly have aroused interest in the Greek-speaking/ Hellenistic cities of the region. And we soon hear of a body of disciples in Jerusalem itself, within months rather than years of Jesus' death and resurrection, who were known as 'Greek-speakers' (Acts 6.1). Since their very designation must indicate that they could function effectively only in Greek (as opposed to the Hebrew/Aramaic speakers — Acts 6.1), they must have heard and used the Jesus tradition in Greek more or less from the first.

The transition would be bound to have an effect on the Jesus tradition. Modern translators know that there is no translation from one language to another which does not involve at least some interpretation. Since the nearest equivalent words in different languages rarely have identical semantic ranges, and since idioms are usually distinctively different between languages, good translations of the Aramaic tradition into Greek would inevitably involve some shift of emphasis and tone.

The point, however, should not be exaggerated. For, as we have already seen, the Aramaic tradition was not fixed; vocabulary and idiom would vary between regions; and the teachers and re-tellers of the Jesus tradition ensured its continuing flexibility (living tradition). Nor should we assume that the transition was immediate, widespread or final. For many years, even decades, no doubt, the tradition continued to be used in Aramaic in Aramaic-speaking churches. Indeed, one can fairly say that the still continuing Syrian churches are the direct heirs of the early Aramaic-speaking churches. In other words, the transition would be long drawn out, and always partial, the first expansion of the Jesus tradition into other languages rather than a transfer of it *en bloc* from one language to another.

Nevertheless, those who are interested in the history of the tradition need to remind themselves that it is only as a result of this transition that we today have immediate access to the tradition. We today have no NT text in

Aramaic; and reconstruction of Aramaic forms is always a hazardous business. Given that we have to be content with the Greek translations, it is only a few scattered words (like 'Abba') which put us in touch with the words whose syllables Jesus actually pronounced.

§2.7. From Oral to Written Tradition

Even more important than the transition from Aramaic to Greek was the transition from oral to written tradition. We are even more in the dark as to when this transition began to take place. It is by no means impossible that there were written versions of sayings and stories of Jesus circulating during his life (as suggested by Ellis). Who can say what scribal activity literary disciples, or government spies(!), engaged in to help circulate news about the Nazareth prophet or potential trouble-maker? Possibly the first literary collections or epitomes were the attempts to put the tradition into Greek for those who could not understand the Aramaic teachers and story tellers.

Whenever the transition began to take place, and in whatever forms, it is sometimes assumed that the transition was something epochal, from highly flexible oral tradition to a script fixed in writing (Bultmann, *History* 3), 'frozen into a static condition' (Kelber 94). Such a view exaggerates both the flexiblity of oral tradition and the degree of fixity of written tradition. The former, as we have seen, retains core, substance and shape, even while the secondary, complementary or interpretative details are varied. The latter, as the literary relations between Gospels themselves confirm, allow quite as much flexibility in transmission. And as we shall see, even when the written text is beginning to be regarded as sacred, the processes of scribal transmission allow for variation, elaboration and correction. Those who have studied the processes of oral tradition most closely point out the difficulty of making clear and consistent distinctions between oral and written tradition in terms of fixity and flexibility (Ø. Anderson).

And as with the transition from Aramaic to Greek, so with the transition from oral to written, the transition did not take place overnight, or all in one place. It was neither once-for-all, nor, once it had happened in any place, did it mean that the now literary community somehow ceased to be an oral community. The oral community assuredly did not jettison its oral tradition when and because it had received a proto-Gospel or complete Gospel. Rather we have to assume a quite lengthy process of tradition being increasingly put into writing, probably in Aramaic but certainly in Greek, while at the same time the same and other material continued to circulate orally and to be used in both Aramaic and Greek in oral forms. Well into the second century, when presumably the transition was well advanced, there were still those inquiring about oral traditions which must still have been circulating and not all 're-duced' to writing. We need recall only the words of Papias (c. 130) cited by Eusebius:

> 'If anyone chanced to come who had actually been a follower of the el-ders, I would inquire as to the discourses of the elders, what Andrew or what Peter said, or what Philip, or what Thomas or James, or what John or Matthew or any other of the Lord's disciples; and the things which Aristion and John the elder, disciples of the Lord, say. For I supposed that things out of books did not profit me so much as the utterance of a voice which liveth and abideth' (Eusebius, *Hist. Eccl.* 3.39.4).

All this needs to be remembered when we consider the more familiar next phases.

§2.8. From Forms to Written Sources

The process by which written sources emerged is still fairly speculative for the twentieth-century inquirer. Presumably the passion narrative was early on put into writing, in one or more versions for different churches' use. Certainly the relatively sustained character of the narrative and the stability of the se-quence of events in the two main Synoptic versions (Matthew/Mark and Luke) suggest a narrative well established by repeated use, where the distinc-tion between oral and written becomes immaterial. Similarly it is quite possi-ble that the collections of Jesus' teaching, like the Sermon on the Plain in Luke 6.17-49 and the collections on parables mentioned earlier (Mark 4; Matt. 13), were put into writing at some early stage.

Gospels research of the last 150 years has concluded that our present Gospels drew on two main sources — Mark as the earliest of the written Gos-pels, and Q as a collection of sayings of Jesus which Matthew and Luke drew heavily upon (see again Tuckett, 'Introduction to the Gospels'). But Mark may well have had earlier blocks of written material to use (the group of contro-versy stories in 2.1–3.6, the collection of parables in ch. 4, the collection of miracle stories in chs. 4–6, the material behind 'the little apocalypse in ch. 13, and the passion narrative running from chs. 14 to 16). And Luke in the pref-ace to his Gospel speaks of many orderly accounts of Jesus' ministry at-tempted before he himself took the task in hand (Luke 1.1). Alternatively, the putting into writing of the tradition in Mark's Gospel, with the ordering, shaping and editing involved, may have been mostly his own work.

In terms of the process of tradition transmission it need not have made very much difference how many layers or phases there were in the process before the tradition reached its present shape in the Synoptic Gospels. Earlier research tended to assume that there must have been innumerable layers between the present Gospels and any original words of Jesus or witnesses to Jesus. On this view, every telling of the tradition, every transcription of the tradition was another layer, each with its own emphases, elaborations or abbreviations, each with its own peculiar characteristics, which in principle at least might be stripped away, like layers of old paint or wallpaper, or layers of varnish, dirt and alterations obscuring the work of some old master, to reveal the original, authentic masterpiece, pristine fresh once again. Not unnaturally, no one thought the in-principle possibility was very realistic. As one attempted to penetrate through each successive layer, more and more would become less and less certain, and in the end, at best, there would be a few sayings or actions which one could confidently trace back to Jesus himself (Bultmann traced only about forty sayings to the earliest layer of tradition).

But the imagery itself is wrong. Above all, it depends too much on an outmoded model of literary tradition — as though it was all a process of cutting and pasting, in which one by extreme diligence might actually be able to peel away and identify the authorship of each phrase or sentence. Or, indeed, as though analysis of Gospel tradition was something like tracing a tradition through a nineteenth-century writer's dependence on Shakespeare, through a mediaeval chronicler available now only in fragmentary condition, and back to some long lost classical text. But we have already noted how much of the process we have been tracing was a process of *oral* tradition, rather than of literary dependence. We have also noted that the character of oral tradition likely to have been followed was not a matter of one teacher building a fresh layer on another, but rather of teachers re-telling the settled core and substance of a respected tradition. The variation and elaboration of any such re-telling did not constitute a fresh layer to be carried forward to the next re-telling; any particular re-telling may have been quite ephemeral. It was the stable core and substance and overall shape of the tradition which was passed on, to be freshly elaborated in the next telling.

In other words, in the course of the process of tradition transmission, the original emphases and features of the sayings and doings of Jesus are unlikely to have become obscured and lost to view by layers of over-telling. On the contrary, it was precisely the original emphases and features which were fixed by the process of re-telling, because it was these emphases and features which encapsulated the original impact and which the process was designed to preserve and maintain. Furthermore, that character of oral transmission has been carried over into the written tradition, as the relationship of tradition between the Synoptic Gospels confirms. For, as we have seen, it is precisely that same respect for tradition, its core and point, together with variation in the use to which that tradition is put, which is such a manifest feature of the Synoptic tradition.

§2.9. The Gospels

We need not pursue the transmission process further in any detail. For the next phase is the written Gospels themselves, and enough detail is given concerning them and their use of the tradition in the pages which follow. It is important to observe, however, that the Evangelists forwarded the traditioning process by the way they themselves shaped the tradition which came to them in ways indicated above. In the history of Gospel research we have now reached the phase of 'redaction criticism', where attention began to turn from the Evangelists as collectors of earlier forms to their own role as editors (below §5.5). Some obvious examples are Mark's use of the Caesarea Philippi confession and Transfiguration narrative as centre and turning point of his Gospel (Mark 8.27–9.13), Matthew's ordering the traditions of Jesus' teaching into five large blocks (chs. 5–7, 10, 13, 18, 24–25), quite possibly in deliberate echo of the five books of Moses, and the way Luke has inserted a perhaps surprising amount of traditional material within the framework of the journey to Jerusalem (Luke 9.51–19.27).

In addition, there are a number of more general points of relevance worthy of note. One is the way in which the Gospels seem to have fixed the nature of a 'Gospel' — that is, as an account of Jesus' ministry which climaxes in his death and resurrection. This seems to have been an early extension of a use of the term 'gospel' already established in Paul's writings (e.g. Rom. 1.1, 9, 16; Gal. 1.6-7, 11; 2.2, 5, 7). We see the transition from 'gospel' = good news of Jesus' life, death and resurrection, to 'Gospel' = written account of Jesus' life, death and resurrection, already in the opening of the earliest written Gospel (Mark 1.1). And since it was Mark's outline ('a passion narrative with extended introduction') which provided the framework for the other three Gospels, we can probably credit Mark with establishing the definitive Gospel shape. In the same connection it is notable that the Q material (a collection only of Jesus' teaching) was not preserved as such, but within the Gospels only as incorporated into the Markan outline. Q as such was evidently not judged to be a

'Gospel'. This Markan outline evidently became the 'canonical shape' of the Gospel and was no doubt a factor in the subsequent decisions of the emerging catholic Church to reject other would-be Gospels which lacked that shape (see again Tuckett, 'Introduction to the Gospels').

Another point deserving of note is what the Evangelists' use of traditions tells us about the character of the Gospels themselves, and whether the achievement of written Gospels marked a significant change in the character and function of the tradition. The point here can be summarized in terms of the debate on whether the Gospels may properly be described as biographies. In the heyday of form criticism (see again below §5.4) it was strongly asserted that the Gospels were *not* biographies (typical was the reaction of Bultmann, *Jesus*). This was in reaction to the late-nineteenth-century abuse of the Gospels by those anxious to write Lives of Jesus which explored his spiritual development and self-consciousness. And the criticism made at that time remains valid: that such a Life of Jesus can only be written by filling in the gaps by imaginative reconstruction (Kähler). For the Gospels were not written to provide such information, and themselves did not express such interest. But to acknowledge this is simply to recognize that the Gospels do not share the interests of the modern biographer. Bultmann and the others of his generation would have been more accurate if they had asserted the Gospels were not *modern* biographies. In contrast, however, they can be adequately classified as *ancient* biographies. For they share the ancient biographical interest in depicting the hero's character by telling stories about him and reporting the sort of things he said. To be precise, the Gospels are *sui generis*. But it nevertheless remains true that they are closer in genre to ancient biographies than to anything else (Burridge).

The point is that as a type of ancient biography, the Gospels do confirm a continuing interest in the life of Jesus, that is, in what he said and did, and that one of the primary reasons for writing the Gospels was indubitably to preserve and spread that tradition.

Add to this the strong evidence of consistency between the traditions as recorded in the three Synoptic Gospels — all the more noteworthy in view of the renewed appreciation of the Evangelists as editors and theologians in their own right (see again below §5.5). For all their variation in structure and individual emphasis, the amount of substantially shared tradition (in character and emphasis as well as detail) far outweighs the amount of variation. To repeat: the respect shown by oral tradition, to retain core and substance and shape within the variation of each re-telling, remains a feature of the tradition as 'fixed' by the Synoptic Gospels.

To be noted here too is the evidence provided by the Gospels as to how widely the tradition had spread round the Eastern Mediterranean. Matthew is usually linked with Syria; Mark has traditional links to Rome; the Q material has links with Egypt; and we might mention also John which is traditionally linked with Ephesus. Even if these geographical associations are speculative and far from securely grounded, they are a reminder of what must have been the case — that is, that the tradition which they embodied was widely dispersed, and in its coherence and consistency provided a solid base of foundation tradition for the many churches throughout the region which treasured and made use of that tradition.

All this highlights one other point worthy of some emphasis. Many explorations of the Gospels tradition seem to work on a series of questionable assumptions: (1) that the traditions of each church or group of churches were distinct and discrete from the traditions of other churches; (2) that the Gospels were written exclusively for their own group of churches and reflect these churches' distinctive interests (the Matthean churches, the Q community); (3) that when a Gospel like Mark or Matthew reached a more distant church, that was the first time the church would have heard most if not all of these traditions; and (4) that the relations between the different versions or collections can be understood only on the model of literary interdependence.

But everything we have considered so far speaks against these assumptions. The reality is much more likely to have been the reverse: (1) that churches possessed a considerable amount of shared foundation tradition — the tradition which the church founders (apostles) would regard as essential for the church to know and be able to use in its own evangelism and apologetic, nurture and worship (see below §3.4); (2) that the Gospels were able to draw on tradition which was not exclusive to one or another group of churches, and were written as an evangelistic, apologetic, catechetical and/or liturgical aid for a wide range of churches (Bauckham, *Gospels*); (3) that when any Gospel first reached such churches they were able to compare their own versions of much if not most of the traditions which that Gospel contained; and (4) that many if not most of the variations within the Synoptic tradition are to be explained precisely because of these variations between written Gospel and still oral tradition being incorporated into further copies of these Gospels.

§2.10. John's Gospel

Finally, we should consider the fourth Gospel, John's Gospel. For it may seem to call in question several of the features and conclusions drawn above. The reason is that John's Gospel does not seem to be simply an extension of the traditioning process evident in the Synoptics. The Synoptic traditions, consisting of linked short sayings characteristic of wisdom teaching and independent of particular miracles, seem to have been wholly replaced by the long Johannine discourses characteristically linked to some typical miracle presented as a 'sign'. The characteristic emphases of the Synoptic Jesus' teaching on the kingdom of God, with little self-reference, seem to have been wholly replaced by the complete Johannine contrast of characteristic self-proclamation with little reference to the kingdom.

At the same time, however, it must be noted that John's Gospel retains the characteristic ('canonical') Gospel shape noted above. Like the other Gospels, but unlike subsequent claimants to the title, John's Gospel drives single-mindedly towards the climax of Jesus' death and resurrection, and the whole Gospel is to be read in that light. Moreover, closer examination of John's material reveals a consistent pattern, where the distinctively Johannine discourse begins from a typically Synoptic-type incident or saying and proceeds to draw out its significance in characteristic Johannine style (cf. e.g. John 3.3, 5 with Matt. 18.3; see Dunn, 'John and the Oral Gospel Tradition'). The point remains valid even if John's Gospel was able to draw directly on one or more of the Synoptic Gospels as such (rather than on similar versions of the Synoptic traditions) as many believe. In other words, even John's Gospel retains the earlier features of the original oral tradition — a core saying of Jesus at the heart, with the overall Gospel shape of the tradition.

The distinctive Johannine elaboration of the tradition seems to draw particularly on the earlier Jewish Wisdom tradition (see Scott). This way of conceptualizing and presenting Christ and his significance was already well developed in first and second generation Christianity, as passages like 1 Cor. 8.6, Col. 1.15-20 and Heb. 1.2-3 indicate. In John's case the Wisdom christology has been meshed both with the more Hellenistic concept of the creative Logos (rational power) of God (John 1.1-18) and with the more characteristic Jewish concept of the divine agent sent by God, as typified by the prophet in particular. That the endeavour thus to fill out the significance of Jesus as expressed in the Jesus tradition seemed to some to take on docetic-like features (Jesus only seeming to be human) was more a hazard of the type of elaboration on which John embarked than any part of John's obvious intention (Dunn, 'Let John Be John').

Particularly noteworthy is the addition of chapter 21, generally reckoned as a (slightly) later appendix. Notable is the way it seems to commend the holding together of potentially diverging patterns of tradition, the one looking to Simon Peter for authentication (Mark, Matthew), the other to the beloved disciple (John). This appendix is a further indication of how earlier

332

tradition could be elaborated, but also possibly indicates an emerging self-consciousness of the need to assert (and maintain) the coherence and consistency of a developing pattern of tradition. Other indications of a similar consciousness may be the commendation of Luke and Mark in the same breath in 2 Tim. 4.11 and the commendation of Paul's letters in 2 Pet. 3.15-16.

John's Gospel should probably be seen, therefore, as a bold re-telling of the tradition which in the event was judged to be acceptable as part of the fourfold Gospel (see e.g. Dunn, *Unity* 296-7). Somewhat like the birth narratives, its detail is not to be recognized as part of the foundation tradition as such. Rather it was an elaboration of the tradition which was seen to be consistent with the foundation traditions, to supplement them and to draw out their fuller significance. As midrash on these traditions, as reflections and meditations on things that Jesus said and did, as still manifestly 'Gospel', John has provided invaluable insights into the meaning of Jesus for further generations. Not least, John's Gospel reminds us of the character of the tradition as living tradition, of the charge laid upon the ministers of the tradition not simply to reverence and repeat rigid and unchanging forms, but to retell it in ways which enable its power to be experienced afresh.

We break off the history of Gospel tradition at this point, not at all because that history 'ceased' with the writing of the Gospels. Quite the contrary, as we shall see (§4). But having reached this stage in tracing the tradition process in the case of Jesus tradition, we pause to let the rest of the NT tradition 'catch up'.

§3. The Rest of the New Testament

The history of tradition in the rest of the NT is both easier to trace and more difficult to trace. It is easier, since as Christian tradition it is post-Easter; if the Gospels tradition begins with Jesus, so other NT tradition begins with the first Christian Easter. So the other NT documents are nearer to the beginnings of their tradition, and the modern inquirer into the history of that tradition does not have to embark on the difficult task of tracing tradition to the far side of Easter, to the period before the Gospel shape and context had even been provided. At the same time, however, the tracing of the post-Easter tradition is more difficult. For, as we have seen, one of the strengths of the Gospels tradition is the coherence and consistency between the Synoptic Gospels. Whereas the post-Easter tradition comes to us in a wide variety of documents, none of which were designed as tradition-carriers as the Gospels were, and from which it is often difficult to disentangle the earlier tradition as such.

Nevertheless, a considerable amount of study has been devoted to these traditions, most of which is still of value, and we can draw on that work a good deal more confidently than with much of the equivalent work carried out on the Gospel tradition. The fact is that the NT writings bear testimony in many ways to earlier tradition and how it was used, both by themselves and by the churches to which these writers belonged. Nor should we fall into the trap of thinking that tradition is to be defined solely as that which lies behind these writings. For as the Gospels are themselves forms which the Jesus tradition took/was given at the time of writing, so the other NT writings are themselves the different forms which the tradition took/was given in a variety of instances. The fact that all these writings were retained for posterity attests to the acceptability of these forms to the churches and church leaders who preserved and cherished them.

§3.1. Early Kerygmatic Tradition

To avoid the confusion caused by over-use of the term 'gospel' it is convenient to use the alternative 'kerygma' to denote the proclamation of the good news or the good news itself. The best-known investigation at this point was that of C. H. Dodd who correlated the accounts of sermons in Acts with references by Paul to his earlier preaching which had given rise to the churches to which he now wrote. Even from Paul alone a common outline could be discerned — the apostolic kerygma. Dodd summarised it as the assertion of fulfilled prophecy and new age inaugurated by the coming of Christ, an outline of Jesus' birth, death, resurrection and exaltation, and the affirmation of his coming again in judgment (*Apostolic Preaching* 17). Key texts behind this excerpted summary were Rom. 1.3-4, 1 Cor. 15.3-5 and 1 Thess. 1.9-10: 1 Thess. 1.9-10 because it comes from what most regard as the earliest NT writing and actually describes the preached gospel which proved successful in Thessalonica; Rom. 1.3-4 because it is Paul's description of 'the gospel of God' which confirmed his 'bona fides' to the Roman believers; and 1 Cor. 15.3-5 because it is Paul's fullest explicit statement of the gospel which he preached and on which his churches were founded —

> Rom. 1.3-4 — '. . . descended from the seed of David in terms of the flesh, and appointed Son of God in power in terms of the Spirit of holiness as from the resurection of the dead';
> 1 Cor. 15.3-5 — '. . . that Christ died for our sins in accordance with the scriptures, and that he was buried, and that he was raised on the

third day in accordance with the scriptures, and that he appeared to Cephas, then to the twelve . . .'

1 Thess. 1.9-10 — 'You turned to God from idols, to serve a living and true God, and to wait for his Son from heaven, whom he raised from the dead — Jesus, who rescues us from the wrath that is coming'.

Dodd's work has been qualified and improved in various ways (cf. e.g. Evans, and Dunn, *Unity*, ch. 2). For example, there has been much debate about the sermons in Acts and whether they contain earlier tradition or simply indicate what Luke thought should or might have been said on the occasion narrated. In the event, careful analysis of sermons like those in Acts 2, 3 and 10 does seem to demonstrate the use of earlier tradition. This is indicated, for example, by the liveliness of the eschatology in 2.16-17 and 3.19-21 (less typical of Luke elsewhere), and by the use of primitive-sounding christology in 2.22, 36, 3.13-15 and 10.38, 42. Other features are more appropriately dealt with in the next section.

Two points worthy of particular note emerge from this. One is the watershed formed by the resurrection of Jesus, or, as some prefer to say, by the earliest conviction that God had raised the crucified Jesus from the dead. Whatever preparation or lack of preparation there had been among Jesus' disciples for this epochal (eschatological) event, it was this event which made the decisive difference — the decisive difference between a tradition which was essentially the remembrance of a dead teacher and a tradition which itself continued to speak of a living Master — the decisive difference of perspective which transformed the tradition from a recycling of Jesus' proclamation to a proclamation of Jesus himself, from good news preached by Jesus to the gospel about Jesus, and subsequently to the Gospel according to Mark, to Luke, to Matthew, to John. The very fact that the Acts sermons and the echoes of Paul's evangel in his letters are *not* simply restatements of Jesus' teaching (as though it was the impressiveness and impact of that teaching which was the real source of the resurrection faith) but focus on the significance of Jesus himself (his death and resurrection in particular) should be enough proof that the kerygma of Jesus' death and resurrection marked a decisive new phase in the history of tradition behind the NT (see also Pokorny).

The other point worthy of note is how central was the interplay with (OT) scripture in the first formulations of this new faith. 'According to the scriptures' (1 Cor. 15.3-4) should be taken with full import. Psalms like 16, 22, 89 and 110 and prophecies like Isa. 53 and Dan. 7.9-14 very quickly (in at least some cases immediately) became luminous for the first believers (Lindars, Juel). It was not so much that the first disciples came to a belief and then sought out and discovered confirmation in scripture (though there was no doubt some of that). Nor indeed the direct converse, that certain scripture gave rise to a kind of wish fulfilment (otherwise resurrection appearances would probably have taken the form of Jesus 'coming on clouds' as Dan. 7.13 would have suggested). It was rather that such scriptures provided the metaphor and analogy in which the conviction could be expressed, provided the imagery and conceptuality which clothed the experience of Christ as risen in communicable language. However the point is put, it is unlikely that this first and most essential element in distinctively Christian faith (the resurrection of Jesus) would have become established among devout Jews had it not been for the confirmation and language which the scriptures provided. The tradition was taking a tremendous step forward, but unless its roots in and continuity with the already sacred tradition of the OT could be affirmed and were secure it must remain doubtful whether the new development would have taken and become established so quickly.

It perhaps also needs to be re-emphasised, that though the resurrection of Jesus marked a decisive new stage in the traditioning process which gave rise to the NT, the gulf(?) between pre-Easter tradition and post-Easter kerygma should not be exaggerated. For as the mid-century debate in the Bultmann school on the relation of historical Jesus to kerygmatic Christ brought out, the Gospels are not other than kerygma, are not simply pre-kerygma, but are themselves kerygma. It would be odd, then, to affirm the continuity of NT with OT (as above) and not also to affirm the continuity between kerygma/gospel and Gospel, when, after all, the gospel shape (both gospel and Gospel) focuses and climaxes precisely in the death and resurrection of Jesus.

§3.2. Liturgical Tradition

Closely related to kerygmatic tradition is the tradition evidently used in earliest Christian worship and teaching. Throughout the twentieth century the task of uncovering and identifying this tradition was a continued topic of interest in NT scholarship (e.g. Hunter, Kramer). The Pauline letters proved especially valuable since they are themselves evidence of the lively character of mid-first-century church life and of the interchange between churches.

In particular, a series of confessional formulae can be readily identified — identified because they are so frequently echoed or alluded to within the Pauline letters and elsewhere in recognizable forms. The most obvious/used are: 'God raised him from the dead' (e.g. Acts 3.15; Rom. 4.24-25; 10.9; 1 Cor.

6.14; 1 Pet. 1.21); 'Christ died for us' (e.g. Rom. 5.6, 8; 2 Cor. 5.14-15; 1 Thess. 5.10); 'He was handed (or handed himself) over (for our sins)' (e.g. Rom. 8.32; 1 Cor. 11.23; Gal. 1.4); 'Christ died and was raised' (Rom. 8.34; 2 Cor. 13.4; 1 Thess. 4.14); and confessional formulas like 'Jesus is Lord' in Rom. 10.9. Here again we see the tradition process in full flow: new beliefs coming to formulation, formulation becoming formulaic by regular use and repetition, formulas becoming so established that they can be simply alluded to or 'quoted' to summarise beliefs which have thus become central to and part of the foundation tradition.

'The church at worship' (Moule) was another obvious focus of interest. Here hymnic tradition has attracted considerable scholarly attention. How soon was it that the canticles preserved by Luke in his birth narrative — the Magnificat (Luke 1.46-55), the Benedictus (1.68-79), the Gloria (2.14) and the Nunc dimittis (2.29-32) — began to be used regularly in Christian worship? The thought that these songs may have been regular features of Christian liturgy for almost as long as Christianity has existed must surely give food for reflection on the character of NT tradition and the mode of its preservation. Certainly they as much as any other tradition within the NT evidence the character of a living tradition, of a tradition which lives through worship and is not simply maintained by worship.

More fragmentary in their influence have been the doxologies, or rather shouts of praise which have been preserved in Revelation: acclamations of God (4.8, 11; 7.12; 11.17-18; etc.); acclamations of the Lamb (5.9-10, 12); acclamations of God and of the Lamb/Christ (5.13; 7.10; 11.15; 19.6-8). What fervour did they originally express? What fervour have they provided expression for ever since!

Less durable as hymns, if they ever were hymns, have been the much discussed passages, Phil. 2.6-11 and Col. 1.15-20, possibly even John 1.1-18. Certainly if they were hymns they have not had the sustained liturgical influence of the Lukan canticles. Other passages like Heb. 1.3 and 1 Tim. 3.16 are frequently classified as early Christian hymns, as also the fragmentary exhortation, Eph. 5.14. In truth it matters not whether they were hymns as such or not. Their value is in showing that tradition took many forms, that some took poetic or hymnic form, and that as such they lent themselves to being quoted in communication between churches. More to the point, several of these hymnic passages were on the cutting edge of reflection on the significance of Christ. In other words, it may have been the poetic or liturgical expression of tradition (and the relative freedom which such format facilitates) which made it possible for the tradition to develop as it did.

There is evidence also of what in later terms can be called sacramental tradition. It is clear that the use of a regular baptismal formula quickly became established — 'in the name of' (Acts 8.16; 10.48; 19.5; 1 Cor. 1.13). It is also clear from Matt. 28.19 that this early formula was soon elaborated into a three-fold name formula — 'in the name of the Father and of the Son and of the Holy Spirit' — to become the regular formula of catholic Christianity more or less from then on (already Didache 7.1). Rom. 10.9 is widely regarded as (one of) the earliest baptismal confessions, quoted with that in mind by Paul. Many other passages (e.g. Col. 1.12-20; 1 Thess. 1.9-10) and even whole letters (Ephesians; 1 Peter) have been linked to baptism, on the assumption that baptism was one of the primary loci round which tradition would have gathered. But since it is unclear how quickly baptismal liturgies developed such speculation needs to be restrained (Dunn, *Unity* 142-3). Nevertheless, the assumption is probably more sound than our evidence actually demonstrates.

Eucharistic tradition is attested as remarkably fixed already in 1 Cor. 11.24-25 (cf. Luke 22.19-20 and the only slight variation from Matt. 26.26-28/Mark 14.22-24). At the same time there are elaborations evident in comparison of the three Gospel texts and 1 Cor. 11: the switch in emphasis from the significance of the cup (new covenant) to the content of the cup (blood); the emphasis on repeating the act ('Do this in remembrance of me'); and the Pauline interpretation ('As often as you [do this] you proclaim the Lord's death until he comes' — 11.26) (Dunn, *Unity* §40). Here again we see the characteristic of fixed core and elaborated (and varied) significance, as also the indications of developing appreciation of the significance of the original words and acts. It is little wonder that the Eucharist and the eucharistic formulations have provided the living heart of the living tradition for so many Christians and for so many centuries.

§3.3. Ethical Tradition

Perhaps the widest and most diverse range of earliest Christian tradition, in terms of source and influence, is to be found in the ethical teaching preserved in the NT letters.

In the first place, there was evidently a widespread appreciation of some of the moral forms and even of the ethical standards upheld in some of the philosophies and by some of the Greco-Roman moralists of the day. The use of vice-lists in condemnation of unacceptable social behaviour was common to all religious and ethical systems (in the NT e.g. Mark 7.21-22; Rom 1.29-31; 1 Cor. 6.9-10; Gal. 5.19-21; 2 Tim. 3.2-5; 1 Pet. 4.3). In the second generation of Christianity use of *Haustafeln* (household codes/rules) became common, in direct reflection of the widespread belief that the household was the core unit of society, on whose stability the common good and flourishing of society depended (see especially Col. 3.18–4.1; Eph. 5.22–6.9; 1 Pet. 2.18–3.7). But already in the first generation Paul shows appreciation of Stoic values ('what is contrary to nature', 'what is fitting' — Rom. 1.26, 28), and was quite ready to appeal to the broadest categories of 'good and evil' and conscience (Rom. 2.7-10, 14-15) and to what would generally be regarded as 'virtue' and 'praiseworthy' (Phil. 4.8-9). Here, in other words, were little communities (a new sect) not setting themselves apart, as though to be fully themselves as Christians they had to be wholly different, but fully prepared to draw on the common wells of human experience and wisdom. To be good ethical tradition it did not need to be distinctively Christian.

Within that broader range of ethical tradition, however, the first believers were able to draw more fully and most consistently on the wells of Jewish wisdom. The letter of James, as a handbook of good, practical advice, is thoroughly Jewish in content and character (e.g. Bauckham, *James*). Paul's advice in passages like Rom. 12.14-21 and 1 Cor. 5–7 (Rosner) is heavily dependent on the OT and Jewish wisdom. Perhaps most striking is the fact that although Paul regarded himself as free from the Torah (law) in one sense, his regular commendation of the law (Rom. 3.31; 7.12; 8.4; 13.8-10) can only be explained by the degree to which he found Judaism's traditional ethical wisdom still basic and sound in directing the lives and life-styles of his churches. The most notable examples of this are his sustained hostility to sexual license and to idolatry (e.g. 1 Cor. 6.18; 10.14) which did indeed set Christian morality in direct contrast to Hellenistic morality. Paul sat loose to such Jewish traditions as food laws and sabbath, but not because he was opposed to Jewish tradition as such; on matters ethical the continuity and contribution of Jewish tradition to Christian tradition was too important to be sidelined (Dunn, *Theology* §§23-24).

In some ways most significant for the present enquiry is the evidence of the importance of and use made of Jesus tradition in Christian paraenesis (exhortation). There are clear signs of this for example in James (1.5, 17, 22-23; 4.12; 5.12), in Didache 1, and at several points in Paul (e.g. Rom. 12.14; 14.14; 1 Thess. 5.2, 4, 13). In the last case there has been much bewilderment caused by Paul's failure explicitly to cite Jesus as the authority for the teaching (apart from 1 Cor. 7.10-11 and 9.14). But such bewilderment reflects a failure to appreciate the character of the traditioning process. The probability, as we have already mentioned and will document below, is that each new church was established on a foundation of Jesus tradition (also kerygmatic and confessional tradition). This tradition would inevitably have formed part of the regular diet of teaching and reflection in the gatherings of these churches — the process, indeed, which we have outlined in the first section above.

Which also means that much of this tradition would have become part and parcel of their communal discourse; as living tradition it would be a present factor in their communal meditations and so also in shaping and determining the character and detail of their own daily living. Paul could thus simply allude to various elements in that tradition with every confidence that the audience gathered for the Lord's Supper or worship would recognize the allusion — much as generations of preachers (or school teachers) have been able simply to refer to 'the Good Samaritan' or 'the Prodigal Son' without further detail and could be confident that their point was sufficiently made by the bare allusion. In such discourse, the possibility of communication by abbreviated reference and allusion is one of the things which gives the discourse its bonding force and which confirms the sense of belonging for those engaged in the discourse. This last is one of the most important roles of tradition in any ongoing community.

§3.4. Pauline Letters

As the history of tradition behind the Gospels came to fruition in the Gospels themselves, so the history of tradition behind the other NT documents came to fruition in the NT letters, Acts of the Apostles and Revelation. And once again not as tradition becoming something other than tradition, but tradition becoming crystallised in particular documents and formulated for particular occasions. The most interesting for our purposes are the Pauline letters, because of their number and range of situations addressed, and because the Pauline corpus (by widespread consensus) extends beyond the first generation.

Of immediate interest for us are, first of all, the confirmation which Paul explicitly provides that the passing on of foundation tradition was regarded as an essential part of the establishment of a new church (1 Thess. 4.1; 2 Thess. 3.6; 1 Cor. 11.2; 15.3; Col. 2.6). And second, the indications of how Paul himself contributed to the development of the tradition which he inherited and passed on. For the latter, it will suffice if we take examples from each of the three categories already discussed.

So far as kerygmatic tradition is concerned, the point is highlighted by the tension between the assertions of Gal. 1.12 and 1 Cor. 15.1-3. In the one case Paul insists that his gospel was given him direct from God; in the other he is equally clear that his gospel came to him as already established Christian tradition. This tension can be resolved only if we recognize that Paul's gospel was indeed the gospel shared by all the churches, but also recognize Paul's conviction that he had been specially commissioned to take this gospel to the Gentiles (Gal. 1.15-16; 2.7-9; Rom. 11.13). It was evidently the slant which this conviction gave to the shared gospel (not requiring circumcision of Gentile believers) which made Paul's gospel so controversial for many of his fellow Jewish believers (Gal. 2). Here again we see the character of living tradition — the same core formulations shared by the range of apostles/missionaries (1 Cor. 15.1-11), but adapted to the new circumstances and challenges of a gospel for Gentiles as well as Jews.

In the case of liturgical tradition we might mention the way Paul seems to have taken up the tradition of an expected baptism in Spirit, stemming originally from John the Baptist (Mark 1.8 pars.), already adapted by the Jesus tradition to depict Jesus' own death as a baptism (Mark 10.38-39; Luke 12.49-50), and now further extended to speak of believers as being baptized into Christ's death and body (Rom. 6.4-5; 1 Cor. 12.13). With regard to the tradition of the Lord's Supper, we have already observed how Paul elaborates on the institution tradition in 1 Cor. 11.26, both strengthening its reference to Jesus' death and injecting a fresh eschatological note. We might also note the debate on what seems to be a traditional formula on Jesus' death in Rom. 3.24-26, as to whether and to what degree Paul may have elaborated and modified it (Dunn, *Theology* 174). In any case, the character of tradition for Paul as living tradition is further illustrated.

So far as ethical tradition is concerned the most interesting examples are provided by the two cases where Paul actually does attribute teaching explicitly to Jesus (1 Cor 7.10-11 and 9.14). For what emerges from a closer examination of both cases is, once again, Paul's readiness to affirm the tradition but also to adapt it as circumstances required. In the former case, the instruction of the Lord seems clear: as a rule, no divorce or separation of husband and wife should be allowed. But the situation of a believer married to an unbelieving partner was new; and in these circumstances Paul ruled that if the unbelieving partner chose to separate, the believer should accept it (7.15). Similarly the Lord's command was clear in the case of missionaries being supported by those to whom they ministered (9.14). But, once again, in the circumstances of his own mission, Paul chose to disregard the tradition and to maintain himself by the work of his own hands, despite the authoritative tradition (9.15-18). Here again, then, we see clear statements of principle derived from the tradition, principles whose authority Paul delberately restates; evidently he had no quarrel with the tradition itself; he reaffirms the point and authority of the tradition. At the same time, however, he adapts its reference and application to the changing circumstances of his own missionary work and churches. Once again, then, we see the character of living tradition, core and substance sustained but adapted, stability with flexibility.

We could say more on Paul's use of scriptural tradition, but have probably said enough. Particular reference should be made, however, to the work of Richard Hays, who through careful investigation of the resonances of intertextuality in the Pauline letters has given further demonstration of the pervasiveness of the influence of tradition, and of the subtle ways in which traditional narratives and texts shape new discourse and are themselves given fresh life by and through the new formulations which they have in part inspired and informed.

On a different front of contemporary interest in Pauline scholarship is the similar evidence of the way Paul has taken over contemporary epistolary and rhetorical traditions and adapted them. Exploration on this front would take us too far from our immediate concern. But it is worth noting how, for example, Paul adapted the traditional pattern of letter opening — the traditional Greek 'greeting' *(chairein)* changed to the distinctive Christian 'grace' *(charis)* and combined with the traditional Jewish greeting 'Shalom' (peace). Also how he made effective use of the Greek philosophical school format of the diatribe — conversation with an imaginary opponent or interlocutor — in Romans (2.1-5, 17-24; 3.1-8; etc). Paul had no hesitation in drawing on and adapting traditional forms and content where they proved effective vehicles for his message (see further Furnish).

Finally we need to note how at the far end of the Pauline corpus (the Pastoral epistles) the traditioning process has become more structured and deliberate. There is a clearer sense of the need for carefully formulated teaching to be affirmed and adhered to — for example, 'the faith' (11 times), the 'sound teaching' (1 Tim. 1.10; 2 Tim. 4.3; Tit. 1.9; 2.1), and the 'faithful sayings' — the last, interestingly, falling into the same three categories, kerygmatic (1 Tim. 1.15; 2 Tim. 2.11; Tit. 3.5-8), ecclesiastical (1 Tim. 3.1; or is the reference to 1 Tim. 2.15?) and ethical (1 Tim. 4.8-9; 2 Tim. 2.11-13). Very striking is the image of the tradition as *parathēkē*, 'deposit, goods left in trust with someone' (1 Tim. 6.20; 2 Tim. 1.12, 14). The image is rather static and the complementary idea of 'protecting' it (the same verb is used each time) encourages the picture of something retained and returned in the form in which it was first received. It is this image which probably above all gives the impression that the Pastorals mark a new phase in the traditioning process, the impression of a theology concerned more to preserve than to develop, of a faith tied to earlier formulations and discouraged from seeking fresh expression. The living tradition is beginning to lose some of its vitality. Also notable is the window suddenly opened to us in 2 Tim. 2.1-2 on to the traditioning process towards the end of the first century — in this case from Paul to Timothy, through many witnesses, from Timothy to faithful people, 'faithful people who will be able to teach others also' — perhaps three or even four generations in all. The traditioning process is stretching out, but still an extension of the same process we have been examining from the first.

§3.5. The Rest of the NT

The main outlines of the tradition process which resulted in the NT have now been illustrated with sufficient detail. The scope of the tradition is further indicated by the other NT documents, the other letters, the Acts of the Apostles and the Apocalypse (Revelation) of John. But to gain a 'feel' for the history of the NT tradition and its character it is unnecessary to review them in any detail.

The other letters display an interesting variety of tradition: James, with its strongly Jewish character and Jesus tradition enmeshed in it, in effect an extension of the older Jewish wisdom tradition; 1 Peter with the fascination of its Pauline character under the name of Peter; Jude and 2 Peter with their unique mutual relationship, and use both of Jewish pseudepigrapha (Jude 14-15 referring to 1 Enoch 1.9) and unique echo of the Gospels transfiguration narrative (2 Pet. 1.16-18); 1-3 John, both extending the character of the Johannine elaboration of the Jesus tradition, and bearing witness to the way the kerygmatic tradition was also being elaborated in the face of new challenges (1 John 2.22-23; 4.1-3; 2 John 7); and the extraordinary Hebrews, with its extended elaboration of the otherwise slim tradition of Jesus as heavenly intercessor (Rom. 8.34), its confirmation of a widespread interest in the figure of Melchizedek at the turn of the millennia, and its ability to express a Jewish apocalyptic perspective in language meaningful to a Hellenistic audience.

In the case of the Acts, the debate on the sources of Luke's tradition has never been satisfactorily resolved (Dupont). Was there, for example, a 'Hellenist' source behind Acts 6-8, and 11.19-30, possibly even a Hellenist tract used for Stephen's speech in ch. 7? Does the 'we' form of much of the later narrative indicate Luke's own personal eye-witness involvement in what he records, or dependence on some travel journal available to him? Whatever the precise facts, we need doubt neither that Luke had sources of information to draw upon nor that he shaped them to his own ends. Both points need to be given due weight. In the case of the much discussed speeches in Acts, for example, we have already noted, on the one hand, the evidence of primitive features (above §3.1); at the same time, however, no one disputes that the speeches are in Luke's style, complete little cameos (three or four minutes in length) of what Luke no doubt judged to be the substance of the gospel for the occasion. Again, Luke had good information about various significant phases of Paul's work; but he deliberately (we may assume) chose both to pull a veil over more controversial aspects of it (no hint of a crisis at Antioch or with the Galatian churches, for example) and to stress Paul's positive attitude to his ancestral faith (e.g. Acts 18.18; 21.26) in a way that leaves readers of Paul's letters somewhat bemused. Here once again we see that respect for tradition does not mean a slavish reproduction of it, but creative use of it to bring out the point of the past for the benefit of the present.

Finally, with regard to the Apocalypse of John (Revelation), we need simply note its presence in the NT. Here was a means of enscribing and expressing the experience of revelation, of eyes opened to the mysteries of God's purpose, expressed in terms of visions of strange and weird beings, which had gained currency in late Second Temple Judaism (Charlesworth). It was not regarded as rendered unnecessary or unacceptable in the light of the primary revelation of Christ. On the contrary, it gained fresh inspiration from the mode (apocalypse) and from the stock of apocalyptic images available in Daniel and other Jewish apocalypses, and adapted them to a fresh vision of heaven in which Christ had central place (with God). The genre and outcome are not the same, but in its use and re-use of tradition Revelation also bears witness to an essentially similar traditioning process.

§4. The Ongoing Tradition Process

It is important to recognize that the tradition process did not cease when the writings of the NT were completed. As the formulation of the Gospels themselves did not mark the end of the oral tradition, so the writing of the other NT writings did not mark a closure of the tradition process which lies behind them. On the contrary, in every case the documents are to be regarded as a stage in the process, a crystallisation of the process at various points in the course of the first and second generations of Christianity. We begin to move beyond our brief at this point, but its importance for our understanding of the history of NT tradition and of the place of the NT as such within it warrants at least a few more words. The key point can be put thus: the impression is often given when NT scripture is set over against tradition, that the NT is fixed whereas tradition is ever fluid and developing; that is misleading. The NT shares at least something of the flexibility (the not-easy-finally-to-tie-down-ness) of tradition. The point can be documented briefly.

§4.1. In Search of the Text

In every case of a NT document, we can obviously affirm that the document was written down at some point in time. Do we have that document? Strictly speaking, No! Was there an 'original'? Not necessarily, since multiple copies may have been made from the first dictation. The intended recipients no doubt preserved the copy they received and probably further copies were made for further distribution. What happened to the originals, we have no idea whatsoever. As the document became better known and more widely used, more and more copies were made and circulated. The earliest copies available to us are products of that process, several generations removed from the originals, various fragmentary scrolls from the 2nd and 3rd centuries, and more extensive manuscripts from the 4th century onwards.

All this brings us into the realm of text-criticism, the science of reconstruction of the 'original' text; at least that is how the science was at first conceived. The point, of course, is that these multiple copies contain very many variations, and the textual critic has to decide which is the 'best' reading. Most of the variations are relatively minor and can be put down to scribal errors in copying. But in a good number of other cases what we encounter in these variations is the evidence that the tradition process was ongoing; the text was subject to modification, elaboration, correction as part of a deliberate scribal enterprise. In other words, the scribes were not merely copying a fixed tradition, but were doing (in a more modest way) what the story tellers of oral tradition were doing before them — re-telling the story in the text, with the sort of modifications, elaborations and improvements which the oral performance had much more readily facilitated. It would be accurate, indeed, to speak of the scribal task as not simply issuing copies of the text, but as providing something more like versions and editions of the text. The traditioning process at this point is in essence not very different from the process which gave rise to what we might call the sequence of editions of Moses' or Isaiah's or David's or Paul's works (Meade), or indeed from the fresh editions of Esther, Daniel and Ezra in the LXX. In the case of the NT tradition it would be all the more marked when translation of the Greek 'originals' into a different language (Latin, Syriac, Coptic, Georgian, etc.) was involved.

A few examples will suffice to illustrate the ongoing character of the tradition process. The Lord's Prayer, in its slightly different versions, was already a good example of a living tradition — a prayer not simply remembered as part of Jesus' instruction, but used, and in the using shaped by the liturgical usage. But the process did not stop with the forms fixed by Matthew and Luke (Matt. 6.9-13; Luke 11.2-4). For the textual apparatus at the foot of the

Matthean text (or margin of the English translation) indicates that the familiar conclusion ('for yours is the kingdom, the power and the glory, for ever') was soon added (already in a transitional form in Didache 8.2). In other words, the traditioning process of liturgical usage provided a more and more suitable liturgical form — a fluidity of tradition which continues to the present day in the use of various/variant forms of the Lord's Prayer in different churches. Here is a pre-eminent case of the character of the tradition process: few doubt that the prayer in its basic form and substance goes back to Jesus; but the use and re-use of the tradition have allowed for a variation of forms whose extent is amazing for such a few lines in such regular use.

Other familiar examples of the problems turned up by textual criticism are the ending of Mark's Gospel, the poor attestation of Luke 22.43-44, the location of the famous pericope about the woman taken in adultery usually to be found as John 7.53–8.11, the much elaborated version of Acts to be found in Western texts, the multiple positioning of the doxology in Rom. 16.25-27 (also after 14.23 and 15.33), etc. If Mark chose to end his Gospel abruptly at 16.8, the scribes and teachers who used it evidently soon became dissatisfied and attempted to improve it by adding different extended endings. Luke 22.43-44 looks like the sort of pious elaboration which later generations delighted in. Presumably the account of the woman taken in adultery was a 'loose' tradition, a kind of rogue oral element which for a time had no settled place within the written tradition. The scribes behind the Western texts of Acts seem to show the same old story-telling impulse to try to tell the same story better (e.g. Acts 8.37). And the various positions of the doxology in Rom. 16.25-27 attest the circulation of abbreviated versions of the letter. But these should not be thought of simply as text-critical 'problems'. They are more positively to be reckoned as evidence of how the tradition process continued, evidence that the NT itself was part of that process. The recent study by Bart Ehrman demonstrates how much the textual tradition was affected by the struggles between 'orthodoxy' and 'heresy' in support of christological doctrine (see also Parker).

As has become clearer in more recent decades, the outcome of textual critical reconstruction is not the 'original' text of the NT. At best the text used by NT scholars is an eclectic text, made up of innumerable decisions (by majority vote) on innumerable details, with its form changing little by little from one edition to another. Of course we can be confident that it is more or less what Matthew, Paul, etc. wrote, in say 95% of significant cases. The eclectic text is substantially what the NT writers dictated. But the text is not as 'hard', not as 'fixed' as some would like to think when they appeal to the NT over against later tradition. For it shares in something at least of the flexibility of the traditioning process.

§4.2. The Emergence of the Canon

Another important part of the ongoing tradition is the emergence of the canon (details again in Kümmel Part Two). The canonisation process should not be oversimplified — as though some third- or fourth-century church council overnight declared some documents canonical and from that moment gave them an authority they had not previously possessed. The process was a good deal more drawn out and consists rather of the NT documents themselves becoming widely known, used and respected in the churches of the Mediterranean region. They were seen to be authoritative witnesses to Christ and expressions of the common faith. In other words, canonisation was a recognition of intrinsic authority, or of the continuing impact of these documents on congregations, rather than the bestowal of an ecclesiastical authority not previously possessed.

Several aspects of the process are relevant for a better understanding of the history of NT tradition. One is the point just made, which relates back to what was said at the beginning. For the word had not merely to be spoken, the document dictated. It also had to be received. As the Jesus tradition began not so much with what Jesus said and did but with how he was heard and seen (the impact he made), so the canonisation process began with the NT writing being heard and responded to, circulated more widely, read frequently and treasured more deeply. This again attests the living character of tradition and the tradition process — the tradition (Gospel, letter, etc.) not simply prized and displayed in a locked cabinet, as it were, but influencing conduct and shaping faith, and being itself shaped in the process. The tradition process takes the form of an ongoing interactive dialogue between scripture and the *sensus fidelium,* summed up early on in 'the rule of faith' and then in the creeds.

Here we should also simply note the fact that as the text of scripture is not so fixed as many assume, so the canonisation process is not quite so closed as many assume. The fact that Luther regarded certain NT documents as of secondary value, and that most denominations have to reckon seriously with the reality that they operate effectively with a canon within the canon, has to be set alongside the continuing confusion regarding the status of the OT canon (with or without Apocrypha?) and the fact that one Christian church (Ethiopic) regards the OT pseudepigraphon, 1 Enoch, as part of the canon. In other words, once again we see repeated that typically traditional feature, of an agreed and firm core and substance, together with a flexible form, and variation in subsidiary detail and scope.

Of course, a primary function of the NT canon was to provide a norm and yardstick by which to judge which forms and variations of the tradition were acceptable within the churches. For all the flexibility we have seen, there emerged a clear consensus *(sensus fidelium)* that there were elaborations of Gospel and other teaching which modified the core and transformed the character of the tradition too much. For example, the birth narratives of Matthew and Luke were evidently regarded as a primary elaboration of the earliest gospel tradition, properly expressive of faith, whereas the subsequent elaborations (e.g. the Protevangelium of James; see Elliott) were judged to be too far beyond the foundation tradition to be counted as foundation tradition; they were not recognized as part of the NT canon. This canonical (normative) function remains a primary function of the NT as such within the traditioning process.

For that reason also, most will want to resist attempts to reinsert a reconstructed Q into the current stock of Christian tradition, or to give the Gospel of Thomas a place alongside the canonical Gospels. For insofar as Q and Thomas ever had a place within the process, they were judged unfit to retain that place; they failed the test of the process itself, being neglected and then lost so far as the great body of churches were concerned. They simply ceased to be effective parts of that tradition which informed faith, stimulated worship and instructed conduct. In the 'natural selection' of the evolution of tradition, they simply did not survive — primarily, we may guess, because they did not assume the normative 'Gospel' shape (climaxing in Jesus' death and resurrection) established by Mark and his three most immediate successors. Historical reconstruction (hypothetical Q) or chance discovery in a desert cache (Thomas) does not change the verdict of that history.

At the same time it should be noted that the NT did not canonise simply the unity of the tradition, it canonised also the diversity of the tradition (Dunn, *Unity,* ch. 15). To overemphasize the former is to overemphasize once again the ideal of a fixed and uniform tradition, rather than a common core and substance with varied and variable detail and elaboration. To overemphasize the latter is to lose both the unity and the continuity of tradition, and consequently to lose also its power to hold together the diversity and to maintain the full richness of the tradition as a resource rather than as a threat.

§4.3. Hearing the Tradition

Finally a word to connect this outline of the history of the NT tradition to the next section ('Investigating the Tradition'). For as Joel Green indicates, attention has recently switched from the attempt to understand the history of the tradition to the attempt to appreciate how the tradition is received. This is important for an understanding of the history of the tradition, since it is the second side of what, as I have tried to indicate, has always been a two-sided process — the hearing and responding to the tradition are as fundamental to the process as are the telling and enacting of the tradition.

This ongoing process of the living tradition has always been well appreciated in the Orthodox churches of the East — that the NT is not something separate from the Church or its liturgy, cannot be read and understood apart from the Church and its worship, can be appropriated only through and with the Church (cf. Meyendorff). In the Catholic West the process has become too formalized and, from a Protestant perspective, too restricted to and by the magisterium. The resulting dispute about the respective roles of scripture and tradition, which the Reformation occasioned, has resulted in an unfortunate polarisation which for many generations lost sight of the history of tradition and the tradition process described above. But perhaps we are now in a better position to appreciate what both sides of that dispute counted as important.

On the one hand, the fluid and flexible character of the process, of the retelling and reusing of the NT tradition, of the hearing and responding to the tradition, needs to be underlined. No one within a Western cultural tradition truly hears the NT as an entirely new experience. The culture has been so shaped by the NT and its resultant tradition that those who are influenced by that culture in any degree (through education, literature, moral values, etc.) have already encountered much that has been derived directly from or through the NT and the ongoing tradition, their pre-understanding shaped by it. Even more so, the responsive hearer cannot stand above the tradition as though divorced from it, but stands already in the stream of tradition, part of the continuum formed by the living, ongoing tradition, and informed by it (Gadamer). Here the distance between the retelling of the earliest oral tradition within the setting of some first-century house group/church and the reading of scripture in some twenty-first-century congregation is not so great as we might at first assume. For it is the same core tradition, the same foundation tradition which was/is being retold each time; and it is in principle the same kind of expositions and elaborations of the tradition which were/are being heard, each reflecting in various degrees the ongoing tradition of the retelling and the changing circumstances in which the retelling is taking place. In the recognition of the NT as part of a living process of tradition, and of the church as the context within which the NT is heard and understood, the millennial gap between East and West is further narrowed.

On the other hand, an appreciation of the traditioning process allows the Protestant concern for the canonical authority of the NT to be given proper weight within that process. The reason why Protestantism emphasised the importance of scripture over against tradition was the realisation that the tradition, the church can become corrupt. NT scripture provided a norm against which the larger tradition could be checked and any abuses identified. One thinks only of St Francis' hearing again the call to gospel poverty, or the Reformation's rediscovery of justification by faith, or the West's denunciation of its own horrific history of Christian anti-semitism. In effect, this function of the NT as the determinative core which provides a check and control on the flexibility and elaboration of subsequent retellings, as *norma normans* within the overarching tradition, is simply a continuation of the process of tradition from the first. Of course hearing the NT both within the tradition of the church and in its critical role within the tradition involves a subtle dialectic, in which NT scholarship has an important part (though only a part) in setting the text into its original context of vocabulary, syntax and idiom — but no more subtle than the hearing which recognized the authority of these writings from the first and the hearing which resulted in them being accorded canonical authority. The tradition still lives (see also Dunn, 'Levels').

§5. Investigating the Tradition

It was originally the intention of the editors to have a separate article on 'Methods for Studying the Tradition'. But it soon became apparent that a description of the history of NT tradition was bound to cover most of the same ground. And so it has proved. Methods for studying the tradition have been developed steadily in the West since the Renaissance. They have provided a steadily clearer view of the history of the NT tradition as the investigations plumbed deeper into that history. What we have done above is in effect to reverse the process: drawing on the insights and findings of generations of investigative scholarship we have been able to trace the history of the NT tradition using both well-informed historical imagination and consensus critical conclusions. It is appropriate, then, to round off this account of the history of the NT tradition by outlining briefly the steps by which the stages of that history became clearer to NT scholarship.

§5.1. Textual Criticism

The publication of Erasmus' Greek New Testament in 1516 marks the beginning of the modern period of NT scholarship. For it signalled the beginning of the now centuries-long quest for the original text of the NT, or, as it would now be expressed, the search for the text which will be closest to the sort of NT text being read and heard in the first few generations of Christianity. The recovery of that text, and its translation into the lingua franca of different countries, in the Middle East and Europe and then more widely, became the first priority and primary task of all NT scholarship, basic to all that might properly be said thereafter in explanation or exposition of the text.

Over the intervening centuries the number of manuscripts of the Greek NT catalogued, in part or whole, amounts to several thousand. Add to that the manuscripts in other languages (translations from the Greek) and quotations in early Christian writers, with all the thousands of variations attested, and the task of reconstructing an 'original' might seem impossible. The early text critics quickly deduced basic rules whose logic still holds good.

Clearly it was not enough simply to count manuscripts in favour of any particular reading. For later manuscripts were all dependent on earlier manuscripts, and some well-supported reading in later manuscripts could easily have been derived from some very early scribal mistake or improvement. A classic case is the longer ending of Mark: what seems to have been a second-century improvement to Mark's more abrupt end at 16.8 quickly established itself in scribal transmission of Mark.

Two other rules quickly developed: *lectio brevior* (shorter reading) and *lectio difficilior* (more difficult reading). The logic is again clear and convincing: it is more likely that scribes added to the text (by way of elaboration or clarification) than that they omitted part of the sacred text; and it is more likely that a scribe will have improved a more difficult reading, than that he will have made more difficult a reading which was straightforward. More details can be found in any textbook on textual criticism (e.g. Aland and Aland).

The consequence is that all commentators on NT texts really do need to check what is the text they are commenting on. If it is unsatisfactory for a would-be scholar to work solely from one or more translations, it is also inadequate simply to assume that the Greek text consulted records the text as it was first dictated by Paul, or Mark, etc. Just as it is inadequate to assume that the text, whatever it was precisely, was either intended by the writer in a wholly unambiguous way or heard by the first circle(s) of recipients in just one way. As noted above, however fixed the text might have been from the first, the way it was heard was not fixed. The uncertainty with regard to the text, which the task of textual criticism highlights, should serve as a constant reminder of this fundamental degree of flexibility in the tradition from the beginning. A word which finally escapes our attempts to tie it down (and thereby control) is a word which can address us with fresh and unexpected authority.

§5.2. *Historical Criticism*

A second important concern and principle also derives from the Renaissance, that is, from the emerging sense of the pastness of the past: that the past was not only *distant* from the present, but was also *different* from the present. The rediscovery of the Greek and Latin classics brought home to Renaissance man that the world revealed in these texts was very different from the late mediaeval western world. The manners and customs, the mode of government and law, the way of conceptualising the cosmos and thinking about society were not as they are now. Significant change had occurred, and if these texts were properly to be understood the differences and changes had to be recognized and taken into account.

The appropriate method as it first emerged was that of historical philology: such texts had to be set in their correct historical context and their language read in accord with the grammatical and syntactical rules of the time. By the careful analysis of meaning of words and sentences, by reference to the way these words and such sentences were used at the time of writing, these texts could be understood as what they were — historical texts, written in what was an ancient and foreign language. It was this principle and method which enabled Humanist scholars to expose mediaeval documents masquerading as classical authorities for the forgeries they were (notably the 'Donation of Constantine'). The result was the great lexicographical studies on which modern NT scholarship still builds.

For the Reformers this awareness of historical distance and method of documenting historical difference became the means by which the corruptions of mediaeval Catholicism could be identified and shown up for what they were. On the question of scripture and tradition, and who determines the meaning of the text, they replied by maintaining that the text should be expounded in terms of its *plain meaning* as seen in its historical context. Of course they recognized that the 'plain meaning' may include allegory or symbolism when the particular text in question is 'plainly' allegorical or symbolical. But they were sufficiently confident of the perspicacity of scripture, that is, of its sufficiency to indicate its own interpretation when read in accord with its plain meaning.

This historical awareness of the character of the NT text is the heart of historical criticism. With the Enlightenment it was developed in accord with the paradigm of the emerging scientific method to appear as the historical critical method. That is to say, it assumed an objectivity to the past, as though facts were like archaeological artefacts to be dug out from under layers of history. It assumed that human reason was a sufficient measure of true and false facts. And it assumed that the cosmos was an intricate machine following immutable laws, a closed system of cause and effect whose explanation required no God hypothesis or divine intervention.

If the above analysis of the history of NT tradition has been followed, however, it will hardly need saying that the historical critical method thus defined has come under severe questioning in recent decades. Each assumption has been tested and found wanting. The ideas of a cosmic system whose future events are all inherently predictable, that reason alone is a sufficient arbiter of values and complex relationships, that the observing subject can be wholly divorced from the observed object, no longer have much currency or leverage. So in literature, the rediscovery of the reader and of the act of reading in the communication and formation of meaning has become integral to the hermeneutical enterprise. At the same time, the earlier principles of historical criticism remain valid, and the role of the NT read as historical text in historical context to provoke fresh hearings and to criticise received readings can still be asserted. In fact, the balance made possible by a recognition of the NT as tradition, and of what the tradition process has involved and still involves, would have prevented such excesses; that balance needs to be more fully recovered in the present.

§5.3. *Source Criticism*

With the next phase of European cultural history came a romantic interest in origins, appreciation of the inspiration of the creative moment of authorship being seen as the key to understanding and appropriating what emerged from that moment. In terms of NT scholarship this interest translated into a desire to appreciate the religious experience and consciousness of Jesus, as the *fons et origo* of Christianity and (if anything, more important) of the Christian values and insights which still endured. And since Jesus himself left no written record, that meant getting back as close as possible to the historical Jesus in terms of the records in which he featured.

Out of this concern emerged the century-long inquiry into the sources of the Gospels. This has been alluded to above (§2.8) and is treated in more detail by Christopher Tuckett ('Introduction to the Gospels'). He will also indicate the somewhat similar debate regarding sources for the Fourth Gospel. We should simply note here, however, one of the benefits of having three of the NT Gospels so obviously in a literary relationship, with one (Mark) as source for the other two (Matthew and Luke), and with the possibility of reconstructing in some degree a second source for Matthew and Luke (Q). I refer to the benefit that analysis of these relationships yields us clear insights into the tradition process both prior to the writing of these Gospels and indeed subsequent to their being 'reduced to writing'. Likewise, the benefit of the Fourth Gospel and the very difficulty of tracing sources behind it is a salutary reminder that the retelling of the Gospel story can absorb (in the retelling) the very sources on which it drew so completely that they can no longer be disentangled with confidence.

On sources for Acts we have already said enough above. As might be expected, the Gospels and Acts are the only NT writings which have raised in a substantial way the question of traceable sources. For the rest the immediacy of the letter format and of the apocalypse (revelation) hardly invites much if any source criticism.

§5.4. Form Criticism

Form criticism emerged in the early decades of the twentieth century as a way of getting behind the earliest *written* sources to the earlier *oral* traditions on which the sources drew. As with source criticism the chief focus of interest was the Jesus tradition. Here too enough has probably been said by way of description above (§2.4). Unfortunately the potential benefits of the new tool were clouded by two factors. One was the translation of the German, *Formgeschichte* (history of the form), into the English, 'Form criticism'. The former emphasised the process nature of the oral tradition prior to its writing down; the latter invited the reduction of the task to the rather sterile labelling of forms uncovered by (quasi-archaeological) form-critical analysis. The other was that the literary model of analysis of the tradition process encouraged the image of layer upon layer of tradition being built one on top of the other. Consequently, the early model of form-critical analysis was largely negative in its results — the impression being usually given that form criticism enabled penetration through only a few layers and left the researcher in inescapable confusion regarding how much of the tradition could be traced right back to Jesus (see again above §2.8). The earlier analysis of the history of tradition (above) has been an attempt to counter that impression by undermining its assumptions and by demonstrating that a 'retelling of tradition' model allows more positive conclusions regarding the retentiveness and stability as well as the flexibility and adaptability of the Jesus tradition.

We have also noted that form criticism had a much wider role to play than source criticism in regard to the NT epistles (above §3). If Bultmann is the name to conjure with in regard to form critical analysis of the Synoptic tradition, Dibelius is the one who most effectively pointed out its wider value beyond the Gospels. In particular, it was Dibelius who more clearly emphasised the purposes to which the various forms were put. Dibelius' insight at this point is neatly summed up in the aphorism: 'In the beginning was the sermon' (*Tradition* chs. 2 and 9). The insight was elaborated by Marxsen in his description of the New Testament itself as 'the oldest extant volume of the preaching of the church' (Marxsen, *New Testament* 46). By means of such insights the living character of the tradition process from individual form to NT as a whole is retained, and form criticism prevented from lapsing into the 'archaeological dig' model, to inform our appreciation of the history of the NT as tradition.

§5.5. Redaction Criticism

For sake of completeness we should mention briefly four further stages in the history of critical analysis of the NT tradition.

The first is the reaction which followed the emphases of the early form critics. In focusing attention on the form and its identifiability, some of the early form critics overemphasised the Evangelists' role as (simply) collectors of the forms (e.g. Dibelius, *Tradition* 3). The lapse was natural, but it indicated clearly enough that they had not fully grasped the character of the tradition process which they were trying to uncover. For the flexibility of the oral tradition, as indeed revealed by the variations in the forms uncovered, should have alerted them to the likelihood that the Evangelists would probably have been equally as flexible in their use of the earlier oral forms. As noted above (§2.8), the assumption that the transition from oral tradition to written tradition meant a fundamental alteration in the traditioning process (oral = flexible, written = fixed) has been at best misleading and has severely inhibited the recognition of the character of the NT as living tradition (or as sermons, if you like).

Whatever the rights and wrongs of the case, the reaction was almost inevitable. For the Evangelists clearly could not be credited simply as collectors of tradition. They had to be recognized as editors and authors in their own right. It does not take much comparison between the Synoptic Gospels to recognize both how stable the basic tradition was and how adaptable it was to each Evangelist's different emphases and concerns. In the sequence of 'criticisms' it was natural to designate this last addition to the pile of critical tools as 'redaction criticism', that is, the study of the way in which the Evangelists redacted the tradition which came to them. The litany of names recited at this point always includes Bornkamm (Matthew), Marxsen (Mark), and Conzelmann (Luke).

The value of redaction criticism for an understanding of the history of tradition is precisely its confirmation that the process of passing on the tradition involved creative ordering, adaptation and elaboration of the tradition. The tradition at the stage of literary dependence was still not fixed but adaptable to the needs of the churches as perceived by the Evangelists. At the same time, we need to note again the weakness of the assumption which came in with redacton criticism — viz. that the Evangelist in his redaction had in view only or primarily the needs of a particular community. Such an assumption runs counter to the indications of a commonality or even large-scale consensus of Jesus tradition across many/(most/all) churches in the Mediterranean region (§2.9). The more appropriate image is not of different composers of different works, but of different variations on the common themes, outlines and emphases of the shared foundation tradition.

§5.6. Narrative Criticism

Another weakness of redaction criticism has been its tendency to focus attention on the points of redaction as the surest and clearest indications of the Evangelists' theological and ecclesiastical concerns. The result here too was inevitable and predictable: the Gospels should rather be treated as a whole, the emphases of particular passages determined more by the function of these passages within the whole (within the individual Gospel's 'plot') than by comparison of these passages with the parallel passages in other Gospels. The point has been well made, and 'narrative criticism' has produced its own textbooks in turn (e.g. Powell). Indeed, the end of the twentieth century sees a whole scholarly and publishing industry in the business of producing 'readings' of the various books of the NT.

The danger in this case is that the heavy focus on the particular document in itself will abstract it too much from the process of tradition. It is all very well to emphasise 'the world of the text' as the primary context for exegesis of individual passages, so long as the world of the text is itself not abstracted from the historical context within which the text emerged. Nor can (or should) readings of the text divorce themselves from the history of tradition and from the history of the text's influence (Wirkungsgeschichte), since it is often this awareness of the history of the tradition which gives the text its resonance for the informed reader/hearer.

A form of narrative criticism can also be applied to the rest of the NT writings — Acts obviously (Tannehill), but also the epistles. In the latter case, the narrative in view is the story of God's dealings with humankind, Israel in particular, and climaxing in Jesus and the inauguration of the new epoch of salvation (e.g. Hays, *Faith,* and Witherington). Here the resonances of tradition are deep indeed, often beyond normal hearing. In this case the danger is that the narrative can become a composite construction or abstraction compiled from other texts which then provides a kind of control over how the NT text should be heard.

§5.7. Rhetorical Criticism

Equally active in the last two decades of the twentieth century, and particularly in reference to the NT epistles, has been rhetorical criticism (e.g. Betz, Kennedy). The primary concern in this case has been to bring to bear on the letters the light which ancient rhetorical practice provides. In what ways, with what tricks and techniques did, for example, Paul endeavour to persuade his audiences in churches round the Aegean and further afield? Here the value for us is a further means of clarifying and coming to a better understanding of how and why Paul adapted his traditions, including his own formulations in earlier letters. The tradition was 'hellenized' not simply in conceptual terms (as became increasingly the case during the Patristic period), but also and already in the communicative idiom in which it was expressed by Paul and the other writers of the NT letters.

The dangers here have been similar to those in form criticism. Particularly in regard to the various forms of persuasive speech — judicial (to persuade in relation to the past), deliberative (to persuade in relation to the future), or epideictic (usually in praise or blame of someone). For there has been a tendency to assume that these were fixed forms, with Paul's intention in disputed passages too much determined by that assumption. Whereas a clearer appreciation of the living character of Paul's gospel and tradition would have facilitated a sounder recognition of Paul's readiness to adapt form as well as content to the situation addressed. Equally misleading has been the assumption that there was a uniform rhetorical system in antiquity; for example, Betz himself did not know what to make of the paraenetical section in Galatians, since there was no place for exhortation in what he took to be an example of judicial rhetoric. In actual practice, however, as R. D. Anderson has pointed out, ancient rhetoric was much more supple. In rhetorical analysis the interplay of topoi or motifs is much more significant for understanding the dynamic of Paul's theological handling of earlier tradition than the possibility of giving the letter a particular rhetorical label.

§5.8. Canonical Criticism

Finally we should mention 'canonical criticism'. In one sense it actually spans the history of the modern investigation of NT tradition. For since so much of the early modern history of NT scholarship is Protestant in character, it is not surprising that an important early concern was to demonstrate the authority of the NT writings. It was, after all, the authority of the NT which provided the counter to the authority of Catholic tradition. So the early great commentaries on the NT documents saw it as important to be able to establish that the writings had been deservedly recognized as canonical. And if the traditional criteria of apostolic authorship proved questionable (Who wrote Hebrews? was an unresolvable question), that simply encouraged the scrutiny of external attestation as well as internal characteristics. In this, of course, it was being assumed that church tradition, the tradition of the document's reception within the churches of the Patristic period, could help establish the authority of the document within the churches and their tradition. Modern commentators rarely feel the need to re-do all this work since it was done so well by their predecessors; that is one of the reasons why the older classic commentaries still hold an honourable place within the libraries of theological institutions.

In its more recent usage, however, 'canonical criticism' is usually understood as referring to an interpretation of the individual NT document which reads it within the NT as a whole (particularly Childs, and differently J. A. Sanders). In this the definitive moment within the NT tradition is consciously shifted from the moment of composition (the intention of the author) and the moment of reception (how it was received by the original recipients) to the 'moment' of canonisation, or, better, to the context provided by canonisation. In so doing it is assumed that the canon provides the determinative interpretative context: that, for example, readings of 1 Corinthians which do not take account of the Pastoral Epistles, or readings of the Synoptic Gospels which do not take account of John's Gospel, should by that token command the less authority; or indeed that OT monotheism has to be understood as the starting point and context for NT christology, or that the OT prophetic concern for the poor remains a constant for NT ethics.

Such canonical criticism may in effect be assuming a roundedness of the NT (the Holy Spirit building in checks and balances in the composition of the NT, as it were) which is less than clear. And it may invite the mistake in turn of abstracting the NT from the flow of the history of the tradition. We have already noted the ongoing debate about the limits of the NT; if the text of the NT is not as fixed as some would like to be able to assume, neither are the boundaries of the canon (§4.2); Childs himself speaks of 'the church's ongoing *search* for the Christian Bible' (*Biblical Theology* 67). At the same time, the wisdom which recognized the importance of canonising the diversity of the NT witness, including four versions of the Gospel (Dunn, 'John and the Synoptics') and the Apocalypse of John within the one canon, has to be commended. Both the process of canonizing the NT and the canon itself, properly appreciated, are valuable witnesses to the character of Christian tradition, both in the tentativeness of some of the judgments made (regarding canonical status of particular documents) as well as in the firmness with which the *sensus fidelium* has affirmed the others. Ambiguity and fuzziness around the edges are an integral and essential part of Christianity's canonical tradition and heritage.

§6. Conclusion

One of the most striking features to emerge from this study is the amazing consistency of the history of NT tradition, the tradition which gave birth to the NT, the tradition which is the NT, and the tradition *(Wirkungsgeschichte)* as which, within which and through which the NT continues to be heard meaningfully.

(1) We began with a tradition which was both the verbalised impact of the ministry of Jesus and of a consequently fresh encounter with the OT tradition. From the first, in other words, the tradition was a matter of hearing and retelling. It encapsulated the impact made by Jesus, first by his life and teaching, and then also by his death and resurrection, and effected to convey that impact to others.

(2) If the process described above has any closeness to reality, the mode of retelling, of transmission, combined a stable core and substance with a variation and variety for the particular occasion. Typically, the particularities did not become part of the tradition (fresh layers of tradition), but examples of how the tradition might be retold; typically the retellings would be fresh remintings of the core and substance. In consequence the heart and fundamental thrust of the tradition and its various expressions were maintained through the process of transmission.

(3) The same features (stable core with occasional variations) can be seen in the post-Easter tradition (kerygmatic, liturgical and ethical). They ap-

pear in the Gospels themselves — presented to us precisely not as four Gospels, but as the one gospel according to four fundamentally coherent and complementary versions, united by common tradition and common Gospel shape. They appear also in the rest of the NT writings, exemplified by Paul in his several expressions of a gospel which is both coherent and contingent (Beker). And they appear, not least, in the continuing history of the NT tradition, where it is precisely the NT which encapsulates the stable, coherent and normative core within the ongoing tradition.

In other words, (4) the traditioning process did not alter in essential character throughout the history of the NT tradition. The various transitions — from one language to another, from oral to written text, from source to document, from individual writings to canon — affected the tradition in various ways, and over all mark an increasing stability in the tradition. But the flexibility of the retelling (in preaching, teaching and practice) which was always there from the first, and the possibility of a revelatory moment which was always there from the first in the hearing even of older forms of the tradition, has remained a consistent feature of the history throughout.

These observations have important theological implications. For they remind us that the revelatory word of God is not something fixed and final, is not to be simply identified with particular words or with a particular form of the tradition frozen in time (even the NT as such). Were it so, then the tradition would have been something fixed and final, beyond modification and improvement, simply to be transmitted lock, stock and barrel from one generation to the next. Were it so, then hearing would be simply reception of words with univocal meaning, there would be no room for diverse interpretations, and the different hearings of the different denominations and different ages would be heresy and blasphemy.

In contrast, the history of the NT tradition reminds us that while the core and substance of the tradition remains stable through time and multiple retellings, the forms it takes are diverse and variable. And precisely because there must be hearing as well as retelling if the tradition is to be received, there is inevitably a degree of intangibility in the word of God, a coming to be as authoritative word in each effective hearing. It is just this appreciation of the history of tradition as a dynamic process which helps prevent the written or spoken word becoming an idol which is overvalued and frees the hearing to be open to the word within the words, the good news which still comes through the tradition in all its various forms.

Bibliography

Aland, K. and B. 2d ed. 1989, *The Text of the New Testament,* Grand Rapids: Eerdmans

Anderson, Ø. 1991, "Oral Tradition," in H. Wansbrough, ed., *Jesus and the Oral Gospel Tradition,* JSNTSup 64, Sheffield: Sheffield Academic, 17-58

Anderson, R. D. 1996, *Ancient Rhetorical Theory and Paul,* Kampen: Kok Pharos

Bailey, K. 1991, "Informal Controlled Oral Tradition and the Synoptic Gospels," *Asia Journal of Theology* 5:34-54

Bailey, K. 1995, "Middle Eastern Oral Tradition and the Synoptic Gospels," *ExpT* 106:363-67

Bauckham, R. 1998, "For Whom Were Gospels Written?" in R. Bauckham, ed., *The Gospels for All Christians: Rethinking the Gospel Audiences,* Grand Rapids: Eerdmans, 9-48

Bauckham, R. 1999, *James,* London: Routledge

Beker, J. C. 1980, *Paul the Apostle: The Triumph of God in Life and Thought,* Philadelphia: Fortress

Betz, H. D. 1999, *Galatians,* Hermeneia; Philadelphia: Fortress

Bornkamm, H. G., G. Barth, and H. J. Held. 1963, *Tradition and Interpretation in Matthew,* London: SCM

Bruce, F. F. 1997, *Tradition Old and New,* Exeter: Paternoster

Bultmann, R. 1934, *Jesus and the Word,* New York: Scribner's

Bultmann, R. 1963, *The History of the Synoptic Tradition,* Oxford: Blackwell

Burridge, R. A. 1992, *What Are the Gospels? A Comparison with Graeco-Roman Biography,* SNTSMS 70, Cambridge: Cambridge University

Charlesworth, J. H. 1983, 1985, *Old Testament Pseudepigrapha,* London: Darton, Longman & Todd

Childs, B. S. 1985, *The New Testament as Canon: An Introduction,* Philadelphia: Fortress

Childs, B. S. 1992, *Biblical Theology of the Old and New Testaments,* London: SCM

Conzelmann, H. 1960, *The Theology of Saint Luke,* London: Faber and Faber

Dibelius, M. 1934, *From Tradition to Gospel,* London: Nicholson and Watson

Dibelius, M. 1937, *A Fresh Approach to the New Testament and Early Christian Literature,* London: Nicholson & Watson

Dodd, C. H. 1936, *The Apostolic Preaching and Its Developments,* London: Hodder & Stoughton

Dodd, C. H. 1952, *According to the Scriptures: The Substructure of New Testament Theology,* London: Nisbet

Dunn, J. D. G. 1977-78/1998, "Prophetic 'I'-Sayings and the Jesus Tradition: The Importance of Testing Prophetic Utterances within Early Christianity," *NTS* 24: 175-98, repr. in *The Christ and the Spirit,* vol. 2: *Pneumatology,* Grand Rapids: Eerdmans/ Edinburgh: T. & T. Clark, 142-69

Dunn, J. D. G. 1982, "Levels of Canonical Authority," *HBT* 4:13-60, repr. in *The Living Word,* London: SPCK; Philadelphia: Fortress, 141-74, 186-92

Dunn, J. D. G. 2d ed. 1990, *Unity and Diversity in the New Testament,* London: SCM

Dunn, J. D. G. 1991/1998, "Let John Be John: A Gospel for Its Time," in P. Stuhlmacher, ed., *The Gospel and the Gospels,* Grand Rapids: Eerdmans, 293-322, repr. in *The Christ and the Spirit,* vol. 1: *Christology.* Grand Rapids: Eerdmans/Edinburgh: T. & T. Clark, 345-75

Dunn, J. D. G. 1991, "John and the Oral Gospel Tradition," in H. Wansbrough, ed., *Jesus and the Oral Gospel Tradition,* JSNTSup 64, Sheffield: Sheffield Academic, 351-79

Dunn, J. D. G. 1996, "John and the Synoptics as a Theological Question," in R. A. Culpepper and C. C. Black, eds., *Exploring the Gospel of John,* D. M. Smith Festschrift, Louisville: Westminster John Knox, 301-13

Dunn, J. D. G. 1998, *The Theology of Paul the Apostle,* Grand Rapids: Eerdmans/Edinburgh: T. & T. Clark

Dunn, J. D. G. 2003, *Christianity in the Making,* vol. 1: *Jesus Remembered,* Grand Rapids: Eerdmans

Dunn, J. D. G. 2003, "Altering the Default Setting: Re-envisaging the Early Transmission of the Jesus Tradition," *NTS* 49:139-75

Dupont, J. 1964, *The Sources of the Acts,* New York: Herder/London: Darton, Longman & Todd

Ehrman, B. D. 1993, *The Orthodox Corruption of Scripture: The Effect of Early Christological Controversies on the Text of the New Testament,* New York/Oxford: Oxford University

Elliott, J. K. 1993, *The Apocryphal New Testament,* Oxford: Clarendon

Ellis, E. E. 1978, "New Directions in Form Criticism," in *Prophecy and Hermeneutic in Early Christianity: New Testament Essays,* Tübingen: Mohr/Grand Rapids: Eerdmans, 237-53

Evans, C. F. 1956, "The Kerygma," *JTS* 7:25-41

Furnish, V. P. 2003, 'Letters in the New Testament', in J. D. G. Dunn and J. W. Rogerson, eds., *Eerdmans Commentary on the Bible,* Grand Rapids: Eerdmans, 1268-76

Gadamer, H. G. 2d ed. 1990, *Truth and Method,* New York: Crossroad

Gerhardsson, B. 1961, *Memory and Manuscript: Oral Tradition and Written Transmission in Rabbinic Judaism and Early Christianity,* Lund: Gleerup

Gerhardsson, B. 1964, *Tradition and Transmission in Early Christianity,* Lund: Gleerup

Gerhardsson, B. 1979, *The Origins of the Gospel Traditions,* Philadelphia: Fortress/London: SCM

Gerhardsson, B. 1986, *The Gospel Tradition,* Lund: Gleerup

Hays, R. B. 1983, *The Faith of Jesus Christ: An Investigation of the Narrative Substructure of Galatians 3.1–4.11,* Chico: Scholars

Hays, R. B. 1989, *Echoes of Scripture in the Letters of Paul,* New Haven: Yale University

Hofius, O. 1991, "Unknown Sayings of Jesus," in P. Stuhlmacher, ed., *The Gospel and the Gospels,* Grand Rapids: Eerdmans, 336-60

Hunter, A. M. 2d ed. 1961, *Paul and His Predecessors,* London: SCM

Johnson, L. T. 1996, *The Real Jesus: The Misguided Quest for the Historical Jesus and the Truth of the Traditional Gospels,* San Francisco: Harper

Juel, D. 1998, *Messianic Exegesis: Christological Interpretation of the Old Testament in Early Christianity,* Philadelphia: Fortress

Kähler, M. 1892, 1964, *The So-called Historical Jesus and the Historic Biblical Christ,* Philadelphia: Fortress

Käsemann, E. 1964, "Is the Gospel Objective?" in *Essays on New Testament Themes*, London: SCM

Kelber, W. H. 1983, *The Oral Tradition and the Written Gospel*, Philadelphia: Fortress

Kennedy, G. A. 1984, *New Testament Interpretation through Rhetorical Criticism*, Chapel Hill, N.C.: University of North Carolina

Kramer, W. 1966, *Christ, Lord, Son of God*, London: SCM

Kümmel, W. G. 1975, *Introduction to the New Testament*, Nashville: Abingdon/London: SCM

Lindars, B. 1961, *New Testament Apologetic*, London: SCM

Lord, A. B. 1978, "The Gospels as Oral Traditional Literature," in W. O. Walker, ed., *The Relationships among the Gospels*, San Antonio, Tex.: Trinity University, 33-91

Marxsen, W. 1969, *Mark the Evangelist*, Nashville: Abingdon

Marxsen, W. 1972, *The New Testament as the Church's Book*, Philadelphia: Fortress

Meade, D. 1986, *Pseudonymity and Canon: An Investigation into the Relationship of Authorship and Authority in Jewish and Earliest Christian Tradition*, WUNT 39, Tübingen: Mohr-Siebeck

Meyendorff, J. 1978, *Living Tradition: Orthodox Witness in the Contemporary World*, Crestwood, N.Y.: St. Vladimir's Seminary

Moule, C. F. D. 3d ed. 1981, *The Birth of the New Testament*, London: A. & C. Black

Parker, D. C. 1997, *The Living Text of the Gospels*, Cambridge: Cambridge University

Pokorný, P. 1987, *The Genesis of Christology: Foundations for a Theology of the New Testament*, Edinburgh: T. & T. Clark

Powell, M. A. 1990, *What Is Narrative Criticism?* Minneapolis: Fortress

Rosner, B. S. 1994, *Paul, Scripture and Ethics: A Study of 1 Corinthians 5-7*, Leiden: Brill

Sanders, E. P. 1969, *The Tendencies of the Synoptic Tradition*, SNTSMS 9, Cambridge: Cambridge University

Sanders, J. A. 1984, *Canon and Community: A Guide to Canonical Criticism*, Philadelphia: Fortress

Scott, J. M. C. 2003, 'John', in J. D. G. Dunn and J. W. Rogerson, eds., *Eerdmans Commentary on the Bible*, Grand Rapids: Eerdmans, 1161-1212

Tannehill, R. C. 1986, 1990, *The Narrative Unity of Luke-Acts: A Literary Interpretation*, Philadelphia: Fortress

Theissen, G. 1987, *The Shadow of the Galilean: The Quest of the Historical Jesus in Narrative Form*, London: SCM

Trocmé, E. 1973, *Jesus and His Contemporaries*, London: SCM

Tuckett, C. M. 2003, 'Introduction to the Gospels', in J. D. G. Dunn and J. W. Rogerson, eds., *Eerdmans Commentary on the Bible*, Grand Rapids: Eerdmans, 989-99

Wansbrough, H., ed. 1991, *Jesus and the Oral Gospel Tradition*, JSNTSup 64, Sheffield: Sheffield Academic

Witherington, B. 1994, *Paul's Narrative Thought World*, Louisville: Westminster/John Knox.

CHAPTER 15

Living Tradition

A Birthday Gift to Henry Wansbrough

For more than four hundred years Protestant and Catholic have been divided on the subject of 'Scripture and Tradition'. To put it (over)simply: at the heart of the Reformation was an appeal to scripture over against the traditions of the mediaeval Church. The criticism was in essence that ecclesiastical tradition had moved too far from the doctrines and practices of the apostles, as definitively set down in the New Testament (NT). It is this role of the NT in serving as the canon by which subsequent developments in Christian faith and praxis are to be evaluated and criticized which Protestants continue to count as fundamental in the 'Scripture versus Tradition' debate. On the Catholic side of the debate the crucial starting point is the perception that the meaning of scripture is by no means always clear and has to be interpreted. In these circumstances the teaching office of the Church has to be determinative of the meaning; otherwise the authority of scripture would in effect be hijacked for every idiosyncratic reading of the NT texts, as the fissiparity of Protestantism and the contemporary explosion of new churches attest.

Central to the Protestant side of the debate has been the sense of the 'fixity' of scripture, the sense that scripture provides a fixed point of reference. Over against a changing, developing tradition stood the NT texts fixed in writing, a stable 'given', the canon closed. Here was a firm and already final authority which all could read for themselves; to exalt the magisterium to the status of equal authority was to compromise and detract from the unique authority of the NT canon.

It is, however, this very contrast, between a fixed scripture and a changing tradition, which has come into increasing question over the period of debate, and particularly in the last few decades. Or to be more precise, the sense of a clearly delimited canonical text and a final authoritative meaning to be read from the text have become more problematic, and so the stable basis of the Protestant position has become problematic.

Of course the Protestant/Catholic debate can be seen at this point as a particular expression of the transformations in perception occasioned first by the Enlightenment and now by post-modernism. The former could be seen as intervening on the Protestant side of the debate — a natural extension of Renaissance and Reformation. The reaction against tradition and the search for historical origins and original meanings seemed at first to support the Protestant claim that apostolic meaning and apostolic age could be clearly perceived, and clearly perceived to be univocal in content and significance. While the latter, in calling into radical question both a historicist perception of the past and the univocity of all speech, seems at first sight completely to undermine that Protestant perspective. If meaning depends on the reading community within which the NT text is read, then the community of the Church can properly claim to determine the meaning to be heard by the members of that community. The trouble is that in a post-modern world all claims to stable meaning and single authority are called in question. So to mount a defence of one over against the other is simply to reinstate the debate in its older terms and to return to the cul-de-sac into which it had long ago entered.

Having reflected on the debate off and on for most of my academic career, a conviction has steadily grown and developed within my thinking that a positive way forward out of any such impasse is to perceive scripture and the NT in particular as 'living tradition'. What I mean by this should become clear as I try to outline my thinking below. But perhaps I should say at once that to reconfigure the older debate into the single phrase, 'living tradition', is intended to be equally affirmative of the points of lasting value on both sides of the debate and equally critical of others. In any event, the attempt is made with a sense of indebtedness to, respect for and friendship with one who understands well both sides of the debate and who will appreciate what I am trying to say, however inadequate my words may be to the task.

My basic thesis is that the scriptural texts embody and crystallize a perception (I am happy to say a God-given perception) of God and of his dealings with humankind which was expressed through the words of these texts, but never to be simply identified with them. Perhaps the most basic of all Israel's insights was that God could not be imaged. The reality of God escaped and transcended all human representation: 'You shall not make for yourself an idol' (Ex. 20.4). But the same applies to the words with which humans speak of God (or hear God speaking). The Word of God transcends and escapes all human words. To identify the two *tout simple* is to make an idol of what should be an icon. To insist that any particular wording or phrase is the only way in which a word from God or an insight into God and his dealings with humankind can be expressed is to make an idol. To insist that any such wording or phrase can or is to be heard in only one way and must evoke a strictly uniform meaning is to make an idol. A fundamentalist, whether a scripture-fundamentalist or a tradition-fundamentalist, has locked the Word of God into human words or praxis, and is in effect worshipping an idol.

The reality is that the authoritative word for the people of God was never single nor uniform, never fixed nor unchanging. From the first it was a living word, which came to expression in diverse words and in changing terms and practices. This is what I will try to demonstrate and illustrate in what follows. (1) I will draw attention, first, to the canonical tradition behind the Old Testament (OT); then (2) ask how final was the final form of the text. (3) My appreciation of living tradition has been given much richer content by recent work on the oral tradition behind the Gospels. (4) Even though many of the letters of the NT would seem to be restricted by the historical particularity in and for which they were written, the same quality of living tradition attaches to them also. (5) Textual critics have recently joined in by observing that they are dealing not with a fixed text into which mistakes have crept, but a more fluid text constituted by variations, as far back as can be discerned. (6) The diversity of modern translations makes the same point even more clearly. (7) Finally, not least the developing science and art of hermeneutics has reminded us forcefully that meaning is in some degree at least the product of interaction between reader and text and not simply of the text alone and therefore inherently diverse.

I

None of the OT writings should be seen as a once-for-all product of a single inspired (or inspiring) writer. None of them should be seen as coming into existence *de novo,* as a creation *ex nihilo.* Each and every one is, in differing degrees, an aggregation and consolidation of earlier material. Thus no serious scholar today regards the Pentateuch as anything other than the end product of a long process stretching over several centuries. That Moses was a key figure in that process can be maintained with some confidence. But behind Moses there was already tradition from the patriarchal period. Units surviving from different stages of the process can be readily distinguished — for example, the Song of Moses (Ex. 15), 'the Book of the Covenant' (Ex. 21–23), the creed of Deut. 26.5-9. And most would agree that it was only in the post-exilic period, under the influence of Ezra, that the Pentateuch assumed more or less its present canonical shape. Likewise the prophets are typically collections of oracles (and other material) spoken out over a longer period. Few today would hold that the prophecy of Isaiah was singly authored; the three Isaiahs are likely to have spanned two or three centuries The Psalms may have begun as a definitive collection of religious poetry and worship with king David; but no one doubts that the present book of Psalms is a much more extensive collection, again spanning several centuries. And the bulk of the Wisdom literature similarly is best understood as a sequence of aphoristic and commonplace rules for good living, not all exclusively Israel's, collected over time.

The point is that it was not the writing down of this material or its final editing which first gave it an authority which it had not previously possessed. There is an important parallel here with the subsequent process of canonization. Despite casual assertion to the contrary, by recognizing these texts as 'canon', the Church did not give these texts canonical authority for the first time, except in a formal sense. Rather, canonization was a recognition and acknowledgment of the canonical authority which these texts were *already* exercising; they were already being cherished as providing a definitively authoritative rule for faith and life. Had they not been accorded that authority previously they would not have been candidates for canonization in the first place. So it was with the pre-OT traditions which were not only incorporated into the OT, but which, in developed form, became the OT. It was not the 'inscripturation' of these pre-OT traditions which gave them authority as scripture. Rather, it was because they were already functioning as authoritative for life and worship that they formed the warp of the further reflections and editing which became what we know today as the OT texts.

This is what I mean by 'living tradition'. What was first heard as 'word of God', to patriarch, prophet, psalmist, etc., was not at once written down, put in a box, and preserved inviolate for future generations. On the contrary, without ceasing to be word of God, these earliest encounters with the divine stimulated further insight, became the vehicle for further revelation, enabled devotees to hear fresh words from God. Each OT writing was not a once-only and only-then inspired writing, but the climax of a process of hearing and responding to what God was being heard to say. The tensions within and among the texts are testimony to the varied ways in which God's word was apprehended and to how changing circumstances called forth different perceptions of what God was saying afresh. But the earlier words were not abandoned as *passé* or regarded as outmoded, even the prophecies which had failed or been realized only in part. Instead they were the generative seed which flowered into renewed expressions and mutated into different forms. Their preservation within the OT texts bears witness to the lasting influence of the fountainheads of canonical authority — Moses, Isaiah, David, Solomon, etc. But the OT equally attests that their authority was not limited to their own time, but stimulated the further reflection and speaking, the further writing and editing which in due course became the OT.

II

The final form of the OT writings did not end the process. The living tradition which had built up into the OT did not cease to be living from that point/ these points onwards. The very problem of defining what the OT is, and when it became finalized as the OT, reminds us just how *un*fixed is the very concept of the 'OT'.

The most obvious manifestation of the problem is the variation between the Hebrew Bible and the Septuagint (LXX), the Greek Bible. I have used the term 'Old Testament' thus far much too loosely, principally because I am writing from a Christian perspective, and partly because it was inappropriate to raise the issue too soon. But now we have to face up to the fact that the 'OT' strictly speaking does not have a single form. The Hebrew Bible had become authoritative scripture by the century before Jesus — 'the law and the prophets and the other books of our ancestors' (Sir. Prologue; 4QMMT C10); the 22 books of sacred scripture (Josephus, *Apion* 1.37-43) — at least for Palestinian Jews. But for the great body of Jews in the western diaspora, whose *lingua franca* was no doubt Greek, it was the LXX which functioned as Bible, as scripture; this included the overwhelming majority of the early Christians. Moreover, the LXX includes more writings than the Hebrew Bible, writings like Tobit and Judith, the Wisdom of Jesus ben Sira (Ecclesiasticus) and 1-2 Maccabees. The flow of inspiration had not ceased; an authority of near equivalence to canonical authority was accorded to them too; ben Sira was nearly included in the canon of Jewish scripture. Moreover, the LXX clearly attests the phenomenon of earlier tradition/scripture elaborated or reformulated which we can deduce from the OT itself — the priestly revision of the Pentateuch, the different slant on Israel's history provided by Chronicles. For the LXX includes additional material for the books of Daniel and Esther, and a further Psalm (151). The law and the prophets were by then more or less stable, but the third division (the writings) still had fluid boundaries. The tradition continued to live. All this is directly relevant to the Protestant/Catholic debate, since the extra material in the LXX is apocrypha, considered by Protestants to be distinct from the OT and non-canonical, but incorporated into Catholic editions of the OT.

Less widely appreciated is the testimony of the OT pseudepigrapha and the Dead Sea Scrolls. For both attest the vigour of a fresh stream of revelatory insight which only just touched the OT proper (Daniel), which was evidently flowing with full effect in the centuries spanning the BC/AD divide, and which clearly affected Jesus and the first Christians to a significant degree. I refer to what is commonly described as 'Jewish apocalyptic'. For example, the collection of writings put together as 1 Enoch influenced Daniel, the Qumran sect, at least one level of the Gospel tradition, is a precursor for the Christian canonical apocalypse (Revelation), and is cited as with prophetic authority by Jude 14-15 (1 Enoch 1.9). The book of Jubilees and the Qumran Temple scroll are now generally regarded as attempts to rewrite scripture, the former Genesis 1 to Exodus 14, the latter legislative material in Exodus to Deuteronomy. And the Dead Sea Scrolls include the sect's own psalms (1QH) and the incomplete Psalm scroll from Cave 11 with seven non-canonical poems interspersed among the canonical psalms (11QPs^a).

In all this any simple division between scripture and tradition quickly erodes and begins to disappear. Previously it was fairly easy to regard scripture as fixed, in final canonical form, so that what came afterwards is clearly demarcated as reaction to, and interaction with, the scriptural given, as *interpretation* formally different and distinct from the *inspiration* which produced the texts now to be interpreted. For now in the pseudepigrapha and Dead Sea Scrolls we see the text itself, acknowledged as scripturally authoritative, nevertheless being modified and supplemented, as the *interpretation* is in effect given the authority attributed to the text (most clearly in the Qumran pesher on Habakkuk). The living word of God was evidently being heard not so much in the text itself, but in the interpreted text; the text, through its interpretation, still spoke with word of God authority. None of this should surprise us, for this was what the Pharisees were doing as the oral Torah began to supplement the written Torah, and the traditions of the fathers came to have *de facto* scriptural authority in matters of daily praxis (cf. Gal. 1.14).

More to the point, Jesus' own use of scripture, as attested for example in Mark 10.2-9 and 12.24-31, indicates one who was ready to hear God's word in scripture but in fresh ways, and in dialogue with his contemporaries equally seeking to discern God's word. The first Christians in effect operated in like manner — Paul, for example, joining with his Pharisaic contemporaries in the interpretation of texts like Gen. 15.6, Lev. 18.5 and Hab. 2.4; and like them, regarding his interpreted text as the authoritative scripture. The word of God was being heard through these scriptural texts, true enough; but the word of God was the interpreted text, the text as living tradition. So, the puzzle as to where texts like Matt. 2.23, 1 Cor. 2.9 and Jas. 4.5 were drawn from becomes of less importance if we are willing to recognize a living tradition through which God's word was heard but which was not simply coterminous with the already acknowledged scriptures.

III

Nowhere is it clearer that the canonical form of the text was not perceived as the beginning and end of the inspiration which gave that text scriptural authority, than in the case of the NT Gospels. For clearly the Gospels are the end product of a process stretching between the ministry of Jesus himself and the actual writing of the Gospels — a period spanning some 40 to 70 years. No one really doubts that the initial stage of the process was oral tradition. However early we may feel able to date the first writing down of some of the Jesus tradition, the great bulk of that tradition probably circulated in oral forms for some twenty years. For most of the Synoptic tradition at least, Jesus was *remembered*, not recorded or interviewed with a written transcript to follow.

Recent studies of oral culture have brought home more clearly what that would have meant. For the prevailing characteristic of oral tradition is its flexibility. The same stories are retold with seemingly endless variation; the substance or core or gist of the story is stable, but the detail can vary with each telling. The same teaching is repeated in seemingly endless permutations and combinations, with varying emphases presumably deemed appropriate to the differing circumstances in which performance of the tradition takes place. Traditional material is expanded and elaborated, or contracted and treated in summary fashion. So we may speculate with the Jesus tradition. Teaching was not regarded as something fixed in the final form in which Jesus gave it out; almost certainly he repeated much of his most important teaching in varied forms and wording. This was how teachers taught, then as today. Likewise, stories about Jesus were not fixed in a final form by some single authoritative witness; different witnesses with differing perspectives would have reported the same episode in differing terms. This is how reporting happened, then as today. Nor was the material cherished as a kind of relic, its joints and sinews fixed in *rigor mortis*, processed in the equivalent of a reliquary, to be venerated from a respectful distance. The material was the lifeblood of the earliest congregations, providing information about the one they called Lord, and guidance on matters of belief and worship, relationships and conduct. It was living tradition in that it was the tradition by which they lived. That was why it took such varied and changing forms — because it was their tradition, because they lived by it, because it spoke to their changing circumstances, and the changing circumstances are reflected in the changing forms in which the tradition has come down to us. Hence, for example, the differing emphases with which Jesus' teaching on divorce or on the laws of purity, by Mark and by Matthew respectively (Mark 7.15, 19/Matt. 15.17; Mark 10.9/Matt. 19.9). But the basic point is immediately evident when one looks at a Synopsis of the first three Gospels with any care.

It should not be assumed that the writing down of Jesus tradition somehow ended the flexibility of the oral period or froze the stream of tradition once for all. For the oral tradition continued after Mark and the others had extracted the material they wanted for their Gospels. The forms of Jesus tradition echoed in later books of the NT and in the apostolic fathers indicate a knowledge of Jesus tradition not derived from any written source available to us. Moreover, in a non-literate culture (most of the early Christians would have been illiterate) knowledge of any written Gospel itself would have come through hearing rather than reading. Their own use of, and reference to, a written Gospel would have been an example of 'second orality'. Nor should it be assumed that the writing of one of the Gospels was radically different from an oral performance of the Jesus tradition. On the contrary, to take one instance, the Gospel of Mark can be readily seen as a written example of an oral performance — written to be heard rather than to be read. The particular variations of the Jesus tradition which the written Gospels enshrine should be taken more as examples of *how* the tradition was performed rather than as defining the way in which it should be performed or as the only legitimate form of the Gospel.

The preceding paragraphs, naturally, are somewhat speculative, since all our evidence regarding the use and transmission of the Jesus tradition comes down to us, of course, only or already in writing. But the same point can be made anyway by reference to the Gospels themselves. For whatever the reason, the Gospels attest the same sort of flexibility which I attribute to, and largely explain by reference to, the orality of the Jesus tradition in the earliest phase of transmission. It is an observation of enduring significance which has not been given the weight it deserves: that the gospel of Jesus Christ has come down to us not in a single form, as though the one gospel could be told or preached in only one way, as though its authority depended on a fixity and strict uniformity of content and form. The Gospels are the gospel (singular) indeed, but the Gospel according to Matthew, the Gospel according to Mark, and so on. And none of the four is precisely the same. The same gospel in basic structure (beginning with the Baptist and ending with the passion) and overall substance, yes. But not in the detailed content of each. This is simply to recognize that the gospel, written as well as preached (or expressed in practice), was a living form; it adapted to differing and changing circumstances. This is both attested and validated by the testimony of the scriptural texts themselves. By the wisdom of God's Spirit the Church did not canonize only one gospel form, or a single composite form, but *four diverse* forms. It was not a case of 'one fits all', or 'all must fit to the one'. Rather, the gospel was seen as a living tradition which could and evidently did speak with differing emphases to differing contexts and situations. The good news of Jesus Christ was from the first a living tradition.

IV

The letters of the NT can be seen in a similar way. It is true that the letters of Paul in particular are the nearest we have in the NT, perhaps in the Bible as a whole, to occasional literature, that is documents written for a specific context and for specific purposes. So they are not fluid and flexible in the same way as the Jesus tradition. But the same living quality attaches to them nonetheless.

For one thing there are sufficient hints that Paul intended some at least of his letters for more than one audience; he instructed that the letter to the Colossians should be read also in the church at Laodicea, and the letter to Laodicea should be read also in Colossae (Col. 4.16). So he recognized that even the particularity of letters to individual churches could be heard with relevance more widely. Moreover, the fact that most of his letters were retained by the churches to which he wrote suggests also that they were not read once only and then forgotten, but functioned as a resource to which the churches referred and on which they drew as the churches grew and developed. Moreover, it cannot have been long before copies of the letters were being more widely circulated and gathered into a collection, for the same reason: even the most targeted of contents could be heard with relevance more widely.

In addition, as with the OT, we can readily discern Paul's use of and dependency on earlier tradition. We need only think of such passages as 1 Cor. 11.23-26 and 15.3-7. It is true that he insists that his gospel came to him direct from God (Gal. 1.12); but it is equally evident that he thereby refers to his understanding of the gospel *as for Gentiles* as well as Jews, and to be received *by faith alone* ('the truth of the gospel' — Gal. 2.5, 14). He makes a point of stressing that his gospel, the gospel for the uncircumcision, was fully acknowledged by the pillar apostles in Jerusalem as gospel, as a valid expression of the gospel (Gal. 2.7-9). In other words, it was central to Paul's understanding of the gospel that it was not something static and unchanging, but living and malleable, able to be experienced as 'the power of God for salvation' (Rom. 1.16) by different peoples in their different circumstances.

Paul treated the tradition of Jesus' life and teaching in the same way. He quoted it when necessary, as in the case of Jesus' teaching on divorce, thereby indicating its abiding authority for him, but went on immediately to indicate that the circumstances he was confronting in the church at Corinth necessitated some modification of Jesus' teaching (1 Cor. 7.10-16). At other times, echoes of, and allusions to, Jesus' teaching (e.g. Rom. 12.14; 14.14; 1 Cor. 13.2; 1 Thess. 5.2, 4) indicate no concern to distinguish that teaching as something inviolate, given special weight as stemming from Jesus, and therefore requiring attribution to him as the authority. On the contrary, the teaching has been absorbed into the life-blood of Christian paraenesis and is used not by evoking some instruction given by Jesus twenty-odd years earlier, but as the contemporary wisdom of his apostolate and of his churches.

Paul's use of the OT has the same character. To be sure he makes explicit quotation of OT passages much more than he does Jesus' tradition; 'as it is written' regularly introduces such an appeal to the authority of Jewish scripture (Rom. 1.17; 2.24; 3.4, 10; 4.17; etc.). In so doing he testifies that he found the OT to instruct him in present concerns, as in passages like Rom. 15.9-12 and 1 Cor. 10.1-11. But the number of echoes of, and allusions to, the OT far outweigh the number of explicit quotations. The OT was a source of living authority for him. Of course for Paul it was to be read in the light of Christ (2 Cor. 3.12-18), and in that light he construed the demand for circumcision as the mark of commitment to God's covenant (Gen. 17.9-14) differently (1 Cor. 7.19). But such fundamentals as the OT's warnings against idolatry and sexual license remained as much part of his continuing rule for life after his conversion as before. The law, as filtered through the prism of Christ, and as summed up in the demand for neighbour love, as 'the law of Christ' (Gal. 6.2), was an ever valid measure of his everyday conduct.

Nor should we forget that the Pauline corpus attests a tradition that ran on beyond Paul's own death. If we follow the large consensus of scholarly opinion, at least Ephesians and the Pastoral Epistles are post-Pauline. As such they suggest not a concern merely to ape the great apostle, and certainly not an attempt (a successful attempt!) to gain authority for the texts by deception. They suggest rather a living tradition of his thought, where fellow workers, assistants and pupils kept alive what Paul had stood for and laboured for and articulated it afresh for the generation following Paul. In this we can see a parallel with the Pentateuch, or the three Isaiahs, or the psalms of David. In each case a living tradition did not cease with the death of the initial voice and originating authority figure but continued to develop in the genera-tion(s) that followed. The living waters flowing from the fountainhead con-tinued through new channels.

V

The oral period belongs to the beginning of the whole process. Even though Papias' high regard for the 'living voice' of the first generation of disciples could endure into the second century, it could not be satisfied much beyond that. Paul's fellow-workers and pupils in turn died; the school of Paul could not maintain the distinctive Pauline theology in fresh compositions beyond a second generation; the later attempts to provide a 3 Corinthians or to replace the lost letter to the Laodiceans are feeble in comparison. Above all, did not the inscripturated tradition steadily, even if not immediately, supersede the oral tradition? And in so doing, did not the written text give the whole a firm-ness and fixity which had not been possessed before? The simple answer is that it did to a large extent, but by no means entirely. Which brings us to the science and skill of textual criticism.

As a scholarly discipline, the original goal of NT textual criticism was to recover so far as possible the original text penned by Evangelist and Apostle. Quite quickly that objective was modified into the aim to reconstruct a text which takes account of the measured testimony of manuscript and other wit-nesses and which can command assent as the best approximation to the texts emanating from the apostolic age and used by the early Church. Typical of this early phase was the modern regard for the 'first edition' of a great literary work. Typical too the assumption that differences between witnesses were the result of careless copying and scribal error. But recently it has come to be more fully appreciated that the concept of a 'first edition' is much less appro-priate to a document no doubt dictated by a particular author, but whose cir-culation beyond any single recipient depended wholly on authorized and un-authorized copying. In a day well before the idea of copyright gained hold, there was nothing to stop others incorporating parts of other literary works, adapting material to their own ends, or improving what might be deemed poor style, or modifying views thought not to be quite as they should have been.

So just as the discovery of the Dead Sea Scrolls has raised further ques-tions about differing forms of the Hebrew Bible, behind the Masoretic text on the one hand and the LXX on the other, similar questions are being raised with regard to the NT text. What does it signify, regarding 'the NT', if the Western text, particularly on Acts, was the NT for a wide range of western churches? What if Marcion's freedom in regard to the Gospel of Luke and the letters of Paul was not an aberration, but only an extreme example of what was the general practice? What if 'orthodox' as well as 'heretic' felt free to modify the text of particular scriptures in order that the scripture might be heard to speak more in accord with their own position? What would be deemed unacceptable in a literary culture, with a high regard for author's copyright, might well be regarded as good practice in a culture where no two manuscripts of a single work entirely agreed as to its wording, and where varied corruptions of a text being considered by a group of students could be taken for granted rather than being an exception. If justification were to be sought for any attempt to bring a group of manuscripts into conformity on a contentious point, it would be enough to argue that this is what the writer surely intended and not the other.

The rather sobering fact, then, is that the writing down of material did not fix it as much as has traditionally been assumed. The so-called canonical or final form of a text was not all that final. The contrast between written text and oral communication, which becomes so sharp and clear in a society long accustomed to the printed page and the 'first edition' of, say, 500 copies, loses all that sharpness and clarity once we move back in history behind Gutenberg and Caxton. Which means that the contrast between fixed text and changing tradition also loses its sharpness and clarity. In a pre-literary and pre-print age the written text had much more a chameleon-like quality, a living quality, than has normally been recognized.

VI

A still further factor is the whole issue of translation. Islam has been able to maintain its belief in the pristine purity of the Qur'an because it regards only the (original) Arabic as inspired and authoritative. Translations into Turkish or Bengali are not properly speaking the Qur'an. In contrast, it has always been recognized that the scriptures of Israel and Christianity needed to be translated — in the case of the OT, from Hebrew into Aramaic (the Targums) and Greek (LXX and others); in the case of the NT into the other ancient languages of the ancient near East, and particularly into Latin in the West. These translated scriptures were the scriptures for generations of national groups. The Vulgate, the Luther Bible and the King James (Authorized) Version of the

Bible, for example, were the authoritatively canonical texts for centuries in Europe. That perception of a particular translation as having a *de facto* canonical authority has only disappeared in the latter half of the twentieth century, marked as it has been both by an increasing accessibility to agreed Hebrew and Greek texts and by a bewildering plethora of new translations.

The point, of course, is that no translation can produce an exact reproduction of the text being translated. Any word in any language has a range of possible significance, depending on how that word has been used in that language. The nearest equivalent in another language will not have precisely the same range of significance; the range will overlap, making translation possible, but not exact. Add in the complexity of words in sentences, idiomatic usage, wordplays possible in the one language but not in the other, and so on, and the problem begins to become clear. Any sense of a meaning fixed by particular words in an original text, even if valid for the 'original', is at once qualified, if not heavily obscured when primary reference is to the translated text. The issue ought to have been more serious for earlier generations of Christians who regarded the text of the NT as a fundamental authority. For the original teaching of Jesus himself comes down to us almost entirely in translation, and in diverse forms at that. The issue was not seen to be serious, since it was the Greek version of his teaching that was thought of as the inspired original. The problem remained rather academic so long as there was only one translation into the vernacular to be reckoned with. But now that a whole range of translations compete for attention the point cannot be ignored. For all these translations are different. To listen to a Bible reading from one translation while following the passage in another translation can at times be a very disorienting experience, so different can the translations be. Any lingering thought of the fixity of the text soon evaporates.

In other words, translations of biblical texts are one of the clearest contemporary demonstrations of the living quality of the biblical text. The meaning of the 'original' Hebrew and Greek simply cannot be pinned down finally and definitively in any single word sequence in English, or German, or Swahili, or whatever. There is an amorphous quality to the very textual form, so that any claim to some translation being the most accurate or as rendering the others redundant is rightly regarded as unrealistic or as mere salesmanship. Twenty-first-century congregations have become accustomed to central liturgies in alternative versions, to a Lord's Prayer in three or four different forms, to Eucharistic prayers which vary according to the season, etc. This is simply because liturgy is one of the clearest manifestations of living tradition, as the amazing burgeoning of new hymnody in the latter decades of the twentieth century shows with particular clarity. The liturgy is adapting to the changing circumstances and needs of the worshipping people of God; that's what we mean by 'living tradition'. My point is that the translated biblical text read within the liturgy shares precisely in that living and developing process. Translations which in their time enabled the biblical text to speak afresh, like the Revised Standard Version, the New English Bible, or the Jerusalem Bible, can quite quickly come to be seen and heard as dated and in need of further revision. The Good News Bible or the Living Bible can bring the Bible to life for a new generation, while leaving an older generation cold. The translated Bible is not a fixed text but a diversity of contemporary performances of the ancient Hebrew and Greek. The Bible in translation has become fully and clearly part of the living tradition of the Church.

VII

Underlying all the above is the increasing recognition of the role of *interpretation* in the reading of the NT, as of any text. Meaning is not simply to be observed in the text and described by the reader, as one might report and describe the physical features of a mountain or church tower. Reading is engagement with the text, personally involving the reader. That is why teachers encourage children to pay attention when reading or being taught a lesson. Without that personal engagement and concentration, the passage or the lesson will 'go in one ear and out the other'. But even a modest degree of concentration brings the life-experience of the reader into interaction with the text read, and to the degree that the text speaks to that life-experience and informs or enhances or extends it we may speak of a successful reading or lesson. In such a case the meaning heard or lesson learned is in some degree at least the product of the interaction of text/speaker and reader/hearer. And in such a case there will be at least a degree of distinctive individuality in the meaning gleaned.

Still further complicating the picture are observations about the more deliberate acts of interpretation long familiar to students of history and of significant texts: that 'historical facts' are each historian's interpretation of the diverse and often inconsistent data still available from the past; and regarding the various forms of the hermeneutical circle, the part helping to illuminate the whole as the whole helps to illuminate the part, and so on. When we take these hermeneutical issues into consideration we find ourselves still further enmeshed in the problem of the historian's or reader's (subjective) input into the quest for facts and for meaning. The old defences of the univocity and definitive meaning of scripture simply failed to appreciate that the issue was not the *inspiration* of scripture but the *interpretation* of scripture. The Catholic side of the scripture/tradition debate had right on its side: no meaning from scripture without interpretation; no authoritative meaning from scripture without an authoritative interpreter; no scripture without tradition! But who determines who or what constitutes the authority? Can there be a finally definitive interpretation any more than a finally definitive scripture? The problem with a post-modern hermeneutic is that it undercuts *all* readings that claim a definitive authority over other readings.

Here, I suggest, is where the understanding of scripture as living tradition can point a way through the impasse.

As living tradition, scripture is not static, with a dead meaning to be somehow dissected from the cadaver of the text. Scripture has potential to evoke a range of meaning and reaction, as the differing translations and disagreements among commentators have long made clear. So long as scripture evokes a faith response (but there are other responses) and so long as faith reads/hears scripture with relevance and profit, it will retain its character as living tradition. Expressed differently, scripture is the basis not only for the unity of Christianity but for its diversity, and only for a unity which, like the human body, consists in the mutual recognition, interdependence and active cooperation of its several and very diverse parts. Without a living tradition the body of Christ will not live.

Since the text is the starting point and point of reference common to all engaged in such faithful reading, the content and structure of the text will itself provide the limit within which the range of meaning can be read/heard. The text is not wholly plastic, vulnerable to being moulded into any shape the reader chooses. There is such a thing as a bad reading. Translations can be recognized to be just plain wrong. The historical context of Hebrew and Greek usage will indicate limits beyond which the reading becomes irresponsible. The one gospel had different versions recognized to be legitimate, but other 'Gospels' were deemed to be illegitimate, and properly so. The discernment of a responsible reading is not the responsibility of any one person or office, but a matter of the *sensus fidelis*, though individual teacher and prophet may well be called by God to speak the word which illuminates a controversial issue.

It is important that the living tradition be not 'frozen' at any point. This was the mistake of the Protestant side of the scripture/tradition debate — in assuming that with the final canonical form of the text the variety and fluidity of scripture's meaning had thereby ceased. But the Catholic side of the debate can fall into the same trap by assuming that the tradition has frozen at various points, into dogma and canonical order. In both cases, the living quality of the tradition means that the tradition must continue to develop and change in response to the changing circumstances of the gospel and the churches. As Jesus saw in regard to 'the tradition of the elders' (Mark 7.9-13), as all three Reformations saw with regard to the developed tradition of the mediaeval Church, as Vatican II saw with regard to the long established tradition of Christian anti-Judaism, tradition can become an excuse to ignore the more obvious meanings to be drawn from scripture. Tradition can give practical expression to the living tradition of scripture, but it can also throttle it and prevent the breath of the Spirit breathing fresh life into and through the scriptures.

In short, when scripture is seen as 'living tradition' its function as word of God for the here and now is clarified and enhanced, its interaction with church tradition, both in expressing its own vitality through the tradition and in providing a check to any excesses of the tradition, becomes clearer and more positive, and its role in renewing tradition, in provoking departure from tradition, and in stimulating new tradition can be given full play.

Bibliography

Barrera, J. T. *The Jewish Bible and the Christian Bible: An Introduction to the History of the Bible,* translated from the Spanish by Wilfred G. E. Watson. Leiden: Brill, 1998.

Barton, J., ed. *The Cambridge Companion to Biblical Interpretation.* Cambridge: Cambridge University Press, 1998.

Brown, D. *Discipleship and Imagination: Christian Tradition and Truth.* Oxford: Oxford University Press, 2000.

————. *Tradition and Imagination: Revelation and Change.* Oxford: Oxford University Press, 1999.

Dewey, J., ed. *Orality and Textuality in Early Christian Literature.* Semeia 65. Atlanta: Scholars, 1995.

Dunn, J. D. G. *Christianity in the Making,* vol. 1: *Jesus Remembered.* Grand Rapids: Eerdmans, 2003.

————. *The Living Word.* London: SCM, 1987.

————. *The Theology of Paul the Apostle.* Grand Rapids: Eerdmans; Edinburgh: T&T Clark, 1998.

————. *Unity and Diversity in the New Testament.* London: SCM, 1977, 2nd edition 1990.

————. 'What Makes a Good Exposition?' *Expository Times* 114 (2002-3) 147-57.

Dunn, J. D. G., and R. W. Rogerson, eds. *Eerdmans Commentary on the Bible.* Grand Rapids: Eerdmans, 2003.

Ehrman, B. D. *The Orthodox Corruption of Scripture: The Effect of Early Christological Controversies on the Text of the New Testament.* Oxford: Oxford University Press, 1993.

Fowl, S. E., ed. *The Theological Interpretation of Scripture: Classic and Contemporary Readings*. Oxford: Blackwell, 1997.

Gadamer, H.-G. *Truth and Method*. New York: Continuum, 1999.

Meade, D. G. *Pseudonymity and Canon: An Investigation into the Relationship of Authorship and Authority in Jewish and Earliest Christian Tradition*. WUNT 39; Tübingen: Mohr Siebeck, 1986.

Moberly, R. W. L. *The Old Testament of the Old Testament: Patriarchal Narratives and Mosiac Yahwism*. Minneapolis: Fortress, 1992.

Parker, D. C. *The Living Text of the Gospels*. Cambridge: Cambridge University Press, 1997.

Rad, G. von. *Old Testament Theology*. Edinburgh: Oliver & Boyd, 1962.

Sanders, J. A. *From Sacred Story to Sacred Text: Canon as Paradigm*. Philadelphia: Fortress, 1987.

————. *Torah and Canon*. Philadelphia: Fortress, 1972.

Schneiders, S. M. *The Revelatory Text: Interpreting the New Testament as Sacred Scripture*. San Francisco: HarperSanFrancisco, 1991.

Shiner, W. *Proclaiming the Gospel: First-Century Performance of Mark*. Harrisburg: Trinity Press International, 2003.

Stone, M. E., ed. *Jewish Writings of the Second Temple Period: Apocrypha, Pseudepigrapha, Qumran Sectarian Writings, Philo, Josephus*. CRINT; Assen: Van Gorcum, 1984.

Thiselton, A. C. *New Horizons in Hermeneutics*. London: Marshall Pickering, 1992.

Watson, F. *Paul and the Hermeneutics of Faith*. London: T&T Clark, 2004.

————. *Text and Truth: Redefining Biblical Theology*. Edinburgh: T&T Clark, 1997.

Index of Gospel and Other Texts Discussed

Index of Modern Authors Referred To

See also Bibliographies at 361-3 and 379-80

Index of Subjects Discussed